Sound Identities

Popular Music and the Cultural Politics of Education

Edited by
Cameron McCarthy, Glenn Hudak,
Shawn Miklaucic, and Paula Saukko

PETER LANG
New York • Washington, D.C./Baltimore • Boston • Bern
Frankfurt am Main • Berlin • Brussels • Vienna • Canterbury

Library of Congress Cataloging-in-Publication Data

Sound identities: popular music and the cultural politics of education /
edited by Cameron McCarthy, Glenn Hudak, Shawn Miklaucic, Paula Saukko.
p. cm. — (Counterpoints; vol. 96)
Includes bibliographical references and index.
1. Popular music—History and criticism. 2. Music and youth.
3. Group identity. 4. Music in education. I. McCarthy, Cameron.
II. Series: Counterpoints (New York, N.Y.); vol. 96.
ML3470.S62   306.4'85—dc21   98-27792
ISBN 0-8204-4139-2
ISSN 1058-1634

Die Deutsche Bibliothek-CIP-Einheitsaufnahme

Sound identities: popular music and the cultural politics of education /
edited by Cameron McCarthy, Glenn Hudak, Shawn Miklaucic, Paula Saukko.
–New York; Washington, D.C./Baltimore; Boston; Bern;
Frankfurt am Main; Berlin; Brussels; Vienna; Canterbury: Lang.
(Counterpoints; Vol. 96)
ISBN 0-8204-4139-2

Cover design by Nona Reuter

The paper in this book meets the guidelines for permanence and durability
of the Committee on Production Guidelines for Book Longevity
of the Council of Library Resources.

© 1999 Peter Lang Publishing, Inc., New York

Printed in the United States of America

Acknowledgments

The editors of this volume are grateful for the funding and research support of the Institute of Communications Research and the Campus Research Board of the University of Illinois. Further research support was provided in the form of a University Scholar Award to Cameron McCarthy. Versions of the essays in this volume by Warren Crichlow, Glenn Hudak, Cameron McCarthy, Robin Small-McCarthy, and Ruth Vinz first appeared in the Australian journal, *Discourse* 3(16). The chapter by Julia Eklund Koza first appeared in the *Review of Education/Pedagogy/Cultural Studies, 16*(2), 1994, and is reprinted with the kind permission of Gordon and Breach Publishers. The chapter by Nina Asher first appeared in *Taboo: The Journal of Culture and Education*, Spring 1997.

Contributors

Sylvia A. Allegretto is a PhD student in the Department of Economics at the University of Illinois at Urbana-Champaign. Her interests include labor economics and human capital theory.

Nina Asher is completing her docorate in the Department of Curriculum and Teaching at Teachers College, Columbia University, and teaches at Penn State University (Delaware County Campus). Her teaching and research interests focus on curriculum theory and critical perspectives on multiculturalism and identity formation in education.

Rhiannon S. Bettivia is a ninth grader at Central High School in Champaign, Illinois. She has co-authored articles with Angharad Valdivia on girl culture and presented a paper on this topic at the 1997 ICA Conference in Montreal, Canada.

Warren E. Crichlow is an assistant professor in the Faculty of Education, York University, Ontario, Canada. He is co-editor, with Cameron McCarthy, of *Race, Identity, and Representation in Education*, Routledge (1993), and "Toni Morrison and the Curriculum," a special issue of the journal *Cultural Studies* (1995).

Greg Dimitriadis is a doctoral candidate in the Department of Speech Communication at the University of Illinois at Urbana-Champaign.

matt garcia is an assistant professor of history and Latina/o studies at the University of Illinois, Urbana-Champaign. His current research focuses on intercultural relations in the citrus growing regions of Southern California from 1900 to 1960.

Glenn Hudak is a professor of education, Pace University, New York City. Glenn's current interests revolve around relationships between the institution of schooling, power, and the struggles over self-representation. To this end he is co-editing (with Paul Kihn) the book Labeling: Politics & Pedagogy. Glenn's focus will be on explicating the dynamics of "addicting epistemologies." His prior articles include, "The technologies of marginality" and "A suburban tale: Representation in special needs education."

George Kamberelis is an associate professor of education at Purdue University, where he teaches courses on literacy, classroom discourse, and interpretive research methods. Informed by critical social theories, practice theories, and theories of discourse, Professor Kamberelis conducts research on situated language practices in school and community settings.

Julia Eklund Koza teaches in the Department of Curriculum and Instruction at the University of Wisconsin, Madison.

Cameron McCarthy is Research Professor and University Scholar in the Institute of Communications Research at the University of Illinois at Urbana-Champaign. His most recent book, *The Uses of Culture*, is published by Routledge (1998). He is also the co-editor, with Warren Crichlow, of *Race, Identity and Representation in Education* (Routledge, 1993).

Peter McLaren is a professor of education, Graduate School of Education and Information Studies, University of California, Los Angeles. Professor McLaren is the author of numerous books on politics and culture, including *Critical Pedagogy and Predatory Culture* (Routledge, 1995) and *Revolutionary Multiculturalism* (Westview, 1997). He lectures worldwide on pedagogies of liberation and political struggle. His work has been translated into Spanish, Portuguese, Japanese, Catalan, French, German, Polish, and Hebrew.

Shawn Miklaucic is currently a doctoral student in the Institute of Communications Research at the University of Illinois. He received a master's degree in English from Illinois State University.

Zena Moore is an assistant professor at the University of Texas at Austin. She teaches courses in teaching and testing culture in the language classroom. Her research interests include work on popular cultures and cross-cultural similarities pertaining to foreign language pedagogy. She is Trinidadian and lives in Austin, Texas.

Chris Richards is currently a senior lecturer in Education at the University of North London, England. He has worked in the field of media education for many years—in schools and in higher education. His book, *Teen Spirits: Music and Identity in Media Education*, was published by UCL Press (Taylor and Francis) early in April 1998.

Paula Saukko is a doctoral student in the Institute of Communications Research at the University of Illinois, Urbana-Champaign. She has studied and published a half a dozen articles on media, youth movements, and the discourse on anorexia, the young women's disease.

Robin Small-McCarthy is the executive secretary for racial justice in the Women's Division of the General Board of Global Ministries (United Methodist Church). As a member of the Section of Christian Social Responsibility, Robin teaches, resources, and develops programs of education and action for United Methodist Women and their affiliates. She is a teaching artist, performer, theatre director, and compassionate activist who works for peace with justice.

Jonathan Sterne is a graduate student in communications research at the University of Illinois at Urbana-Champaign, and has played bass in rock bands since he was 16. He is currently writing a cultural history of sound reproduction in the United States from 1830 to 1930.

Angharad N. Valdivia researches and teaches at the Institute of Communications Research at the University of Illinois. Her main areas of interest are gender, popular culture, and Latin America or US Latina/ Latino Studies. She is the co-editor of *Feminism, Multiculturalism and the Media: Global Diversities* (Sage, 1995) and the forthcoming culture and communication section of the *Global Women's Encyclopedia* (Routledge, 1998). She has just finished a book entitled *Gendered Identities and Media Culture: Essays in Multiculturalism* and has published in numerous journals, including the *Journal of Communication*, the *Journal of International Communication*, *Camera Obscura*, the *Review of Education/Pedagogy/Cultural Studies*, the *Journal of Inclusive Education*, and *Cultural Studies Review*.

Ruth Vinz is an associate professor and director of the English education program at Teacher's College, Columbia University. She taught in secondary schools for over twenty years and since that time has focused her teaching, research, and writing on the dilemmas surrounding the discourses on teaching and learning.

Rinaldo Walcott is an assistant professor in the division of humanities, York University, Toronto, where he teaches in the area of black cultural studies. He is the author of *Black Like Who? Writing, Black, Canada* (1997).

Lise Waxer is an ethnomusicologist and assistant professor of music at Trinity College, Hartford. She specializes in popular musics of Latin America and the Caribbean and has conducted extensive research on salsa and its Cuban roots.

Carrie Wilson-Brown is a doctoral student in the Institute of Communications Research, University of Illinois at Urbana-Champaign.

Table of Contents

Introduction

Anxiety and Celebration: Popular Music and Youth Identities at the End of the Century

Cameron McCarthy, Glenn Hudak,
Sylvia A. Allegretto, Shawn Miklaucic,
and Paula Saukko

> The Right is repoliticizing youth not as an active agent but as a passive victim in much the same way that they are repoliticizing and revictimizing all of the groups that are traditionally seen as oppressed.
>
> Lawrence Grossberg

Popular Music and the Task of Critical Analysis in Education

Contemporary curriculum and educational researchers writing on the topic of schooling have tended to ignore the critical role played by popular culture in the production of the differential social identities of school youth. Though there is a rise of multicultural literature in the field that has from its inception drawn attention to the representations and experiences of minority school youth and women in social and cultural life, such writing has tended to concentrate on the formal and instrumental orders of schooling, particularly textbooks and curriculum content and materials. The marginalization of popular culture comes at a time, particularly in the United States, when educators are everywhere surrounded by inflamed, anti-intellectual, and authoritarian discourses that emphasize static, normative, and disciplinary approaches to the curriculum and the pedagogical needs of youth.

Accordingly, some educators have begun the long retreat into the banner-waving slogans of *Western civilization, virtues, privatization of public schooling* and the like. Typically, these discourses thrive on the aggravated oppositions of *Western traditions* versus *multiculturalism, practice* versus *theory,* and *the classroom versus the extraneous and hostile world.* (Here we are thinking particularly of conservative school critics such as William Bennett [1994], E.D. Hirsch [1987] and Diane Ravitch and Chester Finn [1987] and their culturally narrow-minded texts). In these new conservative discourses popular culture is seen as the enemy—a surreptitious and corrosive force brought into schooling and the public sphere by the minority other and by white working class youth. By all means, then, popular culture must be kept at arm's length lest it corrupt the young and overstimulate the old.

The matter goes further. As Chris Richards (1995) contends, even when there has been innovative research in the marginal areas of the educational field such as media studies, the prevailing concern has been with the visual media to the virtual exclusion of popular music. But as we will argue, music is, after all, at the epicenter of practices of discursive identity formation for the young. The contributors to *Sound Identities,* therefore, seek to go in a radically different direction with respect to the discussion of popular culture than that currently being pursued by mainstream and radical educational thinkers, by presenting substantial studies that join a concern with youth culture centered around music and the concerns of education.

Throughout, our discussion of popular music is framed in terms of the relation between popular cultural identities and the orientation of the school curriculum to "public," "official" versions of what constitutes valid and coherent student identities. We are particularly interested in the popular cultural maps made available to students and the maps of meaning which these young people themselves construct through their engagement with various, often geographically disparate, forms of music. Such cultural maps and identities, which students both engender and decode, need to be understood and worked upon within the school context.

Purposes of This Study

Contributors to this volume seek to fulfill four general objectives. The first is to raise the status of popular music and, more broadly, popular culture in theoretical and practical deliberations in the field of curriculum studies. Among other things, we argue that it is in popular culture and popular music that the differential identities and interests of school youth are constructed, reworked and coordinated, and then infused into the expressive and instrumental orders of schooling. As media critics such as Katherine Frith (1997), Len Masterman (1990), and Michael Parenti (1993) have argued, the school curriculum is rapidly being replaced by the media curriculum. This is an area in which teachers and educators have a lot to learn from the young.

Second, we want, by way of the multidisciplinary theoretical and methodological emphases in these essays, to call attention to the power and relevance of cultural studies analysis to the study of schooling. By cultural studies analysis, we mean the plurality of critical research strategies (phenomenology, semiotics, ethnography, literary analysis, situated history, and political economy) deployed in this volume. These research strategies foreground a radical contextualization and relational evaluation of the popular cultural practices of school youth as reflected in the reciprocal processes of textual production and reception. These critical approaches to lived and commodified cultural forms read these practices of cultural production back into systems of dominant and subordinant relations that characterize industrial societies, even so-called postmodern ones.

Third, we seek to widen the debate over the relationship of popular culture to schooling by incorporating the text of the world: the deeply unstable global setting, the new world order in which "center-periphery relations" are the crude summaries of the hierarchical distribution of repressed interests, needs, and desires of dominant and subaltern groups in first world and third world societies. Collectively, we argue that these stratified interests and desires ride the textual surfaces of popular music and popular culture generally, releasing new energies of communication and normalization as well as critique. These popular cultural texts are produced and consumed by youth in the elaboration of their identities in the school setting and beyond.

Fourth, above all, we want to distance ourselves from the tendency of radical scholars to romanticize the popular culture of contemporary working-class and minority school youth. Not all popular culture is transformative! Indeed, each of the essays in this anthology will call attention to both the transformative and reproductive tensions embodied in the production and consumption of popular music and other cultural forms in contemporary educational and social life. We want to point to the moments of celebration and anxiety within the practices of popular music production and youthful reception and performance.

As a specific instance of the broad social and cultural issues that we seek to connect to youth production and consumption of popular music, we want to call attention to the embattled clothes designer Tommy Hilfiger and the contradictory story of his appropriation of hip-hop cultural form to sell his line of clothing. Tommy Hilfiger's story points to the malleability of music and the social identities of youth. It further indicates the social extendedness of popular culture and the urgent need for educators to enter the world of youth beyond the arena of the classroom and the subject matter curriculum.

Anxiety and Celebration

Alright, I know a lot of people in the hip hop community think his [Tommy Hilfiger] clothes are tight but if every one keeps saying 'keep it real,' then ask yourself, is he real to you?. He is an American designer with a logo that represents "America." Well if you think America is about equality without discrimination and racism and is a country open to all colors, then why are you making a man rich that thinks of AMERICA as WHITE AMERICA? He says he designs clothes with urban youths in mind, does he think we have $200 to spend on a shirt? Are Asians and other minorities not considered "American" too? So to the hip hop community who have made this racist man rich, are you 'keepin it real'? ("Viking," correspondent on the Internet)

The quotation above stems from a current debate raging in the margins of cyberspace. This debate directly engages the denizens of the hip-hop culture, their music, their fashion and meaning of style. In engaging hip hop, the debate spills the complexities and contradictions of youth identities into the grooves of internet list serves and the new hyperactive talking communities of the cyberworld. This debate connects up the longings, needs, and desires of disadvantaged African American youth circulating in popular culture—rap music, pop magazines, the reality bites of BET and MTV and the everyday cultural practices and performative spaces of black youth themselves—to the new-wave marketing strategies of white designers and the culture industry. It is a debate that above all foregrounds the central themes of anxiety and celebration and the radical instability of youth identities and ethnicities announced in this volume. We are talking about the hot contestation over African American youth consumption of a hip-hop derivative line of clothing marketed by the savvy conservative white designer, Tommy Hilfiger. This debate highlights the paradoxes of music identities, ownership of culture, and the proliferation of new essentialisms and new realisms in the politics of culture and consumption at the end of the century. In our introduction we read these developments around the Tommy Hilfiger clothing line back onto the issues that will be raised in the essays by the contributors to this book writing on the topics of youth musics, youth identities, and education.

The Tommy Hilfiger story goes like this. Hilfiger set out in the early 1990s to compete against department store staple lines like Ralph Lauren and Liz Claiborne with an essentially young Republican type of clothing line. In the course of a few years, this basically khaki, crew and button-down WASP-style, while remaining a constant theme in the Hilfiger collections, has undergone radical revisions and variations. New stylistic emphases brought the Hilfiger product closer to hip-hop style: bolder colors, bigger, baggier styles, more hoods and cords, and more prominence for logos foregrounding the colors of the American flag and the Hilfiger name. Targeting the marketing potential of black youth, Hilfiger established himself at the forefront of the new marketing concept known as "mass customization"—a process of marketing that achieved, in this case, the refined extraction and reproduction of the meaning style and attitude of inner-city youth consumers. Critical, here, is the role that music, movies, and black film stars such as Cuba Gooding, Jr., and rap artists like the late Notorious Biggie Smalls played in delivering a black lower-middle-class youth clientele to the Hilfiger line. The Hilfiger line, after all, is a line that was initially targeted at conservative upper-middle-class white youth.

It is the agonizing fact of the radical appropriation of the putative cultural property of black youth, the radical reconstruction of the black "real" by Hilfiger, that set off the debate on the internet and elsewhere about the Hilfiger style. Participants in the debate, both black and white, contest the meaning of black identity and white identity and the lines drawn down between these poles of ethnic affiliation. To whom does the Hilfiger style ultimately belong? Should poor black youth continue to purchase relatively pricey Hilfiger clothing? What does this say about "Air Jordans"? What ultimately are the meanings and consequences of Hilfiger's appropriation of black hip-hop cool?

In all of this, the themes of anxiety and celebration work themselves into contemporary discourses over the cultural practices of inner-city youth. These themes exceed the limits of popular culture, popular music, hip hop, and so forth and enter into the larger arena of the politics of identity at late-century. For instance, one white interloper in the internet discussion about the Hilfiger line insisted that it was "white," not "black," identities that were at stake. The whole Hilfiger line of clothing, according to this Internet rough rider, is a white archive, and it belongs to white youth not black ones. In rather racist language that mockingly appropriates ebonics, the white interloper drew a line in the sand and announced the topics of white popular wisdom simmering beneath the surface of popular discourses on music and fashion in the country:

> Wasup Yall. I'm from Queeeeeeeens NYC and I'm just chilllllin. After reading some of this stuff about Tommy Hilfiger being racist . . . booooooooshit!!! What the F. The fugees are racist too, but I guess that's o.k. Since they are black right? You know what? I don't care who's racist because all you black people do is blame the white for your problems. "I can't get a job because I am black and they have no affirmative action. And. . ." Go to hell stupid!!! Face it, you didn't get the jobs because you are not qualified and you are F. . . ignorant and lazy. So stop blaming us for your problems. (Thabomb, Internet)

The ironies of this Internet interlude on hip-hop culture bring us to the theater of popular music and its reach into the social world of the commodified and lived culture of contemporary youth. The social extendedness of popular music, particularly as it pertains to school youth, is the central concern in this volume of essays. And, here, we are presented with yet another irony; despite its importance in the lives of school youth, popular music is still a profoundly marginalized area of study in the field of education. Education researchers and practitioners have generally taken a hands-off approach with respect to popular culture, seeing it as a lost area of youth pleasures that is corrosive to the minds and hearts of the young and from which we can learn very little that can help us understand the educational enterprise. On the other hand, many of the subcultural theorists writing outside the field of education have tended to cast a happy gaze upon youth music, adopting a celebratory stance toward youth pleasures and consumption practices. It is as though their exploration of youth culture in itself overcomes a frustrated wish fulfillment to go native against the iron cage of their bureaucratic existence. This collection of essays moves back and forth across the lines of anxiety and celebration, sensuality and bodily containment, the local and the global, cultural reproduction and cultural change.

Cultural Studies and Popular Music

As we enter the twenty-first century, music is playing an ever increasing, pivotal role in the lives of youth as the vehicle of new and old ideas and fantasies and as the site of the work of youthful imagination. But music is also the location of the hegemonic thrusts of the culture industry, the site of the fabrication of new market-susceptible subjectivities, and the site of the production and reproduction of conservative ideas outright. To understand these dynamics we must reach outside the field of education. The emergent school of thought of cultural studies informs us that popular music plays a number of important social functions in the lives of children and adolescents. For instance, Simon Frith (1992) argues that the pleasure of popular music, unlike many other forms of cultural life, is experienced directly through the immediacy of the body. In this sense it is argued that music has a powerful influence in shaping who we are, that is in shaping the formation of our individual and collective identities. Theorists such as Christopher Richards (1995) maintain that the social functions of music include: the formation and cultural reproduction of identities, the development of a sense of place and social context, and the organization and management of feelings. Popular music brings together fragmentary elements of youth life through a process of inclusion and exclusion that links youth actors to classed, gendered, and sexually and ethnically specific, yet interrelated publics. Those listening to popular music often identify with a particular musical genre such as heavy metal, rap, ranchero, or reggae. And especially for adolescents, popular music forms part of or helps to cement a larger social constellation linking media images of stars and celebrities and particular musical genres to specific peer groups, cliques, or gangs. Popular music is related to styles of clothes, and the expression of sexuality, class and racial and ethnic affiliation.

Popular music works for some children to bind the fragmentary elements of the child's school experience. In this way, popular music can serve to teach children the meanings of social categories. Michael Apple (1979), for example, argues that one of the most important lessons learned by children in kindergarten is the different social meanings of the categories of "work" and "play." The process of becoming a student in many ways consists of the fragmentation of the child's experiential knowledge base. Indeed, as the child learns to be a student—a process which fragments consciousness—the presence of popular music can work within the affective domain, as Lawrence Grossberg (1992) suggests, to create the sense of a cohesive reality in the lives of adolescents in school.

It is through their engagement with/in popular culture, and especially with/in music, that children can learn to weave together personal and school knowledge in creative ways, and in the process learn to operate within the rules of negotiation, elaborated inside and out-side the school context. In this sense, the formation of identity is an ongoing process which places youth within competing social posi-tions. In the process of identity formation, adolescents find places from which to speak—positions from which to negotiate and use school knowledge—positions of "enunciation." In the varieties of this pro-cess, young people "try out" identities in competing cultural domains.

If it can be argued that young people construct their identities through the social formation of boundaries, then it is important to uncover how social, cultural, and political boundaries are created and lived through popular music. This is both a pedagogical and political concern. For, as writers such as Elizabeth Ellsworth (1989) argue, the task of liberatory education is not to eliminate difference, but rather to create a dialogue across differences such that alliances may be formed in the struggle against oppressive social institutions and structures. In *Sound Identities*, we pursue these themes throughout: across the terrains of the American nation; across the global dynamics of postcolonial music history and present; and ultimately back into micropolitics of the pedagogy of the musical affect. Ultimately, we see music as operating within the context of a plurality of techno-, ideo-, ethno-, finance- and media-scapes—flows and logics of globalization that fragment, rework and reintegrate human experience in the progress of music within the circuits of production, distribution and consump-tion (Appadurai, 1996). We foreground a wide array of theoretical and empirical research that looks at the dynamic role that music plays at the level of everyday life. *Sound Identities* is divided into four sec-tions: "Music in the Nation," "Music in the Postcolony," "Music in the Contested Metropolis," and "The Pedagogy of the Musical Affect."

Music in the Nation: Rap, Hip Hop, and the Flow of Values

The first four essays in the volume, written by Peter McLaren, Julia Eklund Koza, Rinaldo Walcott, and Greg Dimitriadis and George Kamberelis, look at youth music within the local/global dynamics of the nation. Rap and hip hop, originally stemming from the American black and Latino inner city, often vibrate with a strong political mes-sage about the despair and rage caused by racism, deindustrialization, segregation, gaping income differences, and violence stamping out the lives of large sections of contemporary American urban youth

(Rose, 1993). At the same time, these musical genres also seep with current political nihilism, sexism, commodification, crossovers from multiple traditions and practices, and technological and cultural changes. These dynamics often underscore the visual, sometimes ending up imploding the black and brown public sphere as it collapses into the icon of the Americo-centered male body display: the inner-city basketball court (Gilroy, 1997, p. 89). The four essays in this section address these politically loaded and contradictory tendencies in rap and hip hop and the processes through which they have been articulated into a central locus of celebration, despair, condemnation and seduction for inner-city and suburban youth in contemporary United States.

In the opening essay ("Gangsta Pedagogy and Ghettocentricity: The Hip Hop Nation as Counterpublic Sphere") Peter McLaren argues, drawing on DeCerteau's work, that rap is an "oppositional practice" through which exploited and oppressed groups recode and redeploy the laws and traditions of their conquerors to alternative and subaltern ends. Reviewing an array of scholarly and popular criticisms of rap, McLaren argues that contemporary critics fail to grasp the genre's parodization of the "bad nigga." But McLaren is not a cheerleader for the genre. Rap parodization does have its limitations. The problem that McLaren points toward with respect to this genre is that although parody may rupture the image of the subjugated black subject, the ensuing rupture does not always connect to a larger project of political liberation and change.

Julia Eklund Koza ("Rap Music: The Cultural Politics of Official Representation") focuses more specifically on the media representation of rap, arguing that its marginalization in academic research has meant that the translations of its meaning and political implications have been taken over by the popular press, laden as it is with racist biases. Using the work on narrative and representation of Diana Fuss (1989) and John Fiske (1987), she shows the operation of these biases in major news magazines, such as *Time* and *Newsweek*, and the powerful resentment-type binarisms of the suburban middle-class representations of inner-city youth.

Departing in a different direction and announcing new themes in the analysis of rap aesthetics and theories, Rinaldo Walcott ("Performing the (Black) Postmodern: Rap as Incitement for Cultural Criticism") makes the case for rap as the realization of the black postmodern. Reading the moment of the black lost innocence, he suggests that a critique of black diaspora studies as presently constituted is long over-due. He further maintains that such a postmodernist critique facili-tates multiple and varied readings of rap as a diasporic art form which is both a border-crosser and a localized practice.

George Kamberelis and Greg Dimitriadis ("Talking Tupac: Speech Genres and the Mediation of Cultural Knowledge") close out this first section of the volume with a powerful illustration of the merits of empirical work in the area of rap studies. Attempting to get beyond the theoreticism of many cultural studies approaches to the analysis of popular culture, they investigate the meaning of rap in the everyday lives of black youth. They report on a case study of the way black youngsters make sense of the death of the rap star Tupac Shakur. Dimitriadis and Kamberelis argue that black youth make sense about Tupac's death mainly through the "talk show genre." They highlight the contradictory process of production and circulation of meanings within rap and within the world(s) of its inner-city community of read-ers. After all, ubiquitous in American culture, the talk show genre psychologizes larger economic and political issues into questions of self-esteem, individual choice, and interpersonal relations. The case study ultimately serves to model a tightly integrated and rigorous fu-sion of theory, methodology, and empirical work in the study of the popular arts such as rap.

Music in the Postcolony and in the Diaspora

The essays of Cameron McCarthy, Robin Small-McCarthy, Nina Asher, Zena Moore, and Lise Waxer explore the logics of musical production and reception across the divide of "center and periphery"; particularly with respect to the circulation of music that proceeds across the bound-ary lines of genre, nation, and ethnicity. Like rap, this postcolonial music is riddled with tensions. It articulates experiences of subjuga-tion, displacement, and longing but also pride, parody, and celebra-tion. Yet, the various forms of postcolonial music may also be inter-laced with threads of colonialism, gender-based subordination, and rigid and essentialist or exoticizing, commercialized, and touristy no-tions of ethnicity.

Cameron McCarthy ("Narrating Imperialism: The British Influence in Barbadian Public School Songs") argues against mainstream and neo-Marxist analyses that focus on economic and structural factors in the reproduction of center-periphery relations. Through analysis of

Barbadian school songs, he shows how British rule is cemented in this school music. But McCarthy points, additionally, to a powerful cultural phenomenon: the role of the British school music in the production of cultural and social hierarchies in the island community itself. These dynamics underscore the contradictory role of the imperial symbolic in the periphery and in the circulation of music.

Robin Small-McCarthy ("From *The Bluest Eye* to *Jazz*: A Retrospective of Toni Morrison Literary Sounds") analyzes Toni Morrison's novels for how they interweave the African American oral and rhythmic traditions into powerful prose. She argues that through the use of nonlinear narrative techniques and polyrhythmic narrative shifts, Morrison produces a text uniquely capable of translating the intense suffering and pain but also the love characterizing the experience of slavery.

Nina Asher ("Apache Indian's Syncretic Music and the Representation of South Asian Identities: A Case Study of a Minority Artist") foregrounds the contradictory process of identity formation in popular music through a case study of a South Asian British musician, "Apache Indian." She shows the deconstructive and alliance-building capabilities of a minority artist who mocks the western ignorance of India and Native American culture and combines reggae and rap beats with Indian bhangra. Yet, as she demonstrates, this is commercial crossover music that has a tendency to trivialize ethnic cultural traits. "Apache Indian" is being incorporated even as he transgresses received traditions of identity and musical genre.

Zena Moore's essay ("Postcolonial Influences in the Spanish Diaspora: Christian Doctrine and the Depiction of Women in Tejano Border Songs and the Calypso") provides a feminist critique of two postcolonial musical genres, the Caribbean calypso and the Mexican-American corrido. While acknowledging that corrido and calypso musics articulate the subjugation of Latino and Caribbean men and that these musical genres draw on mixed white and mestiza cultural influences, she points out that they also repeat powerful biblical/Catholic themes of good and evil, loyalty and treachery, which are projected onto a denigrating representation of Latina and Caribbean women.

In her essay ("Consuming Memories: The Record-Centered Salsa Scene in Cali"), Lise Waxer presents a case study of the production, circulation, and consumption of popular music in the Latin American periphery that points us beyond the well-worn story of the cultural reproduction and ensnarement of mass audiences. The essay explores

the role of record-centered consciousness-raising in the popular consumption of salsa in Cali, Columbia. Waxer points to a radical cosmopolitanism from "below" in which musical ideas circulate among the
working-class audiences in Latin America and the Caribbean, overriding the narrow constraints of nation and location. In so doing, she
opens up a whole new terrain in the study of popular music audiences: the power, movement, and critical reflexivities that exist among
the subaltern agents in Latin America and the Caribbean.

Music in the Contested Metropolis:
Rock and the Contradictory Politics of Youth

In the third section of the volume, Chris Richards, Jonathan Sterne,
Matt Garcia, and Lawrence Grossberg investigate youth music in the
"belly of the monster," in the northern metropolis and its suburbs.
The essays focus mostly on rock, the musical genre of the "center"
par excellence, only to complicate simple dichotomies or boundaries
by pointing at how the vast terrain of rock merges into a wide variety
of genres, political campaigns, cultures and ethnicities. By examining
the central affective role rock plays in the formation of contemporary
youth identities, and how mainstream politics has often cleverly employed this affect—although not without friction or backfiring—the
essays underscore the urgency of radical scholars' and pedagogues'
need to engage in the struggle over meaning(s), and to initiate dialogue that discusses the impact of this genre.

Chris Richards ("Live Through This: Music, Adolescents, and Autobiography") links questions of genre and cultural boundary crossing
to questions of "taste," à la Bourdieu. Drawing on the autobiographical writing of 12 British adolescents in a selective high school in London, Richards foregrounds the complex ways in which youth use music to represent their identities and trace out their biographies.

Jonathan Sterne ("Going Public: Rock Aesthetics and the Pedagogy of the Political Field") addresses the full range of writing on rock
music and youth. Drawing on the work of Pierre Bourdieu and
Lawrence Grossberg, he argues that while cultural approaches to rock
music have focused on politics, they have ignored mainstream American politics. As a specific instance of the deployment of politics of
youth culture linked to music, Sterne looks at the mobilization of the
category of "youth" by Bill Clinton and the new generation coming
into power. He argues that this conceptual category of "youth" de-
ploys a hypothetical subjectivity in realpolitique that contradicts vio-

lently the way in which real historical youth subjects experience popular culture and live their lives.

As a brilliant riposte to essentialist readings of rock and roll history and the center-periphery divide in contemporary discussions of popular culture, matt garcia ("The Chicano Dance Hall: Remapping Public Space in Post-World War II Greater Los Angeles") offers a fascinating account of the radically transcultural subaltern sphere of Chicano dance halls in late 1950s and early 1960s Los Angeles. He explores the unique history of the El Monte American Legion Stadium and the Pomona Rainbow Gardens as dance halls that served as harbingers of intercultural exchange and cultural fusion among African American, Latino, white, and Asian/Pacific Islander music and genres. Youth who participated in the Rainbow Gardens and American Legion Stadium music scene crossed the boundaries of class and race in forging new (imagined) communities of subaltern Angelenos. In so doing, they linked music to a new postmodern geography.

In an interview with Carrie Wilson-Brown and Cameron McCarthy ("The Organization of Affect: Popular Music, Youth, and Intellectual and Political Life"), Larry Grossberg addresses the rapid repoliticization of youth by the right through the medium of popular music. He argues that the left has been slow to understand or capitalize on these developments in the organization of affect and suggests that the left must more directly engage the politics of representation in popular music in order to broaden the counter public sphere of critique in the academy itself.

The Pedagogy of Musical Affect

In a mode of conclusion to the discussions on the contradictions of youth and popular music, Warren Crichlow, Ruth Vinz, Angharad Valdivia and Rhiannon Bettivia, and Glenn Hudak draw attention to the pedagogical force of popular music in the context of the contradictory logics of identity politics and the conservative restoration and authoritarian populism that appear to have captured the hearts and minds of contemporary youth. The authors also explore what pedagogues might learn from the polyvocal, improvisatory, affective, and cognitive qualities of popular music that allow for airing of grievances within the boundaries of the "acceptable."

Warren Crichlow ("'No Guarantees': Pedagogical Implications of Music in the Films of Isaac Julien") focuses on films of the London-based director for their pedagogical practice. He argues that Julien's way of addressing the contradictory dimensions of black culture—its resistances, homophobia, and transcultural qualities spanning Jamaica to London and New York, carrying within it some of the specificities of all those places—is exemplary pedagogy that does not shun difficult subjects or fall into simplified dichotomies.

Ruth Vinz's essay ("Learning from the Blues: Beyond Essentialist Readings of Cultural Texts") uses Bakhtin's theories of dialogue and polyvocality to ground her vision of a pedagogy of the blues. Vinz explores the multivocal, multicultural, historically sedimented nature of the blues that yields to multiple interpretations as a fruitful tool for a critical pedagogy. Her essay also discusses her experiment with this framework in teacher education.

Angharad Valdivia and her adolescent daughter Rhiannon Bettivia ("Gender, Generation, Space and Popular Music") offer readers a different insight and a very different conversation regarding the participation of contemporary youth in popular culture. In a theoretically grounded conversation, we hear the voices of a feminist scholar and her adolescent daughter grappling with the issue of the role of popular music in the lives of adolescent girls. Ultimately, the dialogue between mother and daughter reaches beyond the matter of cultural consumption and selection to the issue of pedagogical and strategic intervention in the processes of production and circulation of youth music. They maintain that adolescent girls have contradictory needs and desires and that they prosecute these in their participation in popular culture. In this sense, girls like Rhiannon are not the mindless charges of the culture industry and the cultural forms that it produces and circulates.

In the concluding essay ("The 'Sound' Identity: Music-Making and Schooling"), Glenn Hudak both speaks back to and points beyond the general direction of the volume by directing us out of the narrowness of identity politics and cultural affiliation—purposes to which youth music has too often been subordinated. In a social phenomenology of music making, Hudak explicates what he defines as the formation of a "sound identity"—the formation of the musical "We." The importance of the sound identity is best stated in his opening sentence:

> So powerful is the desire to make music with others, that one is tempted to conceive of music-making as an emergent, radical engagement with consciousness: an engagement which can "rattle" the hegemony of everyday life and open up the possibility of common ground where differences might meet, mingle, and engage one another.

Indeed, Hudak's piece asks us to reflect back upon notions of identity and difference in the creation of "common spaces" where "We" might meet, mingle, and engage one another in building a democracy.

References

Apple, M. (1979). *Ideology and curriculum.* New York: Routledge.

Appadurai, A. (1996). *Modernity at large.* Minneapolis: University of Minnesota Press.

Bennett, W. (1994). *The book of virtues.* New York: Simon and Schuster.

Ellsworth, E. (1989). Why doesn't this feel empowering. *Harvard Educational Review, 59* (3), 287–324.

Fiske, J. (1987). *Television culture.* New York: Methuen.

Frith, K. (1997). *Undressing the ad: Reading culture in advertising.* New York: Peter Lang.

Frith, S. (1992). The cultural study of popular music. In L. Grossberg, C. Nelson & P. Treichler, *Cultural studies* (pp. 174–186). New York: Routledge.

Fuss, D. (1989). *Essentially speaking: Feminism, nature and difference.* New York: Routledge.

Gilroy, P. (1997). 'After the love has gone': bio-politics and ethnopoetics in the black public sphere. In A. McRobbie (Ed.), *Back to reality* (pp. 83–115). London: Routledge.

Grossberg, Lawrence. (1992). *We gotta get out of this place.* New York: Routledge.

Hirsch, E.D. (1987) *Cultural literacy: What every American needs to know.* New York: Houghton Mifflin.

Masterman, L. (1990). *Teaching the media.* New York: Routledge.

Parenti, M. (1993) *Inventing reality: The politics of the new media.* New York: St. Martin's.

Ravitch, D. & Finn, C. (1987). *What do our 17-year-olds know?* New York: Harper and Row.

Richards, C. (1995). Popular music and media education. *Discourse 16*(3), 317–330.

Rose, T. (1993). *Black noise.* New York: Routledge.

MUSIC IN THE NATION: RAP, HIP HOP, AND THE FLOW OF VALUES

Gangsta Pedagogy and Ghettocentricity: The Hip-Hop Nation as Counterpublic Sphere

Peter McLaren

Race is the modality in which class is lived.
                    —Eric Lott (in *Social Text 12*, No. 3, 1994)

I was beautiful; after all, my skin was as rich and as dark as wet, brown mud, a complexion that any and every pale white girl would pray for. . . . My butt sat high in the air and my hips obviously gave birth to Creation.
                    —Sister Souljah (No disrespect, 1995, p. 98)

Black athletes . . . white agents
Black preacher . . . white Jesus
Black entertainers . . . white lawyers
Black Monday . . . white Christmas
                    —Chuck D, "White Heaven . . . Black Hell"

It's your world
(and yours and yours and yours)
and what you see,
it was not meant for me.
It's your world,
but you don't have to be lonely
'cause in your world,
you are truly Free!
                    —Gil Scott-Heron (1976)

When Harvard scholar Henry Louis Gates, Jr. defended the imagery and lyrics of 2 Live Crew at their highly publicized 1990 trial, claiming that the group's album, *As Nasty as They Wanna Be*, was not obscene on the grounds that the lyrics and imagery were derived from the venerable African American tradition of "signifying" and "playing the dozens," no doubt many critics were thinking that the controversy over rap would probably go the way of the debates over rock 'n' roll in the 1950s: it would generally "fade away." At the time of the trial it was difficult to imagine not only the public furor over rap music— gangsta rap in particular—but also the extent to which Washington would develop its anti-rap campaign, signaling a "moral panic" destined to become one of the lightning rods in the 1996 presidential campaign and a flash point in the current debate over race relations. As former secretary of education and drug czar William J. Bennett joins forces with C. DeLores Tucker, the conservative activist with the National Political Caucus of Black Women, to publicly denounce gangsta rap as a seductive, immoral force, perennial presidential candidates Bob Dole, Phil Gramm, and Pat Buchanan decided not only to join in the condemnation of Time Warner (which up to the time of this writing owns interests in a number of rap record labels) but also to launch a frontal assault on Hollywood's entertainment industry and all those liberals who were likely to defend affirmative action, government assistance programs for nondocumented workers, or gay-rights initiatives.

Despite the fact that the Geto Boys' lead rapper, Bushwick Bill, recently thanked Dole for $300,000 worth of publicity (Katz 1995, pp. 1, 18, 19; Proffitt 1995, p. M3) the attacks had a considerable negative effect on the rap industry, prompting Time Warner to fire record executive Doug Morris and to be reportedly (as of this writing) negotiating its way out of a $100 million share in Interscope Records, distributor of Snoop Doggy Dogg, Dr. Dre, and the late Tupac Shakur ("Time Warner" 1995).[1]

Gangsta rappers follow a long line of musicians denounced by the moral custodians of U.S. culture as prime instigators of juvenile delinquency—a list that includes, among others, Frank Sinatra, Elvis, the Beatles, the Sex Pistols, Metallica, and Prince. Members of my generation, puzzling over the 2 Live Crew trial or reflecting on the earlier public debates surrounding the subliminal messages purportedly inserted into songs by Judas Priest and Ozzy Osborne, are perhaps reminded of earlier controversies that accompanied the Rolling Stones' hit "Satisfaction," or the two-and-a-half-year analysis by J. Edgar Hoover's G-men of the Kingsmen's 1963 hit, "Louie, Louie" (Katz 1995).[2] The investigation by FBI sound technicians and cryptographers of this pop chant (which merely recounts a lovesick sailor's return to his Jamaican sweetheart) seems ironic now, given the fact that the teen anthem has since appeared as the backdrop of numerous films, charity telethons, and wine cooler ads (Lipsitz, 1994). The debate over gangsta rap has captured the public imagination at a time when the nation is vigorously reevaluating public policies surrounding affirmative action and urban reform. This has given gangsta rap an urgency and public visibility far greater than earlier debates over rock 'n' roll and morality. Sister Souljah had been criticized by President Clinton and others for inciting violence against white people when in fact she had told a journalist only that she could understand why some black people might want to kill white people:

> In the mind of a gang member, why not kill white people? In other words, if you've been neglected by the social and economic order of America, and you've become casual about killing, you would have no hesitancy about killing somebody white (cited in Rushkoff, 1996, p. 163).

In providing a sociological insight she was roundly condemned—unfairly—as a hate-mongerer. Rapper Chuck D. maintains that rappers themselves don't necessarily feel violent towards whites. Rappers are contemporary urban messengers from God:

> It's not me, or Ice Cube, or Sister Souljah's feelings—we're just the messengers, and how you gonna kill the messenger? The best thing about rap is it's a last-minute warning, the final call . . . a last plea for help on the countdown to Armageddon (Rushkoff, p. 163).

Chuck D. sees rap as the 'hood's equivalent of CNN.

As I complete some final editing to this essay, which takes the form of an interrogative excursion into the subject of gangsta rap, the *Los Angeles Times* reports that rap singer Dasean Cooper (J-Dee), a member of Da Lench Mob, was recently sentenced to 29 years to life for the 1993 murder of his girlfriend's male roommate at a party in Inglewood (Mitchell, 1995, pp. 81, 88; Muhammad, 1995, pp. 4, 10). Terry (T-Bone) Gray, another member of Da Lench Mob, has also been charged with murdering one individual—and wounding another—at a Los Angeles bowling alley. Da Lench Mob's 1992 single, "Who You Gonna Shoots Wit Dat," was cited in the Cooper case by the prosecuting attorney in an attempt to paint murders by rap artists as "life imitating art." Rap artists, such as Snoop Doggy Dog and the late Tupac Shakur, have been the target of several criminal charges, including sexual assault, physical battery, and accessory to murder. The widow of slain Texas police officer Bill Davidson once sued Tupac for allegedly inciting a 19-year-old car thief, Ronald Ray Howard, to murder Davidson with a nine-millimeter pistol. After listening to the mantra-like lyrics of Shakur's song "Crooked Ass Nigga," from his album *2Pacalypse Now*, which describes a drug dealer on a rampage with a nine-millimeter pistol and contains a reference to "droppin' the cop," Howard claims that he "snapped" and shot Davidson as a result of being instructed by the lyrics. Dan Quayle cashed in on the media attention by visiting Davidson's grieving daughter and announcing that Tupac's music "has no place in our society." These events have induced the breach birth of the gangsta rap media elite and have added to hip-hop's hype as hard-edged urban drama muscled onto a compact disc. As this chapter is being completed, Tupac lies dead of gunshot wounds that he received in Las Vegas after attending the Mike Tyson–Bruce Seldon boxing match. He was shot while driving in a car with Death Row Records co-founder and president, Marion "Suge" Knight. Although he bragged defiantly about the tough life in the 'hood, and had "Thug Life" and an AK-47 assault weapon tattooed across his abdomen, his Grammy-nominated 1995 hit single, "Dear Mama," was a tender ballad written for his mother. Tupac's mother, Afeni Shakur, was a member of the Black Panther Party and was pregnant with Tupac while she was serving time in a New York prison for allegedly plotting to blow up department stores and police stations. He sang: "Even as a crack fiend always was a black queen." The name Tupac Amaru comes from a sixteenth-century Incan chief whose name means "shining serpent." Tupac Amaru was the last Incan leader to be defeated by the Spanish. He was executed in 1572. The Tupac Amaru Revolutionary Movement led by Nestor Cerpa Cartolini made international headlines in its fateful siege of Japanese diplomats in Lima, Peru, in early 1997. Tupac's posthumous *The Don Killuminati: The 7 Day Theory* is compared to the Beatles' *Anthology 3* as the nation's best-selling album.

Eazy-E's death from AIDS left the hip-hop nation stunned. (Eazy-E was a former member of NWA, a financial contributor to the Republican party, and the head of Ruthless Records, the first significant rapper-owned record label.) Early last April, the Los Angeles Police Department joined with FBI agents in Operation Sunrise, sweeping through a 30-block area of South Central LA, arresting gang members of the Eight-Tray Gangster Crips, a gang that came into public prominence during the 1992 uprising with its involvement in the attack on truck driver Reginald O. Denny and other motorists at the intersection of Florence and Normandie. East LA Chicanos are still recovering from the news of the slaying of Selena, superstar of Tejano music and heroine of Molinatown's Chicano barrio in Corpus Christi. Among gangsta rappers, the mood of the city felt all too familiar.

When jury selection in the murder trial of Snoop Doggy Dogg, his bodyguard, and his friend began in Los Angeles, defense attorneys (including Johnnie L. Cochran, Jr.) were preparing to "play the LAPD card" in their attack on police evidence tampering. In the post-Simpson era, the lawyers representing Snoop Doggy Dogg (a.k.a. Calvin Broadus, former member of the Long Beach Insane Crips) and his associates stand a good chance of landing further blows to the credibility and integrity of the police. A few months earlier Snoop Doggy Dogg was praised by President Bill Clinton and Ice-T for writing a letter to 60 gang sets in Los Angeles and honoring their efforts to "keep the peace." As Snoop Doggy Dogg's words of thanks were sounded at a celebration at the International House of Blues in West Los Angeles, sets from the Imperial Courts, Jordan Downs, and Nickerson Gardens housing projects in Watts sat down with the Fruit Town Pirus of Compton and sets from Long Beach, the Pueblo Bishops 5 Duce Mid-City Gangsters, the 5 Duce BCG, the Santana Block Crips, the V-13s and Shoreline Crips of Venice, and the Parkside Manor Circle City Pirus of Los Angeles. When, at this afternoon gala, a Crip, a Blood, and a Latino gang member cut a cake in unison, gangsta rappers had symbolically joined forces with Bill Clinton's four-member color guard, present at the ceremonies as a sign of "respect."

For someone who grew up listening to Robert Johnson's Delta Blues, who used to frequent the Colonial Tavern on Toronto's Yonge Street to hear musician friends jam with Muddy Waters, who idolized Lightning Hopkins, and who wanted to play the blues harp like Little Walter, rap music was not a natural transition for me. Ska, rock-steady, and reggae helped to broaden my musical sensibilities, but, even so, rap was a taste that was difficult to acquire at first. In recent years I have grown to greatly appreciate gangsta rap as an oppositional political practice, but despite its possibilities for articulating an oppositional performative politics, gangsta rap remains, in some senses, a problematic cultural practice.

In this article I am generally referring to *gangsta rap* and do not wish to conflate this term with those of *rap* or *hip-hop*. When I speak generally about rap music as a form of black cultural address, without specifically calling it gangsta rap, I am emphasizing rap music's situatedness within hip-hop culture, its criticism of the dominant white culture's racial and economic discrimination, and the contradictory urban expressions of African American economic and racial marginality. Here I share Tricia Rose's perspective that rap "is a black idiom that prioritizes black culture and that articulates the problem of black urban life" (1994, p. 4). I am referring to rap artists as cultural workers engaged to a large extent in "the everyday struggles of working-class blacks and the urban poor" (Decker 1994, p. 101). Jeffrey Louis Decker refers to such cultural workers as "hip hop nationalists" who function in the manner suggested by Gramsci's description of organic intellectuals (Katz 1995).

With what some rap critics might call its numbing psychorealism; its fixing of "in-your-face" rhymes to social meltdown and bass rhythms to urban disaster; its commodification of black rage through high-volume and low-frequency sound; its production of sexualizing fugues for an imploding Generation X; its ability to provoke a white hellification of black youth with "attitude"; its seventh sons in blue or red bandanas and ten-dollar gold tooth caps "droppin science" and warning their homeboys against "tell-lie-vision," the "lie-bury," and public school "head-decay-tion"; its dance culture of the Handglide, Flow, Headspin, King Tut, Windmill, Tick, Float, Wave, and freestyle; its production of affective economies of white panic around a generalized fear of a black planet; its sneering, tongue-flicking contempt of public space; its visceral intensity and corporal immediacy; its snarling, subterranean resistance; its eschatological showdown of "us" against "them"; its "edutainers" down with the brothas in the street; its misogynist braggadocio; its pimp-inspired subjectivity; its urban war zone counternarratives; its home-brewed polymerized anarchism; its virulent autobiographical hype; its Five Percenters flashing their ciphers, 7s, and crescent moon and star within a large sun, praising "Father Allah"; its irreverent first-person narratives powered by gats and urban souljahs high on malt liquor; its rhythmic macho boastfests by brothas in Carhartt jackets; and its dissentious themes and high-pitched contempt for the white petit bourgeoisie and the yuppie heirs of the overclass who can afford to sidestep the frenetic dizziness of reality, gangsta rap has occasioned much public debate over the last few years. Gangsta rap is merely the latest incarnation of the rap music industry in general.

Tricia Rose notes that rap music was "discovered" by the music industry, the print media, the fashion industry, and the film industry during the five years after music entrepreneur Sylvia Robinson released "Rapper's Delight" in 1979. Rose further declares that rap music needs to be situated within Afro-diasporic traditions and cultural formations of the English- and Spanish-speaking Caribbean and in the context of specific historical musical junctions such as urban blues, be-bop, and rock 'n' roll. Further, rap needs to be considered in light of such factors as the creation of the postindustrial city and the larger social movement of hip-hop. For instance, rap music can be traced to, among other cultural and social elements, the hip hop nationalism of the 1960s, such as the Black Panthers, Malcolm X, gender politics; New York City's political context of the 1970s; postindustrial shifts in economic conditions, including access to housing, the formation of new communication networks; blaxploitation films such as Melvin Van Peebles's *Sweet Sweetback's Baadassss Song*; deindustrialization; the relocation of people of color from different parts of New York City into the South Bronx; city planning and projects such as the Title I Clearance program; the system of crews or posses as means for alternative youth identities: disco music and the cross-fertilization among rapping, break dancing, and graffiti writing (Loza 1994).

In the 1980s we started to see rap music emerging in other urban ghettos in major cities, such as Houston's Fifth Ward, Miami's Overtown, Boston's Roxbury, and South Central, Watts, and Compton in Los Angeles. The Los Angeles rappers have spawned a specific rap style that, Rose notes, must be seen in the context of narratives specific to poor, young, black, male subjects in Los Angeles. Rose writes that Los Angeles rappers "defined the gangsta rap style" and

> spawned other regionally specific hardcore rappers such as New Jersey's Naughty by Nature, Bronx-based Tim Dog, Onyx, and Redman, and a new group of female gangsta rappers, such as Boss (two black women from Detroit), New York–based Puerto Rican rapper Hurricane Gloria, and Nikki D. (Rose 1994, p. 59).

When examining the roots of rap, or rap's inflection into gangsta rap genres, we need to examine the conjunctural specificity of many factors, including those listed above.

White and black listeners alike are drawn to this surly form of urban apostasy, fashionable deviancy, and stylized outlawry, whose message and transgressive status dig pretty close to the eschatological roots of holy war. Gangsta rap has been accused by some middle-class whites as well as some black professionals of fomenting the anger, racial hatred, and lawlessness that led to the LA uprising of 1992. Of course, in tandem with such dispatches from the bourgeoisie was a studied ignorance about the irreversible structural unemployment faced by many blacks in the inner city, the dismantling of social services, and the progressive hardening of racial lines.

The LA media have not been known for their celebration of rap as a musical genre since the heyday of its Compton rappers: MC Ren, Dr. Dre, Yella, Ice Cube, and Eazy-E (who left groups such as The CIA and World Class Wreckin Cru in order to work collaboratively as NWA— Niggas With Attitude—from 1987 to 1992). Instead, the media have preferred to demonize and hellify the genre that these young Angelenos from Watts, Compton, and South Central—"the nihilistic school of Los Angeles–centered gangsta rappers"—helped to create (Lott 1994, p. 246). Following their more politicized hard-core and hard-beat counterparts in New York (such as Run-DMC and KRS-1) on the East Coast (such as Notorious B.I.G.), in the footsteps of New York's Grandmaster Flash and the Furious Five, and fellow Angelenos Gil Scott-Heron, the Watts Prophets, and the Last Poets (a group of black nationalist lyricists), LA rap artists provided the space for the development of a new form of social criticism. This form of social criticism was apotheosized in Ice Cube's *The Predator*, which offered a potent commentary on the LA uprising of 1992. The cultural power and promise of rap resided in its powerful dramatization of white racism. In "We Had to Tear This Motherfucker Up," Ice Cube (a.k.a. O'Shea Jackson) sentences former LAPD officers Stacey Koon, Laurence Powell, and Timothy Wind to death for the beating of Rodney King.

Like their New York counterpart, Afrika Bambaataa, former member of the Black Spades street gang and founder of the hip-hop community Zulu Nation (made up of African American, Puerto Rican, Afro-Caribbean, and Euro-American youths and based on the Zulu military system), LA rappers Ice-T, Tone Loc, Ice Cube, and Eazy-E were also former gangbangers. Many of these rappers were products of the economic and cultural upheavals that had assaulted and displaced numerous multiethnic urban communities; their futures were bound up in the dimming job market by inner-city trade vocational schooling. For instance, hip-hop originator DJ Kool Herc (whose original rap style was influenced by prison "toasting") attended Alfred E. Smith auto mechanic trade school; Grandmaster Flash studied electronic repair work at Samuel Gompers vocational high school; and Salt 'n' Pepa both worked as telemarketing representatives at Sears and were intent at one time on nursing school (Rose 1994). These working-class black youths were able to escape the uncertain futures constructed for them in an era of deindustrialization. They are some of the lucky few to succeed as part of a financially lucrative musical phenomenon. However, it is a phenomenon often accused of fomenting racial panics and urban youth criminality. Just ask Charlton Heston and Oliver North.

Emerging in the 1970s from the epicenters of hip-hop culture—the blue-collar housing units of America's postindustrial cities—rap music developed among relocated black and Puerto Rican male youths of the South Bronx who celebrated break dancing, graffiti, B-Boy, and wild style fashions (Lipsitz, 1994). Puerto Rican rap has incorporated inflections from salsa, variations of which are drawn from *Santería* rhythms, as is the case of the music of Tito Puente (himself a priest of *Santería*).

Some of the major strands of hip-hop culture (in which rap, style, and politics become mutually informing inflections) can be traced from the jive talkers of the be-bop era to the reggae-based sounds of Jamaican DJ Kool Herc in the West Bronx in 1973 and Jah Rico in north London around 1976. Hip-hop youth in the Bronx and London sympathized with the economic and social struggles of young people in Jamaica and Soweto, wore dreadlocks ("Funki Dreds") with shaved back and sides created by Jazzy B and Aitch for the Soul II Soul crew, or combined the Philly Cut or skiffle with shaved diagonal lines, bleaching, or perms. Shifts in clothes displayed a taxonomy of funky sartorial motifs, from Teenybopper to Home Boy to hard-rocker to Afrocentric; and from Hustler to Superfly to Daisy Age to Cosmic (via Rifat Ozbek). With styles eventually shifting to athletic and leisure wear, Home Boys and Fly Girls started sporting sweatshirts, cropped shorts, "pin-tucked" baggy jeans, baseball caps, chunky gold chains, Dukie Ropes, and leather pendants (Tulloch, 1993). Then came the "hoodies" and the "triple fat" goose down jackets.

Influenced by the music of Curtis Mayfield, the funk of James Brown, be-bop, and rhythmic jazz, rap is an impressive amalgam of complex musical formations. Some ethnomusicologists consider such formations to be extensions of African expressive forms such as "playing the dozens" and "signifying" as well as the praise songs of the African storyteller, or *griot* (Zook, 1992, p. 257).[3] In saying this, however, I am reminded of Tricia Rose's important admonition that hip-hop not be reduced to its African musical origins as oral traditions. Hip-hop needs to be understood, argues Rose, as a "secondary orality" bound up in an electronically mediated reality that is conjuncturally embedded in relations of power and politics. Rose further notes that "rap musicians are not the only musicians to push on the limits of high-tech inventions. Yet, the decisions they have made and the directions their creative impulses have taken echo Afro-diasporic musical priorities. Rap production resonates with Black cultural priorities in the age of digital reproduction" (Rose, 1994, p. 251).

Tricia Rose's discussion of mass-produced repetition undercuts perspectives by Adorno, Attali, and Jameson by arguing that repetition in rap is not always connected to the commodity system of late capitalism in the same way as other musical forms. She argues that repetition in mass-cultural formations can also serve as a form of collective resistance (Rose, 1994a, p. 4).

The operational or performative logics of gangsta rap vary but what is constant is what Lawrence Grossberg calls "affective agency"—its ability to articulate "mattering maps" in which agency is defined as brushing up against the prison of everyday life (Grossberg, 1994). Michael Dyson describes the emergence of rap within a context that emphasizes its situatedness as a cultural form of resistance. According to Dyson:

> Rap music grew from its origins in New York's inner city over a decade ago as a musical outlet to creative cultural energies and to contest the invisibility of the ghetto in mainstream American society. Rap remythologized New York's status as the spiritual center of black America, boldly asserting appropriation and splicing (not originality) as the artistic strategies by which the styles and sensibilities of black ghetto youth would gain popular influence. Rap developed as a relatively independent expression of black male artistic rebellion against the black bourgeois *Weltanschauung,* tapping instead into the cultural virtues and vices of the so-called underclass, romanticizing the ghetto as the fecund root of cultural identity and authenticity, the Rorschach of legitimate masculinity and racial unity (Dyson, 1994, pp. 159–160).

Tricia Rose describes hip-hop culture, from which rap and eventually gangsta rap evolved, in a more global context:

> Hip hop is an Afro-diasporic cultural form which attempts to negotiate the experiences of marginalization, brutally truncated opportunity and oppression within the cultural imperatives of African-American and Caribbean history, identity and community. It is the tension between the cultural fractures produced by postindustrial oppression and the binding ties of Black cultural expressivity that sets the critical frame for the development of hip hop (Rose, 1994, p. 71).

Rap's beginnings as highly politicized and powerfully eclectic music can be seen in such songs as "Rapper's Delight" by the Sugarhill Gang

in 1979, Brother D's (Daryl Asmaa Nubyah) "We Gonna Make the
Black Nation Rise," recorded in 1980, and Afrika Bambaataa and
Soul Sonic Force's 1982 recording of "Planet Rock." According to
Dick Hebdige, Bambaataa "has been known to cut from salsa to
Beethoven's Fifth Symphony to Yellow Magic Orchestra to calypso
through Kraftwerk via video game sound effects and the theme from
The Munsters television series back to his base in James Brown."
Bambaataa—who ran a sound system at the Bronx River Community
Center—would also mix the theme from the *Pink Panther* with bits
and pieces of songs from the Monkees, the Beatles, and the Rolling
Stones (Hebdige, 1987).

Poison Clan, AMG, Hi-C, Nu Niggaz on the Block, Compton Cartel, 2nd II None, Mob Style, and Compton's Most Wanted did not
emerge in a social vacuum. When former LAPD Chief of Police Darryl
Gates proclaimed that "we may be finding that in some Blacks when
[the chokehold] is applied the veins or arteries do not open up as fast
as they do on normal people," he was reflecting the sentiments of the
white dominant culture of law enforcement in Los Angeles (Kelley,
1994, p. 184). Not only was he demonizing African Americans as
biologically subnormal, he was adding to the criminalization of black
youth in general, corralling connotations of black masculinity into the
operative lexicon of unimpeachable white common sense. The LAPD
term describing "African Americans in the vicinity" as "Gorillas in the
Mist" provoked Da Lench Mob to title their album *Guerrillas in tha
Midst*. Some cultural critics were beginning to view rap artists as agents
of revolutionary consciousness. When Operation HAMMER sent Chief
Gates and his minions into the streets of South Central to pick up
"suspicious looking" black youth, harass them, and build up the data
base of the LAPD's task force, gangsta rappers were portraying the
practice of law enforcement as a form of racial and class warfare.

After the release of NWA's 1988 debut album, *Straight Outta
Compton*, white audiences were treated to urban nightmares of white
throats being slit in midscream. NWA's hit crossover recording,
"Efil4zaggin"—"niggaz 4 life" spelled backward—was the first hardcore
rap collection to reach number one on the pop charts. Then "Cop
Killer" hit the airwaves, with Ice-T's hard, pounding, and pimpified
lyrics smashing through listeners' ribs like a brass-knuckled fist, tag-
ging a "don't fuck with me" on their hearts with an aerosol can of his
digitized blood. The media went ballistic in condemnation of this new
transgressive musical form known as "gangsta rap," which was even
propelling white audiences into adopting black inflection and "ghetto"

identification. Ice-T became buoyant after President Clinton publicly criticized "Cop Killer" and sixty congressmen signed a letter condemning the song:

> Very few people have their names said by the president, especially in anger. It makes me feel good, like I haven't been just standing on a street corner yelling with nobody listening all the time. . . . It lets you know how small this country is (cited in Rushkoff, 1996, p. 164).

Ice Cube's 1990 hit "Endangered Species," from the album *Amerikkka's Most Wanted*, captures the attitude that many gangsta rap lyrics reflect with respect to law enforcement agencies:

> Every cop killer ignored
> They just send another nigger to the morgue
> A point scored.
> They could give a fuck about us
> They'd rather find us with guns and white powder
> Now kill ten of one to get the job correct.
> To serve, protect and break a nigga's neck.

This was heavy stuff in a society too preoccupied with consolidating its hegemony through frontal assaults on the welfare state and labor coalitions to concern itself with a bunch of "lowlifes" singing about their crime-ridden hoods. Latino rap didn't really become popular until 1990, during a groundswell of public panic surrounding the growing Latino population in the United States and amidst the reactionary tactics of the English Only Movement. Mellow Man Ace went gold with *Mentirosa*, and Kid Frost's (a.k.a. Arturo Molina) Chicanismo-inspired debut album, *Hispanic Causing Panic*, became the rap anthem of La Raza (Flores, 1994). Chicano rapper ALT (a.k.a. Al Trivette) fuses insights of barrio life in El Monte and Rosemead into African American rap in albums *ALT* and *Stone Cold World*.

The amazing thing about the disjunctive barrage of ghetto moments known as rap was that it sold, turning inner-city homeys such as Mixmaster Spade into deities in gold chains, hawking their rap wares on the very mean streets that they rapped about. Since those early days, gangsta rap has even gone platinum with Dre's *The Chronic* and Snoop's *Doggystyle*.

In the eyes of many ghetto youth, society is going under and gangsta rappers and hepcats from the barrios are the new prophets, sounding their nationalist warnings over a Roland TR 808 drum synthesizer as the world about them swirls into the urban vortex, like DeNiro's ex-convict character in *Cape Fear*, whose savaged and tattooed body writhes while his soul speaks in tongues as both sink beneath the foaming waters.

Death Row Records, run by Andre (Dr. Dre) Young and Marion "Suge" Knight, is the nation's most profitable producer of gangsta rap, grossing a total of $90 million from tape, CD, and merchandise sales in 1993 and 1994 (Cheevers, Philips, and Williams, 1995). Affiliated with media giant Time Warner, this Westwood-based firm boasts a corporate logo of a hooded man in an electric chair. Death Row Records has not escaped the controversies surrounding its stars' involvement in criminal violence. At a party for its out-of-town retailers and promoters held hours after Snoop Doggy Dogg (Calvin Broadus) took top honors at the Soul Train Music Awards, a fan was brutally stomped to death. Young is currently serving a five-month term in Pasadena City jail for parole violation. In 1992 he was convicted of breaking another rap producer's jaw and hitting a New Orleans police officer in a hotel brawl. A year earlier he was convicted of slamming a TV talk-show host into a wall at a Hollywood club. Knight was also convicted of assault with a deadly weapon. According to Dre, "America loves violence. America is obsessed with murder. I think murder sells a lot more than sex. They say sex sells. I think murder sells" (Cheevers et al., p. 18).[4] However, Death Row Records publicly denounces gang violence, and the firm has donated $500,000 to a South Central antigang program.

Russell Simmons, CEO of Def Jam Recordings (the largest African American–owned company in the record business), defends rap as a way to reach kids in Beverly Hills:

> And the most important thing is this. It's very, very important that there be communication between kids that would generally not talk to each other. Your kids may not be bad, but it's pretty sure they know some who are. Your kids are surrounded by those kids. So maybe some kid in Beverly Hills listens to rap and gets a better idea of what some kids in Crenshaw are thinking. And as that kid in Beverly Hills grows up and goes to college, maybe he'll keep a little bit of that in his consciousness, and maybe even grow up to do something about it (Proffitt, 1995, p. M3).

Simmons's justification for rap and gangsta rap as the contemporary hope for shaping the consciousness of rich white kids in Beverly Hills certainly overestimates rap's potential for political resistance and social transformation through the mobilization of Generation X. Yet, it vastly underestimates the power of capitalist hegemony to produce, promote, and protect the vested interests of dominant culture in Western society, and what it takes to construct counterhegemonic social practices.

Shortly after the 1992 LA Intifada, pop singer Michelle Shocked and freelance writer Bart Bull mounted a powerful (if not profoundly misguided) denunciation of gangsta rap in an issue of *Billboard*. Claiming it to be a contemporary recoding of a turn-of-the-century white racist stereotype, a racist revival of the minstrel tradition as embodied in the nineteenth-century "coon song," they proclaimed that the "chicken-thieving, razor-toting 'coon' of the 1890s is the drug-dealing, Uzi-toting 'nigga' of today" (quoted by Grant, 1994, p. 44). Ice Cube is criticized by Shocked and Bull as a "greed artist" who, through albums such as *The Predator*, is profiting from the conditions that produce the underclass through his production of a "Zip Coon Toon Town" version of Los Angeles, "a coon song fantasyland." This perspective is echoed by New York essayist and music critic Stanley Crouch, who calls gangsta rap "the selling of coon images" and who compares record executives who produce gangsta rap to "high tech slave traders" (quoted in Katz, 1995, p. 18). Crouch condemns gangsta rap for portraying black people as wild savages and as badges of black authenticity, as the "real" voices from the hood. Taking issue with Crouch's position, the Geto Boys' lead rapper, Bushwick Bill (whose physical status as a one-eyed midget has not been lost on rap's media critics), describes rap as an "opera to people in the ghetto" (quoted in Katz). Rock critic Dave Marsh argues that the attack on rap is directed at new access to the mainstream media by America's underclass. He condemns the anti-rap campaign by William Bennett and C. DeLores Tucker as 1990s-style McCarthyism. Former *Wall Street Journal* writer and critic Martha Bayles blames the offensive lyrics in much of today's music not on African American music but on the avant-garde European art school thinking that she calls "perverse modernism" (quoted in Katz).

In Mexico border towns like Tijuana, *narcocorrido* ballads (historically derived from the narrative style of Nahuatl epic poetry and Andalusian romantic verse from the sixteenth century) tell stories of drug dealers who prevail in the face of the authorities. Narcocorrido balladeers have provoked the wrath of antidrug spokespeople such as Marta Rocha de Diaz, president of Housewives of Playas de Tijuana. The public debate is similar to that surrounding gangsta rap. Los Tucanes sing *narcocorridos* about smugglers who take heroin, cocaine, and marijuana across the border into the United States. The popularity of Los Tucanes and Los Tigres del Norte has provoked critics to condemn narcocorridos for mimicking U.S.-style gangsta rap.

David Troop's *Rap Attack: African Jive to New York Hip Hop* (1984), Houston Baker's *Black Studies: Rap and the Academy* (1993), and Tricia Rose's brilliant *Black Noise: Rap Music and Black Culture in Contemporary America* (1994) are just a few of the burgeoning scholarly commentaries on rap that offer a much more congenial account of rap's potential for developing forms of counterhegemonic resistance than the account of gangsta rap that is offered by Shocked and Bull. For these critics, it is important to understand how and why the terms governing the popular responses to rap have come into being and how they have, to a large extent, become naturalized. Accordingly, these writers maintain the need to see hip hop in a much broader context: as a global cultural practice that is articulated through the tropes and sensibilities of the African diaspora and the history of Afro-America, and that creates a "diasporic interchange" and "diasporic intimacy" among struggling black peoples the world over who are fighting racism and capitalist exploitation (Lipsitz, 1994). As Nick De Genova emphasizes,

> rather than as an expression of social pathology, gangster rap's imaginative empowerment of a nihilistic and ruthless way of life can be better understood as a potentially oppositional consciousness—albeit born of desperation, or even despair (De Genova, 1995, p. 113).

Common subjective understandings of alienation among oppressed groups are articulated through rap; as a cultural force it is integral in providing black urban youth with both an expression of race and with codes of solidarity. As De Genova puts it, "gangsta rap can be found to transcend the mere reflection of urban mayhem and enter into musical debate with these realities, without sinking into didacticism or flattening their complexity" (De Genova, 1995, p. 114). Rap needs to be understood not so much for its musical poaching through "sampling" as for the way that it is premised on what Tricia Rose calls "transformations and hybrids"—developing "a style that nobody can deal with." She writes that

> transformations and hybrids reflect the initial spirit of rap and hip hop as an experimental and collective space where contemporary issues and ancestral forces are worked through simultaneously. Hybrids in rap's subject matter, not unlike its use of musical collage and the influx of new, regional and ethnic

styles, have not yet displaced the three points of stylistic continuity to which I referred earlier: approaches to flow, ruptures in line and layering can still be found in the vast majority of rap's lyrical and music construction. The same is true of the critiques of the postindustrial urban America context and the cultural and social conditions which it has produced. Today, the South Bronx and South Central Los Angeles are poorer and more economically marginalized than they were ten years ago (Rose 1994, 1994, p. 83).

Strutting apocalyptically across the urban landscape, today's gangsta rappers have, for some listeners, become the new black superheroes invested with dangerous, ambiguous, uncontrolled, and uncontrollable powers, the force of nature bound up with self-conscious and grandiose marginality. You don't fuck with these brothers and sisters and live to tell about it. Shocked and Bull's dismissive appraisal of gangsta rap as a message primarily mediated by whites eager to be titillated by the thrilling despair within aggrieved black urban communities, in the form of "bad nigga" narratives and hyperbolic masculinism, underscores their view that the production and performativity of rap is directly at the expense of the structurally subordinated black subject. But is gangsta rap really "an exaggerated defiance feigned for commercial purposes," signifying steroids for sculpting rage, or perhaps a "mock nihilism that parallels the ambiguous accommodationism displayed in subversive forms of minstrelsy" (Lott, 1994, p. 247), or, to borrow a phrase that Charles Pierce used in another context, a "phony menace that is little more than Tomming with your hat turned backward"? (Pierce, 1995).

Some gangsta songs, for instance, promote a stereotypical (re)framing that depicts the gangsta rapper as both sociopath and criminal. Stereotypes are recast and refigured so that the negative connotations (of laziness, violence, etc.) become positive attributes of strength, of power, and of resistance to white domination. While the mock nihilism in gangsta rap "is an inherently resistive element," it has also "been a key element in its commercial exploitation" (Lott, 1994, p. 246). While Angela Davis has decried the sexism of rap, she comments, somewhat reluctantly, on the power evoked by the image of the black man—as gun-toting revolutionary—that is offered up to the public by gangsta rap:

Many of the rappers call upon a market-mediated historical memory of the black movement of the sixties and seventies. The image of an armed Black man is considered the 'essence' of revolutionary commitment today. As dismayed as I may feel about this simplistic, phallocentric image, I remember my own responses to romanticized images of brothers (and sometimes sisters) with guns" (Davis, 1992, p. 327).

bell hooks argues that much of the sexism and misogyny that riddles rap songs is based on an assertive patriarchal paradigm of competitive masculinity and its emphasis on physical prowess. Decker presents Sister Souljah's role as a member of Public Enemy between 1990 and 1992 as deflecting gender-based criticism away from Public Enemy and constructing "an alibi for the stereotypical hypermasculinity of black men" through her exclusive emphasis on racial politics and her allegiance to a hip-hop nationalism that tends to objectify the black woman as a sign of "Mother Africa" (Decker, 1994, p. 109). Black female rappers, however, have done much to present affirming images of black women outside the binary couplet of good girl/bad girl that dominates the patriarchal culture of gangsta rap. For instance, Queen Latifah (Dana Owens) has challenged racist white America's view of black women as "welfare queens" and unwed mothers as well as the view of some black nationalists that women accept roles subordinate to men. For Latifah, women are not the "bitches" signified by some male rap artists. According to Steven Gregory, the welfare mother (defended by Queen Latifah and other female rappers)

> is a privileged site, where the brutalities of racism, patriarchy, and post-Fordist economic restructuring are mystified and, indeed, eroticized as the reproductive pathologies of black poverty. It is precisely this displacement of a politics of real bodies for a biopolitics of patriarchal desire that renders the iconography of the welfare mother and the inner city serviceable to a wide spectrum of cultural and political projects, ranging from the misogynist beats of gangsta rappers, to the more sober, but no less phallocentric, politics of welfare reform. What these projects share, whether as an appeal for a more "paternalistic" state authority . . . the aggressive policing of "group home turnstiles" or the selective re-tooling of black masculinity à la *Boyz 'N the Hood*, is the conviction that patriarchy is the bedrock of nation-building (Gregory, 1995, p. 20).

Queen Latifah refuses the role given to the black woman within hip-hop nationalism—that of Isis—which merely symbolizes the imperialist glories of Egypt and the African empire. Latifah's Afrocentric expression is remarkable, not only because it is devoid of the concomitant sexism of nationalism but because it challenges the masculine logic of nation as well (Decker, 1994, p. 116).

Rose believes that it is hypocritical of black middle-class critics of rap lyrics not to launch the same level of moral criticism at black urban poverty as well as sexism and racism. She asserts that the problem is: one, that technology brings these vernacular practices, the practices most vulnerable to middle-class outrage, into spaces where they might never have been heard twenty-five years ago; and two, rappers are vulnerable, highly visible cultural workers, which leaves them open to increased sanctions. But sexism, at the level of the toast and the boast, is only a subset of structurally sanctioned sexism. In that way, all manner of cultural practices and discourses that do not challenge the structures upon which these ideas are based wind up confirming them. Why, then, is the concern over rap lyrics so incredibly intense, particularly from Black middle-class guardians? Why not the same level of moral outrage over the life options that Black folks face in this country? It seems to me we need a censorship committee against poverty, sexism, and racism (Rose, 1992, p. 226).

Few cultural formations exist within popular culture that are stronger and more potent politically than gangsta rap. According to Kristal Brent Zook,

To say that rap is no more than a sad by-product of oppression is to take an explanatory, defensive stance when, in actuality, rap is a fundamental component of what may be the strongest political and cultural offensive gesture among African Americans today (Zook 1992, p. 256).

Rap is a powerful offensive medium in the way that it raises havoc with white middle-class complicity in and complacency with institutionalized racism; its dialogic pulsions disarticulate white supremacist governing narratives; it ruptures consensual images of blacks whom middle-class whites wish would "know their place." As De Genova argues,

for its white listeners, gangster rap truly reconstitutes "the tyranny of the real"—both by musically and lyrically reconfiguring the real tyranny of the ghetto-space of death and destruction, and by reconfirming, *through* these phantasms of the "other," the sanitized comfort (and privilege) that comes with the tyrannical tedium of suburban, middle-class reality. It is here that we can discern a shared "culture of terror," a musical conjunction of the terror lived in Black ghettoes, and the enchanting terror *dreamed* in white suburbia (De Genova, 1995, p. 111).

Rap unmakes feelings of security and safety in middle-class homes and neighborhoods. It indexes areas of concrete rage and generalized despair that are normally hidden from the official view of American democracy. De Genova powerfully captures this reality when he argues that gangster rap evokes

a bilateral "culture of terror" in a dislocated "space of death": hegemonic (racist) fantasies about stereotypical "Blackness" and the self-destructive ("savage") violence of the urban ghetto-space, are conjoined with the nihilistic, lawless (oppositional) terror-heroism of proud, unapologetic self-styled "niggers"—Niggas With Attitude, Geto Boys, Compton's Most Wanted, et al.— who fulfill the prophesy and the promise of systemic violence and orchestrated destruction. Thus, gangster rap serves up white America's most cherished gun-slinging mythologies (heroic American dreams) in the form of its worst and blackest nightmares, while it empowers Black imaginations to negate the existential terror of ghetto life (and death) by sheer force of the will (De Genova, 1995, p. 107).

Following Kobena Mercer, George Lipsitz notes that rap is not a radical form in itself but has to be understood as a function of culture. He remarks that

culture functions as a social force to the degree that it gets instantiated in social life and connected to the political aspirations and activities of groups. It is here that hip hop holds its greatest significance and its greatest challenge to interpreters (Lipsitz, 1994, p. 38).

bell hooks lucidly illustrates that the context out of which rap has emerged is intertwined with the public stories of black male lives and the history of the pain suffered by black men in a racist society. She is worth quoting at length:

Rap music provides a public voice for young black men who are usually silenced and overlooked. It emerged in the streets—outside the confines of a domesticity shaped and informed by poverty, outside enclosed spaces where . . . [black bodies] . . . had to be contained and controlled. . . . The public story of black male lives narrated by rap speaks directly to and against white racist domination, but only indirectly hints at the enormity of black male pain. Constructing the black male body as site of pleasure and power, rap and the dances associated with it suggest vibrancy, intensity, and an unsurpassed joy in living. It may very well be that living on the edge, so close to the possibility of being "exterminated" (which is how many young black males feel) heightens one's ability to risk and make one's pleasure more intense. It is this charge, generated by the tension between pleasure and danger, death and desire, that Foucault evokes when he speaks of that *complete total pleasure* that is related to death. Though Foucault is speaking as an individual, his words resonate in a culture affected by anhedonia—the inability to feel pleasure. In the United States, where our senses are daily assaulted and bombarded to such an extent that an emotional numbness sets in, it may take being "on the edge" for individuals to feel intensely. Hence the overall tendency in the culture is to see young black men as both dangerous and desirable (hooks, 1992, pp. 35–36, emphasis in original).

The most politically astute rappers take the racist and sexist stereotypes of black males and recontextualize them so that within popular culture, criminalized and hypersexualized black youths now become fearless rebels "standing up" heroically to the white man's exploitation. This fusion of heroism and criminality, of pleasure and pain, occurs without denying the endemic effects of institutionalized racism, patriarchal structures, heterosexist relations, and class exploitation. De Genova captures this point when he notes that

> gangster rap exposes the multivalence and equivocation of racial essentialism: it evokes all of the conflicted meanings and opposed values which congeal simultaneously around a shared set of socially charged signifiers that comprise a single racial nomenclature (De Genova, 1995, p. 107).

Matthew Grant argues that gangsta rap results from the relationship between the criminalized underclass and the overclass reaching a point "where they can mutually benefit from the destabilization of the middle-class majority." According to Grant, what makes gangsta rap so attractive to the middle-class white consumer is not its attempt to develop a revolutionary consciousness among its listeners, but rather the actively transgressive character of its assaults on middle-class taboos against violence. Gangsta rap provides white consumers who yearn to be part of the hip-hop nation with shocking images in which "the norms of bourgeois liberality are violated in an orgy of paradoxically subaltern elitism" (Grant, 1994, p. 45).[5] Through the politics of voyeurism, white youth can become the menacing urban *baaadman*.

Far from being a dispiriting successor to rhythm and blues, gangsta rap occupies a formidable yet not unproblematic space of resistance to racial oppression. A more productive account of gangsta rap, Grant argues, would examine its "celebration of insanity based as a singularly gendered obsession"—what he calls "the insane investment of the real." Grant writes that

> the fantasy of losing it, of stepping over the limit of reason and civility, of surrendering oneself to the intoxication and ecstasy of violence uninhibited by the strictures of reason, is an important component of male subjectivity (which herein seems to cross boundaries established by class or skin color). Madness, among men, is something that must be endured or overcome (unless one is completely overwhelmed and obliterated by it). The flip side of this adventurist relation to the insane is the wholesale projection of insanity onto women as one legitimation of their exclusion from certain segments of the social order (Grant, 1994, p. 47).

Maintaining that the criticism leveled at rappers—that they wildly sensationalize urban life—is wrongly dependent upon holding rappers

to the same ineluctable standards that inform the genre of social realism, Grant offers a spirited defense of gangsta rap, noting that the

> insanity that speaks through the voice of rap music is not simply a brand of
> psychic exoticism: it is the mental state produced by the process of racist
> oppression to which these bodies are subjected. The radical decentering of
> the subject, either through the use of drugs or through the use of semiauto-
> matic weapons (and what could be more decentering than "a hole in your
> fuckin' head"?), which finds its expression in rap, a decentering celebrated by
> poststructuralists and postmodernists everywhere, results from an intensely
> decentering material configuration of the real. The insane distortions of gangsta
> rap actually make their representations realistic. It's just a psychorealism thing
> (Grant, 1994, p. 47).

Representation, as Grant points out, is not just about adducing an
accurate or realistic depiction of an event from many possible interpretations. It also speaks to forms of political advocacy that, in the
case of gangsta rap, deal primarily with the Kafkaesque and carcereal
universe of the black urban male. (There are also "hard core" female
rappers such as Manhole, a Latina from LA, and Boss, a classically
trained African American musician who did not grow up in the hood
but raps about it as if she did.)

Echoing the music of Dr. Dre and Snoop Doggy Dogg, Grant remarks that prison has become the educational alternative for black
men: "the generalized form of social space for the underclass." Moreover, he argues that "hard core" gangsta rap constitutes a political
program that he describes as an urban guerrilla movement. As a social force, however, gangsta rap overwhelmingly fails in its attempt to
organize effectively, since, according to Grant, it has at its disposal
only an "anarchofascist politics of drug dealership and gang-
bangerism." After all, NWA's drug dealing was decidedly "precapitalist"
and, Grant maintains, no match for "the internationally organized capitalist bloc with its huge armies, advanced armaments, and high-tech
domestic security systems." Despite its failure to bring forth the hegemonic articulations that would make Gramsci proud, gangsta rap does
present what I would call a contingent or provisional utopian longing—a trace, within a tapestry of violent imagery, of what is needed to
bring about social justice. Grant puts it this way:

> Gangsta rap, in spite of its contradictions, in spite of what is retrograde in it
> (like its often vicious sexism and homophobia), at least contains elements that
> give us a glimpse of what a radically oppositional culture could look like (Grant,
> 1994, 51).

De Genova echoes a similar sentiment when he remarks that "rap music flourishes in the contradictory interstices of hegemonic appropriation and a fairly self-conscious and articulate politics of oppositional maneuvering" (De Genova, 1995, p. 105).

I locate gangsta rap as an "oppositional practice" in the sense that Michel de Certeau uses the term. While de Certeau is referring to the actions of the Amerindians, I believe his ideas are applicable to many contemporary groups—for example, African Americans—who find themselves exploited and oppressed. According to de Certeau,

> even when they were subjected, indeed even when they accepted, their subjection . . . often used the laws, practices, and representations that were imposed on them by force or by fascination to ends other than those of their conquerors; they made something else out of them; they subverted them from within—not by rejecting them or by transforming them (though that occurred as well), but by many different ways of using them in the service of rules, customs, or convictions foreign to the colonization which they could not escape. They metaphorized the dominant order; they made it function in another register (De Certeau, 1984, pp. 31–32).

For instance, Shocked and Bull's criticism of rap overlooks rap's oppositional possibilities. It overlooks the fact that, among other things, gangsta rap has conflated the image of the "real nigga" and the "bad nigger" of black urban folklore. However, this distinction is admittedly unclear at times and, as Tommy Lott himself notes, the mass media's politicizing of the "bad nigger" idiom has led to a "troublesome conflation" of the "heroic badman" of folklore and the "bad nigga" of rap (Lott, 1994, p. 249).

The politics of resistance in gangsta rap needs to be located within the globalization of capital, the international circuit of debt and consumption, the deindustrialization, deskilling, and de-unionization of work in the expanding service sector. For instance, while it points to the structural instability of capitalist America and the production of urban rage, and while it wages political war against the white sentinels of the status quo, it remains ideologically aligned with capitalist interests, glorifying crass materialism and celebrating conspicuous consumption. As such, rap as a form of resistance can be conflictually located along a series of semantic axes; it varies, in other words, from song to song, from artist to artist, and from listener to listener, depending upon the performative moments that are meant to be signified. In other words, gangsta rap does not constitute a master trope of urban criticism, an ur-text of cultural resistance but is read differently by different groups. Oppressed minorities are more likely to resonate with rap for its political critique, while middle-class white groups are more likely to be drawn to rap for its aestheticization of transgression. De Genova makes an important point when he claims that

> what emerges in gangster rap, like the figure of Bigger Thomas, is "a snarl of many realities." Gangster rap would seem to provide a very different kind of "therapy" for those who live its nihilism, than the shock treatment it provides for those who live in mortal terror of it (De Genova, 1995, p. 116).

Tommy Lott notes, for instance, that "with the commercializing of gangsta rap we can no longer speak in a totalizing manner of rap music. Instead, this designation must be reserved for specific rap tunes (Lott, 1994, p. 246).

I believe that it is instructive to locate rap as a challenge to the bourgeois political and racialized structures which discursively articulate what counts as the quintessential American experience. Elsewhere I have argued that the cultural logic of late capitalism has reinscribed the moral order within the United States around the practice of consumption and the secular redemption of acquiring wealth (McLaren, 1995). The structural unconscious of American popular culture (the term *structural* is meant to draw attention to the fact that the social structure is folded into individual and collective forms of subjectivity which operate through the language of myth) has been occupied by the figure of the serial killer as the last frontiersperson, the last autonomous subject, the last "true" American who can act.

America—Europe's other—has often been considered the promised land (Stratton, 1993). But when all the old myths based on America as the promised land are demythologized, when the Protestant millenarian project to recreate Zion in the streets of Los Angeles ends in the Intifada of 1992, then the quintessential apocalyptic moment becomes the act of random murder. America is exporting this myth through film (*Love and a .45, Natural Born Killers, Pulp Fiction*), music, and other cultural formations.

The gangsta rapper serves in this context to remind white audiences that Utopia is lost, that the end of history has arrived (but not in the way Francis Fukuyama predicted), that the logic of white Utopia is premised upon white supremacy and exploitative social relations, and that whites have mistakenly pledged their loyalty to the Beast. Gangsta rap reveals the white millenarian project of democracy to be grounded upon a will to sameness, a desire to drive out people of color from the mythic frontier of the promised land. In this sense, gangsta rap transforms the "brothas" into avenging angels who call upon whites to redeem themselves or face the wrath of God—a God who will send forth not locusts or floods but angry black urban dwellers taking to the streets.

Just as the black subject has always operated as a metaphor for chaos and instability, the Los Angeles uprising of 1992 literalized this metaphor as one of physical terror. In a world where history has already been purchased by the wealthy, the losers have no choice but to steal some of history back again. The agents of leadership will not be the good Rodney Kings on television but the "bad niggaz" in the streets.

Before we can answer the question of whether hip-hop culture itself is preventing gangsta rap from evolving into a social movement, we need to gain a deeper understanding of the semantic orbit surrounding the politics of difference in gangsta rap. Do we accept, for instance, the resistive elements of gangsta rap only in the context of the production of aesthetic pleasure, rather than the promotion of a political agenda, only because acts of resistance can be defused as well as diffused into a politics of the sublime? Has the commercialization of gangsta rap imploded into the political such that these two characteristics are indistinguishable? Does the conflation of gangsta rap's commodification and political project effectively cancel both rather than dialectically reinitiate a productive political tension around a project of social justice and a praxis of liberation? Does rap's repackaging of oppositional codes along aesthetic lines merely reduce gangsta rap to a more marketable form of cultural capital that can be traded within existing capitalist frameworks of power and privilege? Can the same questions be raised about hip-hop movies such as *Krush Groove, A Thin Line Between Love and Hate, Set It Off*, and *Booty Call?*

De Genova argues that gangsta rap does escape the nihilistic aestheticism of which it has been accused by linking such aestheticism with the politics of the street:

> Gangster rap, even more than other types of hip hop, raises the free-for-all aesthetic far above and beyond the music's formal level: gangster rap celebrates a free-for-all in the streets. Here it becomes possible to imagine the transcendence of a merely aesthetic nihilism which can be contained by commodification to imagine an articulation of this highly public nihilist aesthetic with the street, the place where the sideshow can become the main event (De Genova, 1995, p. 106).

The street or neighborhood, it should be pointed out, becomes a liminal site:

The symbol of "the ghetto" in gangster rap becomes its fire-brand of "authenticity." The ghetto comes to be valorized not only as a "space of death" (and destruction) but also as a space of survival and transcendence; not merely a "heart of darkness," it is also the heart of "Blackness" (De Genova, 1995, p. 119).

Gangsta rap is concerned with the articulation of experiences of oppression that find their essential character among disenfranchised urban black and Latino populations. Rap helps to communicate symbols and meanings and articulates intersubjectively the lived experience of social actors. The ontological status of the gangsta rapper resides in the function of the commodity of blackness, but a certain quality of blackness that is identified through the expressive codes of the rapper is the "inner turmoil" of the oppressed black subject of history. Here, blackness (or Latino-ness) marks out a heritage of pain and suffering and points to the willingness and ability of oppressed groups to fight against injustice "by any means necessary." Gangsta rap songs are able to demonstrate how popular white constructions of black men and women ultimately seek to instantiate control over people of color in order to contain them culturally as well as physically. Rap exposes the hidden and hardened fissures and fault-lines of democratic social life, revealing the underpinnings of social justice to be little more than a convenient cultural fiction.

Much of the hard-core political gangsta rap provides a type of hallucinatory snapshot of everyday life on America's mean streets—a video canvas of Fortress USA—which evinces fearful images of black rage and destruction, images that typically endure in gangsta rap videos but unfortunately do little to transform the social and material relations which produce them. Violence in gangsta rap has become an Adamic ritual that creates a world of order through disorder that performatively constitutes both the gangsta himself or herself and the object of their violence. In other words, the founding language of the gangsta is violence. It is within this rationality that the image of the gangsta circulates like a political sign within an imagined community of oppressed and resisting subjects. Invading the space of other gang bangers or that of dominant groups in binary-coded struggles (black vs. white, male vs. female, cops vs. black community) helps to stabilize the subjectivity of the gangsta rapper and to contingently anchor identity through a negative interjection of the Other, a negation of whatever threatens it: bitches, rival gangs, the police, and so on. The paramount hegemonic voice that gangsta rappers struggle against—and this is true for its eastern Caribbean and east London counterparts—

is law and order. Gangsta rappers challenge the hegemonic modes of thought that are embedded in formal conventions—educational, legal, sexual, and others.

It is important to understand that while gangsta rap suffers from problems of misogyny and nihilism and while the capitalist culture industry amplifies the aesthetic dimension of rap at the expense of its political pronouncements, rap also produces important forms of nationalistic thought that work to nurture forms of coalition building and community. For instance, Zook notes that

> both the form and content of rap express black autonomy, self-determination, and cultural pride. But what is perhaps most fascinating is not only the way that rap confirms a sense of imagined, metaphorical community, but rather, the fact that this fantasy of "home" is simultaneously constructed materially through the very modes of production, marketing, and the critical discourses which surround it. In other words, just as [Benedict] Anderson argues that literary forms such as the newspaper and the novel made European nationalisms possible, I would say that the forms of television, music videos, film, literary works, and the networks involved in producing these forms are also nurturing a heightened sense of racial collectivity, group solidarity, and even political responsibility—all of which are important elements of nationalist thought (Zook, 1992, p. 263).

Gangsta rappers assume a contradictory attitude to black nationalism. On the one hand, they identify with the liberation struggles in Africa, yet on the other hand, they are wary of focusing too much attention on Africa and Afro-centrism for fear of deflecting concern from the serious problems in America's inner cities. According to Robin D.G. Kelley, rappers "contend that the nationalists' focus on Africa—both past and present—obscures the daily battles poor Black folk have to wage in contemporary America" (Kelley, 1994, p. 212).

While it does little to offer a project of transformation, gangsta rap manages, by bursting through the representational space of whiteness and by advancing political solidarity in the form of an imagined community of struggle, to depict what Grant describes as the "proprietary position that whites occupied during the days of slavery (and *mutatis mutandis* still enjoy today) (Grant, 1994, p. 52). Whites who are most threatened by gangsta rap's aggressive and adversarial masculinity attempt to consolidate their opposition in a white woman/black beast symbolic order mythologized in white supremacist discourses which have lately been discursively reinforced by prominent politicians such as Newt Gingrich, Jesse Helms, Pat Buchanan, and

Pete Wilson. It is possible, too, that white consumers of gangsta rap are drawn to a self-consciously exaggerated display of sexuality, much the same way that rhythm and blues artists captured white audiences in the fifties. As Medovoi notes:

> Of course, sexuality had long been a principal theme of rhythm and blues, but the youthful white audience now took an interest in exaggerating and redirecting its sexual themes symbolically across the race line. Chapple and Garofalo quote R&B artist John Otis recalling: "We found that we moved the white audiences more by caricaturing the music, you know, overdoing the shit—falling on your back with the saxophone, kicking your legs up. And if we did too much of that for a black audience they'd tell us—'Enough of that shit— play some music!'" (Medevoi, 1991–1992, p. 165).

While hard-core rap artists such as Snoop Doggy Dogg, Da Lench Mob, Ice Cube, Eazy-E, Niggas with Attitude, and Naughty by Nature unquestionably create politically motivated music, the politics can often be traced to a black nationalist focus. A key issue emerges here. It has to do with the fact that the aesthetic power of the music creates a pleasure among listeners which may even be against the values of the progressive listeners. Tommy Lott reports on a similar issue when he notes that the rap group Public Enemy (which often expresses black nationalist imperatives) is the favorite rap group in some racist white communities such as South Boston.

The controversial rap single "Fuck Rodney King" by former Geto Boy Willie D. makes the powerful claim that during the LA-uprising of 1992, "Rodney King so willingly took the moral low ground and turned himself into an establishment ad for social harmony" through his plaintive plea, "Can we all get along?" (Lott, 1994, 41).

Fuck Rodney King, and his ass.
When I see the mother fucker I'm a blast
Boom in his head, boom boom in his back
Just like that
Cause I'm tired of the niggers
Sayin increase the peace
And let the violence cease
When the Black man built this country
But can't get his for the prejudiced honkey . . .
But when it's time for the revolution
I'm a click click click, fuck this rap shit
Cause money ain't shit but grief
If ya ain't got no peace
Gotta come on with it

Get down for my little Willies
So they can come up strong and live long
And not be scared to get it on! (Lott, 1994, 41, 43).

Rather than identifying the song as an example of black nihilism—the image typically conjured by the lyrics—Lott suggests that it constitutes an incisive political critique. In Lott's view, Willie D.'s song "demands the autonomy and agency wards of the state lack" (Lott, 1994, p. 42). Willie D.'s rap demands the type of political change that would make the violence he calls for unnecessary.

Tommy Lott's analysis of the term *nigga* is instructive. He claims, rightly in my view, that gangsta rap has creatively reworked and recoded in a socially transgressive and politically retaliatory manner the social meaning of the term in ways that distinguish it from the taboo term used by white racists and from the often self-hating inflections of the term expressed by black professionals (Lott, 1994, p. 467). Not only is the racist meaning of the term *nigga* recoded by the gangsta rappers but its ambiguity now shifts, depending on the contexts of its enunciation and reception. When gangsta rappers revise the spelling of the racist version of the word *nigger* to the vernacular *nigga* they are using it as a defiant idiom of a resistive mode of African American cultural expression which distinguishes it from the way that, for instance, white racists in Alabama might employ the term. Further, Lott notes that the vernacular *nigga* permits a form of class consciousness among the black urban "underclass" or lumpen proletariat in the sense that it distinguishes black urban working-class youth from those middle-class black professionals who feel denigrated whenever the term is used. According to Robin D.G. Kelley,

Nigga speaks to a collective identity shaped by class consciousness, the character of inner-city space, police repression, poverty, and the constant threat of intraracial violence. . . . In other words, Nigga is not merely *another* word for black. Products of the postindustrial ghetto, the characters in gangsta rap constantly remind listeners that they are still second-class citizens—"Niggaz"—whose collective experiences suggest that nothing has changed *for them* as opposed to the black middle class. In fact, Nigga is frequently employed to distinguish urban black working class males from the black bourgeoisie and African Americans in positions of institutional authority. Their point is simple: the experiences of young black men in the inner city are not universal to all black people, and, in fact, they recognize that some African Americans play a role in perpetuating their oppression. To be a "real nigga" is to be a product of the ghetto. By linking identity to the "hood" instead of simply skin color, gangsta rappers implicitly acknowledge the limitations of racial politics, including black middle-class reformism as well as black nationalism (Kelley, 1994, p. 210, emphasis in original).[6]

Within the sociohistorical conjuncture of current US urban centers, the gangsta has become a sign of immanence, an alteration of signification between *nigger* and *nigga* relayed to infinity. Through its cultural fusions, intercultural encounters, and expressive articulations, we are invited by gangsta rap to visit spaces we have never lived physically, nor would *ever* wish to—spaces that function significantly in the manufacturing of identity. George Lipsitz remarks that "music not only shapes and reflects dominant and subordinate social and cultural relations, but . . . music making and other forms of popular culture serve as a specific site for the creation of collective identity" (Lipsitz, 1994, p. 127). Rap artists continue to move within Henri Lefevbre's "theatrical or dramatized space" by creating a new legacy of insurgency and struggle, one that menaces the prestige hierarchies of white supremacy, that constructs critical aperçus about human dignity and suffering, and that sets itself in opposition to melioristic reform and on the side of revolutionary transformation. As such, it serves as a "social force" (Lipsitz, p. 89). Yet I wish to underscore that it cannot be celebrated as a form of oppositional consciousness by uncritically attributing political consciousness to rap artists merely because of their social location as urban "underdog" musicians. Nor can we, as Lipsitz maintains, after Kobena Mercer, argue that music is in itself politically transgressive. Rather, music becomes a "social force" only "to the degree that it gets instantiated in social life and activities of groups" (Lipsitz, p. 90). The political inflections of music need to be understood in terms of their cultural, historical, and geopolitical specificity. Lipsitz further argues that the expansion of transnational capital does not, prima facie, sound the death knell of political resistance but rather that "the reach and scope of transnational capital" can make indigenous musical forms more powerful as forms of resistance.

Gangsta rap is essentially a diasporic cultural politics and positions itself as such against cultural displacement and capitalist exploitation. For this reason we can't unproblematically articulate white rappers ("wiggers" or "white niggers") into the rap resistance movement. Cultural borrowings by white rappers are not necessarily problematic but can be seen as troublesome when consideration is given to the way gangsta rap is cognitively mapped by white rappers: the cultural circuits along which such borrowings travel and how these borrowings become fused to dominant Euro-American "universal" meanings, knowledge claims, and social conventions addressed to "the other." Imitation *of* the other doesn't necessarily mean identification *with* the other, yet at the same time it doesn't necessarily exclude such an identification. The Beastie Boys and House of Pain are examples of white rappers with some crossover appeal to black audiences. However, Lipsitz warns that "powerful institutions attach prestige hierarchies to artistic expressions in such a way as to funnel reward and critical attention to Euro-American appropriators, and because ethnocentric presumptions about the universality of Western notions of art obscure the cultural and political contexts that give meaning to many artifacts from traditional cultures that are celebrated as pure form in the West" (Lipsitz 1994, p. 587). While there is, to be sure, a depoliticizing aspect to commodification, this contradiction is also a primary condition of gangsta rap's political enablement. Following bell hooks, Grant underscores the fact that because consumers could ignore the political message or information disseminated throughout the music that it also implies the contrary: consumers could pay attention to precisely that element (Grant, 1994, p. 407). Gangsta rap creatively exploits the contradictions brought on by commodification to construct a guerrilla warfare of the airwaves—a war waged through what I have called elsewhere the media's "perpetual pedagogy" (McLaren, 1995). Grant speaks to this issue when he writes that

> we could thus conceive of a diffuse war of resistance and liberation being waged against the forces of white supremacy with rap music serving as its communication system. . . . Rap music, as the objectified representative of the gangsta, invades the white world and steals white kids. . . . Ice-T also understands his intervention, his invasion, pedagogically. He teaches white kids about racism and power. In addition, he maintains that this music supplies the white youth with an alternative vocabulary in which to articulate their rebellion against the parental authority structure (Grant, 1994, p. 41).

At its best, gangsta rap urges the creation of cooperatives of resistance, zones of freedom, where strategies and tactics of liberation can emerge, where the opposite of local struggles does not collapse into some abstract universalized call for emancipation in the form of a master narrative that brings premature closure to the meaning of freedom, where the opposite of local struggles brings to mind not the master trope of the universal but rather the concept of reciprocal relations at the level of the social. This alternative points to the idea of peoples' collective struggle to advance a project of hope lived in the subjunctive mode of "as if" yet grounded in the concreteness of everyday life. It is within the dialectical relationship between local and more broad, collective struggles that gangsta rap accelerates the anger and rage that is the very condition of its existence. Unlike more mainstream musical forms such as heavy metal or rock, which tend to displace issues dealing with relations of power between black and white populations onto quarantined spaces and which often elide conflicting and contradictory relations premised upon racialized and differential relations of power and privilege, gangsta rap troubles the certainty and unsettles the complacency of existing power arrangements between blacks and whites. I would argue that the multicultural nihilistic hedonism that Newt Gingrich's authoritarian populist millenarianism hates with such a frenzied passion is really one of the few sources of oppositional popular discourses remaining in a nation morally flattened by the weight of the New Right's rhetorical cant that demonizes, hellifies, and zombifies African Americans, Latinos, the poor, and the disenfranchised.

Yet in saying this there is evidence that gangsta rap is running its course within the circuits of capitalist commodification. In a recent issue of *The Los Angeles Reader*, Steve Appleford writes that "another album cover with a gun thrust in your face is as shocking and dangerous now as Madonna without clothes." He cites MC Ren as saying

> we wanted to put Compton on the map, so we rapped about what went on in Compton. . . . But now it's like everybody's talking the same shit, people talking about shit we did years ago, you understand? You've got to advance, man. . . . Everybody right now is just stuck.

Ren remarks that

> you got all these fools coming out now, they think all you got to do is just cuss, talk about weed, low ridin', shit like that, and you can get a record deal, you know what I'm saying? Rap is fucked up, man. It started a few years ago when somebody realized this shit is making money (Appleford, 1995, pp. 9–11).

According to Appleford, Ice-T now rejects the gangsta label, preferring to describe his music as "reality rap." When gangsta rap restricts itself to the politics of the ghetto, white viewers see it as a threat that is constrained to certain areas of life that they can avoid at the everyday level. When you have easy access to the "black threat" for entertainment purposes, it becomes more familiar and therefore less intimidating. On the other hand, ghettocentricity is a constant reminder to white viewers that they themselves are white. Whiteness—that absent presence that outlines the cultural capital required for favored citizenship status—becomes, in this instance, less invisible to whites themselves. The less invisible that whiteness becomes, the less it serves as a tacit marker against which otherness is defined.

There have been some recent alternative movements within rap, such as G-funk and rap/be-bop fusion. For instance, R&B artists such as Me'Shell Ndegéocello are experimenting with aspects of hip-hop and soul. Recently in the *LA Weekly*, Donnell Alexander (1995, pp. 39–40) surveyed some alternative rap, arguing that while hard core gangsta rap (Big Mike, MC Eiht, Jeru, Treach) is now mainstream, alternative rap groups such as Digable Planets, Spearhead, Justin Warfield, the Broun Fellinis, and Michael "Basehead" Ivey haven't been able to develop much of a following outside of white college students. And there is the question of the powerful forces of commodification from the marketplace. Is rap's restricted code of black solidarity against oppression being elaborated for financial gain by the white-dominated culture industry? Is it being diffused into an aesthetic style that can be danced to or played because of its growing availability as a cultural code (Cushman, 1991)? Is it being depotentiated because it is being wrenched away from the cultural contexts that made it meaningful?

The politics of commodification and appropriation that have been confronting gangsta rap artists in the face of the hypermobility of capital is reminiscent of the phenomena occurring with salsa and *rockero* in the context of Puerto Rico. For instance, Javier Santiago-Lucerna discusses how artists like Ruben Blades and Willie Colon, whose earlier musical productions resonated with a progressive politics, have been absorbed into the politics of the marketplace. According to Santiago-Lucerna, salsa music and the cultural *comarrona* have been transformed into spaces constituted with the cynical sign of consumer culture. In fact, the music being produced in the local rock scene and among local punk bands is currently far more hard-edged politically than salsa, *nueva trova*, and *musica campesina*, as the bands Whisker Biscuit, Kampo Viej, Descojon Urbano, La Experiencia de Tonito Cabanillas, and Sin Remedio can attest. For instance, in "Urban Fuckup," Descojon-Urbano sings:

Oye es que me da gusto
Cada vez que cogen a un politico corrupto
Que cabroneria, que barbaridad

el pobre se jode y el rico tiene mas
[It gives me so much pleasure
every time they catch a corrupted politician
What shit, what an atrocity
the poor are fucked, while the rich have more] (Santiago-Lucerna, 1995, pp. 16–17).

The issue of political domestication and product commodification is on the surface somewhat different in the case of gangsta rap because oppositional political rap is now mainstream. Therefore, it is hard to see what other kinds of music might soon replace rap's hard-edge political critique. Perhaps forms of rap will develop that are not coded in the image of the hypersexualized gang banger and that begin to address issues of economic exploitation, misogyny, and homophobia.

Critics of gangsta rap need to take seriously Rosemary Hennessy's suggestion that "in postmodern consumer culture the commodity is a central means by which desire is organized" (Hennessy, 1994–95, p. 52). In other words, listeners of gangsta rap affectively invest in the music and video productions. The music produces certain structures of feeling, particular economies of affectivity. But the logic of the commodity conceals certain invisible social relations that need to be considered. The commodity, argues Hennessy, after Marx, is not material in the physical sense alone but rather in the sense that "it is socially produced through human labor and the extraction of surplus value in exchange." Commodity fetishism refers to the "illusion that value resides in objects rather than in the social relations between individuals and objects." In other words, commodity fetishism "entails the misrecognition of a structural effect as an immediate property of one of its elements, as if this property belonged to it outside of its relation to other elements" (Hennessy, 1994–95 p. 53).

Gangsta rap as a commercial product needs to be understood not simply in terms of the way it transgressively signifies social life but in terms of the exploitation of human labor and the way in which the social relations of production and consumption organize everyday human life: in short, in terms of its commodity fetishism. De Genova notes that

> commodified rap music was able to proliferate through the virtual pillage of an ever-expanding universe of already-existing commodified music—instantiating the semblance of something like a parodic auto-cannibalization of the commodity form. The very essence of hip-hop music, as a musical genre which begins with the unabashed appropriation of pre-recorded, mass-pro-

duced, commodified music, demonstrates that "public culture" is inevitably and unassailably "public-access culture"—a free-for-all (pp. 105–106).

Gangsta rap's relation to the corporate marketplace, its potential for expropriation, and its reproduction of ideologies historically necessary to commodity exchange—such as patriarchal ones—is an important issue that needs to be addressed. In other words, gangsta rap needs to be viewed not merely as an ideological formation, cultural signifier, or performative spectacle, but also as the product of historical and social relations. Gangsta rap needs to be seen not only in discursive terms but rather in terms of the materiality of discourse. By materiality of discourse I refer to "the ways culture constructs subjectivities, reproduces power relations, and foments resistance" insofar as these relations and practices are "shaped by social totalities like capitalism, patriarchy, and imperialism as they manifest differently across social formations and within specific historical conjunctures" (Hennessy, 1994–95, p. 33). This is not to say, however, that gangsta rap at the level of the oppositional spectacle is not an important popular counterdiscourse.

Thomas Cushman's important work on understanding the diffusion of revolutionary musical codes raises some important questions about rap (which, unfortunately, exceed the scope of this essay). These questions demand an analysis of the social evolution of gangsta rap as a musical style as it is situated within the world capitalist system. This suggests examining gangsta rap as a restricted code (condensed, context-specific cluster of symbols and meanings) that articulates the existential experience of subordinate groups of African Americans and Puerto Ricans and their everyday dissent. It also means tracing rap's diffusion into an elaborated code (context-free, universal) across time and space into new social contexts and analyzing how its original, organic, revolutionary expression as a means of addressing race and class exploitation has been diffused. For instance, what is to prevent gangsta rap from becoming, in Cushman's terms, a casualty of

a highly developed, world-wide culture industry that operates precisely by scanning the world environment for disturbances, selectively amplifying and altering certain aspects of those disturbances and re-presenting them to large audiences who receive them as entertainment commodities? (Cushman, 1991, p. 48).[7]

Gangsta rap creates identity through a racial system of intelligibility that produces binary distinctions between blacks and whites, an us-against-them discursive matrix. As a performative signification anchored in the context of the urban ghetto, it constitutes part of the regulatory practices of the dominant culture while at the same time resisting and critiquing this culture.

Diane Fuss, following Frantz Fanon, argues that under conditions of colonialism, blacks are "forced to occupy, in a white racial phantasm, the static ontological space of the timeless 'primitive'" (1994, pp. 20–21). In this "imaginary relation of fractured specularity," blacks are denied by the white Imperial Subject, the alterity or otherness necessary to achieve subjectivity. Interpellated and fixed into a static objecthood, blacks become neither an "I" nor a "not-I," becoming instead a degraded and devalorized signifier, a fragmented object, a form of pure exteriority.

The transcendental signifier "white," according to Fuss, is never a "not-black," but rather operates from its own self-proclaimed transparency, as a marker that floats imperially over the category of race, operating "as its own Other" and independent from the sign "black" for its symbolic constitution. In terms of the colonial-imperial register of self-other relations, which, as Fuss notes, operates in psychoanalysis and existentialism on the Hegelian principle of negation and incorporation in which the other is assimilated into the self—the white subject can be white without any relation to the black subject because the sign "white" exempts itself from a dialogical logic of negativity. But the black subject must be black in relation to the white subject.

For instance, whereas white rap singer Vanilla Ice was once referred to as "the Elvis of rap," the black singer Al B. Sure was referred to as "the Black Elvis." Lionett cites remarks made by Patricia Williams, who points out the parodic nature of these labels: "Elvis, the white black man of a generation ago, reborn in a black man imitating Elvis." Lionett adds that Elvis is "reborn in Vanilla Ice, a white man imitating the black rapper imitating Elvis: a dizzying thought." The point here is that in the depiction of each rap artist, the major point of reference is white culture (Lionett, 1995, p. 107).

Imperialist acts of assimilation and incorporation are located at the level of the unconscious. The gangsta is simultaneously a mimicry of subversion and subjugation. Drawing on Homi Bhabha's notion that colonial mimicry possesses the possibility of resisting and subverting dominant systems of representation (through the possibility of mimicry slipping into mockery) as well as subtending them, I want to argue that when it ironizes the role of the incorporated black subject, gangsta rap (at least in its video incarnations) undermines the image of the impotent black subject, de-transcendentalizing it and rendering it unstable (Bhabha, 1984, 125–133). However, when the gangsta rapper undertakes a "parodic hyperbolization" (to borrow Fuss's term) of the subjugated black man—in the figure of the gangsta with a gun—but does not connect it to a larger political project of liberation, this may rupture the image of the subjugated black subject but fail to unsettle the exploitative relations connected to white supremacist patriarchal capitalism. By not connecting its subversion to a larger politics of possibility, gangsta rap runs the risk of ironizing its own act of subversion and parodying its own performance of dissent in such an I-don't-give-a-fuck fashion that, rather than erode dominant social relations of exploitation and subjugation, it may actually reinforce them.

The social realism that accompanies much of the gangsta rap of Ice Cube, Ice-T, and others is situated within a larger political agenda and sets the context for portraying the role of the rapper (qua oppositional cultural forms) as a "truth sayer" and noble revolutionary subject fighting the injustices of the white-controlled megastate. It also builds the ground for a more sustained critique of racist and capitalist social relations.

But in some of the rap videos of, say, Sir Mix-A-Lot or 2 Live Crew, unrealistic portrayals occur of the dissenting black male subject, depicting him as living in ostentatious luxury, surrounded by black and white women massaging their breasts on his car window ("put 'em on the glass") or swaying their G-stringed buttocks in his welcoming face. In this instance, there is a tendency to recuperate a reversionary politics, because the lifestyle of the black hepcat dissenter appears to be exaggerated to the point of parody. Such a parodic representation of the successful black consumer (where women are presented as thong-clad commodities to be plucked from swimming pools) tends to defray and to occlude a larger politics of liberation outside of commodity culture. In this case, the landscape of rap is defoliated in terms of race, class, and gender issues, while dissent is defused into issues of who has the most "babes who got back." In another sense, however, it's also possible to look at 2 Live Crew's videos in a different light. It's possible to overlook the sexism and the hyperbolizing of the black male-as-womanizer by focusing on the consumer trappings of the black rapper—swimming pools, fancy cars, beautiful houses, and available sex. Acquiring these "trappings" becomes a form of resistance because they are not available to the average white or black subject. The problem here is rap's apparent legitimation of capitalist social relations of consumption. Do rappers—including gangsta rappers—just want to make the pleasures of patriarchal capitalism available to all black males?

Can gangsta rap move beyond Benjamin's shock effects, its decontextualization as an effect of its mechanical reproducibility, beyond the space of its own commercial structures, beyond its ideological prohibitions, its structures of expectation, its demarcations of despair—all of which create a locus of signifying phantasms and perverse forms of the "other," which, in turn, collaborate with neoliberal approaches to politics that ultimately wrest away rap's oppositional potency? To create a praxis of both opposition and possibility, gangsta rap needs to undertake the construction of new identities that are refractory to commodification. It must continue to perturb society, to shape culture on a deeper level. Hip-hop culture must provide spaces of resistance and transgression, without succumbing to political incoherence. Only in this way will it be able to prevent its revolutionary potential from being articulated to the terms of the official culture of consumption that defuses adversarial codes into the cultural logic of the aesthetic.

Despite the always-present threat of commodification, gangsta rap still poses a serious challenge to the formation of new identities of resistance and social transformation. The new identities surrounding various articulations of gangsta rap hold both unforeseen promises and potential dangers. As Lipsitz remarks, "to think of identities as interchangeable or infinitely open does violence to the historical and social constraints imposed on us by structures of exploitation and privilege. But to posit innate and immobile identities for ourselves and others confuses history with nature, and denies the possibility of change" (1994, p. 62).

The challenge that confronts gangsta rap in particular and hip-hop culture in general is the extent to which it contributes to the de-familiarization of the Western sovereign subject, the Euro-American imperial subject, and the extent to which it can become self-conscious of the relations of power and privilege that create the context for and overdetermine its cultural exchanges. This means, as I have argued above, linking a politics of semiotic subversion to a critique of the material social relations of exploitation that have been largely responsible for the problems faced by people of color in the United States.

Manning Marable speaks to a new articulation of the concept of blackness that is defined not in racial or ethnic/cultural terms but as a political category that speaks to new forms of political mobilization:

We must find new room in our identity as people of color to include all other oppressed national minorities—Chicanos, Puerto Ricans, Asian/Pacific Americans, and other people of African descent. We must find the common ground we share with oppressed people who are not national minorities—working-class people, the physically challenged, the homeless, the unemployed, and those Americans who suffer discrimination because they are lesbian or gay. I believe that a new multicultural America is possible, that a renaissance of Black militancy will occur in concert with new levels of activism from the constituencies mentioned above. But it is possible only if we have the courage to challenge and to overturn our own historical assumptions about race, power, and ourselves. Only then will we find the new directions necessary to challenge the system, to 'fight the power,' with an approach toward political culture that can truly liberate all of us (Marable 1992, p. 302).

In its most politically enabling formations, gangsta rap is able to create a space of resistance in which black identity is not dependent upon whiteness to complete it. It escapes colonial mimesis through a series of cultural relays that keeps identity fluid and shifting. The particular liberatory values that are affirmed in gangsta rap need, however, to co-reside with other resonant values rooted in the contingency and radical historicity of oppressed groups throughout the globe. For white folks this means not simply a *tolerance of* difference but rather a critical *engagement with* difference on a global scale.

The death of Tupac Shakur provides a bitter lesson about the best and worst of gangsta rap. Tupac's reputation as one of the most hardcore of the gangsta rappers and his obsession with living the "authenticity" of the streets as a "real nigga" eventually rebounded against him as he brought together his own brand of what Mike Dyson calls "thuggery and thanatopsis." Dyson remarks that "the Real Niggas are trapped by their own contradictory couplings of authenticity and violence. Tupac's death is the most recent, and perhaps most painful, evidence of that truth." Dyson further notes that Tupac's own project constituted "a sad retreat from a much more complex, compelling vision of black life that gangsta rap and hard-core hip-hop, at its best, helped outline." In his art of "celeterrogation" (what Dyson calls "the deft combination of celebration and interrogation") Tupac embodied the best and the worst of gangsta rap. Dyson eloquently comments:

by joining verbal vigor to rage—about material misery and racial hostility, about the avalanche of unheard suffering that suffocates black lives before they wake, walk or will their own survival—hard core rappers proved that theirs was a redemptive vulgarity. At their best, they showed that the real vulgarity was the absurd way too many black folk perish on the vine of fruit-

less promises of neighborhood restoration, of racial rehabilitation. The hard
core hip-hopper proved that the real vulgarity was the vicious anonymity and
punishing silence of poor black life, with which they broke faith every time
they seized a mike to bring poetry to pain. . . . But, in the end, despite all
his considerable gifts, Tupac helped pioneer a more dangerous, even more
destructive, trend in hard-core hip-hop that, ironically, draws from the oral
energy of the orthodox black culture from which he sought thuggish refuge.
Tupac yearned to live the life he rapped about in his songs. That golden ideal
was the motive behind gospel passions in black culture to close the gap between preaching and practice, between what one said and what one did (1996,
p. 3).

As long as African Americans and other historically marginalized
social groups are perceived by whites to be artificial constructions—in
effect, artificial white people—who exist largely to be economically
exploited or else reinvented and rewarded by whites in the sphere of
leisure culture for their own entertainment, then it is unlikely that democracy will ever be achievable. As long as the rules by which society
functions continue to be defined by the white majority, and the interpretation of such rules continues to be controlled by a dominant capitalist elite, then the concept of equality is nothing but a hollow term.
As long as the liberal pluralistic society in which we all participate is
controlled a priori by our failure to address the problem of material
exploitation, then gangsta rap will operate out of necessity as a serious critique of U.S. cultural life. As long as the politically unifying
cultural understanding that pluralists posit as the framework for democratic social life continues to read narratives such as gangsta rap as
necessarily threatening to social harmony, then success in our society
will always be racially determined.

Equal access to shared symbols of nationhood does not spell democracy for any group when such symbols are discouraged from being interrogated, reanimated, and transformed. More importantly, equal
access to the material necessities of human survival and dignity must
be made a fundamental prerequisite for democracy. Anything less than
this makes a mockery of the ideal of social justice. In this context, the
"brothas" and "sistahs" of gangsta rap are demanding that democracy
live up to its promises. They challenge—by any means necessary—
democracy to rearticulate its mission in view of the current urban
nightmare in which the melting pot itself has melted in a postpluralist
firestorm. How must we rethink identity when the container can no
longer contain, when the ladle dissolves in the mixture, when the signifier ceases to signify?

If British sociologists Scott Lash and John Urry are correct in asserting that "we are not so much thrown into communities, but decide which communities—from youth subcultures to new social movements—we shall throw ourselves into," then what sort of aesthetic (hermeneutic) reflexivity is required in the case of gangsta rap? (1992, 316). What is at issue when the ideographic mode of gangsta-ing is counterposed to conduct regulated by the abstract norm-governed social structure of the state? Is this a question of what Lash and Urry call "race-baiting neo tribes" or the beginning of "new communitarian social movements"? What happens when the wild zones of information flows and networks of the so-called underclass enter into a marriage with the new informational bourgeoisie?

In an era in which the subject is located as ambivalent and grounded in lost referents and instabilities within signifying chains, gangsta rap draws needed attention to the importance, not only of dis-identifying with the cultural obvious but also of recognizing that the difference rendered most invisible in the production of postmodern cultural representations is the difference between rich and poor. We are viscerally reminded by gangsta rappers that cultural identities and practices remain tied to capital's drive to accumulate profits through the appropriation of labor that relies historically on forms of racism, patriarchy, and imperialism (Ebert, 1994, pp. 137–142).

Epilogue

The casket carrying the body of Notorious B.I.G. (Christopher Wallace, a.k.a. Biggie Smalls) rests in a hearse winding its way past 226 St. James Place, in the rapper's old Brooklyn neighborhood, toward the Frank E. Campbell Funeral Chapel in Manhattan's Upper East Side. Two black Cadillacs filled with flowers—the letters B.I.G. are spelled out in brilliant red carnations—are spotted driving through Bedford-Stuyvesant. At the open casket service, fans stricken with grief catch a glimpse of Junior M.A.F.I.A., Flavor Flav, Dr. Dre, Spinderella, and Sister Souljah. For the postmodern theorist, there is a whole lot of signifying going on. For the people lined up outside the funeral home—who don't have the consolation of the sociology seminar room—the issue is not one of semiotics but of survival. It is not an event that calls for interpretation. It is an event that calls for a commitment to struggle.

References

Alexander, D. (1995, March 24-30). Closed border: The hip-hop nation deports alternative rap. Michael Ivey's B.Y.O.B., *LA Weekly*, 17, no. 17.

Appleford, S. (1995, March 3). The rise and fall of gangsta rap. *Los Angeles Reader.*

Baker, H. (1993). *Black studies: Rap and the academy.* Chicago: University of Chicago Press.

Bhabha, H. (1984). Of mimicry and man: the ambivalence of colonial discourse, *October, 28,* 125-133.

Cheevers, J. Philips, C. & Williams, F. (1995, April 3). Violence tops the charts, *Los Angeles Times.*

Cushman, T. (1991). Rich rastas and communist rockers: A comparative study of the origin, diffusion, and delusion of revolutionary musical codes, *Journal of Popular Culture, 25,* no. 3, 17-61.

Davis, A. (1992). Discussion. In Dent, G. (Ed.), *Black Popular Culture* (pp. 325-331). Seattle, WA: Bay Press.

Decker, J. (1994). The state of rap: The time and place of hip hop nationalism, In Rose, T. & Ross, A. (Eds.). *Microphone fiends: Youth music, youth culture* (pp. 99-121). New York: Routledge.

de Certeau, M. (1984). *The practice of everyday life.* Berkeley: University of California Press.

De Genova, N. (1995). Gangster rap and nihilism in black America: Some questions of life and death," *Social Text 13,* no. 2, 89-132.

Dyson, M. (1994). The politics of black masculinity and the ghetto in black film. In Becker, C. (Ed.). *The subversive imagination: Artists, society, and social responsibility* (pp. 154-167). London: Routledge.

Dyson, M. (1996, October 22). Tupac: Living the life he rapped about in song. *Los Angeles Times,* p. 3.

Ebert, T. (1994). The surplus of enjoyment in the post-al real. *Rethinking Marxism, 7,* no. 3, 137-142.

Flores, J. (1994). Puerto Rican and proud, boyee! Rap, roots, and amnesia. In Rose, T. & Ross, A. (Eds.). *Microphone fiends: Youth music, youth culture* (pp. 89-98). New York: Routledge.

Fuss, D. (1994). Interior colonies: Frantz Fanon and the politics of identification. *Diacritics,24,* nos. 2-3, 20-42.

Grant, M. (1994). Of gangstas and guerrillas: Distance lends enchantment, *Appendix, 2*, p. 44.

Gregory, S. (1995). Race and racism: A symposium, *Social Text, 13*, no. 1, 1–52.

Grossberg, L. (1994). Is anybody listening? Does anybody care? On 'the state of rock'. In Rose, T. & Ross, A. (Eds.). *Microphone fiends: Youth music, youth culture* (pp. 41–58). New York: Routledge.

Haymes, S. (1995). *Race, culture, and the city: A pedagogy for black urban struggle.* Albany: State University of New York Press.

Hebdige, D. (1987). *Cut 'n' mix.* London: Comedia.

Hennessy, R. (1994–95). Queer visibility in commodity culture, *Cultural Critique, 29*, 31–76.

hooks, b. (1992). *Black looks: Race and representation.* Boston: South End Press.

Katz, J. (1995, August 5). Rap furor: New evil or old story, *Los Angeles Times*, p. M3.

Kelley, R. (1994). *Race rebels: Culture, politics, and the black working class.* New York: Free Press.

Lash, S. & Urry, J. (1992). *Economies of signs and space.* London: Sage.

Lionett, F. (1995). *Postcolonial representations: Women, literature, identity.* Ithaca, NY: Cornell University Press.

Lipsitz, G. (1994). *Dangerous crossroads: Popular music, postmodernism, and the poetics of place.* London: Verso.

Lipsitz, G. (1994). The bands of tomorrow are here today: The proud, progressive and postmodern sounds of *Las Tres* and *Goddess 13*. In Loza, S. (Ed.), *Musical Aesthetics and Multiculturalism* (pp. 139–147). Los Angeles: University of California, Department of Ethnomusicology and Systematic Musicology.

Lott, E. (1994). Cornel West in the hour of chaos: Culture and politics in *Race Matters. Social Text, 12*, no. 3, 39–50.

Lott, T. (1994). Black vernacular representation and cultural malpractice. In Goldberg, D. (Ed.). *Multiculturalism: A critical reader* (pp. 230–258). Cambridge: Basil Blackwell.

Marable, M. (1994). Race, identity, and political culture. In Dent, G. (Ed.). *Black popular culture* (pp. 292–302). Seattle, WA: Bay Press.

McLaren, P. (1995). *Critical pedagogy and predatory culture.* London: Routledge.

Medovoi, L. (1991-92). Mapping the rebel image: Postmodernism and the masculinist politics of rock in the U.S.A. *Cultural Critique, 20*, 153–188.

Mitchell, J. (1995, February 4). Third trial ruled out in slaying by officer. *Los Angeles Times*, pp. B1, B8.

Muhammad, R. (1995, August 16) LA gangs honored in keeping the peace, *Final Call, 14*, no. 21.

Parenti, C. (1995, November 3). *New Statesman and Society, 1995.*

Percelay, J., Monteria, I. & Dweck, S. (Eds.). *SNAPS.* New York: Quill/William Morrow.

Philips, C. & Abrahamson, A. (1996, December 29). U.S. probes Death Row Record label's money trail, *Los Angeles Times*, pp. A1, A34, A35.

Pierce, C. (1995, April 23). Sunshine is back! *Los Angeles Times Magazine.*

Proffitt, S. (1995, August 27). Russell Simmons: Defending the art of communication known as rap. *Los Angeles Times*, p. M3.

Rose, T. (1992). Black texts/black contexts. In Dent, G. (Ed.). *Black popular culture* (pp. 223–227). Seattle, WA: Bay Press.

Rose, T. (1994a). *Black noise: Rap music and black culture in contemporary america.* London: Wesleyan University Press.

Rose, T. (1994b). A style nobody can deal with: Politics, style, and the postindustrial city in hip hop. In Rose, T. & Ross, A. (Eds.). *Microphone fiends: Youth music, youth culture* (pp. 71–88). New York: Routledge.

Rose, T. (1994c). Give me a (break) beat! Sampling and repetition in rap production. In Bender, G. & Druckrey, T. (Eds.). *Culture on the brink: Ideologies of technology* (pp. 249–258). Seattle, WA: Bay Press.

Rushkoff, D. (1996). *Media virus.* New York: Ballantine Books.

Santiago-Lucerna, J. (1995). Nothing's sacred, everything's profane: Rock isleno and the politics of national identity in Puerto Rico. Paper presented at York University, Toronto, March, 1995.

Souljah, S. (1994). *No disrespect.* New York: Random House.

Stratton, J. (1993). The beast of the apocalypse: The post-colonial experience of the United States. *New Formations, 21,* 35–63.

Troop, D. (1984). *Rap attack: African jive to New York hip hop.* London: Pluto Press.

Tulloch, C. (1993). Rebel without a pause: Black street style and black designers. In Ash, J. & Wilson, E. (Eds.). *Chic thrills: A fashion reader* (pp. 84–100). Berkeley: University of California Press.

Time Warner to abandon gangsta rap (1995, September 28). *Los Angeles Times*, pp. 1, 13.

Zook, K. (1992). Reconstruction of nationalist thought in black music and culture. In Garofalo, R. (Ed.). *Rockin' the boat: Mass music, and mass movement.* (Pp. 255–266). Boston: South End Press.

Notes

1. Time Warner Inc. has formally abandoned its $115 million stake in Interscope Records, blaming the split on contractual provisions that prevented the company from monitoring the content of Interscope's gangsta rappers such as Dr. Dre and Snoop Doggy Dogg. Bob Dole claimed responsibility for this development claiming he "shamed" Time Warner into dropping their gangsta rappers (Time Warner to abandon gangsta rap, 1995).

2. Richard Berry's original hit in 1955, "Louie Louie," was Afro-Calypsonian yet was influenced by the Rhythm Rockers, a Chicano-Filipino band from Orange County, California. Band members had introduced Berry to René Touset's "Loca cha cha," which provided Berry with the model for "Louie Louie" (See Lipsitz 1994, pp. 139–140). "Louie Louie" has been recorded by more than 300 artists, for example, Ike and Tina Turner, the Kinks, the Beach Boys, Tom Petty and the Heartbreakers, Frank Zappa, Iggy Pop, and even the Rice University Marching Owl Band. A resident of South Central Los Angeles, Berry contributed vocals to the Robins' "Riot in Cell Block No. 9" and Etta James's "Roll with Me Henry (the Wallflower)."

3. "Playing the dozens" and "signifying" are variations of African American linguistic practices or traditions which can be characterized as ritualized verbal contests or wars of words. The "dozens" are confrontations of wit, intellect, and repartee played out in lingual games of one-upmanship that are distinguished by lexical originality and creativity, mental dexterity, and verbal innovation and agility in the effective deployment of clever and sarcastic insults or put-downs. A continuation of a rich African diasporic oral tradition that has been distilled through the lens of the African American experience, playing the dozens and signifying are the ultimate expression of brains over brawn— spoken word showdowns that have transformed and elevated a marginalized community's collective humor, anger, joy, and pain in the face of adversity into a game of survival, a ritualized form of entertainment, and a highly valued and respected socio-cultural art form (see Percelay, Ivey & Dweck, 1994).

4. Young and Knight have since broken up their partnership. With a record eight criminal convictions (mostly for assault and weapons charges), Marion "Suge" Knight is currently serving time in a Chino prison while awaiting a Superior Court hearing. In 1995 he entered no-contest pleas to two accounts of assault that involved the beating of two rappers in a Hollywood recording studio. Under a plea bargain he was given a suspended nine-year prison term and five years probation. Since it was discovered that Knight had cut a record deal with the original prosecutor's 18-year-old daughter and had lived in the prosecutor's Malibu Colony house through the summer of 1996, the prosecutor was dropped from the case. At the MGM Hotel in Las Vegas, just hours before Tupac Shakur was fatally wounded in a car driven by Knight, a surveillance videotape showed Knight and several Death Row employees attacking a

Crips gang member. This led to the revoking of Knight's parole. Death Row Records is currently under investigation by the Federal Bureau of Investigation, the Internal Revenue Service, the Bureau of Alcohol, Tobacco and Firearms and the Drug Enforcement Administration for funding crimes by the Mob Piru set of the Bloods street gang, for allegedly engaging in business deals with "drug kingpins" Michael Harris and Ricardo Crockett, and for dealing with entrepreneurs linked to organized crime factions that included New York Mafia figures Joseph Colombo Jr. and Alphonse "the Whale" Mellolla (see Philips & Abrahamson, 1996).

5. See also the important work of Haymes (1995).

6. Kelley also points out that the term *nigger* made a "comeback" at the height of the Black Power movement of the 1960s when a distinction was made between *nigger* and *negro*—the latter signified a sellout or a brainwashed black person.

7. According to Christian Parenti, prisoners are being exploited as cheap labor, and their wages are used to pay for their incarceration. He notes that "the California Department of Corrections is also trying to find a niche in Japan's jeans market with its new line of 'Gangsta Blues.' Thus, the much deplored hip hop culture of African-American and Latino youths—which has embraced the look of denim workclothes—is being imitated, glorified, and sold back to the public by the very criminal justice system that claims to wage war on Gangsta culture" (Parenti, 1995, pp. 20–21).

Author Note

Special thanks to Carlos Tejeda. Ash Vasudeva, Warren Crichlow, Makeba Jones, Karl Bruce Knapper, Michelle Knight, Mike Seltzer, and Nicole Baker for their helpful suggestions.

Rap Music: The Cultural Politics of Official Representation

Julia Eklund Koza

Introduction

Rap music has been in existence for at least twenty years and has been called "the most significant popular innovation" of the past two decades (Leland, 1992d, p. 59), but American music educators have rarely welcomed this diverse and potentially powerful genre into official school knowledge. Instead, for many, rap epitomizes what they have dedicated their careers to opposing. According to a growing body of educators, however, a compelling case can be made for giving serious and respectful attention to many dimensions of popular culture, including rap.[1] Educators who acknowledge that rap is a significant aesthetic experience for countless American students and recognize the merits of understanding and valuing the cultural experiences students bring with them call for a broadened definition of legitimate school knowledge, one that recognizes rap as a significant cultural artifact. As forays into the complexities of cultural politics reveal connections between official knowledge and power, the problems resulting from unquestioned acceptance of traditional definitions of legitimate school knowledge have become clearer. Ignoring or denouncing popular culture—the culture of the people—sends elitist messages about whose understandings of the world do or do not count, both in schools and in the dominant culture. Thus, educators should care about rap, because disregarding this important art form may help to perpetuate dominant power relations. Furthermore, popular culture sometimes serves as a venue for cultural critique, specifically of institutions and the power regimes that support them. Schooling is one such institution, and it is imperative that educators, ensconced as we are, seriously ponder the voices critical of this institution and the regimes of power that shape it.

The uninformed educator who seeks to better understand rap music quickly discovers that the genre has received scant attention in scholarly circles, particularly in music. This silence is a commentary on whose knowledge is deemed most legitimate in academe. More importantly, however, it enlarges the role of the general media as educators of educators on rap. Because the general media may be playing a central role in shaping educators' understandings and attitudes, the manner in which the media represent rap and hip hop culture is of considerable importance.

In the process of becoming more rap literate, I became intrigued by media coverage of the genre and decided to embark on an exploration of this coverage. To that end, I did a close reading of all rap-related articles that appeared in three American weekly news magazines during the ten-year period from January 1983 through December 1992; the three magazines I examined were *Newsweek*, *Time* magazine, and *U.S. News and World Report*. In the following analysis, I will uncover some of the ways that discourses of domination, including inside/outside binaries that construct the outside as the undesirable other, speak through these texts, reinforcing and reinscribing unequal power relations along lines of race, social class, and gender. I will argue that in their representations of rap, rappers, and rap fans, these news magazines participated in a construction and commodification of otherness, integrally related to the perpetuation of hegemony. Construction of otherness was accomplished not only through specific textual content but also by means of what television media specialist John Fiske calls "generic characteristics" or "conventions" of news reporting (1987, pp. 282–283).

Representation and Power

This analysis is based on the assumption that representations are social constructs and on the premise that mass media representations are commodities designed to be marketed to and consumed by vast audiences. The significance of representation, specifically mass media representation, lies in its relationship to power, a relationship that bell hooks explores in her books *Yearning: Race, Gender, and Cultural Politics* and *Black Looks: Race and Representation*. Hooks discusses the critical role media representations play in shaping people's perceptions of themselves and others,[2] and she ties specific representations of race to the perpetuation of unequal power relations:

> There is a direct and abiding connection between the maintenance of white supremacist patriarchy in this society and the institutionalization via mass media of specific images, representations of race, of blackness that support and maintain the oppression, exploitation, and overall domination of all black people (hooks, 1992, 2).

She calls for "radical interventions," for "fierce critical interrogation" of representations, and for "revolutionary attitudes about race and representation" (1992, p. 7, p. 5). hooks' observations about the relationship between power and representation, and her call for new attitudes, are relevant not only in discussions of race, but also in those of social class and gender.

Binary Constructions and Oppression

Examining how oppressive representations are constructed can be a part of the fierce critical interrogation that hooks recommends. Some constructions use what John Fiske calls deep-structure binary oppositions, and what feminist Diana Fuss describes as inside/outside oppositions that depict the outside as the alien, excluded, lacking, or contaminated other (Fiske, 1987, pp. 131–134; Fuss, 1991, pp. 1–3). Fiske explains that deep-structure abstract binaries, such as good/evil, are "metaphorically transformed into concrete representations," such as middle class/lower class, order/lawlessness, light/dark, and masculine/feminine. Fiske points to the theorizing of Roland Barthes, who argued that such binaries are part of a mythmaking that serves dominant classes in capitalist societies (Fiske, 1987, p. 132, p. 134). Fuss relates inside/outside rhetoric to regimes of power by stating that

> the figure inside/outside, which encapsulates the structure of language, repression, and subjectivity, also designates the structure of exclusion, oppression, and repudiation. This latter model may well be more insistent to those subjects routinely relegated to the right of the virgule—to the outside of systems of power, authority, and cultural legitimacy (1991, p. 2).

Fuss maintains that the inside/outside figure can never be completely eliminated, but it can be "worked on and worked over—itself turned inside out to expose its critical operations and interior machinery" (1991, p. 1).

Strategies of Containment and the News

In addition to relating narrative structures such as binary oppositions to the maintenance of unequal power relations, Fiske explains how "generic characteristics" or conventions of news reporting tend to reinforce dominant ideologies, specifically through controlling or limiting meaning. Fiske considers news to be a commodity and news reporting a highly ideological practice, and he maintains that a myth of objectivity tends to obscure the ideological intent of such reporting (1987, pp. 281–283, p. 285, p. 288). He enumerates several general characteristics or conventions of news reporting that he contends are strategies of control and containment; the list includes selection, categorization, metaphor, negativity, and inoculation. Selection and categorization involve decisions about what does or does not constitute news. Fiske points out that to discuss news in terms of "events" gives news an aura of naturalness; however, selection, which is the means by which events become news, is a cultural process (Fiske, 1987, pp. 282–293). Through selection and categorization, events are placed into the categories of news or not news; categorization also refers to sorting news into subcategories and to placing events on a "conceptual grid" (1987, pp. 286–287). Fiske says that such subcategories are "normalizing agents," and as I will show later, choice of category may influence how an event is read and interpreted. Metaphor, according to him, is a sense-making mechanism; choice of metaphor affects how news is understood (1987, pp. 291–293). Negativity is the tendency for the news to focus on the negative or the "bad"; he comments on the ideological messages underlying the convention of focusing on bad news:

> What is absent from the text of the news, but present as a powerforce in its reading, are the unspoken assumptions that life is ordinarily smooth-running, rule- and law-abiding, and harmonious. These norms are of course prescriptive rather than descriptive, that is, they embody the sense of what our social life ought to be rather than what it is, and in doing this they embody the ideology of the dominant classes (Fiske 1987, p. 284).

Finally, inoculation is a metaphor for allowing radical voices to be heard in controlled doses. This practice surrounds the news with an aura of objectivity, but Fiske says it tends to strengthen rather than challenge "the social body" (1987, p. 291).

Selecting the General Media Sources

Before turning to a discussion of how narrative structures and news conventions operated in the texts I examined, let us briefly consider the magazines themselves. *Newsweek, Time,* and *U.S. News* are the three most widely circulated news magazines in the United States and Canada. According to 1991 statistics, *Time's* paid circulation was 4,073,530; the circulation for *Newsweek* was 3,224,770 and for *U.S. News* was 2,237,009 (*Information Please Almanac,* 1993, p. 310). All three magazines are published weekly, all of them may be classified as information rather than entertainment magazines, and two of them, *Time* and *Newsweek,* regularly feature a music/arts column. As Fiske has noted in regard to television, information, and entertainment are "leaky" classifications. He points out, however, that in spite of this leakiness there are "very real differences" in the approaches and understandings that audiences and producers bring to these genres (Fiske, 1987, 282). Information magazines were chosen for this study because of the understandings that audiences likely would bring to such texts.

Rap and rap-related subject headings in *Readers' Guide Abstracts,* which indexed articles for the ten-year period from January 1983 through December 1992, were used to find pertinent articles. Thirty-nine articles were located and read. During subsequent readings, as part of my analytical strategy, excerpts were placed in one or more thematic categories. I acknowledge that my against-the-grain readings are situated in this selection scheme and, thus, partial and incomplete. Furthermore, I recognize that as a white, middle-class female, I hold multiple positions, and I realize that these positions helped shape what I did or did not see.

Selection and Silence

One way to begin to understand how rap was represented is to examine patterns of coverage in the three magazines (Table 1).

Clearly, *Newsweek* provided the most consistent and extensive coverage while *U.S. News,* which did not have an arts/music section, spoke only rarely about the subject. Although the magazines are independent from each other, Table 1 shows that they displayed remarkably similar patterns of decision making regarding when rap was or

Table 1: Frequency of Rap Article Publication, by Year

Magazine Year	Time	Newsweek	U.S. News	Total
1983	1	1	0	2
1984	0	0	0	0
1985	0	0	0	0
1986	1	1	0	2
1987	0	1	0	1
1988	0	0	0	0
1989	0	1	0	1
1990	3	7	2	12
1991	2	3	0	5
1992	7	6	3	16
Total	14	20	5	39
Arts Section	Yes	Yes	No	

was not considered newsworthy. During the seven years prior to 1990, the magazines were nearly silent on the subject, and no articles were published during the years 1984, 1985, or 1988. Two sudden increases in coverage occurred during the same years in all three magazines, and those were the only years when *U.S. News* published any rap articles. Perhaps the most dramatic revelation from this portion of my analysis is that one-third of the thirty-nine articles published during the ten-year period appeared in the four months in 1992 immediately following the Rodney King verdict and the Los Angeles response to that verdict.[3] After those four months, coverage disappeared completely from *U.S. News* and dropped dramatically in the other two magazines. I will discuss the foci of some of these articles a bit later; but for now, let us consider the silences, particularly the silences in the two magazines featuring an arts/music column.

Patterns of coverage can reveal what Fiske calls the strategies of selection and categorization—in this instance, the categorization of rap music as news or not news. As I indicated earlier, Fiske maintains that these strategies are based in ideology. For many years, even those magazines featuring a music/arts column did not think rap was newsworthy; perhaps they did not think rap was art, at least not art of sufficient merit to deserve their attention. Silences and sparse coverage indicate that the magazines were in doubt about whether rap was "socially *legitimate*" cultural capital, to use Michael Apple's phrase (1979, p. 6). The lengthy span when these widely read magazines relegated rap to the right of the virgule in the news/not news or art/ not art binary is a reflection of whose knowledge was deemed worth knowing, and thus, indirectly, a commentary on power relations. In this instance, the role of race and social class as influential factors in the selection and categorization processes should not be overlooked.

Subcategorization: Rap as a Cultural Artifact

Another pattern emerged when I examined which news subcategory was selected when information about rap was published. Rap was more frequently discussed in the music/arts section than in any other single news category in the two magazines that featured such a section. However, in both of these magazines, articles about rap appeared *outside* the music/arts section *in the majority of cases* (e.g., in "Lifestyle," "Nation," "Living," "Sports," etc.).[4] In *U.S. News*, the magazine not featuring a music/arts section, rap articles appeared most often under the "Society" heading.

As Fiske has noted, choice of news category influences the ways that information is understood:

> The categorization of news and its consequent fragmentation is a strategy that attempts to control and limit the meanings of social life, and to construct the interests of the western bourgeoisie into 'natural' common sense. Compartmentalization is central to news's strategy of containment (Fiske, 1987, p. 287).

Placing discussions of rap in categories other than the music/arts sections contributed to a construction of rap as a sociological phenomenon, as political discourse, or as reportage rather than as an art form, and, thus, it changed the terms in which rap was discussed. Regardless of whether articles appeared in or out of the arts/music section, however, there was very little discussion of the music itself, aside from its lyrics. Little attention was paid to its history, its formal characteristics, or even to the practice of sampling, which is a rich and complex musical component of rap. These absences further contributed to rap's construction as a sociological phenomenon, subject to intense social analysis. Thus, even if the magazines recognized that rap is an art form (as opposed to "not art"), they did not discuss it as

such, and certainly not in terms apparently reserved for "high art."
The few journalists to compare rap and "high art" placed rap on a
much lower plane. For example, in a scathing critique of N.W.A.'s
explicit lyrics, Jerry Adler wrote, "The outrageous implication is that
to *not* sing about this stuff would be to do violence to an artistic vision
as pure and compelling as Bach's" (Adler, 1990, p. 58). George F. Will
distanced rap from "high art" music by suggesting it was ludicrous to
compare negative responses to 2 Live Crew to the riots that followed
early performances of Stravinsky's *Rite of Spring* (Will, 1990, p. 64).

Of course, rap *is* a socially constructed cultural artifact, as is all
music; however, a double standard appears to exist, which can be
made visible by comparing the terms in which Euro-American high art
music is usually discussed to those used for rap. Recent attempts to
regard high art music as a sociological phenomenon have often met
with sharp criticism and considerable resistance, at least from within
academe.[5]

One dissimilarity between the left and right sides of the high art/
popular art binary is that a myth of transcendence tends to accompany the high art position, and the myth appears to insulate high art
from discussion constructing it as a cultural artifact. Thus, the myth
accords high art music a measure of freedom from the intense scrutiny and sociological analysis to which rap, constructed as popular art,
not art, or bad art, was frequently subjected. This myth of transcendence suggests (falsely, of course) that "high" or "great" art does not
participate in the racism, misogyny, homophobia, or glorification of
violence with which rap was frequently associated and for which it was
harshly criticized. A handful of the magazines' discussions of attempted
censorship of rap lyrics shattered this myth by pointing out that a net
designed to catch rap would also snag much "high art" music. Ira
Glasser, executive director of the American Civil Liberties Union, was
quoted as saying that there are no words in 2 Live Crew "that have
not appeared in books or in serious literature" ("Should dirty lyrics,"
1990, p. 24). Ironically, although Glasser supported 2 Live Crew's
rap, he also categorized it as not serious and, thus, relegated it to the
right side of the virgule.

Of course, the myth of transcendence does not completely insulate
"high art." For example, controversy over the Mapplethorpe exhibit
made the news during the same period as discussions of 2 Live Crew's
lyrics. However, the strength of the myth of transcendence may have
aided the Mapplethorpe case; significantly, the gallery showing

Mapplethorpe's pieces was acquitted of all obscenity charges while the record store owner who sold 2 Live Crew albums was convicted, a point not lost on Peter Plagens, who wrote about the court decisions in a *Newsweek* article entitled "Mixed Signals on Obscenity" (1990, p. 74).

Pierre Bourdieu (1984) theorized about the role that distinctions between high and popular art play in the perpetuation of unequal power relations along social class lines. These distinctions, and their relationship to power, need to be taken into account when considering representations of rap; in addition, however, the role that these distinctions play in perpetuating unequal power relations along racial lines also should be examined.

Rappers, Rap Fans, and Otherness

Rappers
Now that we have considered some of the ways that strategies of selection and categorization placed rap on the right side of the virgule in inside/outside binaries, let us turn to actual textual content, specifically to that which constructed rappers and rap fans. Rap was generally represented as a genre by and for black, urban, adolescent, males who were poor or from the working class. Evidence of inside/outside binaries was in abundance in comments about rappers' race and social class, the binaries variously taking the form of high/low, good/bad, here/there, and up/down. Rap was usually associated with the right side of the virgule, and with lack or want. For example, Jay Cocks relied upon high/low binaries when he reported that rap "began as a fierce and proudly insular music of the American black underclass (1992, p. 70). David Gates, in his description of rap as "a communiqué from the 'underclass'—or less euphemistically, poor blacks," equated poverty (specifically being "under") with being black. Gates also painted a picture of want and lack when he described athletes and rappers as "the only credible role models for inner-city kids"; since most athletes and rappers are male, his comment has sexist overtones as well (Gates, 1990a, p. 60). In several sources, rap was described as coming from the ghetto, a term not only suggesting a place apart, but also a place of otherness, at least from a white, Anglo-Saxon, Protestant perspective. This place of otherness was represented as dangerous; for example, N.W.A.'s music was described as a "rap mural of ghetto life, spray painted with blood" (Cocks, 1991,

p. 78). One source said rap originated in the "cauldron of New York City's underclass," a phrase evoking images of simmering, poisonous brews (Thigpen, 1991, p. 71). Articles that called rap the music from the streets were connecting it to a specific social-class location; however, as a location of otherness, streets were represented as undesirable places associated with crime, poverty, offal, and moral degradation. For example, one reference explained that a "new musical culture, filled with self-assertion and anger, has come boiling up from the streets. Some people think it should have stayed there" (Adler, 1990, p. 56). The statement not only placed streets on the low side of an up/down binary but also suggested that rap had changed social location and had moved to an unnamed "higher" ground. Finally, the headline "America's Slide into the Sewer," which George F. Will chose for his anti-rap essay, suggested that America, however defined, had participated in a downward movement to a place reserved for offal (Will, 1990, p. 64). We can assume that Will was describing a moral slide; however, sewers are found in or under the streets, and streets represent a social location.

A second component in the construction of rappers was an emphasis on the meteoric rises to fame and fortune that resulted from rap's popularity and success. Rap was represented as an enormously profitable venture, but mixed messages were sent about whether such profit was good. Rap's critics argued that rappers were making fortunes on obscenity and getting rich on offensiveness. Much attention was paid to the successes of controversial groups such as N.W.A. (Adler, 1990, p. 56; Gates, 1990b, p. 52; Leland, 1992b, p. 48). In addition, critics and proponents alike sometimes listed ways that rappers and those affiliated with the sales and promotion of rap were spending their money. For example, rap impresario Russell Simmons was described as "livin' large. His empire brings him an income of $5 million a year" (Simpson, 1992, p. 69). The article enumerated some of his possessions, including a bullet-proof Rolls-Royce and a triplex penthouse. Simmons, the magazine reported, buys Cristal champagne, and abstract art. Sports cars, a private jet, exotic trips, a home in Hollywood, and expensive jewelry were among the other possessions associated with rappers (Cocks, 1990, p. 73; Donnelly, 1992, p. 68; Bard, 1987, p. 71; Gates, 1990a, p. 607). Philanthropic efforts were reported occasionally, but more often than not, the magazines focused on rappers' predilections for luxury items. In addition to symbolizing success and wealth, however, the belongings mentioned can also represent extravagance, excess, and unprincipled spending, at least to a middle-class eye.

Another element complicating the representation of successful rappers was the implication that rap is a quasi-legal means of making money, a just-barely-legal way to acquire capital. The tone was set by references to some rappers' past criminal activities. For example, 2 Live Crew's Luther Campbell was described as an "ex-gang leader turned entrepreneur," and Ice-T was reported to have been very successful as a hustler, spending $500 on sneakers before he changed careers (Gates, 1990b, p. 52; Donnelly, 1992, p. 68). Such reports set the stage for portrayals of rap as "the safe and legal road to riches" (Gates, 1990a, p. 61). One article quoted Ice-T lyrics indicating that friends in crime were now making more money in music (Donnelly, 1992, p. 68). Another reported that one quarter of rap's "homeboys end up in serious trouble with the law" (Gates, 1990a, p. 60).

Some links between successful rappers and crime were more subtle. For example, when N.W.A.'s attitude was described as "jaunty and sullen by turns; showy but somehow furtive, in glasses as opaque as a limousine window and sneakers as white as a banker's shirt," subtle connections were made between N.W.A., crime, and otherness (Adler, 1990, p. 56). The words "sullen" and "furtive" set an ominous tone. Next, reference was made to signs of fortune that have also come to represent criminal activity. Limousines with opaque windows are symbols of wealth, but they also are associated with pimps and drug dealers. Opaque glasses, long worn by highway patrol officers, also suggest drug use and inaccessibility. White banker's shirts are a symbol of legal acquisition of capital, but N.W.A. members were not wearing banker's shirts; instead, they donned sneakers.

Reports indicating that some successful rappers, including impresario Russell Simmons, Tracy Marrow (Ice-T), and members of Public Enemy had not come from poverty, but instead had roots in the middle class (Simpson, 1992, p. 69; Donnelly, 1992, p. 66, p. 68; Leland, 1992b, p. 49), contributed to a representation of rappers as impostors and charlatans, shrewd but unscrupulous business people, who furthered their own interests at the expense of a long list of victims, among them women and poor black people. Of course, rather than recognizing that all musical performances are just performances, such arguments assumed that some are and others are not. One critic charged that Ice-T's heavy metal single *Cop Killer* was not "an authentic anguished cry of rage from the ghetto," but rather a "cynical commercial concoction designed to titillate its audience with imagery of violence"; *Cop Killer*, the critic claimed, is "an excellent joke [by Ice-T and Time Warner, the parent corporation] on the white establishment" (Kinsley,

1992, p. 88). Another article described impresario Simmons as sens-
ing the commercial potential when others thought rap was a gimmick
(Simpson, 1992, p. 69). In a discussion of an N.W.A. album released
in 1991, N.W.A's mystique was said to pay "no attention to where
criminality begins and marketing lets off" (Leland, 1991, p. 63). Finally, when Sister Souljah spoke at a convention of Jesse Jackson's
Rainbow Coalition in 1992, and presidential candidate William Clinton
criticized Souljah, one commentator unflatteringly represented all three
figures (Jackson, Souljah, and Clinton) as self-serving, bottom-line
business people whose primary interest was furthering their own careers; the essay was entitled "Sister Souljah: Capitalist Tool" (White,
1992, p. 88). The proposition that rappers are entrepreneurs, not
artists, overlooked the possibility that they could be both; furthermore, it did not address the reality that most, if not all, artists are by
necessity entrepreneurs as well.

Ironically, stories of rappers' entrepreneurialism and success, boot-
strap stories that would make Horatio Alger proud, sometimes were
viewed with mistrust and suspicion. Controversial rappers, at least
one of whom was a card-carrying member of the Republican party,[6]
were amassing wealth by serving up conservative political fare that
embraced "old-fashioned social norms (even in its take on gender roles
and homosexuality. . .)" (Leland, 1992b, p. 52). Ironically, these conservative voices were being vilified and rebuked by other conservatives. Thus, rappers' acquisition of wealth and their concomitant shift
in social-class status did not necessarily change the representation of
these rappers as outsiders. This representation can be explained, in
part, in terms of power relations. If successful black rappers are viewed
as a threat to hegemony and a challenge to some white middle-class
values, specifically to beliefs about who is entitled to capital, how it
should be acquired, and how it should be used, then mixed or negative
portrayals of these rappers may be seen as attempts to reinforce dominant ideology and to keep black people "in their place."

Rap Fans

As mentioned earlier, rap was represented as originating in a specific
place of otherness; lines of distinction were drawn in terms of race,
social class, and gender. However, as the decade advanced, the magazines indicated that some types of rap were traversing some of these
lines; the race and social class of the typical fan were shifting, but the
age and sex generally were not. Some articles said these shifts or

expansions began in the mid-1980s, but the movement may have started several years earlier.[7] When an article published in 1990 told parents that rap can be heard booming from "your kid's bedroom," the kid in question could have been either black or white (Gates, 1990a, p. 60). As early as 1990, articles began recognizing that music by rap's most controversial groups, for example, Public Enemy and N.W.A., was being consumed primarily by white, middle-class, suburban, adolescent males (Gates, 1990a, p. 61; Cocks, 1991, p. 78). By contrast, according to John Schecter, editor of the hip-hop journal *The Source*, N.W.A. was not liked by most black people (Cocks, 1991, p. 75).

Audience shift or expansion was discussed most extensively in articles appearing during the final three years I analyzed, 1990–1992; this shift may help explain the dramatic increase in 1990 of the magazines' coverage of rap. The scope of the expansion was alluded to in a statement made in 1992 by rapper Tupac Shakur, who opined that rap was no longer a black movement but rather a youth movement (Leland, 1992a, p. 53). Throughout the final three years, however, the perception lingered that rap was, first and foremost, by and for black people.

The term often used to describe the movement of rap's popularity from one racial and social-class group to another was "crossover," and the place to which rap crossed was often called "the mainstream." Inside/outside binaries were evident throughout these discussions. The mainstream, the inside of the binary, was white, middle class, and male. Journalists spoke of rap crossing over from black America "into the mainstream of popular culture" (Gates, 1990c, p. 68). Impresario Russell Simmons was described as moving rap "from the streets of the inner city into the white mainstream of American pop culture" (Simpson, 1992, p. 69). Journalist John Leland mentioned rap's "trip to the white mainstream" (1992b, p. 51), and Jay Cocks talked about "why ghetto rage and the brutal abuse of women appeal to mainstream listeners." Cocks later gave a profile of the typical fan that provided clues about who constituted the mainstream; fans were white, middle class, teenage, and male (Cocks, 1991, p. 78).

Inside/outside binaries took several forms in discussions of rappers and rap fans, one of which was a we/they binary to which the moral judgments good/bad were often explicitly or implicitly attached. At times, "they" were rappers, and at other times, fans. For example, an article appearing in 1990, the year when crossover began receiving substantial attention, was entitled "Polluting Our Popular Culture."

The article described popular culture as "the air we breathe," and 2 Live Crew was termed "a pesky new pollutant"; the journalist, John Leo, called for the elimination of the "2 Live Pollutants" from "our air." In this we/they structure, popular culture was owned by an un-specified "us," and "they," 2 Live Crew, were a foreign contaminant. "They" were rappers and rap music from whom rap fans, constructed as "our daughters," needed to be protected. Leo, in a question that displayed a protect-the-women-and-children logic, queried, "Why should our daughters have to grow up in a culture in which musical advice on the domination and abuse of women is accepted as entertainment?" (Leo, 1990, p. 15). Leo's question appears to be a color-blind plea to all parents; however, in an article focusing on 2 Live Crew's contro-versial lyrics, group leader Luther Campbell observed that he had been making similar albums for years and had received no complaints from the "decency police" until white kids started listening (Gates, 1990b, p. 52). Apparently, protecting daughters was not much of an issue with these watchdog groups until "our daughters" were white. Leo's question is an excellent one; however, as feminist musicians know, serving up the domination and abuse of women as entertainment is not unique to rap or to popular music; much Euro-American high art music does the same. Leo's decision to single out rap indicated that the genre was on the outside of the inside/outside binary, a position offering less protection from scrutiny.

Yet another example of the we/they binary was seen in a scathing criticism of rap fans, whom journalist Jerry Adler described as "work-ing-class" and "underclass" youths "who forgot to go to business school in the 1980s." Adler placed himself in the otherwise unspecified cat-egory of "we" and argued that "we" cannot talk to "them," the rap fans. Adler characterized fans as stupid and uninformed; he main-tained that if they "had ever listened to anything except the homeboys talking trash," if they had studied and read, "[t]hen we might have a sensible discussion with them; but they haven't, so we can't" (Adler, 1990, p. 59).

An especially ugly manifestation of the inside/outside binary was seen in discussions distancing rap from civilization. For example, in a diatribe focusing largely on rap, George F. Will implied that rappers are lower animals (Will, 1990, p. 64). Shortly thereafter, Jerry Adler equated civilization with control and rap with chaos when he wrote, "Civilized society abhors [rap] attitude and perpetuates itself by keep-ing it under control" (1990, p. 57). A letter to the editor responded to the issue in which Adler's article appeared by chastising *Newsweek* for publishing any information about rap. Calling it a "bestial and obscene" subculture, the reader fumed, "I realize that these creatures [rappers] have the right to express themselves. . . . However, you seem to have forgotten your responsibility to your readers to keep within the bounds of decency."[8] To suggest, as these passages did, that members of a predominantly black group such as rappers are uncivilized, low animals is to invoke a racism as old as colonialism itself.

The Other of Others

Some rap and rappers were routinely criticized for making hateful or demeaning comments about whole groups of people. The groups most frequently mentioned were women, gays, Korean immigrants, Jews, whites, and the police; however, from time to time rap also was denounced for furthering hatred toward blacks through the commodification of racist images of black people. With the exception of the police, the groups mentioned were defined in terms of race, social class, gender, sexual orientation, or ethnicity. Social class was described as a separating factor when black people were divided in opinion on the subject of rap. Discussions of black opposition to rap shattered the myth of a unified black voice; however, they also contributed to the perception that rap had and deserved little support from important segments of the black community; anti-rap sentiment was thus portrayed as transcending race. Paradoxically, people who may have viewed themselves as disenfranchised others—women, gays, Asian immigrants, and Jews—were summoned to join powerful dominant groups—whites and the police—in an improbable coalition against rap. In short, not only were rappers and rap fans often represented as the others in inside/outside binaries, they also were constructed as the other of others. A quotation by bell hooks applies: "Black youth culture comes to stand for the outer limits of 'outness'" (1992, p. 34).

Rap and Negativity

It would be inaccurate and misleading to say that every article openly opposed all rap. Indeed, making generalizations about the overall tone of the articles was extraordinarily difficult. It usually was impossible to simplistically categorize an article as patently pro or con, positive or negative. I can say that *U.S. News* had a prevailing attitude toward rap because anti-rap sentiments were expressed in every article; furthermore, four of the five articles were patently opposed to the rap discussed. However, when speaking about the other two magazines, especially about *Newsweek*, which presented the most extensive coverage of rap, there is an ever-present danger of being reductive. In all three magazines an image of balanced reporting, of including multiple viewpoints, was created; one way of accomplishing this was by using side-by-side pro and con arguments. The image of balance confounded attempts to analyze and generalize, and it implied that the magazines were not in the business of telling readers what to think. However, Fiske probably would describe these pro/con presentations as examples of inoculation, of allowing radical voices to speak in controlled environments.

Even though the articles were difficult to characterize and often presented the image of balance, most of them nevertheless participated in reinforcing dominant ideologies through the strategy of containment that Fiske calls negativity. Evidence of this negativity surfaced when thematic content of the articles was analyzed. The vast majority of articles made reference to at least one of the following themes: violence, obscenity, hatred, crime, gangs, and anger. Such references appeared in all *U.S. News* articles and in more than 85% of those published by *Time* and by *Newsweek*. Thus, even when articles were sympathetic to rap, they usually reinforced a link between rap and specific negative themes. A corollary representation was that controversy is rap's constant partner. Concentrating on the negative, focusing on a circumscribed list of rap topics, and constructing rap as controversial, were means by which these magazines placed readers in a position where they likely received a skewed vision of rap, a vision that nearly obliterated its diversity. The vastness of rap and its extraordinary variety—illustrated, for example, by the existence of groups such as DC Talk, composed of students from conservative evangelist Jerry Falwell's Liberty University—was lost in a reductive wash (Rabey, 1991, p. 50). In its relentless search for the negative and the controversial, the reporting made generalizations about the whole after looking at only a very small part. It centered on a few controversial groups rather than on the complete genre, and characteristics of the former tended to be ascribed to the latter. Coverage almost invariably obscured the reality that the rappers and rap discussed were neither necessarily representative nor the most popular with the majority of rap fans. The rare qualifying statement, such as, "The vast majority of rap is healthy," or "Rap is so vast, you can't really categorize it anymore," was barely audible amid the clatter of negativity (Leo, 1992, p. 19, p. 50).

Negative Imagery and the Representation of Rap

Even when articles did not specifically refer to negative themes, they nevertheless sometimes constructed rap as bad in roundabout ways, for example, through use of imagery. As Fiske states, choice of image, specifically of metaphor, influences the understandings people bring to texts. There was imagery of poison and pollution. For example, one headline read "Rap Music's Toxic Fringe" (Leo, 1992, p. 19). In a similar vein, an article suggested that the recording industry was telling consumers to "buy a gas mask or stop breathing"; it described rap as sending "venomous messages" disguised as "harmless fun" (Leo, 1990, p. 19). There also were images of violence, anger, and fear. Ice-T's poetry, it was said, "takes a switchblade and deftly slices life's jugular" (Donnelly, 1992, p. 66). A simile laced with racism described rap attitude as being "as scary as sudden footsteps in the dark" (Adler, 1990, p. 57). Even descriptions of the music itself sometimes relied on violent imagery. For example, a journalist wrote of "the thumping, clattering scratching *assault* [my emphasis] of rap" (Adler, 1990, p. 56). Another said that the group B.W.P served up "a vengeful brand of radical black feminism" in a "snarling hard-core style" (Thigpen, 1991, p. 72).

War metaphors were used occasionally. One passage called rap music "a series of bulletins from the front in a battle for survival," and another referred to members of Public Enemy as "racial warriors" (Leland, 1992b, p. 6, p. 49). In what was perhaps the most vivid example, an image of war was evoked when conservative actor Charlton Heston likened Ice-T to Adolf Hitler, a comparison made at a Time Warner shareholders' meeting held in 1992 (Leland, 1992c, p. 51). By equating a rapper with a war figure who personifies evil of mythic proportions, Heston and the journalist who reported the event constructed Ice-T as the enemy in a battle of good against evil.

Rap, Representation, and Race

The significance of the magazines' negativity and negative representations becomes clearer when one considers that theorists have linked both negativity and negative representation to power relations. John Fiske asserted that negativity is a strategy of containment that tends to reinforce dominant ideologies. Specifically, Fiske noted, ideological practice is evident in news reporting's predisposition to construct "the bad" as an aberration in dominant culture but as normal for others. Fiske commented on the relationship between "otherness," negativity, and power:

> There is, of course, a connection between elitism and negativity: the positive or 'normal' actions of elite people will often be reported whereas those without social power are considered newsworthy only when their actions are disruptive or deviant. In representing the dominant as performing positive actions and the subordinate as performing deviant or negative ones the news is engaging in the same ideological practices as fictional television (Fiske, 1987, pp. 285–286).

Because there is a relationship between representation and power, negative representation that consistently links a black cultural product and black performers to violence, obscenity, hatred, crime, gangs, and anger, and that thus represents hip hop culture as the undesirable other, must be viewed as a factor contributing to the maintenance of white supremacy. Tricia Rose, who has explored some of the complex cultural politics of rap, speaks of a "sociologically based crime discourse" that surrounds "the political economy of rap" (Rose, 1991, p. 277). Rose asserts that opposition to rap is grounded in fear:

> Young African Americans are positioned in fundamentally antagonistic relationships to the institutions that most prominently frame and constrain their lives. The public school system, the police, and the popular media perceive and construct them as a dangerous internal element in urban America—an element that if allowed to roam about freely will threaten the social order, an element that must be policed. The social construction of rap and rap-related violence is fundamentally linked to the social discourse on Black containment and fears of a Black planet (Rose, 1991, p. 279).

According to Rose, this white fear, born in the days of slavery, is of loss of white control, specifically through black uprising or revolt; the fear informs constructions of black people, especially of young black males, who are seen as threats "to the social order of oppression," threats that must be restrained or controlled (1991, pp. 283–284, p. 289).

Fears of a Black Planet and the Discourse of Containment

With Rose's analysis of the cultural politics of rap music in mind, let us examine two cases from the magazines in which the negative representations of rap, rappers, and rap fans seemed clearly linked to fears of a black planet and the social discourse of containment. I will begin with a close reading of George F. Will's essay, "America's Slide into the Sewer," in which Will stepped beyond the observation that some rap lyrics speak of violence to suggest that 2 Live Crew lyrics induce violence. In this article, Will associated rap with an actual act of violence, the brutal rape in 1989 of a Central Park jogger. It is from rap groups like 2 Live Crew, Will suggested, that young men such as the accused rapists learn that sexual violence against women is enjoyable: "Where can you get the idea that sexual violence against women is fun? From a music store, through Walkman earphones, from boom boxes blaring forth the rap lyrics of 2 Live Crew." To prove his point, Will interspersed horrifyingly graphic excerpts of courtroom testimony from the rape case with shockingly explicit rap lyrics from 2 Live Crew. He connected the rapists to rap fans by citing common characteristics of both groups: "Fact: Some members of a particular age and social cohort—the one making 2 Live Crew rich—stomped and raped the jogger to the razor edge of death, for the fun of it." To bolster his argument he quoted the *Washington Post*'s Juan Williams, whom he identified as "black and disgusted"; Williams excoriated 2 Live Crew, claiming the group is "'selling corruption—self-hate—to vulnerable young minds in a weak black America'" (Will, 1990, p. 64). Williams supported his allegation that American black families are falling apart by citing statistics indicating that half of all black children are raised in single-parent households headed by women.

Will charged that liberals are the tools of unscrupulous corporations, which have sold "civil pollution for profit." America's priorities are wrong, Will argued, because protecting black women receives less attention than saving endangered fish: "America today is capable of terrific intolerance about smoking, or toxic waste that threatens trout. But only a deeply confused society is more concerned about protecting lungs than minds, trout than black women. We legislate against smoking in restaurants; singing 'Me So Horny' is a constitutional right" (Willis, 1990, p. 64). Will's parting comments indicated that he believes protection of black women will be accomplished by exercising more control over groups such as 2 Live Crew.

The Central Park rape was horrible and 2 Live Crew's lyrics are graphic and misogynistic; however, these realities do not change the fact that Will's argument was not only flawed, sexist, and elitist but also showed evidence of a racist fear of a black planet. To begin to excavate the racism, sexism, and elitism implicit in Will's essay, the reader must keep in mind a critical piece of information about the Central Park rape: the jogger was white and the attackers were black. Will made no reference to the race of either party, but this information was generally known and widely reported. Thus, Will chose as his example of crime and violence an event that was laden with prejudicial meaning and was a classic scenario for evoking white racist fears. The Central Park rape reinforced the racist perception that young black adolescents are dangerous, out of control, and sexually violent; the event appeared to confirm the belief that uncontrolled, young black adolescents are a threat to vulnerable (female) white America.

Next, Will linked this meaning-laden rape to a black cultural product, even though he did not present one scintilla of evidence suggesting the accused rapists had ever listened to 2 Live Crew or to any form of rap music. Even if Will had found such evidence, he would have faced the formidable task of establishing causation. He grounded his case on the argument that the accused rapists were of the same "age and social cohort group" making 2 Live Crew rich but never articulated salient features of that cohort group. Will and Williams apparently assumed that race was one of those salient features, an assumption encountered in Williams' statement that 2 Live Crew was selling corruption to the black community. However, as noted previously, information reported elsewhere in 1990 indicated that the typical fan of controversial rap groups was a young, white, middle-class boy from the suburbs. Thus, Will's characterization of "social cohort group" probably was flawed. Significantly, his characterization tended to perpetuate negative stereotypes of black adolescents while it permitted members of the social cohort group most likely to listen to explicit rap—white, middle-class boys from the suburbs—to emerge unscathed.

When Will asked the question "Where can you get the idea that sexual violence against women is fun?" he failed to list a whole array of sources unrelated to black music, and in so doing, constructed rap music as the culprit. He did not acknowledge that young males in American society can learn misogyny from countless sources in the dominant culture, the most influential of which are probably outside the boundaries of entertainment. There is implicit racism in Will's decision to single out a black cultural product but never to mention heavy metal, country, opera, and the classical fare typically sung in high school choirs, which often are at least as misogynistic (if perhaps not as graphic) as 2 Live Crew.

Will appears to have attempted to construct his argument as one that transcends race. For example, he included a sentence criticizing Andrew Dice Clay, whom he carefully described as a white comedian. However, that sentence was the only one to indict a white cultural product, and it was dwarfed by the extensive coverage given to 2 Live Crew. Will also appears to have tried to protect himself from the accusation of being racist by quoting a black spokesperson. However, Juan Williams' unflattering assessment of the state of black families and his sexist but commonly believed assumption that single-parent families headed by women are not strong, worked to reinforce white racist constructions of black families as bad families. bell hooks has commented on similar constructions:

> . . . African-Americans need to consider whose interests are served when the predominant representation of black culture both on television news and in talk shows suggests that the black family is disintegrating and that a hostile gender war is taking place between black women and men (hooks, 1990, 73).

Finally, in a particularly patriarchal gesture, Will constructed himself as a protector of black women; one significant aspect of this construction was that it came in response to the rape of a white woman. By placing himself in that role, Will depicted black women as the weak or vulnerable "others" who need to be protected by the strong, more powerful white man. Protected from what? According to Will, from violence caused by black music, his assertion simply assuming that music-induced violence exists. His unspoken, racist message is that trouble in the lives of black people is caused by black people, in this case, by black musicians. Arguments such as Will's deflect attention away from real issues and substantive discussion of the kinds of change that would be necessary to alter the lived realities of many black women's lives. Whose interests are served by such deflection? Greater control of black discursive terrain would tend to reinforce dominant power relations; substantive change that might bring real improvement would threaten hegemony.

Some of the racial politics of Will's essay become visible when one examines the list of who looks bad in this article, that is, who was portrayed as the evil, lacking, or undesirable other. First, there were the rapists, whom the newspapers had widely reported were black. Next, there was rap music, which was generally regarded as a black cultural product, followed by 2 Live Crew, a black rap group. Fourth, there were 2 Live Crew fans, who were assumed to be black (probably incorrectly). In all of these representations, negativity was achieved by linking black people or cultural products to brutality, sexual violence, and amorality. Fifth, there were black families, specifically those headed by women, and finally, there were unscrupulous liberals and corporations, groups whose racial constitutions were not reported. Will's superficial attempts to present himself as color-blind did not mask the racism, elitism, and sexism in his constructions of black people as dangerous, undesirable, others.

Fears of a black planet and a discourse of containment were evident not only in Will's choice of the Central Park rape as the crime to discuss and in his negative constructions of black people and black cultural products, but most significantly, in his cries for more regulation of black discursive terrain. Ironically, a spurious link between rap and actual violence was the foundation for this cry. Will claimed that more control would benefit black women, but the question of whose interests are served and who stands to benefit from black containment typically elicits answers other than black women.

Finally, Will accused liberals and corporations of participating in a pornography of violence for profit. However, news also is a marketable commodity, and an inspection of Will's article for signs of what was being sold there reveals that such accusations may also justifiably be leveled at him. For example, his decision to write about brutal violence, and to include graphic excerpts of the trial transcripts and lyrics, suggests that he himself was participating in this very commodification.

Rap coverage in the four months immediately following the Rodney King verdict and response was a second example in which representations of rap, rappers, and rap fans as the "bad other" seemed clearly linked to fears of a black planet and the social discourse of containment. As I mentioned earlier, the three independent magazines made very similar decisions about when rap and rappers were newsworthy, and all concluded that hip hop culture was big news in the four months immediately following the Rodney King verdict and the Los Angeles response. A rapper, Sister Souljah, even made the cover of *Newsweek* in June 1992. I am not suggesting the publishers were malicious, nor do I subscribe to conspiracies theories. However, in the case of the articles appearing during that four-month period, the timing of this extensive coverage, even if it was coincidental, was of the essence. Through timing alone, rap once again was linked to controversy and violence, and was thus represented as the undesirable other.

The question of why the magazines decided to give rap such extensive coverage during those four months, and why the coverage would nearly disappear after August or September, is an interesting one. Most of the articles appearing during this period focused on (1) a comment about killing whites that rapper Sister Souljah reportedly made at a convention of Jesse Jackson's Rainbow Coalition, or (2) Ice-T and a boycott of Time Warner proposed by police in response to the rapper's heavy-metal single *Cop Killer*. The reproaches leveled at these performers were not new: critics accused the musicians of condoning or inciting hatred and violence. In addition, several rap articles mentioned the Rodney King verdict and response. Typically such references explored the relationship between rap, the verdict, and the response (Leland, 1992a, pp. 52–53; 1992b, p. 48, p. 52; Leo, 1992, p. 19; Zuckerman, 1992, p. 80). Some articles spoke of rap presaging the events; others suggested it contributed to, orchestrated, or incited the insurgence. Just as George Will had done earlier, some journalists were suggesting the unlikely, namely that "bad" art was responsible for real-life events.

If we naturalize the news by saying it is merely about events and if we assume that the Souljah and Ice-T events just coincidentally happened in the wake of the verdict and response, then we lose sight of the role that the cultural process of selection plays in the reporting of news. However, if we assume that the Los Angeles response tapped the deep-seated white fears of which Tricia Rose spoke, then extensive coverage of controversies surrounding black musicians and a black cultural product is less puzzling, especially when the controversy included allegations of promoting or inciting hatred toward whites and the police. A statement in *Time* by Doug Elder, a Houston police officer spearheading the boycott of Time Warner, not only reverberated with white fears but also constructed rappers (and perhaps rap fans) as the dangerous enemies, the evil outsiders in a mythic opposition of good against evil: "'You mix this [*Cop Killer*] with the summer, the violence and a little drugs, and they are going to unleash a reign of terror on communities all across this country'" (Donnelly, 1992, 66).

On August 4, 1992, Ice-T announced that he was withdrawing *Cop Killer*, a decision he reportedly made after employees of Warner Brothers Records, the subsidiary of Time Warner that had distributed *Cop Killer*, had received bomb or death threats. If the controversy over this single is constructed as a standoff between the police and Ice-T, and if this standoff is viewed as a racist concretization of deep-structure myths, then the headlines "Ice-T Melts" and "The Ice-Man Concedeth" sent the message that "good" had prevailed over "evil" (Leland, 1992c, p. 50; "Ice-T Melts," 1992, p. 23). The melting imagery obviously was a play on Ice-T's name; however, images of melting also send messages about power. The Wicked Witch in *The Wizard of Oz* lost her magical powers when she melted. When people melt, they are reduced, weakened, made invisible, or rendered impotent. Ice-T had not merely made a decision to withdraw a single; instead, according to the headlines, he had conceded and melted.

The *Newsweek* article reporting Ice-T's decision spoke of mounting fears that skittish corporations would exercise more internal control over future releases. The Time Warner corporate board, the article reported, "*is* demanding tighter control of what gets made." Journalist John Leland expressed the concern that self-censorship would stifle "controversial ideas before they can ever enter public debate" (1992c, p. 51). Thus, limitations on discursive terrain, on published space, appeared to be a long-lasting outcome of one of the 1992 controversies. Such self-censorship is significant because, as Tricia Rose maintains, control over the art form is a form of containment; self-censorship is another manifestation of what Rose called the "institutional policing to which all rappers are subject" (Rose, 1991, p. 276).

For the most part, 1992 coverage of rap ended with Ice-T's announcement. Rap once again was relegated to the "not-news" category, and the news gaze glanced elsewhere. Significantly, the tone of the two rap articles that appeared in the final months of 1992 was distinctly different from that of most others. One article constructed rap as an extraordinarily successful exportable commodity, and the other spoke largely of a new style, dancehall, that was said to be rapidly supplanting rap (Cocks, 1992, pp. 70–71; Leland, 1992d, p. 59). Both articles intimated that rap was on its way out.

When assessing whose interests were or were not served by the extensive coverage given to rap in the four months immediately following the King verdict and response, it is important to remember that news itself is a marketable commodity. Not only did these magazines link rap to violence and controversy, but the companies owning them profited from such representations, and thus, participated in their own version of what bell hooks calls "the commodification of Otherness" (1992, p. 21). There was potential for Time Warner to reap double benefits, first, from sales of *Cop Killer*, and, second, from sales of *Time* magazine's coverage of the controversy.

There was no indication that the magazines viewed themselves as being in any way responsible for the reduction in discursive terrain that was a promised result of the Ice-T controversy. Journalists rarely reflected on the role they, or the media in general, played in the perpetuation of specific representations of rap, rappers, or rap fans; furthermore, there was little or no discussion of the potential damage media representations might cause. Only one article, an interview with high school students, mentioned media representations of rap and hip hop culture. In this article, several high schoolers indicated that newspapers and other media, obsessed with controversy and negativity, have played a significant role in shaping rap's bad image (Leo, 1992a, pp. 50–51).

Theories on the Appeal of Controversial Rap to White Males

Before closing, let us consider a final related question: Why is explicit, controversial rap especially popular among white, middle-class, suburban males? One theory is that stereotypical constructions of blackness, prevalent in rap, help define whiteness. According to this theory, consuming the "other," in this case listening to rap music, is a transgressive act, performed in defiance of dominant white norms. David Samuels writes,

> Rap's appeal to whites rested in its evocation of an age-old image of blackness: a foreign, sexually charged, and criminal underworld against which the norms of white society are defined, and by extension, through which they may be defied (1991, p. 25).

Thus, for whites, listening to rap may be an expression of adolescent rebellion and a symbol of opposition. A foray into otherness, according to bell hooks, may be viewed by adolescents as a way out of alienation:

> Masses of young people dissatisfied by U.S. imperialism, unemployment, lack of economic opportunity, afflicted by the postmodern malaise of alienation, no sense of grounding, no redemptive identity, can be manipulated by cultural strategies that offer Otherness as appeasement, particularly through commodification (hooks, 1992, p. 25).

Opinions have differed, however, about whether acts of transgression principally reinforce or challenge dominant power relations. Peter Stallybrass and Allon White, for example, argue that transgression tends to unravel dominant discourses: "Transgression becomes a kind of reverse or counter-sublimation, undoing the discursive hierarchies and stratifications of bodies and cultures which bourgeois society has produced as the mechanism of its symbolic dominance" (1986, pp. 200–201). Another perspective is provided by hooks, who maintains that consuming otherness for pleasure is a means by which discourses of dominance are reinforced:

> When race and ethnicity become commodified as resources for pleasure, the culture of specific groups, as well as the bodies of individuals, can be seen as constituting an alternative playground where members of dominating races, genders, sexual practices affirm their power-over in intimate relations with the Other (hooks, 1992, p. 23).

To rebut the assumption that consuming rap is unproblematically counterhegemonic, Samuels points out that although black music historically has been a "refuge from white middle-class boredom," in earlier times forays by whites into black music required face-to-face contact; with the advent of records and videos, whites can now consume without contact. One significant dimension of this no-touch mode of consumption is control; controversial rap can offer exciting, but safe, appearances of danger—semblances of street experience—to consumers who never leave the comfort of their suburban living rooms (1991, p. 29). Media, to use Bakhtinian terminology, have enabled carnival to be transformed into spectacle, and this transformation alters power relations. Records and videos, thus, provide a vantage point similar to that offered by the nineteenth-century balcony, which, Stallybrass and White have observed, was a location from which the bourgeoisie "could both participate in the banquet of the streets and yet remain separated" from it and above it (1986, p. 126).

Some scholars have indicated that fascination with the other is an inevitable consequence of binaries that construct otherness as evil, bad, or disgusting. For example, Stallybrass and White indicate that "disgust always bears the imprint of desire. These low domains, apparently expelled as 'Other', return as the object of nostalgia, longing, and fascination." Furthermore, these margins and sites of otherness may be viewed as growth plates, historically serving as sources of creativity from which the bourgeoisie have drawn sustenance (1986, 191, p. 21). The appeal of rap may thus be its imaginative, creative potential.

Finally, it may be argued that the text, which is what renders some rap controversial, is of little importance to many rap fans, who are drawn to the genre because of its strong, mesmerizing beat and its potential for dancing. Those who forward this explanation argue that white appeal is unrelated to rap's explicit texts and stereotypical representations of race. Perhaps no single factor accounts for rap's appeal to specific groups. However, the topic is an interesting one and merits much further consideration.

Conclusion

Through an analysis of *Time, Newsweek*, and *U.S. News and World Report*, I have explored how concretizations of deep-structure binaries and general characteristics of news reporting have constructed rap, rappers, and rap fans as the deviant, lacking, undesirable, or evil other. I have examined links between specific representations of hip hop culture and the perpetuation of dominant power relations along lines of race, social class, and gender. Specifically, I have explored how these representations were related to fears of a black planet and to discourses of containment. Finally, I have suggested that the magazines themselves engaged in a commodification of otherness, as well as a commodification of violence, and that these news sources did not openly acknowledge their own role as participants in the construction of representations that tend to perpetuate hegemony. In revealing some of the weaknesses of these magazines' coverage of rap, I have also pointed to drawbacks of relying heavily on such media for information about the genre. Like it or not, however, the general media are educating all of us, and television, newspapers, and magazines may be the sole sources of information about rap for a large portion of the population.

Learning about rap from second-hand sources such as the general news media, given the prevalence of the myth that news reporting is objective, presents a special array of problems for educators. These problems may be particularly serious if media information substitutes for actual experience with the genre. As I mentioned at the outset, some circles are urging educators to become more rap-literate and to include rap in official school knowledge. Ironically, however, current goals and conventions of news reporting appear to result in media representations that may bolster narrow beliefs about what constitutes legitimate school knowledge and fuel suspicion of popular culture. Because these magazines' representations are in many respects problematic, educators need to subject them to the "fierce critical interrogations" of which bell hooks speaks, especially as they make decisions about whether and how to include rap in the school curriculum. These fierce critical interrogations are of paramount importance, not only as an essential ingredient when consuming entertainment, but also, as we have seen here, when we consume the news.

References

Adler, J. (1990, March 19). The rap attitude. *Newsweek*, p. 58.

Apple. M. (1979). *Ideology and curriculum*. London: Routledge.

Barol, B. (1992, June 29). The kings of rap, together. *Newsweek*, p. 71.

Bourdieu, P. (1984). *Distinction: A social critique of the judgement of taste*. Cambridge, MA: Harvard University Press.

Cocks, J. (1983, March 21). Chilling out on rap flash. *Time*, p. 73.

Cocks, J. (1990, August 13). U can't touch him. *Time*, p. 73.

Cocks, J. (1991, July 1). A nasty jolt for the top pops. *Time*, p. 78.

Cocks, J. (1992, October 19). Rap around the globe. *Time*, p. 70.

Donnelly, S. (1992, June 22). The fire around the ice. *Time*, p. 68.

Eichelmann, H. (1990, April 9). Letters. *Newsweek*, p. 13.

Fiske, J. (1987). *Television culture*. New York: Routledge.

Fuss, D. (1991). Inside/out, In Fuss, D. (Ed.). *Inside/out: Lesbian theories, gay theories* (pp.). New York: Routledge.

Gates, D. (1990a, March 19). Decoding rap music. *Newsweek*, p. 60.

Gates, D. (1990b, July 2). The importance of being nasty. *Newsweek*, p. 52.

Gates, D. (1990c, December 3). Play that packaged music. *Newsweek*, p. 68.

Giroux, H. & McLaren. P. (Eds.). (1989). *Critical pedagogy, the state, and cultural struggle*. Albany, NY: State University of New York Press.

hooks, bell. (1990). *Yearning: Race, gender, and cultural politics*. Boston, MA: South End Press.

hooks, bell. (1992). *Black looks: Race and representation*. Boston, MA: South End Press.

Information Please Almanac: Atlas and Yearbook. (1993). Boston: Houghton Mifflin.

Kinsley, M. (1992, July 20). Ice-T: Is the issue social responsibility. *Time*, p. 88.

Leland, J. (1991, July 1). Number one with a bullet. *Newsweek*, p. 63.

Leland, J. (1992a, May 11). The word on the street is heard in the beat. *Newsweek*, p. 53.

Leland, J. (1992b, June 29). Rap and race. *Newsweek*, p. 48.

Leland, J. (1992c, August 10). The iceman concedeth. *Newsweek*, p. 51.

Leland, J. (1992d, September 7). When rap meets reggae. *Newsweek*, p. 259.

Leo, J. (1990, July 2). Polluting our popular culture. *U.S. News and World Report*, p. 15.

Leo, J. (1992a, June 29). The lowdown on hip hop: Kids talk about the music. *Newsweek*, p. 50.

Leo, J. (1992b, June 29). Rap music's toxic fringe. *U.S. News and World Report*, p. 19.

Plagens, P. (1990, October 15). Mixed signals on obscenity: Mapplethorpe passes but 2 Live Crew doesn't. *Newsweek*, p. 74.

Rabey, S. (1991, June 24). Rhymin' and rappin' 4D King. *Christianity Today*, p. 13.

Rose, T. (1991). Fear of a black planet: Rap music and black cultural politics in the 1990s. *Journal of Negro Education*, *60*, 32–77.

Samuels, D. (1991, November 11). The rap on rap. *The New Republic*, p. 25.

"Should dirty lyrics be against the law?" (1990, June 25). *U.S. News and World Report*, 24.

Stallybrass, P. & White, A. (1986). *The politcs and poetics of transgression*. Ithaca, NY: Cornell University Press.

Thigpen, D. (1991, May 27). Not for men only. *Time*, p. 71.

Van Den Toorn, P. (1991). Politics, feminism, and contemporary music theory. *The Journal of Musicology*, *9*, 3, 275–299.

White, J. (1992, June 29). Sister Souljah: Capitalist tool. *Time*, p. 88.

Will, G. (1990, July 30). America's slide into the sewer. *Newsweek*, p. 64.

Zuckerman, M. (1992, June 29). The Sister Souljah affair. *U.S. News and World Report*, p. 80.

Notes

1. For interesting work on the relationship between popular culture and education, see Giroux & McLaren 1989.

2. See, for example, hooks (1990, p. 73, p. 220).

3. In Time, six of seven articles were published after the LA response, and five of seven appeared in the four-month window. This within-window count did not include an article appearing in the May 4, 1992 issue. Although the date of the issue technically qualified the article, I assume the issue went to press before the verdict. In *Newsweek,* five of six were published after the LA response. All three 1992 *U.S. News* articles appeared in the window.

4. In 25 of the 39 articles, discussions appeared in a classification other than arts/music. Eleven of twenty Newsweek articles were not in music/arts, and nine of fourteen *Time* articles appeared elsewhere.

5. One obvious example of this resistance is negative response to feminist musicologist Susan McGlary's ground-breaking analyses and deconstructions of opera and symphonic music. For a scathing assessment of McGlary, see Van Den Toorn (1991).

6. N.W.A.'s Eazy-E reportedly "contributed $1,000 to join the Republican Senatorial Inner Circle"; see Leland (1991).

7. For discussions indicating the shift occurred in the middle of the 1980s, see Barol (1992) and Gates (1990c). Jay Cocks (1983) talked about rappers sometimes performing for mostly white audiences in 1981, and Donnelly (1992) said Ice-T held performances for "mostly white crowds" as early as 1982.

8. See correspondence from Eichelmann (1990). Ironically, the same issue included several letters from irate rap fans who charged that Leo had treated rap unfairly.

Performing the (Black) Postmodern: Rap as Incitement for Cultural Criticism

Rinaldo Walcott

I came of age as a teenager listening to the pleasurable and profoundly political sounds of Grandmaster Flash's "The Message," Afrika Bambaataa's "Planet Rock," and Sugarhill Gang's "Rapper's Delight." To link those songs together is to evoke a moment that back then I could not even imagine; a moment that would see rap ascend to valued, reviled, and contested commodity form. Bambaataa's "Planet Rock" made use of computer sounds to animate the refrain "rock, rock, the planet rock, don't stop," and Grandmaster Flash rapped of urban decay and increasing drug related conditions of existence, proclaiming, "Don't push me cause I'm close to the edge," while we played Pac Man in video arcades. Little did I know how the themes and samples of those two songs ("The Message" and "Planet Rock") had anticipated and cited elements which would have a profound effect on black peoples, especially those in urban North America. The profound effects of these two prophetic songs were lost on my youthful exuberance and did not immediately signal how the rampant use of drugs and the ever increasing computerization of the workplace would grossly affect those among the most disadvantaged.

Early rap musicians who made use of either the theme of drugs or computer sounds to animate their raps demonstrated that rap is both an example of cultural politics and enunciative of black cultural politics. Rap is cultural criticism and rap musicians are what Jacques Attali (1989) calls *jongleurs*. They are musicians whose musical practices do not sit easily within an understanding of music as non-political. The very practice of their music is politics.

*

The central concern of this essay is to walk a thin line of "diasporic critique" which loosely embraces a "diasporic postmodern aesthetics." In doing so my concern is to both disrupt narratives of nation in favor of a "diasporic sensibility," while simultaneously demonstrating that nation still matters. By reading black Canadian musicians into spaces and gaps of "diasporic criticism," I hope to demonstrate the possibilities and limits of some diasporic and national narratives while pointing to how black expressive cultures create and require both the locality and specificity of nation and the expansive qualities and "common feelings" of diaspora. However, I argue that the moments, contradictions, and disjunctures of a diasporic sensibility are best read through a (black) postmodern positionality.

Consequently, this essay uses rap and hip hop culture as an incitement to and for cultural criticism. By that I mean that my analysis of rap and hip hop culture aims to address larger questions of black subjectivities, and to consider the meanings of blackness as they proliferate in an age of increasing repetition. I bring black postmodernism into contact with discourses of nation in an attempt at a deterritorialized criticism which is not forgetful of nation. In fact, part of my analysis attempts to demonstrate how using a too-easy deterritorialized discourse of diaspora can (re)constitute nation discourse (as in the case of Tricia Rose and Jeffrey Decker) and at the same time how a critique of nation can point to the why of a diasporic discourse and sensibility (as in the case of the music of the Dream Warriors and Devon).

Rap's Coming Out Party?

In the U.S. presidential election of 1992, two interesting events occurred. Prior to election night the then presidential nominee of the Democratic party, Bill Clinton, attacked the rapper Sister Souljah as a hate-monger. Clinton's comfort in attacking Sister Souljah should not be ignored. Following on the heels of the Anita Hill-Clarence Thomas Senate confirmation hearings, America was prepared to see black women dehumanized and scapegoated. As Toni Morrison (1992) wrote in response to the perversity of the hearings: "As in virtually all this nation's great debates, nonwhites and women figure powerfully, although their presence may be disguised, denied, or obliterated" (p. xix). I would like to suggest that Clinton attacked Sister Souljah not just because her message was disturbing, but also because by doing so he could garner some needed attention.[1] In particular, he could acquire some of the attention that accompanies rap music and its "publics" and have some impact on various African American communities and young people. At the time, Souljah represented the importance of rap's political edge and thus Clinton was forced to engage her because her message called a large public into being.[2]

The other event, which took place on the night of the presidential election, was rapper KRS-One as a commentator on youth response at the polls for the Public Broadcasting Station. The invitation of KRS-One attested to the importance of rap to contemporary cultural politics. KRS-One's appearance on an extended version of PBS news should not be read as some token gesture on their part; PBS realized that rap musicians are political in all senses of the word ("politicians"/jongleurs) and represent a "constituency." This is not unlike Clinton's attack of Sister Souljah. Given such events, rap and hip hop culture must be taken seriously not only as intervention, but also as representative of our political and cultural times.

In the last fifteen years rap music and hip hop culture has proliferated beyond the confines of African American communities. The proliferation of rap and hip hop culture is testimony to two important but different conjunctures. First, the mass marketing of rap and hip hop culture as a commodity, both at home in the United States, and abroad, have meant that rap and hip hop culture has garnered much media attention as a desirable, needed and demanded commodity. American capital has played a major role in the creation of desire and the dissemination of hip hop culture, as American capitalists sought and conquered "newer" markets (youth) and "new" products (rap) to market.

The success of marketing black American culture has been commented on before (Willis, 1989; Garofalo, 1995) and therefore rap and hip hop was merely "new territory" to conquer for American capital. However, the story of rap's commodification is not as neatly packaged as my rehearsal here suggests. Rap and hip hop culture has a conflictual and contradictory relationship to the processes of commodification. Rap artists and their "publics"—the hip hop nation—have created fissures and ruptures in the ways in which transnational corporations seek to market rap and hip hop. The hip hop nation, which is a loose amalgam of folks who identify with various elements of hip hop culture, are as unruly as the music they listen to.

[The hip hop nation might be counterposed to formulations like Generation X and Slackers. *Generation X* has become the hegemonic term or marker for those born in the mid-to-late-1960s and tends to cut across socioeconomic and racial markers while producing a bounty of information about the declining economic opportunities for middle-class white boys. *Slackers* tends to be a term used to pathologize working-class white boys who have been disenfranchised in postindustrial America. Hip hop nation then "blackens" the process of naming "youth" communities by grounding the term in relation to black cultural expressions like rap music and specifically black responses to the postindustrial North American scene. Thus hip hop nation might be understood as a subaltern naming practice for identifying a dispersed and fluid community whose experiences are shaped by postindustrial and postmodern situations. Yet, the hip hop nation is not a racially defined group.]

Indeed, rap and hip hop culture responds to its commodification in the boldest of ways. This is particularly so in an era when it appears that the desire and acceleration for accumulating commodities is excessive across class positions, while working class "aristocratic" jobs continue to disappear and to be replaced by the "unlivable" wages of the service industry. Often rappers and hip hoppers gesture to important political questions through a clear understanding of their cultural habits as commodified, recognizing the exploitation of (black) bodies in the process. In fact hip hop fashion in clothing choices might be the best example of the contradictions of our commoditized era. The vast expense on clothes speaks to a distorted sense of class in terms of access to middle-class shopping habits, but hip hoppers also re-work middle-class implications or desires by wearing the clothes in ways that are entirely outside a middle-class aesthetic and practice. In the music a similar practice is evident. De La Soul raps in "I Am I Be":

> I be the new generation of slaves
> here to make tapes to buy record
> exec rates
> the pile of revenue I create
> but I guess I don't get a cut
> 'cause my rent's a month late. . .
> (*RapPages*, Feb., 1994)[3]

De La Soul's response to their commodification and exploitation is doubled. The song will no doubt be a commodity. But as De La tells it, theirs is a greater mission "to bring peace" so that they can "be." The song is an attempt to articulate the difficulty of "being" within the midst of the late logic of capital. [One further example. Similarly, EPMD, which stands for "Eric and Parish Making Dollars," gestures to the importance of black men making a living in the postindustrial United States where industrial working-class jobs, but black working-class jobs specifically, have disappeared. Those jobs have been replaced by working class service industry jobs where it is common to hear employees blame themselves for not being "well educated" enough to acquire high paying jobs in technological industries—a story repeated all across post-NAFTA North America.]

The second reason that rap and hip hop have proliferated is much more nuanced, and it is one of the main foci of this essay. Many of those who have taken up "citizenship" in the hip hop nation feel that some reference to their personal and collective histories, cultures, memories, desires, needs, pleasures and disappointments is expressed and narrated by rap artists, and this is of crucial importance to them. Rap and hip hop culture is constituted from various threads and traces which often draw on the experiences of the everyday and the ordinary, in many cases to offer critiques of social relations, cultural practices, and societal attitudes. Many of the cultural practices of rap and hip hop challenge normative identity by either exaggerating the everyday or by bluntly and clearly challenging various articulations of the "normal."

Rap and Performance Studies

Hip hop culture has a long and varied tradition in diasporic black communities, drawing on and recycling black traditions of performance while simultaneously rendering those traditions as "new inventions." Rap music stands out as one of the most identifiable elements of hip hop culture as first and foremost a form of talking/singing (rapping) or storytelling that makes use of rhyming and rhythm to produce narratives often about personal accomplishments. In the late 1970s and early 1980s these rhymes were consistently backed up by musical samples to broaden their appeal at parties and other black public events. Sampling involved "lifting" recognizable elements from popular songs or lifting elements from songs that the disc jockey felt would incite the audience to participate in dancing or some other response (verbal) or simply in order to accentuate the narrative of the rapper (Toop, 1984; Rose, 1994; Potter, 1995).

The practice of rapping—whether enhanced by technology, like sampler machines, or merely practiced through the use of the voice, the way many black preachers talk—is a shared black diasporic or "black

Atlantic world" cultural form. By cultural form, I mean that the practices of rapping suggest certain qualities that are evident in diasporic
black expressive cultures that have survived the trauma of the middle
passage to become the basis of black cultural memory and performance. Thus black cultural form characterizes a relationship to Africa,
as well as the syncretic inventions of (black) modernity in the Americas, forged in the crucible of the violent encounters between Europe,
Euro-Americans, and aboriginal Americans.

I take the term "black Atlantic world" from Paul Gilroy (1992a,
1993), who writes that the black Atlantic world is an "intercultural
and transnational formation" (1993). For Gilroy (1993), the black Atlantic is

> the stereophonic, bilingual, or bifocal cultural forms originated by, but no
> longer the exclusive property of, blacks dispersed within the structures of
> feeling, producing, communicating, and remembering (p. 3).

The sociohistoric mapping of the black Atlantic allows us to explore
how numerous cultural exchanges among black communities have
contributed in important ways to the conversation that we might call
rap and hip hop culture. Thus, despite the official histories of rap
which ground it in the United States (Rose, 1994; Potter, 1995), other
claims can and must be made for rap's nonsovereign status (Gilroy,
1993; Flores, 1994).

Central to hip hop culture is the idea of performance or rather acts
of performativity. Manthia Diawara (1993) in "Black Studies, Cultural
Studies: Performative Acts" called for a theory of black cultural studies which addresses the performative qualities of black expressive cultures. Diawara wrote:

> Black "performance studies" would mean study of the ways in which black
> people, through communicative action, created and continue to create them-
> selves within the American experience. Such an approach would contain sev-
> eral interrelated notions, among them that "performance" involves an indi-
> vidual or group of people interpreting an existing tradition—reinventing
> themselves—in front of an audience, or public. . . Thus, the notion of "study"
> expands not only to include an appreciation of the importance of performative
> action historically, but also to include a performative aspect itself, a reenact-
> ment of a text or a style or a culturally specific response in a different medium
> (p. 25).

Hip hop culture is particularly characteristic of the performative. Hip
hop participants rewrite "both hegemonic and ambiguously (non)

hegemonic discourse" (Henderson, 1989, p. 138), through an engagement in continuous practices of parody, deferral, bricolage, pastiche, collage, indirection, reversal, and numerous other "postmodern" practices to articulate and invent representations that are excessive and push the limits of normativity.

Rap music and hip hop culture's "postmodern" practices play with the notion of an original and normal, often parodying what is cited. Judith Butler (1990, p. 138) writes that parody can often call into question the very notion of an original. Calling into question notions of origins while hinting that some trace of an "origin" might be present in the "new" invention is crucial to parody and its performative acts. Butler further states that parody is not necessarily subversive but "what makes certain kinds of parodic repetitions effectively disruptive, truly troubling, and which repetitions become domesticated and rearticulated as instruments of cultural hegemony" are important considerations for hip hop's commodification and its parodic identity play. Repetition and parody are key to understanding hip hop's rewriting of "original" signs and artifacts. Thus the performative acts of hip hop are a "dramatic and contingent construction of meaning" (1990 p. 139) that refuses being pinned down for long periods of time.

The performative is key for understanding the moves of hip hop culture and its limits or lack thereof. Hip hop's continual reinvention (even in its largely unimaginative gangsta period) and rewriting of itself is performative in the senses that I am outlining here. The "showing out" of hip hoppers in style and dress is one element of the performative; various articulations around political positions, political disagreements, and political formations are other elements of the performative in hip hop.

Following Diawara's (1993) formulation of performative studies, hip hop is a citational, referential, and resignification act. By that I mean that hip hop draws on the historicity of black experiences and practices, but, as Butler (1993) suggests, the constituent elements of any historicity can never be fully disclosed. Butler alerts us to the fact that performativity is primarily a discourse that only becomes actual when put into practice. "Performativity is not a singular 'act,' for it is always a reiteration of the norm or set of norms, and to the extent that it requires an actlike status in the present, it conceals or dissimulates the conventions of which it is a repetition" (1993, p. 12). The citations, references, and performances of hip hop are the "foundations" and repetitions of what James Snead (1990) in "Repetition as a Figure of Black Culture" identifies as the sites/cites that continually reproduce the circularity of black cultural expressions. Hip hop's circularity places it in line with black postmodern expressions.

Consequently hip hop as a method or way of knowing sets up the possibility to engage black cultural politics as "critical organic catalyst" (West, 1990, p. 33), while simultaneously resisting any form of amputation (Fanon, 1967, p. 140). By this I mean that both Fanon and West open the realms of possibilities to push the limits of what black studies can bear to know, hear, or bear witness to, when as Diawara (1993) writes we move from "oppression studies" (the study of racism and exclusion) to performative studies.[4] This essay explores what performative studies might look and sound like. Clearly one of the primary elements of performance studies is its polyphonic qualities and its ambivalence about certainty. This is so despite Mae Henderson's (1996) recent critique of (black) cultural studies in favor of Black Studies.

The Conditions of Black Postmodernism?

The Canadian rappers Dream Warriors (1990) on their first album announced that they were taking listeners on a "voyage through the multiverse," signalling the importance of multiplicity to their music. The multiverse that they rap on the album is a complex postcolonial articulation of community and identifications constituted through a continuous decentering of territory and identity as they collage numerous elements to make a statement about the postmodern profoundness of rap and hip hop culture. What rappers like the Dream Warriors are able to do in their music is to articulate the creolized and hybridized actuality of life in postindustrial North America in ways that some other forms of representation can not do. But they are also able to trouble and worry national discourse and bring the black Atlantic into being through political identificatory moments.

A proliferation of black identificatory positions has emerged from which to understand black political actions. Politicizing and problematizing notions of "nation" (Lubiano, 1993), "family" (Gilroy, 1992b), and other concepts (like sexuality) which can be used to reproduce black patriarchal positions of ruling has been an important part of (re)conceptualizing what blackness means in the contemporary era. I believe the reconceptualizations are articulated and constituted from a desire for an ethical and just world. Processes of fashioning new possibilities for political identifications are important in that they open up spaces to understand the "messiness" of categories that History offers.

While it is true that many black scholars have been tentative around using the term or describing their work as postmodern (Christian, 1990; Joyce, 1991), the theoretical positions of postmodernity have clearly impacted on persons who argue for recognition of black differences. As bell hooks (1990), in a "cautiously and with suspicion" endorsement of some elements of postmodern theory, wrote:

> Postmodern culture with its decentred subject can be the space where ties are severed or it can provide the occasion for new and varied forms of bonding. To some extent, ruptures, surfaces, contextuality, and a host of other happenings create gaps that make space for oppositional practices which no longer require intellectuals to be confined by narrow separate spheres with no meaningful connection to the world of the everyday. Much postmodern engagement with culture emerges from a yearning to do intellectual work that connects with habits of being, forms of artistic expression, and aesthetics that inform the daily life of writers and scholars as well as a mass population (p. 31).

hooks states this position after systematically and clearly demonstrating that postmodernism had been a theoretically elitist position that codified intellectual speech in ways that often did not lead to the decentering of the authority its proponents desired. The practices of indirection, circularity, collage, and hybridity have long been argued as important subversive strategies by black scholars. It may not be surprising that when those very same practices are advocated in theories of postmodernity, many black scholars remain skeptical of the intention or motives of the theoretical turn. Such has been the response to postmodernity by a number of black scholars. While some critics have written off many of the skeptics of postmodernity as antitheoretical, I do think that the resistance is one that is far greater than "a fear of theory."

I pose black postmodernity as a counter to emergent discourses of black nationalism and Afrocentrism which seek to produce narratives of black sameness as the basis from which large groups of heterogenous black people might act politically. Black postmodernity argues for understanding memory as a site that is contested. Thus while black postmodernity does not dismiss the historicity of remembering, black postmodernity also articulates memory and remembering as a complexly layered practice that opens up other possibilities concerning community. For example, one's relationship to the Sixties might not only be conditioned by the civil rights movement but it might also be conditioned by women's liberation and gay liberation movements. Therefore, an act of memory might well put into place an understanding of community that exceeds the category of any too-easy sameness.

By the conditions of a black postmodernity I mean to signal a number of important post-civil rights/postcolonial conditions. I want to suggest that a specific type or form of black postmodernity exists in an effort to make clear the changed relations of black Atlantic exchanges and dialogues in the age of digital and technological reproduction. Those conditions are: (a) the collapse of notions of a unified black body politic; (b) an excavation of past relations and an insistence on continued closer transglobal black connections and dialogues; (c) the emergence of black feminisms; (d) black queer theory and activism; (e) the varied representational practices of black artists and other cultural producers, with specific attention to the use of technology; (f) the continuation of the emergence of discourses of black difference and heterogeneity; and (g) the emergence of an anticolonial and postindependent "black world" and debates within, across, and outside that world. While this is by no means an exhaustive list of conditions, what I hope to point out by naming those above is a shift in how debates about blackness are currently being waged. These conditions exist at the same time that a virulent strain of cultural nationalism has re-emerged and avidly engages large (black) audiences.

Paul Gilroy (1993) has referred to some of the elements of postmodernity as elements of an unfinished modernism for blacks. By this he is gesturing towards the importance of repetition and allegory in black cultures and the relationship that such practices have had to the survival of a collective memory and more importantly to the survival of bodies—the still lingering issue of liberation. Liberation and the repetition of its promise are of particular importance to black Atlantic cultures and to African cultures generally. For people who have to live their lives in the sphere of oppression and domination, processes of allegory are often developed not only to throw off the smell of danger, but to subvert while maintaining dialogue.

In fact, it is obvious that resistance to domination continues as a part of the conditions of black postmodernity. In a black postcultural nationalism in North America, arguing for aesthetic criticism to toe a specific and particular line or else risk collective condemnation is no longer feasible. Attempts at condemnation are now greeted with spirited debate and contestation of ideas that opens up new and important avenues. For example, the debates around Wynton Marsalis and jazz are but one moment of this scene. Postmodernity in black communities is the continuation of the project of modernity, and while black postmodernity differs profoundly from black modernist projects like the Harlem Renaissance, black postmodernity signals in numerous ways that postmodernity is not a break with modernism.[5] Debates continue concerning emancipation, reason, rationality, the unified black subject, and so on. These debates, while seeking to bring to the fore the various ways in which black peoples conceive of themselves, are often wrapped in Enlightenment project narratives. In fact the continuing debates concerning "nation" and "family" are an example of this (Lubiano, 1993; Gilroy, 1992b).

However, it is the representational that has garnered the most intense debates concerning black (postmodern) practices. The insistence on representational practices that do not speak in terms of monolithic categories has been one of the key moments for locating the contested nature of contemporary black political positions. Hal Foster's (1985) distinction between two types of postmodernism (neoconservative and poststructuralist) is useful to keep in mind:

> Poststructuralist postmodernism, on the other hand, rests on a critique of representation: it questions the truth content of visual representation, whether realist, symbolic or abstract, and explores the regimes of meaning and order these codes support (p. 129).

While Foster focuses on visual representation, his comments are important for two reasons. First, it is a "poststructural postmodernism" (to borrow his term) that I believe to be at play in black postmodernity. Second, he echoes the ways in which realist, symbolic, and abstract practices have been contested and questioned in black political debates.

The writings of bell hooks, Adrian Piper, Coco Fusco, Michele Wallace and Wahneema Lubiano might be said to represent the conditions of a black feminist postmodern positionality. Each, in different ways, articulates a decentering of essentialist positions. Each engages with dominant claims to truth and knowledge while producing new truth claims grounded in oppositional histories and practices that both complement and disrupt dominant and "marginal" discursive formations. Fusco (1990), in "Managing the Other," writes of postmodernism:

> Some of the more germane theoretical inquiries that have occurred in various strains of post-colonial studies have looked at the effects of technologically

facilitated intercultural intercommunication, and have looked at *the vernacular post-modernisms* found in the cultures of the uprooted peoples of the world, whose experiences have been shaped by interactions with foreign cultures. Appropriation and syncretism. *This used to be called creolization, or mestizaje. It also used to be called derivative, while Euro-American borrowing was called ethnographic film, Cubism, neo-primitivism, and bricolage.* As the cultural practices of the third world extend further into the first world, more white, North Americans become aware of *living between cultures*, something that white minorities in Latin America have confronted, managed, poeticized and theorized for centuries (p. 82, emphasis added).

Embedded in Fusco's analysis is the earlier mentioned skepticism of some black academics toward postmodernism. The fact that some of the key markers of postmodernism have been for a long time elements of the cultural practices of the formerly colonized is highlighted. What is of vital importance in Fusco's claim is the awareness that "living between cultures" has been a part of the existence of black "Atlanticers" for five hundred years. W.E.B. Du Bois's (1903) "double consciousness" and "the veil" are but two signifiers of how the trope of "in-between-ness" has been and continues to be integral to black Atlantic consciousness and existence.

Black Canadian Performativity and Black (Cultural) Studies

Significantly, black cultural studies might move beyond merely identifying black forms of appropriation and syncretism to demonstrate how those practices can and do impact on black cultural expressions and black cultural debates. The latter part of this essay attempts a reading of the in-between by turning to Canadian rap artists and reading them as interventions into debates on blackness, rap criticism, and histories. The dialectic of appropriation and syncretism opens up some of the messy areas of black cultural borrowing and its relationship to other kinds of borrowing. Also, appropriation and syncretism are crucial to the practices of black collective remembering and desire. Black collective memory and desire are often engaged in rewriting dominant narratives of knowing as dominant narratives seek to institute amputations—cultural and otherwise.

Rap music and hip hop culture are among the sources through which forms of black postmodernity might be explored. In particular the constitution of hip hop's cultural practices of sample and version, in specifically the music, but in clothing choices as well, demonstrates rap's postmodern concerns with pastiche, collage, and bricolage. More importantly rap's postmodern style lies in its multiplicities of voices and politics. Yet Tricia Rose (1994) in *Black Noise* articulates these voices as one, and a great part of that has to do with her conception of the History of rap, which she too neatly packaged through an urban African American narrative.

Rose reads "Afrodiasporic forms, traditions, and practices" (p. 25) in her analysis of hip hop but does not sustain a diasporic analysis. Rose's failure to continually engage a diasporic analysis in her argument might be the most important weakness of her study. The mononarrative of rap's history that she eventually produces is *all* nation, despite overtures to the contrary. There is literally no development of the role of Caribbean migration to New York and its impact on the pleasure and leisure economies but also on the material, social and employment economies. Therefore how would her analysis help us to make sense of Canadian Maestro Fresh-Wes, who titled his third album *"Naaah Dis Kid Can't Be from Canada?!!"*. Fresh-Wes's hypercommentary is a critique of the official history of rap as American, but he is also speaking to the ways in which official nation-state practices place him and more generally black people outside what is Canadian.

The politics of migration, both actual and imagined, as well as metaphors of migration are missing from Rose's analysis. Yet terms like Afrodiasporic signal a moment of migration. Fresh-Wes forces us to consider how practices of migration both metaphorically and literally interrupt narratives of nation. In particular, the album in question was released from the United States. He did not only call Canada as nation into question but he actually left it. Yet he refused to easily identify with any nation in his narrative but rather to play a game of doubles whereby his commentary could speak to the ambivalence that national narratives represent for many diasporic peoples. But what is significant about the lost discourse of migration in Rose's argument is that rap and hip hop culture is packaged and textually accomplished as an African American cultural form once the conceptual terrain of Afrodiasporic is evacuated. This has important consequences for thinking about histories of rap and hip hop and importantly the reinvigoration of black studies as Baker (1993) argues rap can aim in.

Let us return to Henderson's (1996) recent critique of (black) cultural studies. She has argued that black cultural studies has not paid its due respects to Black Studies and that (black) cultural studies seeks to undermine a discourse and a field—Black Studies—which gave rise to it. While I am in agreement with her genealogy of black cultural studies (grounding it in Du Bois), I differ with her on what is at stake in the move to a more fragmented and, need I say, postmodern, black cultural studies. Black studies tends, despite claims and overtures, to be locked into a nation discourse, and while recognizing the limits and (im)possibilities of nations are always important, Black Studies has often not moved beyond the national narrative. Depending upon the location one reads from, Du Bois is situated as a diasporic figure who, though important to African American and American culture, is deeply implicated in black Atlantic histories (Gilroy, 1993).

This is especially so once we consider the antagonistic relationship between him and Garvey and the ways in which Garvey's diasporic nationalist project was rejected by Du Bois's nation-centered position. As well we must consider the ways in which nativist and immigrant discourses played out in this debate, because these have implications for contemporary debates where blacks in America have become African Americans or black Americans, the latter signifying immigrant status. This "problem" of Black Studies might be what Slavo Zizek calls "the national thing" (p. 165). The national thing reoccurs time and again in rap histories and criticism. So while I understand Henderson's concern for the (re)marginalization of Black Studies in favor of (black) cultural studies, she does not fully address the implications of why such a move might have occurred. Black cultural studies, despite being mired in national discourses in its U.S. Practices, has attempted to bring a diasporic sensibility to the fore.

Jeffrey Louis Decker (1994), in "The State of Rap: Time and Place in Hip Hop Nationalism," argues that two different forms of nationalism exist in rap music. He identifies those forms as (a) a nationalism that harkens back to black nationalism of the 1960s and appropriates the images of Malcolm X, Angela Davis and so on as exemplified by Public Enemy (P.E.); and (b) a nationalism that is Afrocentric and sees Africa as the base through which its politics will ultimately be expressed as exemplified by X Clan. Decker analyzes the lyrics of P.E. and X Clan to demonstrate how the two groups differ in articulated politics. Yet his analysis demonstrates that eventually both groups produced a kind of sexism that places women in very proscribed, restricted, and limited positions. While his exercise is an interesting one, Decker's project does not address the overall problematic of a nationalist politics but instead focuses on "the language of nation to rearticulate a history of racial oppression and struggle which can energize the movement toward black empowerment and independence"

(p. 100). I would contend that the use of nation as a conceptual tool continues to produce a disabling politics of inconsistency, domination, and imperialism and thus leaves Decker's argument in a weak position. Both Decker and Rose are somewhat trapped by the discourse of the "national thing" within which they work.

Decker turns to the music and videos of Queen Latifah to recapture any moment of possibilities in what he terms nationalist rap. Decker wants to hold on to the discourse of nation, but by moving to Latifah he is forced to jettison nation in favor of a diasporic gathering—a fluidity of borders. I would suggest that Latifah's rap, especially "Ladies First," is about the thin line between nations and diaspora. Latifah's music is a diasporic and dialogic black Atlantic expression. Money Love from England raps on the album and the specific song; while Winnie Mandela's image and township uprisings in the video all point to moments that exist beyond the strict confines of nation to address the more interesting and complex relations of transAtlantic identifications, historical relations, practices, memories, and desires.

In fact Timothy Brennan (1997), in an excellent rereading of George Lipsitz's (1994, especially chapter 2) reading of Latifah's "Ladies First," makes the point that

> "[t]he national and ethnic dissonances within the African diaspora are exactly what the rhetoric of globalism obscures, along with (as here) its political stakes. To put it another way, the struggle represented by a career-enhancing artistic performance is just not comparable to the struggle that forced an apartheid regime to the negotiating table. One of the ways imperialism works is to suggest that it is" (p. 8).

Because Decker never questions nation or state, his "state of rap" is to reduce the complexities of "Ladies First" to what can only be interpreted as American imperialism in blackface. Decker's is a deterritorialized criticism which speaks volumes about nation—his nation—in an uncanny way.

The Canadian rapper Devon is rather instructive on questions of time or temporality, diaspora, (sonic) communities, and political identifications. In his song "Mr. Metro," a plea to end police violence in North America, the main narrative is located and positioned in the locale of Toronto, Canada. Yet, Devon makes cross border identifications with African Americans. He raps:

No, no, no, no, LAPD; ease up RCMP; ease up
Orange County; ease up

No OPP; ease up 52; ease up
Peel Region; ease up Don't shoot the youth

His naming of police both in Canada and the United States speaks to a concept of time and nation which sits outside modernist notions. His identifications are postcolonial and postmodern because of the ways in which assumptions of oppression and community are gestured to. Devon's practice is particulary postmodern because the communities that his music calls into being exist only sonically—many African Americans might not know or recognize Peel Region, 52 Division and even the RCMP (Canada's national police force) as policing institutions in Canada. His sense of time and nation is constituted quite differently from what Decker (1994) offers in "The State of Rap." Devon's "state" is locally constituted but yet he can make political identifications across nations, like recording a song to raise funds for voter registration for the first South African elections. His diasporic sensibility does not appear to be an imperialist gesture like Latifah's, who must "rule" the "black world" to really make the point for "ladies first" at "home."

In another way, the Dream Warriors' innovative and now classic first album *And now the legacy begins. . .*, is an important commentary on blackness in Canada and North America generally. In their appropriation of the theme song of the game show *Definition* for their "My Definition," there is the suggestion of what I call a grammar for speaking, writing, and thinking Canadian blackness (Walcott, 1997). The song "My Definition" does not offer a definition of blackness lyrically; rather the definition is offered in the method of the song. In fact, the Dream Warriors seem to suggest that creative appropriation—improvisation, resistance, variation and inventiveness— are what constitute blackness for them. In a sense this is a "blackness without blood" as Gates (1992, p. 51) puts it in an attempt to articulate an anti-essentialist blackness. By that I mean, the Dream Warriors' appropriation of the Definition theme song both disrupts white Canadian normativity and recasts that normativity in "blackface" by recirculating the *Definition* theme song and reinventing its meaning.

The black diasporic expressive form, rap music, is the vehicle for reinvention. The Dream Warriors' practice takes from and remakes the very terms of how we might think and talk about nation. The Dream Warriors announce their presence in the nation, even as they dissent from nation by stopping short of rapping lyrics that would place them firmly within Canadian national borders; instead they take us on a "voyage through the multiverse." Elsewhere on the album, "Ludi" charts routes and roots across nations and regions. The Caribbean and Canada are named as homespaces in "Ludi" by the Dream Warriors. When reading "Ludi" alongside "My Definition," an ironic moment occurs. The fact that the theme song they sample and represent for "My Definition" was composed for the Canadian show by Quincy Jones speaks to a diasporic, postmodern, outer-national black sensibility instructive for black studies, Canadian studies, and studies of national discourses.

To conclude, I have tried to suggest in this paper that the relationship between nation and diaspora is a dialetic. Given the dialetical nature of the relationship, cultural readings and criticism should be aware of the ways in which discourses of nation and diaspora impact on configurations like black studies and Canadian studies, but that the talismanlike use of diaspora does not preclude a descent into national discourse. In effect I have tried to suggest and argued that diaspora discourses might only be useful insofar as the disciplinary and regulatory apparatus of nations remain intact for its subaltern "citizens." At the same time that I have tried to make use of a diasporic sensibility, I have tried to call into question masquerades of diasporic discourses which are covering nation-centered criticism.

If diaspora claims are useful for anything, they are useful for creating doubt in our analyses of the transmigrations of blackness. Attentiveness to how our locations within specific nations shapes our diasporic analyses might be the first order for the use of diaspora as a conceptual tool.

Bibliography

Allinson, E. (1994). "It's a black thing: Hearing How Whites Can't." *Cultural Studies*, *8*(3), pp. 438–456.

Attali, J. (1989). *Noise: The* political economy of music. (B. Massumi, Trans.). Chicago: University of Chicago Press.

Baker, H. (1993). *Black studies, rap and the academy*. Chicago: University of Chicago Press.

Brennan, T. (1997). *At home in the world: Cosmopolitanism now*. Cambridge: Harvard University Press.

Butler, J. (1990). *Gender trouble: Feminism and the subversion of identity*. New York: Routledge.

Butler, J. (1993). *Bodies that matter: On the discursive limits of "sex."* New York: Routledge.

Chandler, N.D. (1996). The economy of desedimentation: W.E.B DuBois and the discourses of the negro, *Callaloo*, 19(1), pp. 78–93.

Christian, B. (1990). The race for theory. A.R. JanMohamed and D. Lloyd (Eds.). *The nature and context of minority discourse*. New York: Oxford University Press.

Decker, J.L. (1994). The state of rap: Time and place in hip hop nationalism. In A. Ross & T. Rose (Eds.). *Microphone fiends: Youth and youth culture*. (pp. 99–121). New York: Routledge.

Diawara, M. (1993). Black studies, cultural studies: Performative acts. In C. McCarthy & W. Crichlow (Eds.), *Race, identity and representation in education* (pp. 262–267). New York: Routledge.

Dream Warriors. (1990). *And now the legacy begins* [CD]. Canada: Island Records.

DuBois, W.E.B. (1903/1969). *The souls of black folk*. New York: Signet Classic.

Fanon, F. (1952, tr. 1967). *Black skin, white masks*. New York: Grove.

Flores, J. (1994). Puerto Rican and proud, boyee!: Rap Roots and amnesia. In A. Ross & T. Rose (eds.), *Microphone Fiends: Youth Music and Youth Culture* (pp. 89–98). New York: Routledge.

Foster, H. (1985). *Recordings: Art, spectacle, cultural politics*. Seattle: Bay Press.

Fusco, C. (1990). Managing the other. *Lusitania*, *1*(3), pp. 77–83.

Garofalo, R. (1995). Culture versus commerce: The marketing of black popular music. *Public Culture*, *7*(1), pp. 275–287.

Gates, H.L. Jr. (1992). *Loose canons: Notes on the culture wars.* Oxford University Press.

Gilroy, P (1992a). It's a Family Affair. In G. Dent (Ed.). *Black Popular Culture* (pp. 303–316). Seattle: Bay Press.

Gilroy, P. (1992b). Cultural studies and ethnic absolutism. L. Grossberg, C. Nelson, & P. Treichler (Eds.). *Cultural studies* (pp. 187–198) New York: Routledge.

Gilroy, P. (1993). *The Black Atlantic: Modernity and double consciousness.* Cambridge: Harvard University Press.

Henderson, G.M. (1989). Speaking in tongues: Dialogics, dialectics and the black women writers literary tradition. C. Wall (Ed.). *Changing our own words: Essays on criticism, theory and writing by black women* (pp. 16–37). New Brunswick: Rutgers University Press.

Henderson, G.M. (1996). Where, by the way, is this train going?: A case for black cultural Studies. *Callaloo,* 19(1), pp. 60–67.

hooks, b. (1990). Black postmodernism. In hooks, b., *Yearning: Race, gender, and cultural politics* (pp. 23–31). Toronto: Between the Lines.

Joyce, J.A. (1991). Black woman scholar, critic and teacher: The inextricable relationship among race, sex, and class. In J. Hartman & E. Messer-Davidow (Eds.). *(En)Gendering knowledge: Feminists in academe* (pp. 159–178). Knoxville: University of Tennessee Press.

Knight, R. (1992). Anti-hero. *Spin Magazine,* October, pp. 96–99.

Light, A. (1992). About a salary or reality?—Rap's recurrent conflict. A. Decurtis (Ed.). *Present tense: Rock and roll and culture* (pp. 219–234). Durham: Duke University Press.

Lipsitz, G. (1994). *Dangerous crossroads: Popular music, postmodernism and the poetics of place.* London: Verso.

Lubiano, W. (1993). Standing in for the state: Black nationalism and "writing" the black self. *Alfabet City,* 3, pp. 20–23.

Lubiano, W. (1996). "Mapping the interstices between Afro-American cultural discourse and cultural studies: A prolegomenon." *Callaloo,* 19(1), pp. 68–77.

Lyotard, J. (1984). *The postmodern condition: A report on knowledge.* (G. Bennington & B. Massumi, Trans.). Minneapolis: University of Minnesota Press.

Lyotard, J. (1992). *The postmodern explained.* (D. Barry, B. Maher, J. Pefanis, V. Spate & M. Thomas Trans.). Minneapolis: University of Minnesota Press.

Morrison, T. (1992). "Introduction: Friday on the Potomac." In T. Morrison (Ed.). *Race-ing justice, en-gendering power: Essays on Anita Hill, Clarence Thomas, and the construction of social reality* (pp. vii–xxx). New York: Pantheon Books.

Potter, R.A. (1995). *Spectacular vernaculars: Hip hop and the politics of postmodernism.* Albany: SUNY.

Rose, T. (1994). *Black noise: Rap music and black culture in contemporary America.* Hanover: The University Press of New England.

Snead, J. (1990). Repetition as a figure of Black Culture. In R. Ferguson, M. Gever, T. Minh-ha and C. West. *Out There: Marginalization and contemporary cultures* (pp. 213–230). New York: The New Museum of Contemporary Art and MIT Press.

Toop, D. (1984). *The rap attack: African jive to new york hip hop.* London: Pluto Press.

Walcott, R. (1997). *Black like who?: Writing, black, Canada.* Toronto: Insomniac Press.

West, C. (1990). The new cultural politics of difference. In R. Ferguson, M. Gever, T. Minh-ha & C. West. (Eds.) *Out there: Marginalization and contemporary cultures* (pp. 19–36). New York: The New Museum of Contemporary Art and MIT Press.

White, S.K. (1991). *Political theory and postmodernism.* Cambridge: Cambridge University Press.

Willis, S. (1989). I shop therefore I am: Is there a place for Afro-American culture in commodity culture. In C. Wall (Ed.). *Changing our own words: Essays on criticism, theory and writing by black women* (pp. 173–195). New Brunswick: Rutgers University Press.

Zizek, S. (1991). *Looking awry: An introduction to Jacques Lacan through popular culture.* Cambridge: The MIT Press.

Notes

1. See Robert Knight (1992) "Antihero." Clinton attacked what he read as an anti-white people message on Sister Souljah's debut album, *360 Degrees of Power*.

2. It is important to point out that Sister Souljah prefers to think of herself as a political activist who uses music to get her point across to her constituency. In terms of constituencies, Clinton's appearance on MTV (music television) was also an attempt to broaden his appeal to a younger voting public.

3. For a discussion of the tensions between rap and reality, Alan Light, "It's About a Salary or Reality?—Rap's Recurrent Conflict"; or for a different and racialized take on the inability to read any moment of fantasy into rap see E. Allinson, "It's A Black Thing: Hearing How Whites Can't."

4. This question is particularly important in light of the recent essays by Mae Henderson, Wahneema Lubiano and Nahum Chandler, all in *Callaloo*. Henderson's essay most explicitly takes on (black) cultural studies. The other essays are more nuanced in their critique but are clearly also making a case for thinking otherwise about (black) cultural studies. What is also not apparent is whether or not (black) cultural studies is being used as a metaphor in the place of a particular "European" variant of literary studies masquerading as cultural studies which has been celebrated in the American academy.

5. See Gilroy (1993); many postmodernists, especially those in architecture, conceive of postmodernity as a complete break with the traditions of modernist practices. However I take a literal meaning to "post" which signals for me a change, but a continued relationship to what came before. See Jean-Francois Lyotard (1984) *The Postmodern Condition: A Report on Knowledge*; Lyotard (1992) *The Postmodern Explained*; Stephen K. White (1991) *Political Theory and Postmodernism*.

Talkin' Tupac: Speech Genres and the Mediation of Cultural Knowledge

George Kamberelis and Greg Dimitriadis

Much recent work within cultural studies, communication studies, cultural psychology, and anthropology has retheorized liberal-humanist notions of knowledge and identity, demonstrating that both are more provisional, politically contested, historically unfinished, and inventive than previously imagined (e.g., Bhabha, 1994; Clifford, 1988; Grossberg, 1992; Hall, 1996; Markus & Kitayama, 1991; McCarthy, 1998). These theorists have argued, quite convincingly, that knowledges and identities are constructed/produced in specific historical-social-cultural sites through the appropriation of specific discourses and practices salient within those sites (Bourdieu, 1990). Central to these appropriation processes is their mediation by speech genres, which are conventionalized and codified patterns of discourse. From this perspective, an articulation of theories of discourse with theories of speech genres provides a productive theoretical framework for empirical investigations of how young people construct social and cultural knowledges and identities on complex, uneven, and shifting discursive landscapes (Dimitriadis & Kamberelis, 1997). More specifically, examining how young people appropriate and transform specific speech genres as they think and talk about the culture(s) they inhabit provides important understandings about how these genres enable and constrain their efforts to reproduce and resist the power arrangements that constitute their lives and to construct social knowledges and identities within these arrangements.

In this chapter, we focus on one group of youth—urban African American middle school children—and we examine some of the discursive tactics they used to construct their cultural knowledges and identities on fast-moving and sometimes violent social and cultural terrains. More specifically, we map how these adolescents deployed an adaptation of the "television talk show" genre to discuss the life and death of rap star Tupac Shakur. Importantly, we began our study of these young people focused on their investments in rap music and rap artists, hoping to understand the complexities and nuances of their musical tastes and dispositions, as well as how these tastes and dispositions contributed to their identity construction processes. Our interest in speech genres (and the television talk show genre more specifically) emerged during the course of the study because it was such a salient dimension of our participants' everyday talk and patterns of social interaction. As the study progressed, rap music and rap culture became less a primary research focus and more an arena for the study of local discursive tactics and their effects on children's processes of knowledge and identity construction.

The primary argument promoted in this chapter is that appropriating the television talk show genre to frame their understanding and communication about Tupac's life and death resulted in certain epistemological and practical possibilities and constraints. Specifically, this speech genre seemed to afford discussions of complex and subtle personal and interpersonal issues more readily than it did discussions of analogous economic, social, and political issues. Indeed, the primary focus of talk among our research participants centered on a series of conflicts that occurred between Tupac and fellow rapper, Biggie Smalls. This intense and almost exclusive focus helped constitute the field of "possible selves" and "possible worlds" (Bruner, 1986) that were visible to these young people within this situated activity. Before saying more about the empirical dimensions of our work, we will elaborate on our theoretical understandings of identities, discourses, and genres.

Theoretical Framework: Identities, Discourses, and Genres

Identities

Theorists of race, class, and gender have argued recently that these social categories are less "essential" than they are "positional" (Alcoff, 1988; Appadurai, 1996; Bhabha, 1994; Grossberg, 1992; Rosaldo, 1989). Raced, classed, or gendered identities involve positioning oneself at the intersection of various identity axes within a changing historical context of identity markers. From this perspective, being black or Latina or working class or female (or various combinations of these and other social categories) is to take up a position within a moving historical context, to choose how to interpret this position, and to imagine how to alter the context that made such positioning available in the first place. This way of thinking about identity seems to avoid reducing agency to the intentions of a homunculus while also escaping antihumanist assaults on the very notion of agency by reconceptualizing identity as the activity of positioning oneself within (and against) existing social and cultural networks and ideologies. Instead, identities are recognized as multiple, complex, porous, and shifting sets of positionings, attachments, and identifications through which individuals and collectives understand who they are and how they are expected to act across a range of diverse social and cultural landscapes (Hall, 1996).

According to Foucault's notion of power/knowledge, people invariably construct racial, class, and gender identities in ways that partially reproduce the power matrices of specific historical-social-cultural hegemonies. As Gramsci (1971), Fairclough (1992), Foucault (1990), and others have shown, people also resist such power matrices through the discursive construction of their positions within those matrices. In short, identities (and the meanings assigned to them) are actively constructed through specific social practices and not merely discovered or passively assumed. These local identities constitute compromises or articulations between resistance and accommodation to larger social formations and their concomitant practices and ideologies. Identities, then, are always tentative and partially unstable because they are continually constructed within particular configurations of discursive and material practices that are themselves constantly constituting and reconstituting themselves.

Discourses and the Power/Knowledge Nexus
Foucault (1972, 1979, 1990) was fundamentally interested in the power of discourse to produce social formations, as well as how discourses define, construct, and position individuals within those formations. According to Foucault, discourses "systematically form the objects of which they speak" (1972, p. 49). Such forms of social production occur by constructing "truths" about both the natural and social worlds, which eventually become received or taken-for-granted definitions and categories. Drawing largely upon the work of Foucault, Fiske (1996) noted that discourses provide a "social formation . . . with ways of thinking and talking about areas of social experience that are central in its life" (p. 7). Different discourses provide different interpretive lenses for constituting reality, lenses which are selectively brought to

bear upon particularly salient social experiences. Some discourses dominate others at particular historical moments, and some are more powerful and more durable than others. Culture itself, according to Fiske, can be conceived as a "river of discourses" (p. 7). Such discourses "are deep, powerful currents carrying meanings of race, of gender and sexuality, of class and age" (p. 7), and individuals often embrace them in uncritical ways. Yet Fiske himself pointed out that there are limits to the "river" metaphor.

> The naturalness of a river can imply an inevitability in flow and counterflows, can reduce media events to tourist spectacles that people watch from a safe distance . . . and can reduce or even eliminate political intervention, social agency, and discursive struggle (pp. 7–8).

We want to suggest that some of these problems with reduction can be avoided by focusing on moment-to-moment discursive practices as mediated by speech genres. Speech genres, as we note below, mediate between the macrolevel discourses and microlevel practices that constitute the engines of both social reproduction and social change.

Speech Genres

Bakhtin (1986) defined speech genres as discursive forms that organize utterances into coherent ensembles of structures and practices. A speech genre

> is not a form of language, but a typical form of utterance; as such the genre also includes a typical kind of expression that adheres in it. . . . [Speech] genres correspond to typical situations of speech communication, typical themes, and consequently, also to particular contacts between the *meanings* of words and actual concrete reality under certain typical circumstances (p. 87).

Bakhtin went on to argue that all utterances are constructed not from individual words but from speech genres:

> We speak only in definite speech genres, that is, all our utterances have definite and relatively stable typical *forms of construction of the whole.* Our repertoire of oral (and written) speech genres is rich. We use them confidently and skillfully *in practice,* and it is quite possible for us not even to suspect their existence *in theory* (p. 78).

Although Bakhtin posited speech genres as the fundamental templates and building blocks of discourse, he was careful not to represent them as static or ossified structures, but ones that are continually reconstituted within new contexts and in the hands of new users. "A genre lives in the present," he noted, "but always remembers its past" (1984, p. 104).

As such, genres are historically and ideologically saturated "aggregate[s] of the means for seeing and conceptualizing reality" (Bakhtin & Medvedev, 1985, p. 137). Genres are indexical, signaling the ideologies, norms, values, and social ontologies of the communities of practice in which they typically function. Indeed, it was central to Bakhtin's theory of genres that the thematic and stylistic construction of texts embody ideological values rooted in socio-cultural-historical contexts (Bakhtin & Medvedev, 1985, p. 21). No elements of texts are pure form; texts are also populated with ideological intentions or value orientations. In the appropriation of genres, then, people also appropriate these ideologies as obvious and familiar, as horizons against which their actions and the actions of others make sense.

Bakhtin's discussion of how speech genres mediate identity practices and the social discourses within which they are embedded provides a particularly powerful framework for describing the particular discursive practices through which the urban African American youth with whom we have been working construct their social knowledges and identities. Such a theoretical framework helps demonstrate precisely how these young people take up certain subject positions through the enactment of certain speech genres. Central here is an examination of what typified forms of discourse (i.e., speech genres) young people deploy when discussing events that are salient to their lives and constitutive of their identities. This articulation of speech and event provides insights into what kinds of knowledges are enabled (and constrained) by what kinds of discursive practices and frames, as well as what kinds of frames are preferred for understanding what kind of experiences. The durability or resiliency of certain kinds of knowledge will thus be located (at least in part) in the durability of speech genres and/or the durable ways in which they are taken up.

Conversationalization and Popular Media Discourses

It is necessary to situate any cultural analysis both historically and culturally, and our analysis depends upon understanding one of the strongest trends in contemporary American culture (and various other cultures as well), the trend toward "conversationalized" discourse. According to Fairclough (1992, 1995) public discourse has tended to take on an increasingly conversational character. Affected by this tendency are not only printed media and advertising but also official documents such as employment applications and insurance forms, radio and television programs, formal government reports and academic texts. Among the more salient discursive features that characterize discourse as conversational are utterances replete with affective verbs (e.g., feel, love, want); the use of the present tense to relate past events (e.g., and he tells me, "I'll be back"); an abundance of reported speech, colloquial lexicons and idioms; a proportionally large number of personal (and often inclusive) pronouns; many oral discourse markers (e.g., oh well, yeah, like, really); dense intertextual links to the public media and other forms of popular culture such as song lyrics or advertising slogans; and thematic content that might be considered private such as sexual affairs and financial dealings.

A cursory historical analysis of media communication in almost any domain of public interchange would show that the boundary between "news" and "entertainment" has become increasingly fuzzy during the past several decades (and perhaps even longer). This trend, for example, is evidenced in tabloids such as *The National Enquirer*, in television news magazines such as *A Current Affair*, in reportage of special events such as the Olympics, and even in the "official" news programs of network television. In relation to this historical trend, Fairclough (1992) provides microlevel analyses of more personal/informal forms of discourse within the public sphere across a number of different texts, including university advertisements, television shows, and newspaper headlines. For example, he shows how newspapers routinely represent the voices of powerful individuals or social forces in informal or colloquial ways, using a headline from the *Daily Mirror* to support his claim: "Di's Butler Bows Out . . . in Sneakers!" He points out that "the voice of the royal butler . . . is a popular speech voice, both in the direct discourse representation . . . and in the attributed use of 'sneakers'" (pp. 111–112). Princess Diana, in turn, becomes "Di," and she is described as "'nice,' 'ordinary,' 'down to earth,' and 'natural'" (p. 112). In the very commercial context of this newspaper, information about the royal family revolves around personal and personalized issues and concerns. This personalization is instantiated in the texts themselves, which are markedly colloquial.

Fairclough notes that the use of more informal language in public texts is indicative of two tendencies: "the tendency of public affairs media to become increasingly conversationalized" and "its tendency to move increasingly in the direction of entertainment—to become more 'marketized'" (Fairclough, 1995, p. 10). As market forces overtake media such as records, radio, and television, they become more personal or conversational. Quite often, efforts to render news and information more informal and approachable are deemed democratic. More people have access to news and other public information because media events are "brought to the level" of the average citizen. However, such "marketization undermines the media as a public sphere" as well (p. 13). As a particular manifestation of liberal-pluralist ideologies, conversationalized public discourse renders the meanings of social and political events and issues in terms of individual agency and everyday social practice. "There is a diversion of attention and energy from political and social issues which helps to insulate existing relations of power and domination from serious challenge" (p. 13). Conversationalized discourses routinely collapse personal and political issues, quite often reducing conflict to individual differences, which can ultimately be resolved by individuals through dialogue. Additionally, conversationalized public discourse blurs the line between information and entertainment and between public and private. Among other things, this blurring functions to render commodified possible selves and worlds durably real. It also encourages bringing issues traditionally considered to be private into the public sphere for discussion and evaluation. This point will be amplified below in our discussion of the television talk show genre.

Conversationalized discourses are realized and sustained in and through a number of different speech and activity genres. Two of these are particularly relevant for our purposes here. First is the emergence of the popular/psychologized public icon in rap, an idiom that had earlier been the locus of more collective, party- or event-oriented activities (Dimitriadis, 1996). Tupac Shakur was such an icon, and the struggle between his "positive" pro-black side and his "negative" "gangsta" side was as important to his very public career as his music. Second is the emergence of popular television talk shows in the mid 1980s. Shows such as *Phil Donahue*, *Oprah Winfrey*, *Ricki Lake*, *Jenny Jones*, and *Geraldo* encourage their guests to voice—and increasingly often, to fight over—interpersonal concerns and issues with the goal of resolving them through talk.

Rap and the Psychologized Hero
Recent trajectories in rap music seem linked constitutively to the emergence of conversationalized discourses. Indeed, hip hop began as a largely party-oriented music, almost entirely dependent upon face-to-

face action and interaction. The musical event itself was more important than any particular verbal or vocal text that might occur in it and later be lifted out for reproduction and marketing. Loose collectives such as The Sugarhill Gang and The Furious Five traded verses in live interactive settings, all with the primary goal of getting live crowds involved in an unfolding event. As rap grew in popularity, however, the individual icon and the self-contained vocal text became increasingly important. The first such figure or character type was "the gangsta." Gangsta rappers, including Dr. Dre, Ice Cube, and Ice-T, told first-person (often three-part) narratives which relayed their criminal exploits in explicit and thrilling detail. These gangstas became the most visible and important part of hip hop culture during the late 1980s as rap became wildly successful in recorded commodity form.

In large measure, the gangsta was a larger-than-life character or figure whose exploits existed at the surface of exaggerated violence and brutality. During the early to mid 1990s, however, more personal and more complex portraits of these figures began to emerge. Most importantly, rappers like The Geto Boys, Biggie Smalls, and Tupac Shakur "psychologized" the gangsta type, adorning their stories with disturbing personal and psychological insights. The goal was no longer only to present a violent snapshot of gangsta life, but to help us understand what was happening "inside" the figure of the hero. Biggie Smalls (or Notorious B.I.G.), for example, framed his debut album *Ready to Die* as an aural/musical biography, beginning with his birth and ending with his suicide. Smalls thus used his biography to contextualize his music, blurring the line between the personal and the public, between information and entertainment. This album was not only intended to get dance crowds dancing (as in early hip hop), or to relate violent exploits (as in gangsta rap), but also to give us a peek into Biggie Smalls' psyche—his motivations, desires, and feelings as explicated in deeply psychological narratives.

Tupac Shakur is another prime example of the psychologized rap hero. His biography is a crucial part of his public image, and the details of his life, which are talked about on record and off, have become almost legendary. In a key example, the song "Dear Mama" chronicles his early life in explicit detail, including his lack of a father, his reliance on his mother, her use of crack cocaine, and his turn toward crime. Again, Tupac goes beyond a two-dimensional sketch of his life to present a complex, deeply structured, and highly textured portrait of it. In weaving together the narrative of his mother and her struggles, he simultaneously constructs an "account" that functions to justify or explain the choices he made (Buttny, 1993).

Tupac's self-revelations often position him at the nexus of complex and seemingly conflicting social forces. In fact, "Dear Mama's" personal narrative is made all the more poignant by the widely known fact that Shakur's mother, Afeni Shakur, was a famous Black Panther—one of the Panther 21 who were arrested for allegedly attempting to orchestrate a series of bombings in New York City. According to popular accounts, Tupac inherited much of her militant black-power world view. These accounts emphasize, for example, the fact that Tupac has a black panther tattooed on his arm and the fact that a number of his songs depict or celebrate the struggles of black people (e.g., "White Man'z World" and "Keep Ya Head Up"). To a large extent, Tupac is heralded as a contemporary bearer of 1960s-inspired black nationalist attitudes and sentiments.

Yet Tupac is as much gangsta as revolutionary. He was involved in a number of shootings (including one with two off-duty police officers); he was sentenced for up to four-and-one-half years in prison for sexual abuse; he was almost fatally injured in an assassination attempt and robbery; and he ultimately was murdered in a drive-by shooting. Much of his music reflects this gangsta lifestyle, as evidenced, most especially, on *All Eyez On Me*, which was recorded on the Death Row Records label (see, for example, "Ambitionz az a Ridah," "2 of Amerikaz Most Wanted," and "Can't C Me"). Many interviews and news stories on Tupac have stressed his complex and divided soul, pointing out how his internal struggles between "good" (fighting for black rights) and "evil" (his uncritical gangsta posturing) were central to his music, which, again, ran the gamut from the more "positive" to the wildly "negative." *Rap Pages,* for example, subtitled their December, 1996 tribute to Tupac "Exploring the Many Sides of Tupac Shakur" and included a feature article entitled "Loving Tupac: The Life and Death of a Complicated Man."

Many rappers, such as Biggie Smalls and Tupac, have become near-mythic public figures whose personal struggles were and are an integral part of their music. This fact was set into high relief in the feud that erupted between Tupac (and his record label, Death Row Records) and Biggie Smalls (and his label, Bad Boy Records). The history of this feud is complex. According to Tupac, he and Biggie had been friends early on in their careers. In 1994, however, Tupac was ambushed and shot while heading to a recording studio to meet Smalls.

He was shot five times but survived. Although the shooting was never solved, Tupac publicly accused Biggie Smalls of setting him up. A number of seemingly related and popularly disseminated incidents followed. A friend of Suge Knight (head of Death Row Records) was killed at a party, and Knight blamed Puff Daddy (head of Bad Boy Records) for the murder. An entourage of Death Row Records' members then threatened Biggie Smalls at an industry award party, brandishing guns. Finally, Suge Knight, reputedly associated with the L.A.-based gang, the Bloods, was rumored to have threatened Puff Daddy's life.

These real-life events overlap and blur into events chronicled on a number of recorded singles released by these two artists. Biggie Smalls, for example, released the caustic "Who Shot Ya?" in 1995 as a b-side to the hit "Big Poppa." This single plays off the phrase "Who Shot Ya?" presumably alluding to Tupac's earlier and apparently unsolved shooting. Thus, Tupac is the private audience targeted by this ostensibly public message. Lines such as "Cash rules everything around me/ Two Gloc 9s for any mother fucker whispering about mines" abound in this track, along with various threats and boasts by Biggie and Puff (e.g., "Didn't I tell you not to fuck with me! . . . Can't talk with a gun in your mouth?").

Tupac, in turn, released his scalding "Hit 'Em Up" in 1996 in which he viciously attacked both Smalls and Junior Mafia (Smalls' group; his protégés). This track explores in explicit detail the personal falling out between Tupac and Biggie. Tupac begins the track by saying "That's why I fucked your bitch, you fat mother fucker," an allusion to the rumor that he slept with Biggie's wife, R&B singer Faith Evans. Faith has denied the claim but, as we will note later, it has gained factual status within the popular imagination. Tupac goes on, during the course of this track, to threaten Tupac, Junior Mafia, and all of Bad Boy Records with attacks grounded in their personal histories. At one point, Tupac raps about their early friendship, "Biggie, remember when I used to let you sleep on the couch?" Yet, as he raps, "now it's all about Versace? You copy my style/ Five shots couldn't drop me/ I took it and smiled." According to Tupac, Smalls returned his friendship by trying to imitate Tupac's musical style (which revolved around the expensive tastes of the "playa" lifestyle, as evinced in the reference to Versace), and eventually orchestrating his attempted assassination.

This particular conflict demonstrates how the line between what artists portray through their lyrics and what happened in real life gets blurred. This blurring is in no small measure related to the tendency within the rap music industry in the early nineties to foreground the inner lives, experiences, and conflicts of its artists—artists who are portrayed as mythic figures with complexly explicated biographies. Equally important for our argument, this particular moment in hip hop's history seems constitutively linked to more global cultural imperatives marked by a tremendous increase in conversational or personalized discourses in the public sphere.

Television Talk Shows

A primary function of contemporary broadcast media is to render information or news more informal and entertaining. Rap, with its alternative stress on reality ("we're like reporters") and entertainment ("we're like actors"), is entirely linked to this move. Fairclough argues that television talk shows are particularly salient, even exaggerated, generic forms of these conversationalized discourses. For example, he notes that Oprah Winfrey—who addresses a wide range of topics on her wildly successful hour-long talk show—is an "accomplished performer" who is "witty, humorous," and has a "winning smile." Her warm and open demeanor serves to construct her as "an ordinary person sharing the lifeworld of people in the studio and home audiences" (Fairclough, 1995, p. 142). Yet, Fairclough also emphasizes that Oprah Winfrey provides more than entertainment alone for her audience. Oprah "is also at times a moralist and educator, directly addressing viewers on the themes of the programme" (p. 142). Like many talk show hosts, she is both teacherly and friendly, peddling information in an entertaining and informal manner. Indeed, commercially successful venues such as *Oprah Winfrey* effectively link seemingly personal interactions between and among participants with educational and moralistic discourses, helping to present news or information in an easily digestible form. Perhaps more cynically, the television talk show is a kind of "suburban" genre that functions to domesticate a turbulent social world in its fascination with multiple and contradictory forms of titilation (McCarthy, 1998). As a polysemic discursive practice that blurs public and private, news and entertainment, and underclass, working-class, and middle-class sensibilities, the television talk show is an exaggerated and almost caricatured embodiment—and thus a particularly potent exemplar—of the general trend toward conversationalized public discourse.

Drawing on the work of Fairclough, Janice Peck has called attention to the fact that the therapeutic imperatives so important for talk shows foreground conversation and "communication" as primary ways to resolve disputes that might otherwise be located outside the individual and within larger social structures or cultural frames:

> The programs' personalization strategies, parasociâlity, and therapeutic framework organize social conflict within narratives of individual and interpersonal dysfunction. Within those confines, all problems seem to be amenable to therapeutic intervention—to treatment via the "talking cure". . . . Therapeutic discourse translates the political into the psychological—problems are personal (or familial) and have no origin or target outside of one's own psychic process (Peck, 1995, pp. 75–76).

Ricki Lake is one of the most popular talk show figures to enact such a translation. As Lake herself notes, "Being in therapy and talking about my own problems and being able to communicate honestly has affected my work" (quoted in Star Talker, 1994, p. 57). Although violent conflicts between participants—"high-decibel confrontations that draw hoots and cheers from the studio audience" (Zoglin, 1995, p. 77)—are often characteristic of these shows, the ability to talk through problems is valorized as one of their most important messages. The discourse that occurs on *Ricki Lake* and similar shows locates what could be constructed as social or political issues or problems in and within individual psychological processes. These talk shows personalize issues and make all news entertainment as well. Although this effort to make news accessible as entertainment is, in many ways, democratic, Fairclough notes that it also functions to naturalize dominant ideologies by constructing a cultural imaginary about social relations that renders them less asymmetrical and more benign than they really are. Talk shows and similar media venues promote the idea that because we are all the same underneath, we can talk across and outside of our social positionings.

In relation to this point, Bakhtin's notion of dialogism is particularly useful for understanding precisely how self and other are constituted through the appropriation and redeployment of popular cultural resources. By dialogic, Bakhtin meant not only that people use language to engage in dialogue but, more importantly, that any stretch of discourse (e.g., phrase, utterance, text) tastes of the past texts and discourses from which it was constructed. Ongoing social discourse is always constructed from multiple intersecting languages and systems of meaning drawn from various local, social, and cultural environments. From a dialogic perspective, certain social and historical conditions partially determine what meanings can and cannot be assigned to utterances within particular discursive contexts. Yet, individuals exercise historical forms of agency in the ways that they appropriate, use, and transform extant forms of discourse. Moreover, some historical conditions (and their concomitant discourses) index the real and ward off critique more powerfully and pervasively than others. Thus, the precise articulations between the durability and transformability of social discourses and the concrete possibilities for individual agency are always empirical problems.

Thinking about the speech of an individual as dialogic rather than as originating from the speaker is critical for explaining how people represent themselves in what Clifford (1988) referred to as a "diversity of idioms." It affords insight into how the power of social formations both enables and constrains the various self-constructions they attempt by enacting various speech genres. Key questions in this regard include the kinds of genres people have access to, which ones they prefer, and which ones they deploy comfortably and competently. These are the questions that guided our investigation of how one group of urban African American youth worked to construct their identities, social relations, and visions of the world around them as they "talked through" their understanding of the life and death of perhaps their most important cultural hero, Tupac Shakur.

Youth Heralding the Psychologized Rap Icon
In and Through the Television Talk Show Genre

The empirical work that we report here was conducted as part of a larger program of community service and research at a local youth-based community center. The participants were 10- to 12-year-old African American children. Although most were boys, several girls also participated. Some children participated on a routine basis; others participated only occasionally. Although most children attended the center daily, our formal meetings with them were conducted once a week. During these meetings, we talked about, wrote about, listened to, and watched videos related to various forms of black vernacular culture, including gospel, blues, jazz, soul, and rap. Participants in the program committed to various short-term projects such as publishing a newsletter. These projects grew out of participants' interests and included listening to, reading articles about, watching music videos and documentaries about, and writing about figures such as Mahalia

Jackson, B.B. King, Snoop Doggy Dogg, and Tupac Shakur. When not working on specific projects, these young people engaged in more open-ended discussions focusing on artifacts suggested by members of the group. Most of these discussions were tape recorded. Segments of these tapes were transcribed and used as prompts for future group discussions and as material for generating written products. These written products allowed the children to extend and deepen their discussions, to put momentary closure on their work together, and to create tangible products for public consumption.

The particular project that we focus on in this chapter came out of a series of open-ended, child-initiated, and child-led discussions about Tupac Shakur. Since Tupac had died less than a week before we began this project, he had been a constant focus of discussion. Indeed, we discussed his life during the first six project sessions. During the seventh session, we suggested working on a written project together, perhaps a tribute to Shakur. We elicited or suggested a number of different kinds of texts that the members of the group might write including biographies, music reviews, movie reviews, personal reflections, and essays. We encouraged the children to use tape recorders as they generated ideas for their texts (either alone or in small groups). Their recordings functioned both as data for us and as props for subsequent texts and performances that the children created.

The "talk show" genre as a key frame for organizing talk about Tupac emerged in the discussion session after we introduced the idea of producing some kind of tribute to Tupac. Several children launched into a lively discussion about Tupac and his recent album (under the pseudonym Makaveli), *The Don Killuminati*. During this discussion, Kris (a pseudonym, as are all other participant names) talked about the introduction to the song "To Live and Die in L.A.," which is a skit framed as a question-and-answer session from a fictitious radio "call-in" show called *Street Science*. On this track, the female host of the show begins and a male caller responds:

Host: *Street Science*, you're on the air. What do you feel when you hear a record like Tupac's new one?
Caller: I love Tupac's new record.
Host: Right, but don't you feel like that creates tension between East and West? He's talking about killing people. "I had sex with your wife." Not in those words. But he's talking about, "I wanna see you deceased."

Kris's reaccented version of this exchange, which embodied the speakers' intonations almost perfectly, was "Biggie Smalls, how do you feel, how Tupac been saying, he had sex with your wife?" Laughing, Lakisha pitched in the comment, "but not in those words." Still laughing, she added, "You ain't dead yet? You still talking? Roaches!" Interestingly, Lakisha's utterance indexed another skit from the same album. This skit precedes the song, "Bomb First," in which Tupac calls himself a "bad boy killer." The skit is framed as a news report about Tupac's new album and the East-West conflict that constitutes much of the thematic material of the album. In the context of this fictitious news report, Tupac yells, "You niggas still fucking talking? You niggas still breathing? Fucking Roaches!"

Kris's and Lakisha's performative exchange emerged spontaneously and produced the discursive context within which many subsequent talk show interactions took place. For example, directly following this exchange, three other young people took recorders, separated themselves from the group, and produced talk shows. In all of these shows, both the primary thematic material and the talk show frame were appropriated by our participants as devices for talking about their knowledge of and affiliation with Tupac Shakur and the cultural world in which his life and work was embedded.

Because the television talk show genre had not come up in our brainstorming sessions, we were a bit surprised that the children fastened onto it so intently (and intensively). We were even more surprised that this genre remained so central to their work on the Tupac anthology. Once the talk show format was introduced, it was appropriated consistently and pervasively in a majority of the work sessions that occurred during the subsequent five weeks. In all but a single week, at least one child or group chose to produce a talk show no matter what kind of text we asked them to produce (and we specifically asked them to produce facsimiles of a real news report, a biography, and a rap song).

As we mentioned earlier, the use of this speech genre seemed to have concrete effects on how our young participants framed the events they reported. This was not particularly surprising since a primary function of speech genres is to fuse form, thematic content, and practice (Kamberelis, 1995). One concrete effect of deploying the television talk show genre was that the thematic content that the children foregrounded in their dialogic discussions and projects were ones that are typically foregrounded in media coverage of rap artists (and other pop culture icons), most of which are highly personal and psychological. More specifically, the children constantly gravitated toward discussions about Tupac's murder, including his betrayal by Biggie Smalls and his conflict with Biggie over Biggie's wife, Faith. These topics dominated both formal discussions and informal conversation among peers and between peers and adults during the months that both preceded and followed Tupac's murder.

In most of the remainder of this chapter, we demonstrate some of the ways that these youth fused the dialogic talk show format with psychologized content from the world of rap music in their discursive practices. We do this by analyzing segments of transcripts from two of the talk shows that different children or groups of children created and performed. Importantly, there was considerable thematic and stylistic overlap across the many different talk shows produced by various children. For example, all of the talk shows showcased the privileging of affective and conflict-laden discourse and the power of talk to resolve the conflicts. However, each show was also unique in the particular themes that it foregrounded, the particular speech genres that it laminated onto the television talk show genre, and the particular ways that it fashioned the fusion of conversationalized discourse and psychologized social facts. For example, the first transcript that we analyze embodied a fusion of these two discursive features with exceptionally rich intertextual links to the lyrical content of certain rap songs and albums, as well as the myths that grew up around them. Within the second transcript we analyze, these two features were woven together with confessional discourse, which Foucault (1979, 1990) has argued is a particularly powerful normalizing technology of the self. Through our analyses of these two transcripts, we hope to show some of the ways in which the television talk show genre both enabled and constrained children's efforts to construct social knowledges and identities.

On the first day of the sessions devoted to the Tupac anthology, Kris and Rufus created and performed the first full-blown television talk show. As they performed their show, several other boys and girls pitched in comments from the audience rim. A segment of the transcript from this performance appears below:

R: Biggie Smalls, how do you feel what Tupac did to you?

K: Well, I'm, I ain't sweatin' it really because, all he's saying is ain't nuttin' but a joke to me.

R: Tupac, how do you feel? (*Voice deepens as he enacts Tupac's response*) Man, you stole my lyrics, my jewelry, so I stole your wife, you big fat mug (*Laughter*).

K: Well, nigga you wanna sport with my wife, ooh, cause I ain't even like that old girl anyway. She wasn't a little girl. You played your own self nigga, 'cause I don't like her, and you can have her nigga, 'cause I got more money than you do. That's why I'm gonna have Junior Mafia and them smoke your punk tail.

R: Oh, Junior Mafia ain't gonna do nothin'. Now, now, you all gonna try to smoke me. Then I'm gonna fake my death, and West Side gonna come on y'all and shoot y'all up (*Sound effects*). Now, what you gotta say about that? Huh? Wanna square? Wanna square? Huh?

(Section omitted where Kris and Rufus stop recording and regroup)

K: (*Voice shifts back to that of talk show host*) Back to me men, back to me please. Stop the arguing, all right.

R: (*Aside*) Back to Biggie.

K: Back to Biggie now. Biggie Smalls, how do you feel, about, Tupac saying that he want you d- deceased, dead? He said he gonna get his West Coast on you. He said he had his West Coast in the back. So (*Pause*)

R: (*Whispered prompt*) How do you feel?

K: How do you feel?

R: Well, I can kill any of them niggas anyway, 'cause guess what? I got my North Coast and South Coast on y'all niggas.

This performance is interesting both thematically and interactionally because it foregrounds key personal and interpersonal events in Tupac's and Biggie Smalls's lives. Rufus (who is playing Tupac) says "you stole my lyrics, my jewelry, so I stole your wife, you big fat mug." This utterance indexes a number of accusations made by Tupac in his single "Hit 'Em Up," where he charges that Biggie stole his style and his jewelry (during the shooting mentioned earlier), and that he ultimately got revenge by sleeping with Biggie Smalls' wife, Faith. Rufus also seems to index this single when he refers to "West Side!," a phrase that gets repeated in the song.

When asked to create a text that has something to do with Tupac Shakur, Rufus and Kris chose to take the psychologized struggle between Tupac and Biggie that is the thematic content of this single and re-situate it within the interactional frame of the television talk show

(Bakhtin, 1981; Kamberelis & Scott, 1992). This fusion of psychologized thematic content, the dialogic format of the talk show genre, and the quotidian practices of "street talk" is quite predictable from the theoretical perspectives offered by Fairclough and Peck. It is also very important in terms of the kinds of knowledge it enables and constrains about these folk heroes and the wider world in which they operate. A closer look at some of the discursive features used by Rufus and Kris will bring this point into relief.

Many of the features that both Fairclough and Peck have argued are central elements of contemporary broadcast culture (especially insofar as this culture is embodied in television talk shows) are embedded in this constructed dialogue. For example, the interaction is framed by Rufus in terms of "feelings." He begins by asking, "Biggie Smalls, how do you feel what Tupac did to you?" He then asks a similar question of Tupac, "Tupac, how do you feel?" Importantly, this line of questioning, including its wording, thematic focus, and syntax, mirrors the line of questioning Kris first broached when attempting to mimic the introduction to the Tupac song, "To Live and Die in L.A." Although Rufus's version of it is different both from the original version and Kris's version, both foreground feelings. As we demonstrated above, the version from the album is directed to a radio listener and focuses on the new Tupac album—"What do you feel when you hear a record like Tupac's new one?" Kris appropriated this feeling-focused question and redeployed it in relation to the conflict between Tupac and Biggie, which had been so much a part of their talk for several weeks: "Biggie Smalls, how do you feel, how Tupac been saying, he had sex with your wife," to which Lakisha added, "but not in those words," which is a near-verbatim appropriation from the dialogue of the album's introductory skit.

Importantly, these kinds of "therapeutic" questions are relatively uncommon in much rap music, which tends to focus on physically impenetrable male characters. Yet, there is some overlap here between the kinds of issues treated in talk shows and the kinds of issues central to rap music, especially recent variants of this musical form. Interpersonal conflict and its resolution, for example, tend to be foregrounded in both media forms, albeit somewhat differently. Talk show discourse focuses on "therapeutic" solutions, which are "formulated around intimate, revelatory conversation" (Peck, 1995, p. 61). The goal of such discourse is to restore to good health the "individual psyche" through open communication and speech about feelings (p. 60). In contrast, conflict in much rap music often includes yelling, screaming, and physical confrontation, which is deployed rhetorically to build tension, sometimes almost to the breaking point. The goal of these conflict-resolution tactics is not usually therapeutic restoration, at least insofar as such restoration has been normalized within "mainstream" society. When conflicts are resolved, they are typically resolved through physical violence. Gangsta rap is a key example of this tendency.

The articulation of these partially incommensurable conflict-resolution strategies in the dialogue created by Kris and Rufus is very interesting. Kris (acting as a talk show host) asks Rufus (acting as Tupac) to express his feelings about his conflict with Biggie, positing faith—at least provisionally—in the ability of open communication to resolve it. However, this provisional faith is continually disrupted when they threaten to break into a fight. Interestingly though, these disruptions are often smoothed over by sliding back into the discourse of the television talk show genre. For example, role-playing the parts of Tupac and Biggie, Kris and Rufus almost come to blows. First Kris says, "That's why I'm gonna have Junior Mafia and them smoke your punk tail." Rufus replies with:

> Now, now, you all gonna try to smoke me. Then I'm gonna fake my death, and West Side gonna come on y'all and shoot y'all up (*Sound effects*). Now, what you gotta say about that? Huh? Wanna square? Wanna square? Huh?

Kris restores order by assuming the interviewer role once again, "Back to me, men, back to me, please. Stop the arguing, all right." Once order is restored, Kris reinvokes the feelings-centered dialogue of the television talk show, "Biggie Smalls, how do you feel, about, Tupac saying that he want you d- deceased, dead?" In short, the eruption of conflict and the escalation of emotion are contained with a performative and discursive frame that privileges personal feelings and open communication about these feelings.

This general communication pattern, which blends television talk show discourse with the discourse of rap and revolves around psychological/interpersonal issues of rap artists, was central both to media coverage of the real life conflict between Tupac and Biggie over Faith Evans and in the talk of our young participants. The claim that Tupac slept with Biggie's wife as a form of revenge was a recurring motif throughout their interactions. Recall that we discussed this fact in relation to the mock television talk show created and performed by Kris and Rufus. It was also the central motif of a mock television talk show created and performed by John a week later. In this show, he played three different characters (talk show host, Faith Evans, and Biggie Smalls), the latter two of whom were brought together to "work on" their conflict in the controlled space of national television and under the arbitration of the show's host. As John performed various roles, he switched voices, postures, and seating positions. Marco and Rufus pitched in snippets of dialogue, comments, and questions from their audience positions. As the performance emerged, all three boys seemed to contribute to each other's knowledge and construction of relevant facts and events:

J: (*Playing talk show host*) All right. What is this with you and Biggie Smalls getting into it over Faith? (*Long pause*)

(*Pause and some background noise, perhaps coordinating an answer*)

J: (*Whisper*) All right, let's get back. (*Pause*)

M: Right, you know, I tried to get hooked up with, I (*Indecipherable*). Who is Faith?

J: (*Laughter*) Forget it. We'll bring in a magazine.

R: (*Laughter*) I'll bring in the magazine. I'll bring a picture of her.

J: (*Playing talk show host again*) Ladies and gentlemen, bring out Faith!

     (*Playing Faith and enacting a high-pitched voice*) Oh, thank you, thank you.

     (*Playing talk show host*) Faith, did you have a relationship with Biggie Smalls?

     (*Playing Faith*) John, yes I did.

     (*Playing talk show host*) Faith, did you love Biggie Smalls?

R: John, yes I did.

J: (*Playing Faith*) No, I didn't.

     (*Playing talk show host*) Faith, (*Background commotion and laughter*) Faith, did you ever make love to Tupac?

R: (*Playing Faith*) Yes, I did.

J: (*Playing Faith*) John, yes.

     (*Playing talk show host*) How did you make Notorious Big feel?

R: (*Playing Faith*) Sad, mad, very, very (*Pause*)

J: (*Playing Faith*) I don't know, John. I can't answer that.

     (*Transcript continues with an interview of Biggie Smalls*)

Playing the role of talk show host, John opens this monologue by explicitly positing Faith as the nexus of the conflict between Tupac and Biggie when he asks, "What is this with you and Biggie Smalls getting into it over Faith?" This is important because the conflict between the two men was very complicated, involving many factors including the exchange (legitimate or otherwise) of economic, cultural, and symbolic capital within the music industry. Indeed, the conflict began (as noted above) with an attempted robbery in New York City, during which Tupac reputedly lost $40,000 worth of jewelry. According to Tupac, Biggie knew this robbery would happen and told him nothing about it. Although it is easy to see how their conflict could be reduced to "getting into it over Faith," it is important to note that there are many equally plausible alternatives. Why not, for example, attribute the conflict to the prevalence of rampant materialism, the increase of black-on-black crime, the victimization of women, or the extremes of social Darwinist thinking? Given these (and other) plausible alternatives, the fact that John (and others) selected a personal and intimate subject (i.e., the exchange of sexual capital in the context of romantic betrayal) as the major reason for the conflict between Tupac and Biggie is both interesting and important to our argument. This selection seems related in no trivial way to the ideological constraints of the television talk show genre that John chose as the discursive format for rehearsing and exploring his knowledge about Tupac. This genre affords or encourages conversationalized discourse such as emotional, intimate, and self-revelatory questions. As a cursory survey of these kinds of shows would reveal, they typically feature subjects that involve "painful relationship problems, the kind everyone can relate to" (Zoglin 1995, p. 77). And conversely, such shows tend to steer people away from discourse about macro-economic, social, and cultural explanations for human and social problems.

In addition to foregrounding interpersonal relationships, intimate subjects, and feelings, John's monologue embodies a "confessional" quality. For example, he asks Faith to reveal the details of her relationship with both Biggie and Tupac (i.e., Did she sleep with Tupac? Did she ever really love Biggie?). As Foucault and others have noted, the "confession" is a primary technological apparatus of bio-power through which individuals are made into subjects:

> The confession is a ritual of discourse in which the speaking subject is also the subject of the statement; it is also a ritual that unfolds within a power relationship, for one does not confess without the presence (or virtual presence) of a partner who is not simply the interlocutor but the authority who requires the confession, prescribes, and appreciates it, and intervenes in or-

der to judge, punish, forgive, console, and reconcile (Foucault, 1990, pp. 61–62).

Foucault's explanation of how oppressive or restrictive forms of power are reproduced through the enactment of the confession is particularly helpful for understanding how subjects are produced within discursive regimes such as the television talk show. Whenever the confession is enacted—and this is usually in particular discursive sites such as the ones highlighted by Foucault (schools, churches, prisons, therapy sessions, etc.)—the subject of the discourse is simultaneously constituted by it and subjected to it. Things are yet more complex than this, however. Because confession is multifunctional and because confessing is experienced as "personal," it tends to render brute and restrictive forces of power as nonexistent or benevolent. This is especially true in the late twentieth century since, as Fairclough has noted, the confession has become more widespread and more public due to the increasing presence and power of the media. This is particularly relevant for our purposes in this chapter because "the compulsion to delve into and talk about oneself, and especially one's sexuality, in an ever widening set of social locations . . . appears on the face of it to be a liberating resistance to objectifying bio-power" (Fairclough, 1992, p. 53).

From this perspective, the act of confession seems to transform the confessee. It "exonerates, redeems, and purifies him [sic]; it unburdens him [sic] of his wrongs, liberates him [sic], and promises him [sic] salvation" (Foucault, 1990, p. 62). However, according to Foucault and many of his followers, this sense of freedom and resistance is an illusion. In reality, confession draws more of the person ever so subtly into extant networks of power (Fairclough, 1992; Foucault, 1990). With its semblance of agency, confession constitutes a marvelous technology of the self, a paramount instance of bio-power at work.

The discourse of television talk shows, with its privileging of affect, creates a context ripe for confession. One typically does not probe affective domains (e.g., loss, guilt, shame, sin) for sport but to excavate and exonerate the negativity and heaviness associated with such feelings through talk. So, the purpose of asking questions such as "How did you make Notorious Big feel?" is to help addressees confess their sins, hear the confessions of others, renew themselves, and move forward with their lives.

Like other features of the discourse of contemporary media, its confessional quality contributes to the translation of economic, social, and political questions into personal ones. And because confession is an instrument of disciplinary bio-power, confessing feels like a liberating experience, not a restrictive one. Yet, as Peck noted, the material function of confession is to reproduce extant arrangements of power. Within the discursive frameworks created by John (as well as by Kris and Rufus earlier), Tupac, Biggie, and Faith are constrained by the requirements of the television talk show genre. They must play according to a set of rules that, ironically, constitutes an effective technology of disciplinary power.

Discussion and Conclusions

The examples of discourse that we analyzed were highly representative of the thematic content and style of much of the talk that the children engaged in throughout the many weeks during which we discussed the life and death of Tupac Shakur. The preponderance of this talk seemed to focus on the role of Faith Evans in the ongoing set of disputes between Tupac and Biggie Smalls, and the form of this talk resembled the conversationalized discourse of the television talk show, wherein "talking about feelings" is posited as a primary discursive means through which to resolve such disputes. Importantly, the discourse requirements of the television talk show genre (as well as contemporary broadcast media discourse more broadly conceived) encourage the use of psychologized iconic discourses, which promote liberal-humanist ideologies of individual agency, intention, and choice.

Among other things, our findings underscore the fact that understanding young people's access to, preferences for, and competencies with different forms of talk is essential to understanding how they come to understand cultural events that are salient within their lives. Because they are primary carriers of ideologies, different speech genres enable and constrain different kinds and degrees of cultural knowledge (Fairclough, 1992; Hymes, 1996; Kamberelis, 1995). Thus, understanding how young people appropriate and deploy the various speech genres that are available and/or salient in their lives is crucial for understanding how they reproduce and/or disrupt dominant cultural discourses. As we noted at the beginning of this chapter, popular culture provides many of the discourses (and speech genres) in which and through which young people constitute both their personal and cultural identities and their knowledge about the world. What speech genres young people gravitate toward and how these genres are rearticulated within their microlevel speaking practices are fundamental both to the reproduction and disruption of cultural discourses and to children's ongoing processes of identity production. Thus, understanding how specific speech genres enable and constrain how young people talk about their lives and their worlds is crucial for understanding the trajectories of their "thinking" and "acting" (Fairclough, 1992; Fiske, 1996; Kamberelis, 1995; Wertsch, 1991).

As we demonstrated through our analyses, one speech genre that seemed particularly compelling for the young people in our study was the television talk show genre. We are not claiming, however, that this genre is a singularly important one for young people. Whether or not such a claim could be supported would require a much more ambitious study than the one we conducted. Among other things, it would require comparisons across a number of different speaking genres, a range of discursive settings, a large number of participants, and an extended time span. Our claim is much more modest and may be summarized as follows: the young people in our study did, in fact, repeatedly choose to deploy the television talk show genre to discuss the life and death of Tupac Shakur, and this genre had concrete discursive effects on how they constructed and positioned themselves in relation to these issues and events.

To understand why these patterns were so salient in our data requires some understanding of the wider set of discursive practices that are common currency within the lives of many urban African American youth. In the many different formal discussions, informal conversations, and observations that we have conducted in the community in which our study took place, we have found that television talk shows have a tremendous appeal to a wide range of audiences across a wide range of ages. We have also found that personalized and conversationalized discourse and the psychologization of social issues are extremely common discursive practices among the people who constitute these audiences. We will elaborate on each of these issues, focusing first on the conversationalization of public discourse.

During a discussion that focused on the viewing practices of our participants and their family members, it became clear that television talk shows were a staple of family entertainment. For example, *Ricki Lake* and *Jenny Jones* were mentioned repeatedly as favorite shows by many of our participants. Interestingly, both of these shows seem to be targeted at younger audiences in comparison with shows like *Oprah Winfrey* and *Maury Povich*, which are targeted at older viewers. Moreover, shows like *Ricki Lake* and *Jenny Jones* tend to showcase more extreme examples of the kinds of animated interpersonal conflicts that we have discussed throughout this chapter, a fact that was not lost on our young viewers. Rufus, for example, noted that "the best one is *Ricki Lake* and *Jenny Craig* [*Jenny Jones*]." He continued, "it's funny, they be start fighting and stuff; it be looking funny; . . . they be doin' cat fights, them girls." Later in the conversation he added that he found it more enjoyable to watch shows filled with arguing and fighting than shows where the guests "just be talking." That this preference was pervasive and durable for most of our participants was reinforced many times when we viewed television shows and films with them. Almost without exception, they were riveted to the screen during intense action scenes. In contrast, they lost interest and began to talk among themselves (often about issues unrelated to the show or film) during scenes that involved mostly talk or narration.

The viewing practices of our participants were also closely linked to their family lives and social lives. Many young people told us that they watched these television talk shows with members of their families. Marco, for example, said, "Everyday after school, I see my grandma watchin' it, and I sit down and lay on the couch and I start watchin' it, and he [his brother] come in and start watchin' it. And then it be me, him, and my grandma." Indeed, we got the impression from various discussions that our participants' viewing practices were intensely social.

Our discussion of television talk shows also led to discussions of other kinds of television shows that our participants watched. For example, during one discussion of *Ricki Lake*, Marco brought up another show, *The Love Connection*. Mention of this show prompted Rufus to share his recollection of a particular episode in which a man refused to pay for gas needed while on a date. Rufus broke into laughter as he told us, "She dumped him!" Although television shows like *The Love Connection* differ from television talk shows in many respects, both types of shows foreground overtly conversationalized discourses, focus largely on personal issues and interpersonal conflicts, and encourage confessional discourse. Extreme interpersonal conflict is also central to another set of media events commonly consumed by our young participants—professional wrestling. Indeed, watching and talking about professional wrestling was a very popular "sport" among them. The television at the community center where they "hung out" was almost always tuned to professional wrestling when it was being broadcast; most of our participants had accumulated a rich body of knowledge about the spectacle; and most engaged in fairly frequent discussions about particular contestants, emphasizing their idiosyncratic personalities, their antics, and their recent contests. Like rap music and many of the "events" featured on television talk shows, professional wrestling features violent conflicts between and among highly stylized and psychologized individual icons. These characters typically engage in complex psychodramas, and their actual matches are interspersed with interviews and antics that heighten their interpersonal conflicts. Wrestling is indeed embedded within its own mythological narratives with definable characters who engage in both physical and psychological drama. As such, wrestling is another key, albeit paradoxical, example of the tendency toward "conversationalized" discourses within the contemporary broadcast media.

These findings about the broader reception practices of our participants, their friends, and their families reinforce our general argument that there is a certain discursive reciprocity between their viewing practices and the "forms of talk" with which they are most comfortable and most competent. This reciprocity suggests that understanding the forms and functions of certain speech genres is essential to understanding the productive (and restrictive) articulations between young people's consumption practices (e.g., viewing, reading, listening) and their production practices (e.g., speaking, arguing, performing).

We turn now to the psychologization of social and political issues. We have already shown that our participants tended to provide psychological explanations for social and political problems and events. We also noted that this tendency is central to the discourse of the television talk show genre, which we argued is a particularly powerful instance of the trend toward conversationalization within the contemporary broadcast media more broadly conceived. Indeed, during the very first discussion in which we discussed Tupac's death and before any mention of *Ricki Lake*, one participant, Latrice, commented that Biggie didn't have anything to do with Tupac's murder because Faith wasn't "worth all of that." In making this assertion, Latrice implicitly attributed Faith Evans as the primary source of the conflict between the two men, and she justified her claim about why Biggie did not murder Tupac with the warrant that Faith was not attractive enough to motivate a murder. During this discussion, Lakisha and John brought up the single "Hit 'Em Up," which is presumably about Tupac's affair with Faith. As we mentioned in our earlier analyses, this single became a common "prop" around which many subsequent discussions and performances were staged. Predominant themes that were played out included the presumed fact that Tupac let Biggie sleep on his couch when he [Biggie] was down and out, that Biggie had stolen some of Tupac's jewelry (during the robbery), that this act had caused animosity between the two men, and that Tupac slept with Faith as an act of revenge.

We witnessed numerous other interactions and performances during which these young people constructed the facts of Tupac's life and death in a highly psychologized way. Almost exclusively, they linked the murder to the conflict between Tupac and Biggie, and they foregrounded personal and interpersonal issues gleaned from albums, videos, news reports, fanzines, and so on to flesh out the motives of the actors involved. For example, when asked why Tupac chose to target Faith to get back at Biggie for his robbery, Rufus volunteered, "like that's what he likeded the most. And like Tupac likeded his jewelry the most and Biggie Smalls likeded his wife the most." When asked what he thought about Tupac's revenge tactics, Rufus replied "he [Biggie] shouldn't have stole his rhymes, shouldn't stole none of that junk. He stole his jewelry." Rufus also located some of the agency for these events in Faith, noting that she had been unfaithful to Biggie because she liked Tupac more, a claim that added yet another layer of psychologized explanation to the narrative that Rufus constructed to account for the conflict between Tupac and Biggie.

To summarize much of what we have already said, both the thematic content and the form of our participants' talk about Tupac's murder were modeled after the television talk show genre, at least in large measure. We concluded from this tendency that the television talk show genre (and the discourses of contemporary broadcast media more broadly conceived) were discourses with which our participants had tremendous familiarity and fluency. We also suggested that understanding how young people construct themselves and their worlds requires excavating locally specific linkages among societal discourses, consumption or reception practices, and microlevel speaking practices (especially in relation to speech genres), and we provided modest empirical support for this claim. As the primary vehicles of societal discourses, speech genres are discursive "combinations of specific blindnesses and insights. Each is adapted to conceptualizing some aspects of reality better than others" (Morson & Emerson, 1990, p.

276). Or as Burke so astutely noted many years ago, all discursive frames constitute "terministic screens," which are at once reflections, selections, and deflections of reality (Burke, 1966, p. 45). Thus, fastening onto the television talk show genre both enabled and constrained the ways that the young people in our study processed the complex events in the world of rap that so captivated their attention. For example, it seemed that certain structural social and political facts and implications relevant to Tupac's life and death were elided when the television talk show genre became the primary lens through which these facts and implications were viewed, even though this speech genre is socially potent and discursively complex. If we are right here, it is incumbent upon us to imagine how and why these issues were not constructed otherwise. In relation to this point, Charlie Braxton wrote:

> In the absence of absolute truth about the murder of Tupac Shakur, many people attempt to fill the void by proposing countless theories as to who may have killed him and why. Theories range from the plausible to the straight up imbecilic, but very few, if any, examine the critical socio-political issues that ultimately led to the conditions surrounding Shakur's death (1997, p. 97).

We have suggested all along that, in their appropriation of the discourses and discourse formats of the contemporary broadcast media, our participants avoided asking certain kinds of questions and generating certain kinds of explanations. More specifically, they tended to avoid wider social and political questions and explanations in favor of personal and psychological ones, which have "no origin or target outside of one's own psychic process" (Peck, 1995, p. 76). The restricted set of questions and explanations that resulted from these specific appropriation practices made visible some kinds of knowledges and rendered others relatively invisible. Framed as they were within the discourses of contemporary broadcast media, a certain inevitability plagued their accounts of the controversy between Tupac and Biggie. At the heart of the conflict were two individual personalities with strong wills, idiosyncratic compulsions, individual desires, and specific sets of goals. Given this construction, the two most salient solutions available to Biggie and Tupac were to fight it out or to talk it over—or perhaps to fight it out and then talk it over. This kind of resolution is not necessarily a bad thing. Indeed, many, including us, would argue that it is the best of these options. Whether or not this is true is irrelevant to our argument, however. What is relevant is that the conversationalization and psychologicalization of the conflict between

Tupac and Biggie suppressed the possibility of generating economic, social, and political explanations for the conflict and, therefore, the envisagement of more structural kinds of resolutions.

This fact indexes some larger issues about the relations among discourses, communicative practices, and knowledge. What people actually do with language in concrete acts of communication has important implications for how they understand and explain public events, as well as how they, themselves, act. This nexus turns on issues of public access to cultural resources. How people come to understand themselves and their worlds depends in no small measure upon what kinds of access they have to what kinds of discursive frames within the public sphere, because these frames are fundamental to appraising and evaluating social reality. Moreover, specific ways of speaking and ways of knowing are embedded within wider social practices, such as television watching. Like the "confession," engaging in these speaking practices interpellates people into specific subject positions wherein they are both subjects of and subjected to certain ways of processing the world—ways that are good for some things and not so good for others (e.g., Hymes, 1996).

Several implications follow from this assertion. First, we need to understand more fully how and why society makes readily available certain cultural resources and not others. In relation to this point, might viewing social events with the possibilities made available through the lenses of different genres help young people become more astute social critics? With respect to the data that we analyzed in this chapter, for example, what knowledges might have been constructed had our participants resisted "common sense" choices about what genres were most appropriate to discuss Tupac's life and death, processed these events through a variety of generic lenses, and compared the results of doing so? Finally, might such interpretive practices have promoted more open and critical stances toward the constitutive relations between language and reality?

To conclude, we would like to make two summary points—one that is theoretical/methodological and one that is empirical. The work we have presented in this chapter suggests the power of theorizing and investigating speech genres as primary mediators between societal discourses and everyday social practices. Speech genres are the instruments deployed by young people as they actively construct their social knowledges and identities in the context of specific sociocultural practices. Moreover and more importantly, they are also instruments that are differentially available to young people, depending upon a whole set of contingent microsociological and macrosociological factors. Though often theorized, empirical research is necessary to understand more fully the constitutive linkages among discourses, knowledges, and identities, and how speech genres mediate their co-constitution.

Although we ventured into this empirical terrain, we emerged with claims that are both tentative and modest. We found that the genres that the young people in our study gravitated toward and trafficked in (as well as the speech events within which they were embedded) are ones that have been popularized recently within the contemporary public media industries. Although these genres allowed children to construct fairly complex psychological understandings and explanations, they rendered invisible (or at least eclipsed) more global and more structural social and political understandings and explanations. More research of the sort we have conducted is necessary to map more precisely how specific speech genres enable and constrain young people's efforts to reproduce and resist the power arrangements that constitute their lives and to construct social knowledges and identities within these arrangements.

References

Alcoff, L. (1988). Cultural feminism versus post-structuralism: The identity crisis in feminist theory. *Signs: Journal of Women and Culture, 13* (3), 405–436.

Appadurai, A. (1996). *Modernity at large.* Minneapolis: University of Minnesota Press.

Bakhtin, M. M. (1981). *The dialogic imagination* (C. Emerson & M. Holquist, Trans.). Austin: University of Texas Press.

Bakhtin, M. M. (1984). *Problems of Dostoevsky's poetics* (C. Emerson, Trans.). Minneapolis: University of Minnesota Press.

Bakhtin, M. M. (1986). *Speech genres and other late essays* (V. W. McGee, Trans.). Austin: University of Texas Press.

Bakhtin, M. M., & Medvedev, P. N. (1985). *The formal method in literary scholarship: A critical introduction to sociological poetics* (A. J. Werhle, Trans.). Cambridge, MA: Harvard University Press.

Bhabha, H. K. (1994). *The location of culture: Literature related to politics.* London: Routledge.

Bourdieu, P. (1990). *The logic of practice.* Stanford, CA: Stanford University Press.

Braxton, C. (1997). Who killed Tupac Shakur? In M. Datcher & K. Alexander (Eds.), *Tough love: The life and death of Tupac Shakur* (pp. 97–100). Alexandria, VA: Alexander Publishing Group.

Bruner, J. S. (1986). *Actual minds, possible worlds.* Cambridge, MA: Harvard University Press.

Burke, K. (1966). Terministic screens. In *Language as symbolic action: Essays on life, literature, and method* (pp. 44–62). Berkeley: University of California Press.

Buttny, R. (1993). *Social accountability in communication.* London: Sage.

Clifford, J. (1988). *The predicament of culture: Twentieth century ethnography, literature, and art.* Cambridge, MA: Harvard University Press.

Dimitriadis, G. (1996). Hip hop: From live performance to mediated narrative. *Popular Music, 15* (2), 179–194.

Dimitriadis, G., & Kamberelis, G. (1997). Shifting terrains: Mapping education within a global landscape. *The Annals of the American Academy of Political and Social Science, 551,* 137–150.

Fairclough, N. (1992). *Discourse and social change.* Cambridge: Polity Press.

Fairclough, N. (1995). *Media discourse.* London: Edward Arnold.

Fiske, J. (1996). *Media matters*. Minneapolis: University of Minnesota Press.

Foucault, M. (1972). *The archaeology of knowledge and the discourse on language* (A. M. Sheridan Smith, Trans.). New York: Pantheon Books.

Foucault, M. (1979). *Discipline and punish: The birth of the prison* (A. Sheridan, Trans.). New York: Vintage Books.

Foucault, M. (1990). *The history of sexuality. Volume 1: An introduction* (A. Sheridan, Trans.). New York: Vintage Books.

Gramsci, A. (1971). *Selections from the prison notebooks of Antonio Gramsci* (Q. Hoare & G. N. Smith, Eds. and Trans.). New York: International Publishers.

Grossberg, L. (1992). *We gotta get out of this place: Popular conservatism and postmodern culture*. New York: Routledge.

Hall, S. (1996). Who needs "identity"? In S. Hall & P. du Gay (Eds.), *Questions of cultural identity* (pp. 1–17). London: Sage.

Hymes, D. (1996). *Ethnography, linguistics, narrative inequality*. London: Taylor & Francis.

Kamberelis, G. (1995). Genre as institutionally informed social practice. *Journal of Contemporary Legal Issues, 6*, 115–171.

Kamberelis, G., & Scott, K. D. (1992). Other people's voices: The coarticulation of texts and subjectivities. *Linguistics and Education, 4*, 359–403.

Markus, H., & Kitayama, S. (1991). Culture and the self: Implications for cognition, emotion, and motivation. *Psychological Review, 98* (2), 224–253.

McCarthy, C. (1998). *The uses of culture: Education and the limits of ethnic affiliation*. New York: Routledge.

Morson, G. S., & Emerson, C. (1990). *Mikhail Bakhtin: Creation of a prosaics*. Stanford, CA: Stanford University Press.

Peck, J. (1995). TV talk shows as therapeutic discourse: The ideological labor of the televised talking cure. *Communication Theory, 5* (1), 58–81.

Rosaldo, R. (1989). *Culture and truth: The remaking of social analysis*. Boston: Beacon Press.

Star Talker. (1994, December 12). *Broadcasting and Cable, 124*, 56–57.

Wertsch, J. V. (1991). *Voices of the mind: A sociocultural approach to mediated action*. Cambridge, MA: Harvard University Press.

Zoglin, R. (1995, January 30). Talking trash. *Time*, 77–78.

MUSIC IN THE POSTCOLONY
AND IN THE DIASPORA

Narrating Imperialism:
The British Influence in Barbadian
Public School Song

Cameron McCarthy

> Beasts of England, beasts of Ireland,
> Beasts of every land and clime
> Hearken to my joyful tidings
> Of the golden future time. . .
> George Orwell, *Animal Farm*

> The gay Dons sing of Oxford, the Cantabs laud their pile,
> Then let us humbler mortals praise our school in this fair isle;
> So we'll sing not of Tiber's flow, nor of Parnassus tall,
> But our song shall burst from hearts that glow
> With love for Washington. . .
> Washington Junior Public School Song

Introduction

The Barbadian public school song has been accepted as part of a complex of ritual and folklore handed down from the British public school system during the extended period of British colonization and settlement of the island country. The Barbados school system goes back to the beginnings of colonization in the third decade of the seventeenth century. Though the island declared its independence in 1966, these school songs still thrive in Barbados today. This essay explores structure and meaning in 24 school songs. Particular attention is paid to the themes of empire, class, and gender. I will also explore the tensions and contradictions within the school song as an apparatus of social normalization linked to the project of maintaining British hegemony in the Caribbean long after the decline of an active imperial presence and ascendancy in the region.

History and Context

The modern history of Barbados can be fairly clearly demarcated. It begins with the arrival of British settlers in 1627. When these settlers arrived over 350 years ago, the island had already been abandoned by its original Amerindian inhabitants, whose presence in Barbados stretches backward to around 500 B.C. and forward to around A.D. 1500. Though both Spanish and Portuguese traders had visited the island briefly during the sixteenth century, it was the British Captain John Powell who claimed the island for the British crown. Barbados would remain a British colony until 1966. Barbados is a pear-shaped island consisting of a mere 166 square miles. Its landscape is generally flat or undulating. And it is entirely surrounded by the beautiful turquoise and aquamarine waters of the Atlantic Ocean.

Barbados's history is steeped in constitutionality. The antiquity of its House of Assembly is only third to the British House of Commons; the second being that of Bermuda in the northern reaches of the Caribbean sea. Executive power, even now in the postindependence era, remains vested in the British monarch, represented by the island's governor general, Dame Hilda Barrow. Legislative power is exercised through a bicameral parliament, comprising a 21-member Senate and a 27-member House of Assembly. The Barbados Westminster-style government is led by a prime minister; currently, Owen Arthur is the leader of the Barbados government. From inception, there was a special love affair between England and Barbados which the early settlers found "better agreeing with the temper of the English Nacion" (Harlow, 1925, p. 42) than its more mountainous Carib-dominated island neighbors. For a significant part of the seventeenth century, Barbados was predominately settled by English and Irish descended freehold or yeoman farmers who grew tobacco for export and vegetables and fruits for subsistence. With the introduction of sugarcane to the island in the 1640s, African people were imported as slave labor in the plantation economy that would dominate the island's economic life for over three hundred years. By the last quarter of the seventeenth century, African people would make up the majority of the island's population. Over 70% of the current population of 254,000 is of African descent, 20% is mixed race, while about 7% is of European descent; the remaining

2–3% of the population consists of recent immigrants from Asia and the Middle East.

Africa and Europe provide the two powerful cultural presences that so strongly exert themselves in Barbadian historical and contemporary reality. While a British predominance undergirds the formal institutional apparatuses of the country, there is a subterranean current of African survivals in Barbadian popular culture. Africa and Europe therefore exist in genuine accommodation and in sharp tension in Barbadian cultural life. This is expressed in a kind of cultural schizophrenia. For example, when one drives into Bridgetown on the main highway from the Barbados Grantley Adams Airport, one is greeted with an extraordinary symbol of Barbadian Africanism. In the center of a roundabout on the outskirts of the principal city, Bridgetown, one sees a massive, towering bronze statue of a slave in revolt. With his head held high and his fists raised, breaking the shackles of slavery, the slave looks across the verdant, rolling landscape that is Barbados. It is an arresting and impressive statue that signals an eruptive emergence of a cultural and political independence almost leaping from the ground. But if you were to continue on your journey and enter into the heart of Bridgetown, you would be struck by another arresting statue. It is that of Horatio Nelson, the late-eighteenth century British naval commander famous for his victories at sea against the French and the Spanish. Standing as Barbados's preeminent centurion, guarding the ocean sea that surrounds the island, the Nelson statue is of a man fully clothed in military attire, poised, commanding and in control of all he surveys. It is of special note that the Barbadian statue of Nelson was erected in Bridgetown some thirty years before its counterpart in London.

This schizophrenic tension, this intense duality, expresses itself throughout the length and breadth of Barbados's cultural and social institutions and in its popular culture. Barbadians still retain a portion of the imperial seal, the prong of Neptune's trident, in the center panel of their national flag. The Barbados economy, historically dominated by sugar cultivated by black labor, is now dominated by tourism. Tourism is an industry that principally caters to European and Euro-American visitors served by an Afro-Barbadian waiting staff. In the area of religion, this contestation over culture is reflected in the opposition between the established Christian religion, Anglicanism, and the more African-inspired Baptist sects.

But nowhere is this cultural dualism more acutely articulated than in the educational system. The Barbados educational system is quite diversified. At its base are some 200 primary schools spread out across the island. There are over 30 public and private secondary schools. The University of the West Indies at Cave Hill is the principal tertiary institution. But, historically, the entire system has been structurally integrated into the British educational system. In the postindependence era, the British model of education continues to flourish on the island. And, Barbados, for instance, retains the Eleven-Plus Examination, long after the British school system has more or less abandoned it. In addition, at the end of secondary school, Barbadian students sit two types of examinations: one at age 15, set by the Caribbean Examinations Council; and another at age 17, set by the London and Cambridge Examination Boards. These examinations play a critical role in the determination of social possibilities for students beyond school, as they do in England. Despite these contradictions, Barbadians are very proud of their educational system. And with its 98% literacy rate, it is touted as a success story of both of colonization and traditional Barbadian obsession with educational success.

Schooling and the Transaction of Empire

In his excellent book, *Black Marxism*, Cedric Robinson (1983) calls our attention to a very revealing interview in which C.L.R. James recounts a conversation between himself and Aimé Césaire. The tête-à-tête between these two great postcolonial intellectuals highlights the paradoxes of a classical colonial education, the instability of the subaltern relationship to Western intellectual traditions, and indeed the very instability of the canon itself as a normative project. It more importantly provides, obliquely, the founding principles for what I wish to call, following historians like Dominick La Capra (1994) and literary critics like Gerald Graff (1987), a noncanonical reading of canonical texts. In this case, the texts are musical texts, the Barbadian public school songs, part of the lineaments (along with school crests, emblems, flags, and so forth) of a borrowed or imposed tradition of English school ritual that thrives in Barbadian schools today in the postcolonial era. I will analyze some of these songs later in this chapter. James and Césaire's conversation highlights a contradiction in the whole amour of empire that I want to call attention to:

> Aime Césaire and I were talking one day, and I asked him: 'Where do you come from?' He said, 'Well, I grew up in Martinique [and went to] the Victor Schoelscher School'. . .So I said: 'What did you do there?' He told me:

'Latin and Greek and French literature.' And I said: 'What did you do next?'
He said, 'I went to France, and I went to the Ecole Normale Superiore.' I said,
'Yes I know that school. It is famous for producing scholars and communists.'
(Césaire was one of the first in each department: he was one of the finest
scholars and he was a notable Communist.) And I said, 'What did you do
there?' And he said: 'Latin and Greek and French literature.' And then I said:
'Where did you go from there?' And he said: 'I went to the Sorbonne.' And I
said, 'I suppose you did there Latin and Greek and French literature?' And he
said: 'Exactly.' He said, 'But there is one thing more.' And I asked: 'What is
that?' He said, 'I went back to teach in Martinique, and I went to the Schoelscher
school, and there I taught Latin and Greek and French literature.' So when
Césaire wrote his tremendous attack upon Western civilization, in *Return to
My Native Land*, and said that Negritude was a statement for some concepts
of civilization which the black people had and which would be important in
any development of civilization away from capitalist society, he was able to
make this ferocious attack upon Western civilization because he knew it inside out. . . He had spent. . . years studying it (Robinson, 1983, p. 259).

I want to suggest the central paradox raised here in James's recollection, the paradox of Franz Fanon's (1967) "black skins/white masks,"
playing itself out in full contradictory form in the public school songs
of Barbados. These school songs have been accepted as part of the
normal ritual of Barbadian public school life. They represent part of
the lineaments of a borrowed or imposed tradition of English school
ritual that still thrives in Barbadian schools today in the postcolonial
era. They form part of the taken-for-granted life of the primary and
secondary schools of Barbados, and as such are often dismissed, even
by ordinarily insightful school critics, as mindless school routine. Public school songs are regarded as school-specific, serving the purpose—
along with other supporting rituals and symbolic practices—of foster-
ing school solidarity, consensus and group identity. However, a more
sustained exploration of the symbolic meanings of these songs alerts
us to a fascinating universe of messages not only complexly and prob-
lematically situated in the stratified local and indigenous landscape but
also conjuring up an otherworldly context full of references and allusions to battles, service, and empire that link Barbados to England.
These songs are part of what Basil Bernstein (1977) calls the performance ritual of schooling.[1] They help to make up a complex of practices of daily morning assembly in Barbadian schools that include: a
general whole-school congregation, public announcements, "topic for
day," the recitation of the pledge of allegiance, the singing of the
Barbados national anthem, the raising of the Barbados flag, the singing of hymns, the recitation of prayers, and the showcasing of particu-

lar examples of academic or athletic success of individual students. The songs also serve as a particularly sharp ritual of individual school definition at interschool athletic meets or academic competitions. Often in the former context the riotous element in adolescent high school behavior can take over and, in my school days at least, the songs lost their high culture formal quality and were taken over by the will to the popular. A school song like Merecomb's "Lives Are in the Making Here" could be easily spliced with spicy invective, racy and raunchy sexual innuendo, or sung to the melody of Carlos Santana's "Samba Patti" or Jimi Hendrix's "Hey Joe." The formal, British-derived meters of these songs could be lost in antiphonal chanting, African drumming, and cacophonous bugle playing or punctuated by the rhythm and riffs of the latest calypso or reggae hit. In other words, all hell could break loose as the songs descended into an unpredictable world of kitsch, adolescent self-assertion, and resistance to the oppressive formalities of schooling. However, in this essay it is the formal properties of the songs, their content and meaning to which I pay special attention.

Theories and Method

I review a sample of songs obtained from 24 Barbadian high schools.[2] It should be noted that not every song in the sample will be commented on specifically in this essay, but the 24 songs do inform the entire analysis presented. These schools have all been assigned pseudonyms. All the songs except three were obtained from government supported public schools. However, it should be noted that at the high school level, the Barbadian education system is bifurcated into elite grammar and comprehensive or secondary modern schools. There is also a system of private schools for students of both upper middle-class and lower-class backgrounds who did not make it through the grueling Eleven-Plus Examination to the grammar schools.[3] Unlike the United States, it is the government supported grammar schools rather than the fee-paying private schools that have highest status in Barbados. It is the school songs of the grammar schools that receive special attention in this study. These songs were obtained from the Barbados Department of Archives and the Barbados Public Library. This sample of songs is representative of Barbadian public school songs in general. The sample can be subdivided as follows. Eight of the songs were written for historically all-girls schools and the other sixteen were writ-

ten for all-boys schools. Seven of the songs in the sample come from
elite grammar schools. The other seventeen are divided between working-class elementary and comprehensive secondary schools. It should
be said that though most of the schools in Barbados are currently
making the transition to a co-ed system of organization, the lyrics and
the content of these school songs have not been changed. In addition,
the schools are regarded in popular memory and public common sense
in terms of their original or historic designation as a "girls school" or
a "boys school."

In an important sense, my work departs from earlier sociological
and linguistic analysis of school ritual to be found in the work of Basil
Bernstein (1977), who, drawing on the structuralist analyses of Emile
Durkheim and Karl Marx, tells a story of the function of school songs
and school ritual in the reproduction of age and class divisions among
British school youth and their role in legitimating school and societal
authority. It also departs somewhat from the work in the cultural studies tradition from Raymond Williams's *Culture and Society* (1958) to
Stuart Hall's "Encoding/Decoding" (1980) essay and the writings of
others who talk about "structure in dominant." In all these analyses,
the text of culture ultimately corroborates the world outside in some
way.

The method applied in this reading of Barbadian public school songs
is defined by Edward Said (1993) in *Culture and Imperialism* as the
"historically situated" or "contrapuntal" reading of culture. This is the
idea that a literary text, particularly a canonical text, must be read as
part of a complex configuration—must be read against and with the
grain of other texts, other contexts, histories, geographies, literatures,
and so forth. My project here, then, is to map the relations of the
global to the local in the micropractice of the school song. But this
project, as I will show, cannot fulfill or procure a linear or guaranteed
result, a homology between culture and imperialism. It is a little ironic
then, that on this reading and application of the method of situated
history to the Barbadian public school song, I find Said's analysis of
the relationship between culture and imperialism incomplete—incomplete in the sense that in Said's own work, like that of Adorno and
others of the Frankfurt School, the text is still a site of self-coloniza-
tion, operating as a conduit for the expression of economic and political power. The result here is that we have lost the sense of the text as
a field of play, as a set of maneuvers, as a practice laden with its own
troubles as well as the troubles of the world. I want to add to this

model/method a theory of interests, needs, desires, and contradiction, and the concept of "articulation" used in the later work of Hall (1986). By articulation I am referring to Hall's notion that culture is a site of a configuration of practices—a site of both centripetal and centrifugal forces or dimensions—lines of encounter and transformation—lines of consolidation and dissipation. Secondly, these songs will be read against the grain of other texts, other colonial documents and literature and popular music, nascent and contemporary, reproductive as well as resistant, traditional as well as subaltern that point to an inner as well as an outer logic of the cultural and social divides that exist in Barbados itself.

Unlike Said, I situate the Barbadian public school songs not in the fulfillment of British empire but in the context of its waning. British declining interest in administrative control of its overseas colonies is well articulated and anticipated as early as the eighteenth century in Adam Smith's *An Inquiry into the Nature and Causes of the Wealth of Nations* (1776). This waning control was the result, paradoxically, of overacquisition, overregulation, and overcentralization in the metropole. As Said (1993) points out, by 1914 the major powers of Europe and the United States exercised imperial suzerainty over 85% of the countries and peoples of the earth. In the late eighteenth and early nineteenth centuries the administrative costs of colonization were simply too great. I am suggesting that the idea of empire, the idea of rule overseas, imposed constraints on the small polities of Europe themselves. In addition, colonial administration, though directed from and answerable ultimately to the metropolitan government, also embodied a whole complex of accommodations with national, indigenous elites that conflicted with British long-term economic and political interests in cultivating these colonies/ex-colonies as markets for its goods and services.[4]

The Barbados school songs emerged at a time in the late nineteenth century when Barbadian schools, fueled by British colonial investment in the 1830s and 1840s, had reached a relatively stable economic footing. According to the British historian, William Green (1976), in the nineteenth century:

> Barbados had the most cohesive and symmetrical education system [in the British West Indies]. . . During the 1850s—a period of considerable distress in the colonies, the Government spent more money per capita for education than the British Government (Green, p. 349).

The emergence of education for Barbadian lower classes, whom the historian Sidney Greenfield (1968) called "English rustics in black skin," was perceived as a major threat by the local white planter class. The great fear here was that an educated working class population might no longer want to work in the sugarcane fields. The planters thought they stood to lose the labor power that drove sugarcane production, as this statement published in the *Barbados Agricultural Reporter* in January 1892 indicates:

> The sons and daughters of the labouring classes have become impregnated with the idea that the education which is imparted to them makes them better than their fathers; and they have begun to look with disdain upon mere manual labour. Rather than work in the fields they prefer to gravitate to town and recruit the army of loafers to be seen about Bridgetown (quoted in McCarthy, 1983, p. 180).

To be a child of the Empire meant that one could not be at the same time a child of the planter class. One type of paternalism threatened to undermine or cancel out the other.

The Public School Songs

The Discourse of the Child of Empire

The discourse of the Barbadian public school songs creates a world of contrived equivalences into which the colonial/postcolonial child enters as an agent of Empire. In the matter of the defense of Empire the Barbadian child and the English are one. The lyrics of Merecomb Grammar suggest this connection:

> Lives are in the making here
> Hearts are in the waking here
> Mighty undertaking here
> Up and on, Up and on.
> We are arming for the fight
> Pressing on with all our might
> Pluming wings for higher flight
> Up and on, Up and on. (Merecomb Grammar School Song)

Or the lyrics of this song from Berlin Grammar School:

> Here we stand where our fathers standing
> Thought the thoughts that are ours today;
> Yielded their hearts to the School's commanding

Tuned their lives to accept her sway;
One with theirs is the prayer we pray
One with theirs is our Hope, our Light
One with theirs is the game we play
One with theirs is our rule for Fight.
Still in the lore of her legend's pages
Truth like a quenchless star
Set for a sign for future ages
Shines on the years that are.
Here in the games that are ours for playing
Find we more than the moment's prize
Shoulder to shoulder our ranks arraying,
Face the future with fearless eyes.
Hence with doubting and vain surmise!
Standing firmly we front the foe;
Whatsoever the days devise,
Life shall call us and we will go.
Ay, and the lesson of this our chorus
Still we will bear in mind;
Draw for the fight of the years before us,
Might from the years behind.
Here in the tasks that are ours for learning
Read we more than the pages bear
Fan the flame in our spirits burning
Not to be less than our fathers were. . . .
Memory born of old days shall bind us
Though we return no more
Still shall the light of the year behind us
Brighten the years before. (Berlin Grammar School)

Participating in school is a higher calling to serve a greater cause. The "fathers" in the narratives of these songs are not Barbadian, the ancestors here are British, or not even British, some sort of cultural supermen—nameless, yet proprietary. This line of association was maintained in the 1875 *Mitchinson Commission Report*—a report that lays out the British project for Barbadian Education in the nineteenth century. In its report, the commission appointed in 1875 by the Colonial Secretary, Augustus Frederick Gore, laid out an educational program to cultivate the "best and the brightest" in the high school population in the island by sending them off to Oxford and Cambridge:

It would be a very desirable thing if every youth that proved to be at all susceptible of culture could go through a course of higher academic training before settling down to his life-work. . . . It is needless to observe that this education in its most perfect form can best be had in the two great seats of learning in the Mother Country, the Universities of Oxford and Cambridge. It would indeed be a great advantage to the Colony, if she could send her very best raw material to be worked into a cultivated article. Few may be worth the cost implied in so doing; of these fewer still perhaps would return to the colony to enrich it with the fruits of their higher culture. Yet the advantage to the cause of education in this island would be great and worth the cost of one or even two exhibitions per annum. For it would be regarded as the great annual prize to which every boy would look with hope, and to which he would direct his best efforts (Mitchinson Commission, 1875, pp. 27–28).

In other words, education in Barbados was committed to producing an intellectual elite—a sponsored elite that would, interestingly, be black rather than white, would be deeply invested in the state, and mechanisms and technologies of symbolic control—a middle-class that was positioned with the British and the empire and between the lower classes and the national white planter-mercantile elites.

But there is yet another level of reading with respect to the question of the relationship between the purposes and projects of empire and the themes underscored in the school songs. This is related to the epistemological status of school knowledge as defined in the songs. Knowledge, like the imperial center, is described in the school songs as an external commodity residing outside the child. This tight classification and framing of knowledge as the object one pursues like Parsifal, emphasized the authority of the teacher, and obedience. On this reading, the school songs embody elements, then, of what Bernstein (1977) calls "the collection code," the tight insulation and bounding of knowledge. It is a knowledge form that Jamaica Kincaid's Annie, in her novel *Annie John* (1985), resists when she describes Christopher Columbus—presented in history textbooks as the great explorer and discoverer—as the old man "who could not get up and go." Knowledge as an external commodity is something to strive for—a goal that links Barbados to England through a set of processes of authentication and authorization. Educational achievement required a preparedness to discipline and postpone desire, "per ardua ad astra" (through suffering to the stars), maintains the school songs for one of the elite girls' school (Helen's Grammar School).

But it is precisely the value of this imposed worldview that is contested in Caribbean popular music. For instance, speaking back to his education in pre-independence Trinidad, the calypsonian Winston Bailey (the Mighty Shadow) contests the official story of Columbus' discovery of the Caribbean:

Columbus lie, Columbus lie, Columbus lie, lie, lie
He said he discovered the whole of America
He never tell nobody

How he had to run from Apache
Columbus lie, Columbus lie, Columbus lie so bad
I believe Columbus was mad. . ..
Nowadays you enter a strange land, they call you an alien
You get to explain to immigration what is your intention
Columbus didn't have to do that
It just didn't make no sense
His authority was a cork hat
And his passport was violence
(Bailey, 1988).

This anxiety about received knowledge in a British-derived educational system is already announced in the late nineteenth century in a Barbadian public school song such as that of the Washington Junior School. Here parody and self-mockery are interspersed with obvious adoration of British educational institutions. "Mimicry," in the language of Bhabha (1994), turns to mockery in the postcolonial context. Washington Junior's public school song contains traces of the contradictory practices indicated by Bhabha:

The gay Dons sing of Oxford, the Cantabs laud their pile,
Then let us humbler mortals praise our school in this fair isle.
(Washington Junior).

"Empire Day"

But the project of Empire was in earnest, and Barbadian school life was expected to uphold imperial tenets and values. George Lamming (1975), in his autobiographical novel, *In the Castle of My Skin*, describes the celebration of Empire Day in the 1930s in Barbados. The commemoration of Empire Day originated around 1904, three years after the death of Queen Victoria, whose long reign saw both the consolidation and nascent decline of Britain's imperial might (Rohler, 1990). Empire Day was instituted by the Earl of Meath to shore up the ideology of Empire. It was a time when Barbadian primary schools, like schools in the British colonies all over the world, celebrated:

The anniversary of the birthday of our late beloved sovereign, Queen Victoria, during whose glorious and beneficent reign the British Empire practically assumed its present gigantic proportions (Earl of Meath quoted in Rohler, 1990, p. 183).

In Lamming's novel, it is Empire Day, May 24, 1930. Barbadian schools are being visited by a British school inspector, much as Mathew Arnold did in English school districts in his day. It is a context in which the British anthem is sung and the school song is performed along with other ritual academic and theatrical events for the benefit of the English inspector. The inspector is a proxy or stand-in for the monarch (George V):

> The school was a uniform of flags: doors, windows and partitions on all sides carried the colours of the school's king. There were small flags and big flags, round flags and square flags, flags with sticks and flags without sticks, and flags that wore the faces of kings and princes, ships, thrones and empire. Everywhere the red and the white and the blue. In every corner of the school the tricolour Union Jack flew its message. . . The children in the lower school looked with wonder. They seemed to see a mystery that was its own revelation, and there was no need to ask questions (Lamming, 1953, p. 28).

Empire Day was a wellspring of ritual aimed at securing the ultimate mythology of the English monarch as "the patron saint of Emancipation to generations of descendants of enslaved Africans" (Rohler, 1990, p. 183). The dream of ideological closure sutured up the identities of Caribbean people into the fold of Empire. Incongruously, Empire Day annexed the history of struggle for emancipation of Afro-Caribbean people, and a dead queen was declared the liberator of the slaves.

However, the mythology of Empire Day would not be complete without a school song. Meath's anthem for Empire Day ("The Flag of Britain")—written for performance throughout the colonies—had all the tenor of the Barbadian public school song:

> Flag of Britain! where-so-ever
> Thy bright colors are outspread
> Slavery must cease forever
> Light and freedom reign instead. . . .

But, like the public school song, the Empire Day song registered uncertainty and contradiction.

> Flag of Britain, proudly waving
> Over many distant seas
> Flag of Britain, proudly braving
> Blinding fog and adverse breeze. . .
> ("The Flag of Britain" quoted in Rohler, 1990, p. 183).

According to Rohler, it is "The Flag of Britain" that George Orwell (1951) satirizes in the memorable animals' anthem in his *Animal Farm*:

Beasts of England, beasts of Ireland,
Beast of every land and clime
Hearken to my joyful tidings
Of the golden future time. . . .
(Orwell, 1951, p. 13)

Themes of Class

But the school songs, like other aspects of school ritual, also turned inward, and this is a point not quite pursued by Said (1993) in his examination of culture and empire. They worked inward, perhaps more sharply than they worked outward, to define class and gendered differences in Barbados itself. As I have written elsewhere, an historical class bias undergirds the Barbados educational system from its founding (McCarthy, 1985). While in theory all Barbadian students have access to its most elite grammar schools, only a small percentage of students actually make it into these schools. The Common Entrance Examination or Eleven-Plus Examination (popularly known, until recently, as the "Screening Test") is used for determining the transfer of students from elementary schools to secondary schools. It is a rigidly competitive examination, the principal purpose of which is to select some 10–15% of the "best and brightest" for an elite educational preparation in the grammar schools. The Barbados Eleven-Plus Examination is a facsimile of the British Eleven-Plus Examination, and it seals the social fate of school children at a very early age.

The school songs fabricate this class divide, separating the Barbadian grammar schools from the rest of the society's schools, comprehensive or primary, which are regarded as inferior. For example, while the school songs in the grammar schools situate the Barbadian school child as an autonomous agent of empire—within some discursive language of common heritage and fate with the British school child—the songs of the primary and comprehensive schools have a different ring to them. Here is one from Washington Junior—a school founded in the nineteenth century by a Barbadian educator who, like Booker T. Washington, emphasized industry and hard work for the black working-class youth:

The gay Dons sing of Oxford, the Cantabs laud their pile,
Then let us humbler mortals praise our school in this fair isle;
So we'll sing not of Tiber's flow, nor of Parnassus tall,
But our song shall burst from hearts that glow
With love for Washington. . .
We are taught the good and useful, the noble and the true,
And surely all these indicate what when men, we ought to do.

Here, the primary school child sets his/her sights on England. Knowledge is the path to liberation. But the students of Washington must first know their place: as the step-children of the Empire they are not first among equals. The song therefore rejects—and with a great deal of self-mockery—the idea of an academic or professional future of "cultivation" at Oxford or Cambridge.

Typically, the school songs of middle-class schools (Berlin, Merecomb, Royal College, Helen, and so forth) abound with messages of transcendence and convey no explicit reference to work. Schooling is seen instead as a courtly aristocratic joust: the leisurely acquisition of knowledge in congenial settings. For the middle-class child, or the child aspiring to a professional middle-class future, schooling is a corridor that leads them out of and beyond the hardships and mundaneness of ordinary life to the promise of the better social future. The lyrics of the school song of Barbados's most elite grammar school for girls (Royal College) holds out the better life beyond working-class toil:

> Life is a road to tread
> In dust and labor and heat
> But the light shines over our head
> And the thought of the goal is sweet.

This culture and politics of clarity, the idea of knowledge, like light, demystifying and emancipatory, runs throughout the school songs irrespective of gender as in this song of St. Theresa's:

> There's a word that wakes our spirits,
> Lifts our thoughts on high,
> Where St. Theresa's own emblem
> Sparkles in the sky.

Barbados is well known throughout the Caribbean for its relatively short geographic distances but what the historian Gordon Lewis (1968) calls its "huge social distances." The lines of demarcation in these songs are also severe. If through one's school institution one can soar above the turmoil of labor and life, one can also soar above one's social others. There is, consequently, a transparent connection between messages of transcendence and covert messages of class snobbery. The school song of Royal College illustrates this thin line of connection between transcendence and separate social destiny:

The world waits on our way,
And the gate swings slowly apart,
And around us rises the stir of the fray
But it comes not into our heart.

This general mythologising of school life present in the school song of the middle-class grammar schools contrasts sharply with the down-to-earth tone of the song of the working class comprehensive schools such as St. Magna's Secondary Modern. Here schooling is more explicitly identified with work:

We work and play together. . .
Preparing for the future
So to face our destiny. . .
Inspired by faithful teachers
dedicated to their task.

Also, in this song schooling is seen as a worthy activity sui generis. The acquisition and the production of knowledge is described in terms of the metaphor of labor ("task," "preparing," and "dedicated") and not in terms of the metaphor of the joust, as is the case of the school songs of most of the middle-class grammar schools.

Generally, then, the Barbadian public school songs effectively draw down lines between manual and mental labor, desire for "cultivation" and the desire for doing the "tasks at hand." The lines of demarcation between the genders are also effectively drawn. I will discuss these lines of demarcation in the next section of the essay.

Themes of Gender

In *The History of Sexuality, Volume I*, Michel Foucault (1978) calls attention to the role of proliferating institutional discourses around sexuality in regulating, disciplining, and differentiating whole populations. It could be argued that the discourses of the Barbadian public school songs are part of a proliferating discourse around gender and social identity that help to demarcate lines of social divide in the school at the same time as they regulate adolescent desire. Deeply associated with the theme of class is the theme of gender.

The school songs of the eight all-girls schools in the sample are far less heroic and militaristic in tone than those of the all-boys schools. These songs emphasize values of passivity and service as the role function for the girls. That this is the case irrespective of the class orientation of the schools underscores the fact that there is a general practice of gender typing in the regulation of school life in Barbados

(Cole, 1981). Whereas, for example, the songs of the historically all-male schools are inhabited by "foes," "hunting," "Lodges" and "jousting," the songs for the girls schools typically emphasize service, duty, neatness, taste, restraint, and propriety. The tone of the school songs for the girls is noticeably subdued, as illustrated in the "quiet and ordered hours" celebrated in the school song of Royal College. In keeping with this, girls, unlike boys, are expected to have "weary feet" but paradoxically to "carry the lamp" of service to all humankind, somewhat like Florence Nightingale:

> Here we learn for the love of our land
> Handled and made for the service of right
> We shall lift our lamp with a loyal hand,
> We shall carry the light.

The boys by contrast are in the thick of the fray:

> We are arming for the fight.
> Pressing on with all our might
> Pluming wings for higher flight
> Up and on, Up and on. . . .

Service for the girls is presented as a role that was almost divinely ordained and sanctioned, a legacy of yesteryear. In the school song of Helen's Grammar School, the domestic function is seen as something handed down from generation to generation and therefore beyond question.

> We are following the pathway
> Laid by those of yesteryear
> Who have left behind a challenge,
> Joyfully we hear the echo
> Per ardua ad astra [Through suffering to the stars]

Hence passive suffering and self-denial are promoted as the paragon of values and ideals for the girls. These messages of self-denial and patient suffering would of course become important for the girls as they fulfilled their adult roles as mothers and wives.

Conclusion

My description of the internal workings of the Barbadian public school songs paints a picture of normative consolidation at the level of the imaginary, or the level of representation. This is not to be understood as a story of social guarantee of adolescent school behavior. Between the idealistic designs and representation of the school songs falls the shadow of the active role of adolescents as told, for instance, in the stories of Lamming and Kincaid, and the popular response of school children in their magazines to school life. In the wider popular culture and literary production colonial education has been critiqued. But it must also be said that the school songs embody paradoxes that go beyond a constructed loyalty to empire. They embody ideas of ownership of knowledge, ownership of fate, emancipation through learning. Education would become the means of production for black lower-class children to rise out of poverty. A means for the children of slaves to claim the professional and intellectual sphere in Barbados and ultimately to take over the reigns of power in the formal institutions of the State. Barbadian public school songs both affirm loyalty to what Derek Walcott (1993) would describe as "something bigger than you" as well as the possibility for agency. But they also affirmed a past at a time of the waning of British Empire as an administrative and coercive system of overlordship. They represent a cultural, normative transaction of new identities in empire through the seduction of knowledge. In this sense, the school songs are to be understood as a special form of musical high kitsch, lying somewhere between the formalism of schooling and the subaltern irregularities of popular culture.

Notes

1. Drawing on the work of Emile Durkheim and Mariam Douglas, Basil Bernstein offers the following definition of ritual:

   Ritual in human beings generally refers to a relatively rigid pattern of acts specific to a situation, which construct a framework of meaning over and beyond the specific situational meanings. Here the symbolic function of ritual is to relate the individual through ritualistic acts to a social order . . . (Bernstein, 1977, p. 54).

2. The names of the 24 schools are: Gerome Primary, Washington Junior, Morgan Primary, Liston Primary, Bloomsbury, Swift Primary, St. Lucia Girls' Primary, St. Martin's Primary, Lancaster, William Hill, Bishop's Primary, South City, St. Magna's Secondary Modern, Princess Diana's Secondary Modern, St. Ann's Secondary, Robert Marley Secondary, Excelsior Secondary—all elementary and comprehensive secondary schools; Helen's Grammar, St. Mary's Grammar, Berlin Grammar, St. Theresa's Grammar, Merecomb Grammar, Milhouse Grammar, Royal College—all secondary grammar schools. Over half of these schools are located in the main city of Barbados, Bridgetown. The others are scattered across the country side in the more rural parts of the island.

3. The Eleven-Plus or Common Entrance Examination determines the transfer and placement of students from elementary to secondary schooling in Barbados. This competitive examination was based on the British Eleven-Plus Examination and persists in Barbados today well after the British have abandoned this method of determination of transfer from elementary to secondary schooling. The examination is berated by Gordon K. Lewis (1968) in his *The Growth of the Modern West Indies*:

   It meant the subjection of the school population to a murderously competitive regimen, with pupils exercised like race horses in a steeple chase only a chosen few could hope to win, and producing in those few, the well-known phenomenon of the colonial Oxonian only too often made unfit, by experience for creative service to his community (p. 230).

4. As Eric Williams (1964) points out in *Capitalism and Slavery*, West Indian planters and merchants bought seats in both houses of the British Parliament and used their considerable financial resources to protect their sugar interests and to maintain a monopoly in the area of sugar (1964, pp. 92–97).

References

Bailey, W. (1988). Columbus lie. *Pressure point [LP]*. Bridgetown, Barbados: West Indies Records Limited.

Bernstein, B. (1977). *Class, codes and control, Volume 3*. London: Routledge.

Bhabha, H. (1994). *The location of culture*. New York: Routledge.

Césaire, A. (1970) *Return to my native land*. Middlesex: Penguin Books.

Cole, J. (1981). *Women in the Caribbean: Official ideology and the education of women in the English-speaking Caribbean, 1835–1950*.

(Occasional Paper). Cave Hill, Barbados: Institute for Social and Economic Research.

Fanon, F. (1967). *Black skins, white masks*. New York: Grove Press.

Foucault, M. (1978). *The history of sexuality, Volume 1: An introduction* (R. Hurley, Trans.). New York: Vintage.

Graff, G. (1987). *Professing literature: An institutional history*. Chicago: University of Chicago Press.

Green, W. (1976). *British slave emancipation: The sugar colonies and the great experiment, 1830–1865*. Oxford: Clarendon Press.

Greenfield, S. (1968). *English rustics in black skin*. New Haven: Yale University Press.

Hall, S. (1980). Encoding/decoding. In S. Hall (Ed.), *Culture, Media, Language* (pp. 128–138). London: Hutchinson.

Hall, S. (1986). On postmodernism and articulation: An interview. *Journal of Curriculum Inquiry, 10*, 45–60.

Harlow, V. (1925). A briefe description of the ilande of Barbados. In V. Harlow (Ed.), *Colonising expeditions to the West Indies and Guiana, 1623–1667*. London: Hakluyt Society.

Kincaid, J. (1985). *Annie John*. New York: Plume.

Lamming, G. (1975). *In the castle of my skin*. London: Longman

Lewis, G. (1968). *The growth of the modern West Indies*. New York: Monthly Review Press.

McCarthy, C. (1983). *The imperialist motive in the introduction of popular education in Barbados, 1833–1876*, University of Alberta, Department of Educational Foundations.

McCarthy, C. (1985). Ritual as ideology: An analysis of Barbadian public school songs. *Cimaron* 1(1), 69–90.

Mitchinson Commission. (1875). *Education commission report—1875*. Bridgetown, Barbados: Barbados Government Printers.

Orwell, G. (1951). *Animal farm*. London: Penguin.

Reid, and W. Barney (Eds), *Learning history in America: Schools, cultures and politics* (Pp.120–138). Minneapolis: Minnesota Press, 1993.

Robinson, C. (1983). *Black marxism: The making of the black radical tradition*. London: Zed Press.

Rohler, G. (1990). *Calypso and society in pre-independence Trinidad*. Tunapuna: Rohler.

Said, E. (1993). *Culture and imperialism*. New York: Knopf.

Smith, A. (1776/1937). *An inquiry into the nature and causes of the wealth of nations*. New York: Modern Library.

Walcott, D. (1993). *The Antilles: Fragments of an epic memory*. New York: Farrar, Straus and Giroux.

Williams, E. (1964). *Capitalism and slavery*. London: Andre Deutsch.

Williams, R. (1958). *Culture and society: 1780–1950*. New York: Columbia University Press.

From 'The Bluest Eye' to 'Jazz': A Retrospective of Toni Morrison's Literary Sounds

Robin Small-McCarthy

The novels of Toni Morrison make reference to the sites, sounds, and functions of African-American music in a variety of cultural and historical contexts. Drawing on the aesthetics of spirituals, field songs, the blues, and jazz, Morrison's progressive development of musical discursive strategies began with subtle allusions to sound in *The Bluest Eye* (1970), and gradually moved toward a comprehensive jazz aesthetic in *Jazz* (1992a). Morrison's literary sounds—her polyrhythmic narrative shifts, improvisations on words and themes, antiphonal dialogue and plot structures, and jazz-inflected speech patterns—are deeply rooted in African-American oral and musical traditions (Holloway, 1987; Berret, 1989). Thus, a retrospective analysis of Morrison's use of tone colors and rhythms specific to black American music can serve as a means by which an oral interpreter can decode and convey the poetics and the substance of her literature.

Morrison, Transmodal Discourse, and Oral Interpretation

Attention to the convergence of the performing and literary arts in the process of analyzing, transforming, and performing the novels of Toni Morrison can enable interpreters to take an active role in accessing and expressing the cultural knowledge, the ideas, and the perspectives imbedded in these classics (Moffett & Wagner, 1992).

Rendering a jazz novel for an audience, moreover, can deepen and display reading comprehension while awakening the participants to the potential of the synesthesia of language and music—the transmodal perception that can give words a new power to evoke auditory images that can become symbols for a variety of ideas and themes (Moffett & Wagner, 1992). In the process of textual transformation, the participants can learn to experiment with oral language and expression, heighten their understanding of the text, internalize the rhythms, patterns, and lyrical qualities of language, model the syntactic phrasing and music found in the written text, and provide additional interpretive supports and vocal nuance to collectively convey denotative and connotative meaning to an audience (Diamond & Moore, 1995; Kleinau & McHughes, 1980). In performance, moreover, oral interpreters "activate the imaginative, perceptual, and empathic abilities of an audience" (Kleinau & McHughes, 1980, pp. 179–180).

Whether literal or literary, music can evoke the cultural milieu of which it is a part (Moffett & Wagner, 1992). Music can trigger a response in movement or language. Music can liberate bodily response and evoke poetry. Music can therefore be both a sensory stimulant and an effective accompaniment to the oral interpretation of texts that were themselves the result of musical inspiration, texts that mirror the phrasing, tonality, and rhythms of the music from which they were engendered.

In this essay, I will present a retrospective analysis of the "sound structures" (Kleinau & McHughes, 1980, pp. 31–35) embedded in each of the novels of Toni Morrison, not as an exhaustive treatment but rather as a cumulative representation. Beginning with *The Bluest Eye* (1970) and ending with *Jazz* (1992a), I will select and explicate passages from each work that lend themselves well to demonstrations of the ways in which Morrison's discursive strategies operate within African-American musical aesthetics and the ways in which Morrison's texts can be transformed and interpreted in performance. By explicating the author's use of tone color, diction, and rhythm, I hope to clearly demonstrate that the denotative meanings of her words are enriched by alliteration, assonance, consonance, onomatopoeia, rhyme, and the speech patterns, attitudes, and vocal tones characteristic of black vernacular English, and that the regular and syncopated drumming of sounds, words, images, scenes, and narrative shifts can be felt in the muscles of the perceiver. Such an analysis would be of primary interest to those who intend to discover and to lend voice to the soundscape of Toni Morrison's *The Bluest Eye* (1970), *Sula* (1973), *Song of Solomon* (1977), *Tar Baby* (1981), *Beloved* (1987), and *Jazz* (1992a).

Textual Analysis and Transformations

While most fully realized as a jazz aesthetic, Toni Morrison's literary sounds are rooted in ancestral wisdom (Koger, 1989; Morrison, 1984) and in the voices of such blues and jazz writers as Amiri Baraka (Bentson, 1976) and Ralph Ellison (Bigsby, 1987). With bebop lyricism and polyrhythmic structures, she shapes the stories of African-American women and men struggling to maintain their individuality and personal dignity while remaining vital members of their communities—women and men who, like jazz improvisers, "exercise personal freedom within the framework of the group" (Bigsby, 1987, p. 177). This new world griot tells and re-tells the stories of a people for whom music has traditionally been a source of solace and a means of expression and which is entirely dependent on shared or communal knowledge:

> Improvisation is at the core of jazz; its essence is the spontaneous composition of its players. The ability to improvise successfully rests on the musicians' familiarity with the traditions of African American music, his or her knowledge of music theory, and an indefinable "feel" for the music (Koger, 1989, p. 109).

The Bluest Eye

These are the principles that ground Morrison's improvisational techniques in *The Bluest Eye*. Her improvisation of the basal reader, the "Dick and Jane" primer, depends simultaneously on her familiarity with the formulaic structure of the banal narratives of middle-class white Americans found only in basal readers and her familiarity with the tragedies that can occur in the lives of poor African Americans, particularly those who have wasted their lives trying in vain to live up to white supremacist standards of living and of beauty. Here, Morrison's literary improvisation is a form of signifyin' which effectively destroys and lays bare the vapidity of the original text, much like John Coltrane's jazz improvisation of Rodgers and Hammerstein's "My Favorite Things," and much like Jimi Hendrix's acid rock interpretation of "The Star-Spangled Banner."

Morrison prefaces *The Bluest Eye* with a triple improvisation of the Dick and Jane reading primer. The first version, though grammatically correct by conventional standards, tells the story of a lonely Jane whose Mother laughs when Jane asks her to play, and whose Father smiles when asked the same. This passage foreshadows the tragic story of Pecola Breedlove, whose mother has little time for her,

and whose father rapes and impregnates her when his barely concealed rage and frustration finally explodes at the seams. Subsequent
improvisations are presented within the faltering frame of a grammatical structure that parallels the changing of the seasons and the
progressive breakdown of the Breedlove family, and Pecola's mental
health, under the duress of a system of racist, sexist, and classist ideology which privileges white over black, male over female, and the
rich over the poor—and which engenders circumstances and situations that teach Pecola Breedlove time and time again that she is too
Black, too female, too poor, and thus too ugly to live. With each progression, Morrison rejects punctuation and thus exposes the conventions that uniformly structure authoritative texts in so-called Standard
American English. She takes her readers from

> Here is the house. It is green and white. It has a red door . . . (p. 7)

to

> Here is the house it is green and white it has a red door . . . (p. 7)

and finally to

> Hereisthehouseitisgreenandwhiteithasareddoor . . . (Morrison, 1970, p. 8)

The final effect is an accelerated, claustrophobic, chaotic text which
forces the perceiver—the reader, the interpreter, or the audience member—to make meaning for him—or herself. Morrison leaves the perceiver to either struggle for meaning by imposing the presumed missing punctuation, or by accepting the text as it is and trusting his or her
ability to decode any text which visually and aurally reflects the sensory and emotional reality of its subject. In either case, like any jazz
musician, Morrison expects her silent readers, her staged readers, and,
by implication, her audience members to be active participants in the
transformation of the written text from print to meaning and to willingly go with the flow.

Active participation on the part of an oral interpreter would require
the performer to enter into a give-and-take collaboration with the director in order to discover, develop, and express the lyrical vocal patterns—the tones, rhythms, tempo, sounds, and silences—suggested by
the progressive absence of conventional grammatical structure and
the progressive intensity of the narrator's emotional state and sensory
experience. Patterns of vocal action can be discovered through the

development of an intellectual and an emotional understanding of the nature of the written text and the narrative persona. Lyrical vocal nuances can be expressed when the performer allows the narrative persona, in a sense, to possess her voice and her body (Kleinau & McHughes, 1980).

In *The Bluest Eye*, Morrison structures the written text such that the arrangements of the print, punctuation, and spacing are a series of visual and literary improvisations. Alternating between the deceptively simple and the seemingly obscure, her writing represents the versatility of the collective African-American voice as a nuanced discursive instrument capable of signifyin' and of expressing a wide range of critical stances, group identities, and individual eccentricities (Berret, 1989). As stated earlier, Morrison's literary improvisations can be read as a poetic representation of the individual's attempt "to exercise personal freedom within the framework of the group" (Bigsby, 1987, p. 177). For in each of her novels, through improvisation and through various other sound structures, she repeatedly symbolizes the contradictory demands of tradition and innovation, and of social mores and personal desire, experienced by individuals who form communities.

Sula

In *Sula*, Morrison's second novel, this motif finds expression through Morrison's creation of dissonance in the persona of her central character. Throughout the novel, Sula struggles with the dissonance between her free-spirited self-image and the whorish image she attains in the eyes of her childhood friend, Nel, and in the eyes of her neighbors. Harsh minglings of clashing sounds are struck as Morrison explores the dissonance in Sula's image, which stems in part from the dissonance in her relationship with Nel—a relationship that from the beginning posited each woman as opposite ends of a madonna/whore polarity, with each finding in the other the missing part of herself (Demetrakopoulos, 1987, p. 53).

As Morrison puts it, Nel and Sula "was girls together" (1973, p. 174), but as women they fall apart, the final split occurring when Sula betrays Nel by sleeping with Nel's husband, Jude. The harmony that previously characterized Sula and Nel's relationship bleeds into dissonance with the advent of Sula's betrayal of Nel and with the gradual realization that while Sula's sexual transgression was wrong, it was also inevitable. Sula and Nel shared everything as girls—boyfriends, secrets, mischief, and private girlhood rituals. So, from Sula's perspective, it is difficult to understand why Jude should be off limits to her. Sula believes that Jude should have been low on the priority of things she and Nel will not share.

The reader's initial assessment of Sula as a wanton seductress falls flat in the face of Sula's pain. For Sula's pain is not the pain of guilt or remorse, but the pain of rejection. Sula's pain is engendered by Nel's inability to understand Sula and, more importantly, by Nel's seeming disbelief in the primacy of their friendship. At the time of the betrayal, Sula was entrapped in a web of sexual freedom "maintained by her usually callous denial of needs other than her own" (Demetrakopoulos, 1987, p. 59). Dissonant chord that she is, Sula's greatest mistake was in recklessly embracing every pleasure, however brief, and in having earned the status of community pariah by acting on the belief that she had nothing to lose. By hurting Nel, she hurt herself. By crossing one too many boundaries, she bounded herself. Because she had alienated her community, news of Sula's death was received as good news.

Shortly before her death, however, Sula confronts Nel with the hypocrisy of her piety, the contradictory nature of Nel's refusal to forgive and be reconciled. Nel does eventually forgive Sula and turns out to be as much a dissonant chord as Sula, as capable of being right and wrong at the same time, and as capable of seeing the good in a supposedly evil friend. The two sides of Sula are so vastly discordant, and in combination so dissonant, that in performance Sula would be best portrayed by two performers working in close proximity to each other: one representing the Sula that emerges initially as a freedom-loving rebel, a sexual wanton, and a mocker of community mores, the other representing the Sula that emerges finally as a trapped and wounded soul who, especially in her last days, wants a reconciliation with her best friend.

Morrison's narrator describes Nel's last words, "We was girls together. . . . O Lord, Sula . . . girl, girl, girlgirlgirl" as a "fine cry—loud and long—[with] no bottom and . . . no top, just circles and circles of sorrow" (1973, p. 174). The structure of Nel's epiphanic cry is typical of Morrison's strategic rendering of high-pitched emotions with repeated and broken phrases that express the oral in print and which remind the reader of the primal bonds of music and emotion embedded in the voice of one soul crying out to another (Berret, 1989). Morrison's tendency to interconnect music with grief is also in line with the ancient African belief that "the spirit will not descend without song" (Koger, 1989, p. 41). Morrison explores the function of music as an emotional release, as a communal mode of discourse, and as an irrevocable tie to the ancestors more explicitly in *Song of Solomon* (Berret, 1989).

Song of Solomon

Song of Solomon is the story of a family whose members live in a state of tension and unhappy adaptation (Berret, 1989). It is the story of Milkman Dead, the son of a Michigan landlord who is respectably married to a doctor's daughter but who has built for himself and his family, nonetheless, a life devoid of love and warmth. In the house of Pilate, his father's bootlegging sister, Milkman finds "wine, laughter, and close family ties, and feels completely happy for the first time in his life" (Berret, 1989).

In this mystical re-vision of African-American folklore and mythology, images of flight are evoked by blues and folksongs that hearken back to slave songs and spirituals which posited the act of flying as a "symbolic opportunity for slaves to free themselves spiritually from the shackles of slavery" (Holloway, 1987, p. 102). Morrison revises the myth of the flying Africans by characterizing Milkman as a mythic hero, a blunderer, who discovers a song "which immortalizes his family and revives in him their ancient faith in flying" (Berret, 1989, p. 276). In Morrison's re-vision, Milkman is a descendant of the legendary tribe of flying Africans, and her multilayered semiotics posit flight as spiritual release, political resistance, escape, and desertion.

Through the tale of Milkman Dead, the reader comes to realize that music can melt the heart, that music can connect family and friends, and that music can create a sense of community. When Reba and Pilate sing

> O Sugarman don't leave me here
> Cotton balls to choke me
> O Sugarman don't leave me here
> Buckra's arms to yoke me. . .

Hagar joins in,

> Sugarman done fly away
> Sugarman done gone
> Sugarman cut across the sky
> Sugarman gone home. . . (Morrison, 1977, p. 49)

and Milkman responds. He loses his breath, he nearly falls into a faint under the weight of his own emotion, and for the first time in his life he experiences with another human being the bittersweet pain of love and loss—and connection. Despite himself, his initial reluctance, and his tendency to hide from Hagar and her desperate love for him, Milkman becomes a member of Pilate's household—that is, until he learns from his father that the family inheritance in gold is being kept in a large sack belonging to Pilate.

Milkman breaks into Pilate's house to steal the sack. But in the sack he finds only rocks and bones, and he is arrested for burglary. After his release, Milkman sets out on a search for the family gold but instead discovers a more valuable inheritance among the family members he finds in Shalimar, Virginia: community, connectedness, and a song that roots him to his past and helps him to come to terms with his present—a song that releases in him the impulse to fly.

As he watches and listens to children playing in a ring game and singing a folk version of the blues song that Pilate sang before, substituting *Solomon* for Sugarman . . . he imagines a stage of childhood that passed him by. As he listens further, he grows homesick and more understanding and forgiving toward the members of his family, especially considering the trials that they have suffered (Berret, 1989, pp. 275–277).

In *Song of Solomon,* the antiphony, the unified (re)interpretations of songs and mythology, and the narrative shifts that move between the past, the present, and, implicitly, the future reflect an African worldview which holds that music is not a diversion or an escape mechanism on the periphery of life, but rather a spiritual and political force woven throughout day-to-day existence "mediated between . . . the living, the ancestors, and the unborn" (Koger, 1989, p. 104). Morrison's message seems to be that when we respond to the call of our ancestors' songs, and when we revive these songs with contemporary aesthetics and attitudes, the images and the words preserved can liberate us and give meaning to our lives.

In order to reflect the oral rhythms of the text, an oral interpretation of *Song of Solomon* should plainly distinguish between the voices of the separate characters and the groups represented in the text, with each performer maintaining the discourse modes, speech patterns, and musical styles Morrison attributes to his or her character. The vocal arrangements should reflect the major throughline of *Song of Solomon* (i.e. that men are more inclined to value individualism and that women tend to value community), and the blues as the overriding musical mode (Wegs, 1982).

So, in addition to the individualized vocal patterns of especially the principal male characters, Milkman, Guitar, and Macon, the story would also lend itself well to the creation of a predominantly female chorus, alternately representing the family units and communities Milkman discovers at home and in Shalimar, and Milkman's African ancestors. The primary choral action would likely begin as a horizontal sound structure, pitting Milkman's voice against the voices of his friends and family members, moving toward a more harmonious contrapuntal structure created by Milkman's interaction with, say, the chorus formed by Reba, Pilate, and Hagar when they sing the "Sugarman" song, and ending with Milkman singing his own "Sugarman/Sugargirl" song, backed by his chorus of ancestors. Consequently, the voice of Milkman would progress from a solitary voice performing virtually alone; to a singular voice playing opposite a chorus of family, community, and ancestors that fluctuates in terms of size and makeup; and finally to a voice compelled by a new understanding of himself, his family, and his origins to speak and sing with the chorus.

Song of Solomon ends with a climax that carries the senses along with Milkman himself as he seems to soar toward magical heights. To bring home the historical and mythical connections between death, flying, and song and to communicate Milkman's grief, anger, and newfound courage, Morrison makes a gradual break away from conventional description and grammar:

> Milkman moved his hand over her chest and stomach, trying to find the place where she might be hit. "Pilate? You okay?". . . "Sing," she said. "Sing a little something for me." Milkman knew no songs, and had no singing voice that anybody would want to hear, but he couldn't ignore the urgency in her voice. . ."Sugargirl don't leave me here/Cotton balls to choke me/Sugargirl don't leave me here/Buckra's arms to yoke me/". . . Now he knew why he loved her so. Without ever leaving the ground, she could fly. . . (1977, pp. 339–340)

into the short, antiphonal tones and rhythms of Milkman's ambiguous escape:

> He stood up.
> "Guitar!" he shouted.
> *Tar tar tar,* said the hills.
> "Over here, brother man! Can you see me?. . . Here I am!"
> *Am am am am,* said the rocks.
> "You want me? Huh? You want my life?"
> *Life life life life. . .*

> . . .Guitar smiled over the barrel of his rifle. "My man," he murmured
> to himself. "My main man". . .

and finally into a sweeping epiphany of sound, feeling, and truth:

> Without wiping away the tears, taking a deep breath, or even bending his
> knees—he [Milkman] leaped . . . and it did not matter which one of them
> would give up his ghost in the killing arms of his brother. For now he knew
> what Shalimar knew: If you surrendered to the air, you could *ride* it. (Morrison,
> 1977, p. 341)

Polyrhythmic, multicolored sounds, words, and phrases that reflect
the musical qualities of black vernacular—short, staccato rhythms mixed
with sweeping, uninterrupted streams of sound—have become
Morrison's usual means of communicating intense emotions. This discursive style resembles the bebop drumming of Max Roach and the
long and short interwoven, chromatic phrases of trumpeter Dizzy
Gillespie (Davis, 1985). It is a style that makes yet another appearance in Toni Morrison's *Tar Baby,* but this time as a means of inflect-
ing the voice of her central character, Son, "social critic and mythical
hero" (Berret, 1989, p. 280).

Tar Baby

Tar Baby is a modern morality tale. The narrative shifts in focus between Jadine, a young black woman brought up in a white bourgeois
household in the Caribbean, and Son, an American exile who "charms
his way into the house of Valerian Street [Jadine's guardian] to rescue
Jadine from what he sees as the hell of an alien culture" (Berret, 1989,
p. 278).

Having earned a degree in art history at the Sorbonne, and having
rejected her black heritage, Jadine is herself an exile—a cultural and
spiritual exile whose limited view of her people and thus herself has
led her to immerse herself in European culture. As an international
model and a student of art history, she attempts to transform herself
into a conventional beauty, by European standards. She sees herself
as being different from and thus better than other black people, and
yet her self-aggrandizement has the paradoxical effect of self-denigra-
tion. Jadine's pretensions provide no release, or relief: the fact of the
matter remains that Jadine is Black.

Jadine's warped view of herself and her people leaves her impervi-
ous to the significance of a number of events that occur—events which
can be interpreted as warnings, or invitations, to leave her self-destructive track. One such warning takes the form of an encounter with

an African woman dressed in yellow, who spits at Jadine outside a Parisian market, and in whom Jadine recognizes the power nonetheless of an authentic beauty free of alterations made to suit Eurocentric tastes. Jadine dismisses her own response to this woman and, in doing so, she dismisses herself. When she comes to the island to visit the Streets for Christmas and to decide whether she should marry her white lover, she misses yet another warning and yet another opportunity to assert her authentic self by trying unsuccessfully to brush off her first of many confrontations with Son—the day he comes into her room uninvited.

Like many of Morrison's characters, Son is a musician. For him, "music means continuity with the past, friendship, the suggestion at least of love and sex, and the art of communicating. . ." (Berret, 1989, p. 278). He plays the piano to underscore the solos of others and he plays for himself. But Son's musical genius is most apparent when he speaks. For when he speaks, "he demonstrates all of the freedom, passion, and rebellion of a jazz virtuoso" (Berret, 1989, p. 278).

Unlike Jadine, Son finds all the trappings and ideology of contemporary culture destructive for black people, and tries his best to rescue Jadine from the products and designs of today's culture. Within the frame of Son's improvisation of the Tar Baby fable, Jadine is a child who has not yet learned to apply life's lessons to the living of her life. She is a tar baby who has, nevertheless, as much a stranglehold on Son as he has on her. She is a tar baby who has rejected the ancient female power and wisdom needed to hold herself together in a culture that has taught her to disintegrate.

In his attempts to reach Jadine, Son falls into polemical rages against contemporary culture and most eloquently and furiously against the idea of black women bearing white babies. But Son turns out to be nearly as eloquent when he helps Jadine to see the beauty that exists deep inside her being—the beauty of the images and sensations that live inside of her:

> "Would you like to know what it's like to be one? A star?" "A movie star?"
> "No, a star star. In the sky. Keep your eyes closed, think about what it feels like to be one." He moved over to her and kissed her shoulder. "Imagine yourself in that dark, all alone in the sky at night. Nobody is around you. You are by yourself, just shining there. You know how a star is supposed to twinkle? We say twinkle because that is how it looks, but when a star feels itself, it's not a twinkle, it's more like a throb. Star throbs. Over and over and over. Like this. Stars just throb and throb and throb and sometimes, when they can't

throb anymore, when they can't hold it anymore, they fall out of the sky (Morrison, 1981, p. 214)

Son wants Jadine to see more than the planes and angles too many art history classes have taught her to see. In a voice as seductive and lonely, plaintive and painful, melodious and rhythmic as a Miles Davis trumpet solo, he helps her to liberate herself from the strictly visual so that she can learn to "integrate her senses into a wholeness of perception" (Berret, 1989, p. 279).

A man of complex and varied emotions and opinions, the voice of the seductive, smitten Son is a world apart from the voice of the raging turbulence residing in the mind of the Son who denounces all the alienating contrivances of contemporary culture:

That was the sole lesson of their world: how to make waste, how to make machines that made more waste, how to make wasteful products, how to talk waste, how to study waste, how to design waste, how to cure people who were sickened by waste so that they could be well enough to endure it, how to mobilize waste, legalize waste and how to despise the culture that lived in cloth houses and shit on the ground far away from where they ate (Morrison, 1981, p. 203).

Literary critic Anthony J. Berret (1989) writes that:

The repetitions and the rhythms in this passage amplify Son's rhetorical polemic against modern culture, but they also create overtones of ritual incantation which harmonize with the primitive ideal expressed in "cloth houses". . . Dial Africa . . . Son [Son's diatribe] resembles the improvisations of John Coltrane on such albums as Transition and achieves the same mixture [of rhetoric and ritual] and adds other techniques comparable to Coltrane's music: abrasive diction, verbal links and coinages, and prolonged effusions without pause or conventional logic. (p. 280)

Son's speeches emphasize the strongest of Morrison's messages. Like the music of a jazz revolutionary, they refute the reader's initial appraisal of Son as a good-for-nothing vagabond and reveal in him fierce intelligence and artistic ability. Son's speeches are also heavy with righteous anger and pride; they appear in the text at moments of tension and crisis, much like the songs that pour forth from the mouths of performers in musical theatre productions. For these reasons, I am suggesting here that in an oral interpretation of Tar Baby, Son's discourses would be most effectively staged as jazz arias underscored with revolutionary bebop inspired by the likes of Miles Davis and John Coltrane but composed to suit the specific diction, tones, and rhythms of Son's speech patterns. The goal would be to underscore Son's messages by achieving a co-equal relationship between the oral interpretation and the music. This is an aesthetic reminiscent of the rhythmic performances of beat poets and musicians in the Black Arts movement of the 1960s, and of jazz poets like Ntozake Shange (1972) who have carried on the aesthetic.

The syncopated rhythms and the inventive harmonic variations of bebop became popular in the early 1940s (Davis, 1985), but the roots of bebop also lie deep in the rhythmic orientations of traditional African music (Benston, 1976). Bebop musicians set out to revolutionize the functions of their instruments, to reinvent the basic blues impulse in black music, and to build an intellectual artistic culture evolving out of a contemporary, urban black fluency with the cultural symbols of Western civilization. Bebop is 'roots' music because of its African origins and because of its contemporary initiation of a true cultural advance.

Beloved and *Jazz*

In Morrison's last two novels, *Beloved* and *Jazz,* the cultural and temporal shifts embodied in historical analyses of the origins of bebop are strongly mirrored in the author's progressive use of the literary jazz aesthetic. Facilitated by the dynamics of memory and re-memory (Morrison, 1984), the informing perspective in *Beloved,* for instance, shifts between the turn of the century, antebellum, and the Middle Passage. The narrative is constructed such that the reader witnesses Sethe's many returns to a past she would rather forget, as well as the changes that these excursions have wrought in her life—including, most significantly, the appearance of the ghost of her slain daughter.

Conventional literary devices meant to ease the reader along from one scene to the next—e.g. logical cause-and-effect patterns, explicit transitions, chapters named for the character whose turn it is to speak—are absent. As the narrative shifts from the present to the past and then back to the present again, the text takes on a nonlinear structure that may at first appear to be without logic or design. But Morrison's logic is born of her desire to prevent a "cool and distant acceptance of data" (Morrison, 1984, p. 387). Her organizing principle is the jazz aesthetic, which allows the character and the narrative persona to freely move between various streams of consciousness inspired and linked by images that trigger memories of the past and inevitable returns to the present.

In *Beloved*, scenes and narrative perspectives shift frequently. "Sethe's story—her life under slavery, the conception and care of her children in the most dire of circumstances, her escape and her liberation, and her desperately violent and loving act of infanticide" (Hirsch, 1990, p. 428)—is told from a multitude of positions and by more than one character. Sethe's memories are layered in with the memories of Beloved, Baby Suggs, Paul D, and Denver, whose alternating presences are invoked through the process of re-memory that Sethe undertakes to come to terms with her past. Sethe's memories are triggered by contact with sights, sounds, and other sensations that remind Sethe of her past:

> Nothing else would be in her mind. . . Then something. The splash of water, the sight of her shoes and stockings awry on the path where she had flung them; or Here Boy lapping in the puddle near her feet, and suddenly there was Sweet Home rolling, rolling, rolling out before her eyes (Morrison, 1987, p. 6).

The phrasing of Sethe's narrative reflects the rhythm of Morrison's improvisational style. The repetitive and emphatic description of "Sweet Home rolling, rolling, rolling out before her eyes" (p. 6) amplifies the narration while moving the reader into the following scene, without much further ado. Barely a moment later, the reader finds himself or herself—and Sethe—confronted with the arrival of Paul D, "the last of the Sweet Home men" (1987, p. 6).

In order to retain this effect, an oral and physical representation of Sethe's scenic and temporal transitions from Cincinnati, Ohio, in 1873 to Sweet Home in the days of slavery, would do well to allow the performer to stay put as the sights and sounds of the plantation roll out before her, and around her. Staging of this sort is, like Morrison's text, in direct opposition to conventional staging in which the director tends to establish changes in time and location by having the performers move from station to station.

Moving from pre- and post-Civil War Ohio in *Beloved* to the Harlem Renaissance in *Jazz,* Morrison retains the devices of re-memory and antiphony that served to make *Beloved* a polyrhythmic, nonlinear narrative—episodic by nature, cinematic in scope. In both novels, the narrative shifts from scene to scene, and from perspective to perspective, as one moment's sight or sound immediately calls to mind another time or place, and as one character's perspective is redressed by another character's opposing or more detailed perspective.

Antiphony in *Beloved* occurs between characters, reaching its peak when Sethe finally acknowledges that Beloved is the spirit of her dead child. Sethe sings the call of rapturous motherhood:

> BELOVED, she my daughter. She mine. See. She come back to me of her own free will and I don't have to explain a thing. I didn't have the time to explain before because it had to be done quick. . .But my love was tough and she back now. . . (1987, p. 210)

And Beloved responds:

> I AM BELOVED and she is mine. I see her take flowers away from leaves she puts them in a round basket . . . I would help her but the clouds are in the way how can I say things that are pictures I am not separate from her. . . her face is my own and I want to be there in the place where her face is and to be looking at it too a hot thing All of it is now it is always now there will never be a time when I am not crouching and watching others who are crouching too (1987, p. 210).

Both mother and daughter make the claim of ownership, but Beloved's response takes us as far back as the slaveship, where many lives were lost on the middle passage from Africa to the Americas. Beloved's voice is that of her own and of the multitudes of Black people whose bodies were painfully crouched in the hulls of ships. Beloved's speech patterns are not quite human; her thoughts are expressed in broken phrases that shift, like Morrison's narrative, from past to present to future. In *Jazz*, antiphony is but one of the structural devices Morrison uses to create a comprehensive literary jazz aesthetic. In *Jazz*, the narrator is a soloist who performs the call to which the other characters respond. She is alternately a new world griot and a neighborhood gossip telling the story of Violet and Joe Trace. The dialogues that develop between Violet and Alice are constructed as duets, and ultimately as a dissonant relationship that arises out of the story's own peculiar logic. Harsh minglings of clashing sounds are struck when Alice befriends the crazy woman who tried to deface her niece's corpse. Dissonant chords are also struck when we learn that Joe Trace killed Alice's niece in order to preserve his errant love for her.

And dissonant chords likewise sound in the voice of this unnamed persona whose bebop riffs present a soundscape of the City streets below in this strange place and time—the Harlem Renaissance, the Jazz Age, when black people were idolized as musicians and at the same time denied the full expression of our humanity:

I'm crazy about the City. Daylight slants like a razor cutting the buildings in half. In the top half I see looking faces and it's not easy to tell which are people, which the work of stonemasons. Below is shadow where any blasé thing takes place: clarinets and lovemaking, fists and the voices of sorrowful women. A city like this one makes me dream tall and feel in on things (Morrison, 1992a, p. 7).

This inexplicably unnamed storyteller is perhaps one of the strongest narrative personas to ever tell a tale. From the first "Sth" (p. 3), her onomatopoeic tones, her syncopated rhythms, and her variegated phrasing effectively communicate the story's central conflict—and with much attitude:

Sth, I know that woman. She used to live with a flock of birds on Lenox Avenue. Know her husband, too. He fell for an eighteen-year-old girl with one of those deepdown, spooky loves that made him so sad and happy he shot her just to keep the feeling going. (Morrison, 1992a, p. 3)

The tone color and the incessant beat of her speech, along with the dissonant thematic issues and the bird motifs imbedded here and throughout the story, allude to the jazz aesthetic at work in both the structure and the substance of the narrative. Her bebop stylings pay homage to the legendary jazzman Charlie Parker and reveal the often tense and sometimes tragic situations of the three women affected by a man who attempted to assuage his pain by doing the unthinkable.

In the insular world of jazz musicians, and in the public arena, Charlie Parker was known as "Bird." In the jazz vernacular of the 1920s, "the [often marginalized] girl singer was called names like sparrow, wren, warbler, chirp, [and] regardless of her talent she first had to fill the bill as a beautiful, charming, gracious, delicate, softspoken ornament" (Gossett & Johnson, 1980, p. 66). Like the star-struck fans and the wealthy patron who idolized Bird to the point of destruction, Joe Trace idolized his young lover, Dorcas, and killed her when he could no longer keep this bird locked in a gilded cage, when she could no longer fit the bill as his own beautiful and gracious ornament, and when she could no longer bolster Joe's wounded and insecure ego. At the moment of her death, Dorcas's speech patterns take on the heightened tones and rhythms of an aria—a jazz aria:

He's here. Oh, look. God. He's crying. Am I falling? Why am I falling? Why am I falling? Acton is holding me up but I am falling anyway. Heads are turning to look where I am falling. It's dark and now it's light. I am lying on a bed. Somebody is wiping sweat from my forehead, but I am cold, so cold. . . (Morrison, 1992a, p. 192)

Truly, the strongest oral interpretation of *Jazz* has been performed by Toni Morrison (1992b) herself. In her recorded reading, Morrison's voice captures all the tone colours, rhythms, and nuance suggested by her jazz-inflected text. The volume and the pitch of her voice rises and falls with an exactness that distinguishes each character and emphasizes each turning point. Her utterances and her pauses are timed with a keen sense of rhythm and duration. The result is an extended beat poem, at times talk-sung, and in all ways pleasing to the ear. The result evokes in the listener a clear sense of the emotion, the images, the characters, the places, and the ideas Morrison must have imagined when she wrote this bittersweet love song.

Conclusion

Into each of her novels, from *The Bluest Eye* to *Jazz*, Toni Morrison works images and patterns of music, especially those associated with the free speech and casual intimacy of jazz. By this "fusion of artistic forms . . . she enriches the novel itself by bringing to it the influence of a music that is alive and social and that attempts a spontaneous and reciprocal conversation with its listeners" (Berret, 1989, p. 283).

The black aesthetics and the "presentational forms" (Kleinau & McHughes, 1980, pp. 9–10) operating in the novels of Toni Morrison—the literary improvisations, the dissonant characterizations, the call-and-response patterns, the nonlinear narrative shifts, the rich and evocative language, the strong narrative personas, and the ritual and mythic patterns—validate the integral role oral and musical traditions play in the lives and literature of Black Americans. These devices guarantee that no matter what they take from the process of textual analysis and performance, performers and their audiences cannot remain passive (Koger, 1989). Nor can they become so "caught up completely in the story being told . . . [or] so submerged in the emotional experience that they lose sight of the structure and the style of the text" (Kleinau & McHughes, 1980, p. 180). With the guidance of a skillful and culturally literate director, every participant—interpreter and perceiver—can become actively immersed "in a communal activity that 'provides relief and release for all involved'" (Koger, 1989, p. 111).

References

Benston, K. (1976). *Baraka: The renegade and the mask*. New Haven, Yale University Press.

Berret, A. (1989). Toni Morrison's literary jazz, *CLA Journal, 32*, 267–283.

Bigsby, C.W.E. (1987). Improvising American: Ralph Ellison and the paradox of form. In K.W. Benston, (Ed.), *Speaking for you: The vision of Ralph Ellison* Washington DC: Howard University Press.

Davis, N. (1985). *Writings in jazz*. Scottsdale, AZ: Gorsuch Scarisbrick.

Demetrakopoulos, S. (1987). Sula and the primacy of woman-to-woman bonds. In S. Demetrakopoulos & K.F.C. Holloway (Eds.). *New dimensions of spirituality: A biracial and bicultural reading of the novels of Toni Morrison* (pp. 51–66). New York: Greenwood.

Dianond, B., & Moore, M. (1995). *Multicultural literacy: Mirroring the reality of the classroom*. White Plains, NY: Longman.

Gossett, H., & Johnson, C. (1980). Jazzwomen: They're mostly singers and piano players: only a horn player or two: hardly any drummers. *Heresies, 3*, 65–69.

Hirsch, M. (1990). Maternal narratives: "Cruel enough to stop the blood". In H.L. Gates Jr. (Ed.). *Reading black, reading feminist* (pp. 413–430). New York: Meridian.

Holloway. K. (1987). The lyrics of salvation. In S. Demetrakopoulos, S. & K.F.C. Holloway (Eds.). *New Dimensions in spirituality: A biracial and bicultural reading of the novels of Toni Morrison* (pp. 101–114). New York: Greenwood.

Kleinau, M. & Hughes, J. (1980). *Theatres for literature: A practical aesthetics for group interpretation*. Sherman Oaks, CA: Alfred.

Koger, A.K. (1989). Jazz form and jazz function: An analysis of Unfinished Women Cry in No Man's Land While a Bird Dies in a Gilded Cage, *MELUS, 16*, 99–111.

Moffett, J. & Wagner, B.J. (1992). *Student-centered language arts, K–12*. Portsmouth, NH: Boynton/Cook.

Morrison, T. (1970). *The bluest eye*. New York: Pocket Books.

Morrison, T. (1973). *Sula*. New York: Plume.

Morrison, T. (1977). *Song of Solomon*. New York: Signet.

Morrison, T. (1981). *Tar baby*. New York: Plume.

Morrison, T. (1984). Memory, creation, and writing. *Thought*, *59*, 385–390.

Morrison, T. (1987). *Beloved*. New York: Knopf.

Morrison, T. (1992a). *Jazz*. New York: Knopf.

Morrison, T. (1992b). *Jazz* [cassette]. Random House Audio Publishing, RH/213.

Shange, N. (1972). *Nappy edges*. New York: St Martin's Press.

Wegs, J. (1982). Toni Morrison's *Song of Solomon*: A blues song, *Essays in Literature*, *9*, 211–223.

Apache Indian's Syncretic Music and the Re-presentation of South Asian Identities: A Case Study of a Minority Artist

Nina Asher

Introduction

[I]dentity is never an a priori, nor a finished product; it is only ever the problematic process of access to an image of totality.

(H.K. Bhabha, 1994, *The Location of Culture*)

The issues of identity and self-representation have become central to my life as a graduate student at Teachers College, Columbia University, and an Asian-Indian woman in New York City. For instance, I realize that here I am part of a "minority population," that I have been perceived (quite incorrectly) as speaking English with a British accent, and that I am now used to the notion of thinking of myself as a "person of color." As I reflect on the broader contextual factors impinging on me, I negotiate and articulate new interpretations of my identity. Identity and representation, then, are determined by more than just external societal factors but also by an individual's internal sense-making of and response to them.

This process of negotiation also occurs between "minority" communities and the larger "dominant" culture. For instance, my interaction and involvement with the South Asian intellectual and activist communities in New York have brought home for me how, in countries like the United States, immigrant communities and peoples of color struggle to define, express, and locate themselves within the larger context. In particular, young people from these communities find themselves grappling with the differences they encounter between the contexts of their homes and the larger society, as they attempt to define their identities and represent themselves—witness Sengupta's (1996) article, in *The New York Times*, entitled "To Be Young Indian and Hip: Hip-hop Meets Hindi Pop as a New Generation of South Asians Finds Its Own Groove" (pp. CY 1, 11).

Minority cultures distinguish themselves from the mainstream or dominant culture by employing a range of such strategies as adopting particular modes of dress and cuisine, and generating their own literature, art, music and film.[1] They also organize and engage in activism around specific issues. For instance, during the 1990s, the South Asian community (comprised largely of the Asian-Indian, Bangladeshi, and Pakistani populations) in New York has witnessed the emergence of such organizations as Sakhi (a women's group addressing domestic violence within the South Asian community) and SALGA (the South Asian Lesbian and Gay Association), and such publications as *SAMAR* (South Asian Magazine for Action and Reflection). In addition, filmmakers, artists, and writers of the South Asian diaspora have raised issues relevant to the community in their works. For instance, Gurinder Chada, a British filmmaker of South Asian descent, focuses on issues pertaining to South Asian women in Britain, particularly intergenerational and interminority relationships, in her film *Bhaji on the Beach*. Manuel (1995) notes, "South Asian migrants have been sources for some of the most creative postmodern artworks, from Salman Rushdie's *Satanic Verses* to Srinivasan Krishna's Toronto-based film *Masala*" (p. 235).

Similarly, one who considers performance as a means of negotiating identity can interpret music as a form of expression and self-representation. In this article, I focus on the music of Apache Indian, a British-born artist of Asian-Indian descent, as an example of performance reflecting the dynamic process by which young people of the South Asian diaspora negotiate identities.[2] Apache Indian (né Steven Kapur) combines bhangra—a form of folk music and dance from the state of Punjab in northern India—with reggae and dancehall music to create his particular form of syncretic music.

In the sections that follow, I provide an historical perspective on syncretic forms of South Asian music, particularly British bhangra (bhangra originating from Britain), in light of the colonial relationship between South Asia and Britain. I then present an analysis of Apache's music and the messages it conveys. I interpret and discuss the evolution of this music in light of the literature on identity and representation of minority populations. In doing so, I focus on the following three issues: How does syncretic music serve as a site of resistance and self-representation for marginalized peoples? How does it enable them to shift the margins and relocate themselves within the context of the dominant culture? And what are some of the paradoxes inherent in this process of negotiating new identities and representations?

Syncretic Music of the South Asian Diaspora: An Historical Perspective

It is useful to contextualize the history of British bhangra within the larger relationship of South Asian migrants to Britain. Observers have noted that South Asians in Britain have typically filled gaps in the lower orders of the labor market and have been treated as an underclass (Clarke, Peach, & Vertovec, 1990; Robinson, 1990), whereas in the United States, until recently, they have been characterized by high levels of education and high status occupations (Clarke et al., 1990; Glazer, 1980; Lorch, 1992).

Further, Clarke et al. (1990, pp. 21–22) have noted that institutionalized racism and low status in Britain's class structure have been impediments to the social mobility of British South Asians and, possibly, have led to greater political participation on their part, as compared to the relatively affluent South Asians in other countries.[3] Given this historical location of South Asians among Britain's underclass, it is understandable that syncretisms in British South Asian music reflect, in this postcolonial period, alliances with other minority communities.

While various syncretic South Asian music forms have emerged in recent years, bhangra is the most popular and perhaps, therefore, has been the subject of considerable scholarly scrutiny (see Banerji & Baumann, 1990; Ganti, 1995; Gopinath, 1995; Manuel, 1995).[4] For instance, Gopinath (1995, p. 307) has noted that bhangra was brought to Britain by Punjabi immigrants in the 1950s and 1960s and became a cultural marker of such Punjabi enclaves as areas of London, Birmingham, and Manchester. The early practitioners of bhangra in Britain were mostly middle-aged, first-generation male immigrants who saw the music as a means of constructing a shared notion of "Asian-ness."[5] Bhangra, therefore, became a staple at Hindu, Muslim, and Sikh social and religious functions but remained confined to working-class South Asian communities until the late 1970s. Gopinath has noted further that at this time bhangra groups began incorporating such "western" sounds as keyboards and synthesizers, and by the mid-1980s it was enormously popular among young, British-born South Asians. The late 1980s saw thousands of young South Asians attending bhangra concerts in London and other cities, and more recently, bhangra has incorporated such genres as reggae, rap, techno and house. According to Manuel (1995),

> The 1980s and early 1990s have witnessed the emergence of 'bhangramuffin' substyles, synthesising Punjabi texts and folk rhythms with Jamaican reggae-dancehall-raggamuffin declamation style, and also incorporating elements from rap and Hindi film music (p. 236).[6]

Today, British bhangra represents a range of styles, from those that maintain it in the more traditional form, to the more recent ones that have synthesized the original form into new, distinct sounds. In fact,

> bhangra has become the locus of a diasporic South Asian youth culture, with young South Asians outside of Britain adapting British bhangra to their own local contexts of Toronto, Vancouver, Port-of-Spain, New York, Delhi and Bombay" (Gopinath, 1995, p. 308).

Syncretic bhangra music, then, represents multiple interpretations of identity among the youth of the South Asian diasporic community.

Accordingly, although British bhangra might have originated spontaneously out of a simple desire to perform and hear the music of one's homeland, in effect, it has contributed to the evolution of hybrid cultures and the creation of new locales of expression and identification. That is to say, although the early exponents of bhangra in Britain were not consciously attempting to establish a location from which to develop new musical styles as expressions of resistance to the dominant culture, they provided a base for such syncretic styles of today as the one Apache has popularized. These more recent styles are clearly "hybrid," in that they synthesize the original music form with elements of music borrowed from other minority cultures. Or, as Bhabha (1994) observed, they provide the "interstitial passage between fixed identifications [which] opens up the possibility of a cultural hybridity"

(p. 4), [and this] "hybrid cultural space . . . forms contingently, disjunctively in the inscription of signs of cultural memory and sites of political agency" (p. 7). These syncretic forms of music draw on histories of oppression and marginalization, hold popular appeal for young people in diverse locations, and exemplify the porousness of cultures, even as they emerge as sites of resistance. Further, it is the discursive, interactive process through which the individual artist struggles to give expression to new interpretations of culture and related identifications, even as s/he negotiates with and in the very social context s/he is attempting to change. British bhangra, then, serves as a location from which South Asian youth can represent themselves and negotiate new identities, by means of their alliance with other marginalized populations.

Interpreting the notion of "location" more literally, the section on bhangra music at an establishment as commercial as Tower Records, in New York City, is located under "dance music," rather than being clubbed with other "international/world music." Bhangra, then, is now recognized as a new, legitimate form of dance music in the United States. This acceptance indicates that the process of accommodation is not unidirectional, with only the immigrant peoples adjusting to the host culture. Rather, syncretic bhangra serves as a site of political agency, exemplifying how immigrant and other minority communities rewrite the mainstream culture by creating new, hybrid spaces of expression and self-representation.

Apache's Music: A Site of Resistance and a Vehicle of Relocation

Apache, located as he is in the reggae section at Tower Records, pursues more deliberate and conscious efforts than his predecessors to create a new kind of music and redefine the identity of the Asian Indian in Britain. In the following paragraphs, I discuss the messages his lyrics convey; the political implications of the syncretisms he employs and the way he is marketed; and the direct and indirect impact his music has on the rewriting of the identities of South Asian youth.

I was first introduced to Apache's music in Toronto in January of 1993. At that time, in a review for SAMAR (Asher, 1993), I wrote that I was "struck by the unmistakable reggae sound and the blend of Hindi, Punjabi, and Jamaican patois. The following lines from his latest single *Arranged Marriage* are a good example of Apache's evoca-

tive use of Jamaican patois combined with his easy command of Hindi
and Punjabi:

> So next time you pass a' see Apache,
> Just say *badhaiya* (congratulations) to congratulate me.
> But if me yard you a pass and you want greet me
> Bring the *laddoo*, the *besan*, and the *barfee* [names of Indian treats]" (p. 46).

Similar syncretisms appear in his more recent album, *Make Way for
the Indian* (Apache Indian, 1995). In the title track, Apache has appropriated the persona of the Jamaican "rude boy" and alludes to
himself as the "rude-raggamuffin-Indian."[7] Further, in the song entitled "Boba" (Apache Indian, 1995, track 3) he talks about discovering "the new music a' the bhangra-ragga" in England. These examples
indicate the fluidity with which Apache transgresses geographic, linguistic, and cultural boundaries through the medium of music.

Paying closer attention to his lyrics, I began to analyze their political implications. In "Chok There" (Apache Indian, 1993, side A, track
2) he says,

> Chok there! See me face upon the television.
> Chok there! Hear me voice upon the radio station.
> . . . .
> Me bring a bran new style upon the island,
> Fe the black a fe white I know a fe the Indian,
> So each and everyone come follow fashion.
> Chok there, dip your knee cork out your bottom.
> Chok there, everyone in a the bhangra fashion.

In these lines, Apache refers both to employing the media to make
himself visible and audible to the larger society and declares it his
mission to forge a "bran new style" meant for everyone, not only
Asian Indians or other minorities, but those of the dominant race as
well. In "Come Follow Me" (Apache Indian, 1993, side A, track 8)
Apache reiterates, somewhat defiantly, this message of crossing borders and being open to other cultures:

> *Chaar, paanch, chhay* [four, five, six]
> Come after one, two, three, . . .
> But if you can't understand the words of Apache,
> You better stick to your *Ingrayjee* [English] . . . .

In both these songs Apache talks of replacing existing Anglocentric
norms with new ones, determined by him as a representative of a
once silent, invisible group. And through this very act, Apache suc-

ceeds in creating a cultural reality which pushes the margins and attempts to open up a new space for Asian Indians, other South Asians, and symbolically, other minority communities from which they can represent themselves as members of the larger British society.

The following excerpts from Apache's more recent songs "Ansa Dat" and "Back Up" (Apache Indian, 1995, tracks 6, 8) reflect his continued concern with issues of representation of and voice for marginalized peoples:

Me have a question for all de youth them:
Who dem a follow? . . . who set the trend?
Ansa dat. Why you justa be copycat? (Ansa Dat)

Me no take back no chat,
. . . .
If a boy diss me, I be right after.
Long time me watch you, a' you a' watch me,
You a' push up yo'self in a society.
Is the program in a' the community. (Back Up)

These lyrics reflect the recognition of years of oppression and silencing experienced by peoples of color, and the need to act for change, for self-recovery. Rejecting a passive compliance with existing norms established by a dominant white culture, Apache urges young people of color to think and act for themselves. While one finds a continuity in the themes reflected in Apache's songs, one also finds differences worth examining. A comparative analysis of the titles and cover inserts of his 1993 and 1995 albums reveals how the artist is negotiating new identities through his medium.

Apache's stage name and the title of his 1993 album, *No Reservations,* can be construed as a play on words hinting at the historical confusion that first invited and then legitimized the misidentification of Native Americans as Asian Indians.[8] Implied here is the casualness with which various peoples of color get lumped together, labeled as "minorities" and "immigrants" and so on, and treated as mutually interchangeable, thereby rendering their particular identities inconsequential. Or, as Spivak (1993) puts it, "Subterfuges of nomenclature that are by now standard have almost . . . obliterated the fact that that name [Indian] lost some specificity in the first American genocide" (p. 54).

Further, one can interpret the title *No Reservations* as a statement of the artist's intention to lower the barriers and transgress boundaries imposed by a dominant white population. Crossing borders by blending reggae and bhangra, and incorporating references to Native American peoples, Apache defines and uses new spaces of representation and resistance as an icon of marginalized peoples of color.

The title of the 1995 album, *Make Way for the Indian*, pushes the margins even further. It appears to be both an unqualified demand for what Apache claims is the rightful space and deserved recognition of Indians in a white-dominated Britain, and a redefinition of what it is to be "Indian." The tracks on *Make Way*, like the ones on *No Reservations,* combine Hindi and Punjabi lyrics and South Asian themes with reggae and dancehall music, but they rely more heavily on reggae and less so on bhangra. By making this shift, Apache, who has identified himself as a "proud Indian" (Gopinath, 1995, p. 312), writes his "bhangra-ragga" music into Indian culture and adds a new facet to an Indian identity. This rewriting of identity also appears in the contrasting images of himself that Apache presents on the cover inserts of the two albums.

The five images of Apache on the fold-out cover of the *No Reservations* audiotape focus less on the face than on the overall bodily posture. Apache, bedecked in gold jewelry, sporting a "fade" (a razored style with patterns cut into the hair), and dressed in Rastafarian colors of red, gold and green, looks into the camera almost defiantly. At first glance, he resembles a "rapper," and even at second glance, one would probably not identify him as an Asian Indian. The single definite indicator is the flag of India in the background of the first of the five images. This cover also presents a collage of images that represent Jamaica and India.

In the five images on the cover insert of the *Make Way* compact disc, Apache is foregrounded, his face now the focus. He is clad in a black fishnet shirt, with a black bandana covering the top of his somewhat straggly hair. His visage—intent, thoughtful, absorbed, with the eyes never looking directly into the camera—gives the impression that this recording is a matter and a moment of great import. Gone is the defiant rapper, replaced by a more subdued, reflective persona.

These 1995 images contrast starkly with the ones on the cover of his 1993 album, and as expressions of representation, the two sets convey different messages. The earlier set, from the *No Reservations* album, established Apache's identification with the West Indian population in Britain. The subtext is a statement of the alliance of one minority community with another. These images, along with the lyrics, seem to speak to the need for various minority communities to

cross borders and find common sites of resistance in order to represent themselves. By contrast, the 1995 images do not portray the
"rapper": Apache's hair is longer, the Rastafarian colors are gone,
and the jewelry is limited to a couple of bracelets and rings as opposed to several chains, rings and bracelets in the earlier set. It is
almost as if Apache himself is "making way for the Indian." The double
entendre here lies in his representation of "Indian" as projected by the
persona in these images, and in his demand of Britain, Indians in
Britain, and his audiences elsewhere to accept this hybrid music and
the new images as Indian. The consistency of the sounds and the
themes of his music, coupled with the new look and title, underscores
Apache's rewriting of an Indian identity and his message of alliance
with other minority cultures.

According to Bhabha (1994),

> Each time the encounter with identity occurs at the point at which something
> exceeds the frame of the image, it eludes the eye, evacuates the self as site of
> identity . . . leaves a resistant trace, a stain of the subject, a sign of resis-
> tance. . . . [T]he demand for identification becomes, primarily, a response
> to other questions of signification and desire, culture and politics" (pp. 49–
> 50).

Apache's "encounters with identity," as expressed by the two albums discussed above, serve as efforts to expand—perhaps even break—
the frame within which the image of "Indian" has historically been
contained, at least in Britain. Furthermore, Apache directs his message of resistance not only to those representative of the dominant
culture, but also to those on the margins, making them accountable
for their agency in re-locating themselves. Also implied here is the lack
of fixity and the blurring of boundaries that this effort entails, as the
artist himself makes a shift in representation and identification from
one album to the next. This notion of lack of fixity can be further
extrapolated to the artist herself/himself—that it is not the individual
artist who is the site of resistance, but rather that it is the "traces" and
"stains" resulting from the endeavors of such agents which serve as
the signifiers in the process of cultural and political change.

Apache's resistance to existing patterns of domination stops short
of addressing gender issues; in fact, critical perspectives on these issues are noticeably absent in his work. For instance, the following
lines from his song, "Arranged Marriage" (Apache Indian, 1993, side
B, track 2), seem to perpetuate the objectification of women:

Say the Don *Raja* [king] me want a Princess,
Me wan gal a fe me Don *Rani* [queen],
Me wan gal dress up in a *sari* [Indian garment for women],
Me wan gal say *sohni lagthi* [pretty-looking],
Me wan gal sweet like *jalaybee* [an Indian treat].

If Apache intends these words to be a disparaging commentary on the secondary status to which women have been historically relegated, his jaunty song fails to convey that intention.

Shifting the Margins: Struggles and Paradoxes in Negotiating Identities and Representation

Marginality: who names? whose fringes? . . . Identity: the singular naming of a person, a nation, a race, has undergone a reversal of values. Effacing it used to be the only means of survival for the colonized and the exiled; naming it today often means declaring solidarity among the hyphenated people of the Diaspora. . . . Identity is a way of re-departing. . . . It is hardly surprising then that when identity is doubled, tripled, multiplied across time (generations) and space (cultures), when differences keep on blooming within despite the rejections from without, she dares, by necessity. She dares mix; she dares cross the borders to introduce into language (verbal, visual, musical) everything monologism has repressed. . . . The challenge is thus: how can one re-create without re-circulating domination? (Minh-ha, 1990, 328–329)

In trying to understand how disenfranchised minority communities establish and declare solidarity, I wonder about the strategies they use and how they implement them. What are some of the struggles minority communities encounter in re-departing, in re-locating themselves across cultures and borders, in reinventing themselves? How are their acts of resistance paradoxical? As Cornel West (1990) noted, cultural critics and artists who choose to align themselves with disenfranchised peoples are simultaneously progressive and co-opted because they function within the very power structures they are attempting to change.

I analyzed Apache's commercial, political, and cultural success in light of these issues and questions. What challenges has Apache met in crossing borders? How has he created spaces for re-departure? In what ways has he re-created patterns of domination?

Success and Selling Out: A Paradox

Apache's success has been well-documented. As Magic Mike, a South Asian DJ in New York, remarked, Apache's song, "Boom Shack-a-lack" was fifth on the "western" charts in Britain, not just the bhangra or reggae charts (Ganti, 1995), and in India, Apache has played to packed audiences (Gopinath, 1995). Zuberi (1995) writes, "But now, Apache Indian is on the BBC's primetime Top of the Pops, and though he is something of a novelty, he has definitely 'opened doors.' Brit Asian music culture has entered the nation's cathode ray consciousness" (p. 36).

Success of this kind, particularly by a minority artist in a highly competitive industry, implies both immense popular appeal and a shrewd marketing approach. The paradox I highlight here is that while the marketing and publicity strategies underlying Apache's success have worked to open doors, they are not entirely unproblematic and may actually serve to work against some of the issues Apache's music addresses.

When researching the evolution of Apache's music for the review I wrote for *SAMAR* (Asher, 1993), I learned how the musician and his music were being packaged and marketed. Drawing from the "bio" I received from the publicity representatives at Island Records, I wrote,

> According to the "bio," Apache . . . grew up in a multi-racial neighborhood . . . learning Jamaican patois at school, hearing English on the radio, and then going home and hearing Indian [sic]. . . . I gather from it that the 25 year old Apache grew up in the town of Hansworth where (t)he pot started stewing. . . .—a town known for the reggae of Steel Pulse and the multi-racial configurations of bands like UB40. . . . where East and West Indians grow up side by side hearing East Indian film music and its western incarnation, bhangra, compete with the boom-boom of reggae (p. 46).

Troubled by the glib distortions used to highlight Apache's multiracial context, I continued:

> As any South Asian knows, there is no language such as "Indian." Besides, bhangra—originally a Punjabi folk dance—is described in the "bio" as the "western incarnation" of popular Indian film music, and even more mystifying is this quote attributed to Apache: "Bhangra comes from England and combines the more traditional East Indian music of artists like Ravi Shankar with western sounds. . . ." Misinformation of this kind is particularly disturbing in this instance, where the artist himself is representative of . . . diverse cultures and, therefore, is more likely to be able to convince relatively uninformed audiences that statements like this are indeed true! This kind of marketing approach serves only to sell the currently fashionable product of "multiculturalism" by building on existing stereotypes instead of unfolding the complex layers of the so-called "minority cultures" and adding depth to current knowledge in the West (p. 46).

In addition, Manuel (1995), who refers to Apache as the "Punjabi-Birmiyite rapper," notes that

> Kapur's lyrics are light rather than profound and on the whole are not de-
> voted to any particular explicit message. . . . Indeed, the concept of "India" in
> Kapur's lyrics is consistently and self-consciously shallow, reduced to jumbled
> lists of familiar foodstuffs, personages, and stray Hindi and Punjabi phrases,
> garbled together with Jamaican patwa and intertextual invocations of other
> DJs (p. 236).[9]

The shallowness of Apache's evocation of India, and the misinfor-
mation peddled in the pursuit of publicity are certainly troubling and
underscore the point that his success is based, in part, on his "selling
out." The deleterious effects of such shallowness notwithstanding,
however, Apache's success is proof that his music provides young
South Asians born or raised in Britain, America, and elsewhere with a
meaningful form of expression and identification. Besides, this same
marketing strategy has contributed to Apache's visibility on British
television, which suggests an audience that now includes members of
the dominant culture.

The Appeal of Popular Culture
In analyzing Apache's international success, one must understand its
timing and the popular appeal it holds for today's youth. As noted
earlier, the immigrant generation brought bhangra to the Punjabi neighborhoods in Britain. Yet, young British-born South Asians like Apache,
having grown up in oppressed, working-class neighborhoods alongside other minorities, seek to create new voices of self-representation.
The earlier generation's silent acceptance of its invisibility in Britain
has now been replaced by Apache's "voice upon the radio station"
and "face upon the television."[10]
    The appeal of Apache's music for young South Asians lies in its
catchy rhythm, as well as in its openness to reinterpreting identities,
its acceptance for the need for re-departure, and its message of self-
representation. The very shallowness Manuel (1995) noted may offer
young people in different parts of the world a source of identification
to which they can relate easily. In fact, bell hooks (1990b) noted that
rap music serves as a critical voice for the black underclass (p. 27),
and theorized that, "art that engages with popular culture may well be
the central future location of the resistance struggle" (p. 31).

Border Crossings and the Negotiation of Representations and Identities

Apache has chosen to resist by forming alliances with other marginalized communities. He has entered "that space in the margin that is a site of creativity and power, as an act of intervention, to recover ourselves" (hooks, 1990a, pp. 341–343). In this act of intervention Apache uses the distinctive sound of his music along with other strategies—particularly his use of semiotics and of the media—to make himself heard across borders.

Language is a place of struggle (hooks, 1990b), where producers of messages construct a social identity for themselves and their hearers (Hodge & Kress 1988). Further,

> an accent is a particular inflection which gives a different social meaning to an apparently common set of signs, just as happens with various accents of speech which mark class and regional identity. . . . [T]he processes of struggle, negotiation and creation and resolution of differences are both social and comprehensible . . . (Hodge & Kress, 1988, p. 19).

Apache's effective play on words in his choice of stage name and album titles, his blending of accents and musical styles, and his changing visual representations of "Indian" all serve as border crossings that create new interpretations and meanings of Indian identity.[11] This semiotic zigzagging underscores the point that racial differences and identities are socially constructed, cultural rather than biological realities (Brantlinger, 1990; McCarthy & Crichlow, 1993).

Brantlinger (1990, p. 109) and McCarthy and Crichlow (1993, pp. xvi–xvii) discuss the inability of those on the margins to represent themselves accurately through the channels and institutions of the dominant culture, and the related question of who represents whom and when and how. In light of these propositions, it is worth examining Apache's strategic use of the media and himself as a showperson. Chambers (1985) wrote of the mods and their "recognisable bric-a-brac of affluence," in the Britain of the 1960s. "They created themselves as 'mods,' living their lives in that most public of theatres—the market-place of commodities—as self-proclaimed 'artists' or 'actors'" (p. 78). Similarly Apache is creating and re-creating himself as an icon through the marketplace of his medium. Using the media to project changing images of himself, he is a self-proclaimed creator of a new style, a new voice. He has shifted the balance of power to make accessible to minority youth those channels of expression historically controlled by the dominant race for the purposes of self-representation.

The Paradox of Appropriation

Although at an obvious level, Apache's music reflects his alliance with other marginalized peoples as he attempts to break away from patterns of domination and oppression, Apache, himself as a British South Asian musician, appropriates and recycles themes and materials from other cultures, including the culture of his "origin."[12] Chambers (1985) noted that ska music evolved out of the Jamaican appropriation of Black American rhythm-and-blues, and later the interracial 'Brum beat' of Birmingham's UB40 and the Beat built on ska, reggae, and other novel musical indications (pp. 74, 192). Such musical appropriations from other cultures and genres often appear in the history of the development of new styles. But in Apache's case, this appropriation is compounded by the circular process of importing "raw materials" (bhangra) from the country of origin (India), recycling them, and exporting the "finished product" (his "bhangra-ragga" music) back to it. A British national and a producer of a very British music (Gopinath, 1995), Apache, in selling his music to India, creates a parallel to the historical and colonial relationship. It appears then, that his international success rests, in part, on the very re-creation of an historical situation from which he wants to break away.

At the same time, however, Apache's music redefines the boundaries of British culture and identity. By creating and claiming a space for himself on British prime-time television, Apache rewrites British popular culture. As Gopinath (1995) notes, "Bhangra acts as a means of asserting membership and locating a space within the national culture, thereby disrupting and redefining the very nature of that culture" (p. 313). Moreover,

> The fact that this hybrid notion of 'Indianness' [as projected by Apache] is produced within and deployed from the former colonial power, and is being consumed within the former colony, complicates a standard cultural imperialism argument, where Britain could be seen as merely exporting another commodity—this time Indian identity—to India. Rather, the movement gestures toward a refashioning of what it means to be British through a refashioning of what it means to be Indian, and vice-versa; it is a movement that disrupts the sanctity of the borders of the nation-state on all sides (pp. 313–314).

Just as Apache is "making way" for a new Indian identity, so is he creating that "interstitial passage" for a new British identity. In Apache's case, then, the paradox of approximation is comprised of interrelated patterns of recycling. While, on the one hand he evokes the colonial relationship, on the other he recycles "raw materials" borrowed from the former colony and other minority cultures in order to re-define the former colonial power itself.

Conclusion

At this point I should return to Minh-ha's question: "How can one re-depart and re-create without re-circulating domination?" As we have seen, Apache's creation of new representations and identities necessarily involves appropriation, perhaps as an inevitable consequence of the need to establish alliances. It also complements patterns of domination, particularly when it comes to the economics of success. But his music does open up a hybrid cultural space from which to re-depart, re-invent identities. Apache has created new sites of resistance and self-representation for minority youth, which allow them to begin rewriting the dominant context itself. As this process of re-departure recurs over time, we can

> force the limits of the social as we know it to rediscover a sense of political and personal agency . . . within the civic and psychic realms. This may be no place to end but it may be a place to begin. (Bhabha, 1994, p. 65)

References

Apache Indian. (1993). *No reservations* [Audiocassette]. St. Laurent, Quebec: Island Records.

Apache Indian (1995). *Make way for the Indian* [CD]. New York: Mango/Island Records.

Asher, N. (1993, Summer). Don Raja: Britain's multicultural music phenomenon. *South Asian Magazine for Action and Reflection (SAMAR)*, 46–47.

Baily, J. (1990). *Qawwali* in Bradford: Traditional music in a Muslim community. In P. Oliver (Ed.), *Black music in Britain: Essays on the Afro-Asian contribution to popular music* (pp. 153–165). Philadelphia: Open University Press.

Banerji, S., & Baumann, G. (1990). Bhangra 1984–8: Fusion and professionalization in a genre of South Asian dance music. In P. Oliver (Ed.), *Black music in Britain: Essays on the Afro-Asian contribution to popular music* (pp. 137–152). Philadelphia: Open University Press.

Bhabha, H. K. (1994). *The location of culture*. New York: Routledge.

Brantlinger, P. (1990). *Crusoe's footprints: Cultural studies in Britain and America*. New York: Routledge.

Chambers, I. (1985). *Urban rhythms: Pop music and popular culture*. New York: St. Martin's Press.

Clarke, C., Peach, C., & Vertovec, S. (1990). Introduction: Themes in the study of the South Asian diaspora. In C. Clarke, C. Peach, & S. Vertovec (Eds.), *South Asians overseas: Migration and ethnicity* (pp. 1–29). Cambridge, UK: Cambridge University Press.

Ganti, T. (1995). *Gimme somethin' to dance to! what is bhangra?* [Videocassette]. New York: Chutney Productions.

Glazer, N. (1980). Foreword. In P. Saran & E. Eames (Eds.), *The new ethnics: Asian Indians in the United States* (pp. vi–viii). New York: Praeger.

Gopinath, G. (1995). "Bombay, U.K., Yuba city": Bhangra music and the engendering of diaspora. *Diaspora, 4*, 303–321.

Hodge, R., & Kress, G. (1988). *Social semiotics*. Cambridge, UK: Polity Press.

hooks, b. (1990a). Marginality as site of resistance. In R. Ferguson, M. Gever, T. T. Minh-ha, & C. West (Eds.), *Out there: Marginalization and contemporary cultures* (pp. 341–343). New York & Cambridge, MA: New Museum of Contemporary Art and MIT Press.

hooks, b. (1990b). *Yearning: Race, gender, and cultural politics*. Boston: South End Press.

Lorch, D. (1992, January 12). An ethnic road to riches: The immigrant job specialty. *New York Times*, pp. 1, 20.

Manuel, P. (1995). Music as symbol, music as simulacrum: Postmodern, pre-modern, and modern aesthetics in subcultural popular musics. *Popular Music, 14,* 227–239.

McCarthy, C., & Crichlow, W. (1993). Introduction: Theories of identity, theories of representation, theories of race. In C. McCarthy & W. Crichlow (Eds.), *Race, identity, and representation in education* (pp. xiii–xxix). New York: Routledge.

Mercer, K. (1990). Black hair/style politics. In R. Ferguson, M. Gever, T. T. Minh-ha, & C. West (Eds.), *Out there: Marginalization and contemporary cultures* (pp. 247–264). New York & Cambridge, MA: New Museum of Contemporary Art and MIT Press.

Minh-ha, T. T. (1990). Cotton and iron. In R. Ferguson, M. Gever, T. T. Minh-ha, & C. West (Eds.), *Out there: Marginalization and contemporary cultures* (pp. 327–336). New York & Cambridge, MA: New Museum of Contemporary Art and MIT Press.

Robinson, V. (1990). Boom and gloom: The success and failure of South Asians in Britain. In C. Clarke, C. Peach, & S. Vertovec (Eds.), *South Asians overseas: Migration and ethnicity* (pp. 269–296). Cambridge, UK: Cambridge University Press.

Sengupta S. (1996, June 30). To be young, Indian and hip: Hip-hop meets Hindi pop as a new generation of South Asians finds its own groove. *New York Times*, pp. CY 1, 11.

Spivak, G. C. (1993). *Outside in the teaching machine*. New York: Routledge.

West, C. (1990). The new cultural politics of dfference. In R. Ferguson, M. Gever, T. T. Minh-ha, & C. West (Eds.), *Out there: Marginalization and contemporary cultures* (pp. 19–36). New York & Cambridge, MA: New Museum of Contemporary Art and MIT Press.

Zuberi, N. (1995, Summer). "Paki" Tunes. *South Asian Magazine for Action and Reflection (SAMAR)*, 36–39.

Author Note

I am grateful to Professor Glenn Hudak, formerly of Teachers College, Columbia University, now at Pace University, for encouraging me to undertake this project and sharing generous and insightful comments as I wrote.

Notes

1. For instance, Kobena Mercer (1990, p. 248) argues that Black people of the African diaspora, located in capitalist First World societies, have developed distinct patterns of style across a range of practices from music, speech, dance, dress and even cookery, that are politically intelligible as creative responses to the experience of oppression and dispossession.

2. I use such words as "Indian," and "Indian-ness" to refer to India and Asian Indians, unless otherwise specified. Also, rather than discussing the issues in terms only of "Indian" identities and music forms, I choose the broader term "South Asian" in light of the undeniable historical, cultural, and linguistic connections among the countries in that geographic region.

3. Unlike in the U.S., South Asians in Britain have identified themselves as "Blacks." For instance, women of South Asian descent are members of Southall Black Sisters, a London-based women's organization.

4. See Manuel (1995) for a discussion of such Indo-Caribbean music as "chutney soca," and Baily (1990) for a discussion of *qawwali* music in Bradford.

5 For instance, when I interviewed Bittu's bhangra band in New York City during the summer of 1995, I learned that Bittu, who immigrated from the state of Punjab, in north India, to England nearly a decade ago, speaks very little English and continues to use Punjabi or Hindi. When I asked the band members how their music evolved, and what message, if any, it carried, they told me that they were simply trying to make bhangra available to young people who particularly enjoyed the consistent rhythmic beat of the *dhol* (a kind of drum) and the sound of the *thumbi* (a string instrument). Since young people seemed to like western sounds, however, they had added the synthesizer and keyboards to their repertoire but otherwise had tried to maintain bhangra in its original form.

6. Various terms like "Bhangramuffin," "Ragga," and "Bhangra-ragga" have been used to describe styles evolving from the blending of bhangra and reggae.

7. Iain Chambers (1985, p. 168) describes the persona of the "rude boys" as rebellious models for black youth in Britain. They were "too bad" and "wicked" in their relations with society, twisting commonsense definitions in the hope of finding a localized negotiation within the spaces of ghetto life. By contrast, the Rastas point blank refused even to engage with that reality. See Chambers (1985) for a detailed discussion of the history of urban music in Britain.

8. Gopinath (1995, p. 312) notes that Apache's choice of stage name is also a reference to Jamaican raggamuffin artist Wild Apache.

9. Punjabi is the language of the state of Punjab in north India, and "Birmiyite" refers to a resident of Birmingham in Great Britain.

10. With reference to the West Indian community in Britain, Chambers (1985, pp. 164–165) writes, "The passage in the 1950s and 1960s of West Indians to yet another country, this time the colonial "Mother Country," also threatened to widen the gap between the experience of Afro-Caribbean popular culture and the optimistic hopes these black immigrants invested in British possibilities. By the 1970s many of these hopes had faded. If older generation Jamaicans had adopted a defensive stoicism, young Blacks were increasingly embittered. . . .

 Second generation West Indian youths—many British born and bred—began to turn away from their parents' attempted, but largely foiled, efforts to enter the tepid mainstream of British society. . . . It had become clear by then that racism and racial discrimination was neither personal nor accidental, it was a structural problem. Black youth became increasingly aware of its profound dilemma: caught between a fragmented colonial inheritance and a present that was daily denied."

11. For instance, Kobena Mercer (1990, p. 248) theorizes Black hair-styling as a popular *art form* articulating a variety of aesthetic "solutions" to a range of "problems" created by ideologies of race and racism. Further, she notes that hair is a key "ethnic signifier" (p. 250). Caught, as it is, on the cusp between self and society, nature and culture, the malleability of hair makes it a sensitive area of expression (Mercer, "Black Hair/Style Politics").

12. As Kobena Mercer (ibid.) notes, "Black practices of aesthetic stylization are intelligible at one 'functional' level as dialogic responses to the racism of the dominant culture, but at another level involve acts of appropriation from that same 'master' culture through which 'syncretic' forms of diasporean culture have evolved. . . . In additon there is another 'turn of the screw' in these modern relations of inter-culturation when these creolized cultural forms are made use of by other social groups and then, in turn, are all incorporated into mainstream 'mass' culture as commodities for consumption . . . to strengthen its dominance and revalorize its own symbolic capital" (pp. 257–260).

Post-colonial Influences in Spanish Diaspora: Christian Doctrine and the Depiction of Women in Tejano Border Songs and Calypso

Zena Moore

Popular Culture and the Classroom

Educators have traditionally resisted attempts to include popular culture in the high school curriculum. The reasons most commonly advanced have to do with perceptions and values, and the perpetuation, promulgation, and retention of these values. Schools are socializing agents and as such serve as transmitters and preservers of middle-class values (Apple, 1990; Garcia, 1982). As a consequence, the curriculum reflects, reinforces, and reproduces these values. Working within the school curriculum that both excludes and includes, that places barriers and limitations on things "different," educators, while intellectually recognizing the merit of popular cultural art forms, hesitate to include them in their classroom, an argument Koza presents in this volume.

A common belief is that popular art forms are the sites of the "Other," largely of the people of the "working class," a belief that clearly is a holdover from the bourgeois classist definition of the term "popular." If we recall, the word "mass" was first used at the time of the French revolution and it was a term of contempt for the working class.

Theorists in the field of education traditionally use the term "mass culture," as against a structurally complex high culture (haute culture), so the signifiers carry with them certain emotional attitudes associated with other binaries: superior/inferior, good/evil, high-brow/low-brow, decent/vulgar, middle-class/working-class. Franco (1982) referred to the binary opposition when he described popular culture as a spectrum of signifying practices and pleasurable activities which fall outside the controlling discipline of official schooling.

Bourdieu (1984) also referred to popular culture as embodying class distinctions and stratifications, subtle subcultural distinctions and differentiations acquired largely in noninstitutionalized settings. Since it is generally accepted that schools are largely a middle-class affair, it stands to reason that there will be resistance to the inclusion of any material believed to be inferior or working class.

The language teacher who attempts to move beyond the textbook to include everyday, authentic linguistic samples of the "real world," because she believes that she must teach language as a product of a culture from which it derives meaning, is caught in a paradoxical dilemma. On the one hand, she is aware of the controversies that surround attempts (pedagogically defensible though they be) to include samples of popular cultures in the language classroom. On the other hand she knows that she must be "authentic" (true) to her own code of ethics as a pedagogue. She must expose students to as many different forms of linguistic and cultural input as is possible.

In addition, leaders in the field have applauded the merits of music, deeming it an authentic source of culture and advocating the use of music as a valuable way of helping students develop an ear for the authentic sounds of a different language. According to Brooks (1976), the element of culture that is closest to language is music, which should find a place in the language class not because it teaches language but because it represents other elements of culture in a most appealing form.

Even more recently, Miller and Coen (1994) argued for the inclusion of music in the national core curriculum for all students, stating that music is essential for the development of aesthetic appreciation, citizenship, and thinking.

In spite of the fact that we promote the teaching of music, per se, in the classroom, there is the unspoken, undeclared assumption that the music to be taught is not the music of the "margins." According to bell hooks (1984), although there is willingness to give audience to diverse voices, the diversity does not include the literature and other art forms from the margins. Such literature still struggles for inclusion in mainstream classes (see also Koza in this volume).

In this chapter I present an argument for the inclusion of popular music in the language and culture curricula, be it foreign language, second language, the traditional language/arts classrooms, the social studies classroom, critical studies, women's studies and multicultural education classes. If, according to Blacking (1969), the interpretation of musical activity can serve as a key to understanding other aspects of a group's culture and social organization, there is much to be learnt by introducing popular music into the curriculum.

Border Music: Calypso, Corrido and Romance

I focus specifically on discussions and comparisons of Tejano border songs (*romances* and *corridos*), and the *calypso* of Trinidad. Geographically situated thousands of miles apart, the two postcolonial communities have one major link. They are part of postcolonial Spanish diaspora. I theorize that, as cultural products of Catholic domination and influence (French and Spanish), the two art forms will reflect the Catholic teachings about women as inferior, as fulfilling roles of submissive handmaids of the lords, and as responsible for the fall of men. In other words, I theorize that these beliefs promulgated by the Catholic Church will inform the male artists' definition of the role of women.

First of all, let me give a brief historical account of the emergence of the art forms. The two musical art forms are popularly referred to as music of the oppressed working class. Peña (1985) described Tejano *conjunto* music as "musica de la gente pobre" and acknowledges the *corrido* and *romance* as the most popular lyrical expressions of Tejano *conjunto* music. Herrera-Sobek (1982) spoke of the *corrido* and the *romances* as folk music of the lower classes that traces its roots to the Spanish romances of the 15th century.

If the roots of the *corrido* and the *romance* can be traced back to the 15th-century Spanish romances, it is not surprising to find that there will exist similarities in lyrical content. The *calypsoes*, too, are "songs of resistance" produced by people in the margins (Rohlehr, 1990). As expressions of "border music" the two art forms document the social conditions, values and belief systems of "border people." But, in addition to this significant role of documenting the lives of the people, they are also rich sources of linguistic expressions, and as examples of oral art forms, they have been described as more resilient and flexible (volatile even, as in the case of gangsta rap, signifying and doing the dozens) than the written mode. As such, then, critics describe them as highly resistant to cultural domination and extremely innovative and creative in their responses to new pressures.

In addition to the features mentioned above, I hypothesize, that as art forms of Spanish diaspora, the *calypso*, the *corrido* and the *romance* will have other features in common. Principally, they will reflect the values of the dominant religion, Catholicism, manifested in patriarchal rule and control in societal and family relationships.

As a consequence of the hypothesis, this paper looks specifically at the depiction of woman in the two art forms in what I call postcolonial Spanish culture. I will examine border music of the *tejanos*, specifically the *corrido* and the *romance*, and the *calypso*, called the music of "jamette culture," and I will compare the depiction and portrayal of women in these songs. To facilitate the discussions, I think it is useful to begin with a brief historical outline of the historical context in which these art forms emerged.

Spanish/French Catholic Influences

Trinidad was discovered by Christopher Columbus in the name of the Catholic monarchs in 1492. The British gained control and dominion of the island in 1786 as a result of the conquest of Spanish forces in the colonial wars of the late 18th century. So, for almost three hundred years, the island was under European and Catholic domination. This influence is still seen today, particularly in education.

The most prestigious schools in Trinidad are owned and run by members of the various Catholic orders. All schools on the island are structured according to the Catholic calendar, and the school holidays are marked by three principal Catholic festivals, Christmas, Easter and the season of Lent. The annual national celebration of Carnival, a period of bacchanalian celebration closely followed by the harsh season of lent, is a perennial reminder to the people of the frailty of the flesh and the need for repentance.

The interplay of festivity and repentance, of good times and remorse, is part of the bigger concepts of the Catholic doctrine, of good and evil, of the sinner and saint. One of the weapons used by the Church in those colonies where it was allowed to function, was the power of excommunication. Trinidad was no exception. The effect was to create in the minds of the people a dichotomy between the sacred and the secular, between decent and obscene, between ladylike and whorish, and in the case of music, between the Lord's songs and the songs of the Devil. For years the calypso music associated with the pre-Lenten celebration of Carnival was considered evil and a form of devil worship.

In the process of socialization to the wider society in postslavery Trinidad, the landless "freed slaves," exhibited behavior patterns common to most immigrant groups. They compromised early with French Creole Society in two very significant ways. They adopted Christianity, with its practices and belief system, and they learned the language and culture of the dominant group, while at the same time maintaining their own cultural practices. In so doing they not only selected ways of assimilation into the mainstream culture without abandoning essential features of their cultural art forms, but they also reproduced the dominant ideological beliefs of the colonial masters.

Songs of Resistance or Sermon Songs

Thus, according to Rohlehr (1990), the role and function of the ruling planter class to control and censor behavior, were perpetuated and reinforced by the Catholic Church, amply supported by the "decent" folks, mainly of the middle-class and upper-class, who sought constantly to purge and censor song and dance. As an oral art form with origins in African song with French lyrics, the *calypso* emerged out of the "barrack yards" of a working/lower class substratum, people of a "jamette" culture (Fr. *le diametre*/the margin). The newspapers of the time, according to Hill (1975), recorded numerous comments and complaints by members of the "upper echelons of society," about the lewd and diabolic behavior of the "jamette" people, who were the creators and singers of the *calypso*.

It was from a milieu of confrontation and resistance, of violent self-assertiveness and verbal artistry, that the *calypso* was born. Little wonder that it is still a male-dominated form of verbal "warfare" in which themes of manhood, glory, and identity are celebrated within the group. It is not surprising, then, that many of the lyrics focus on denigrating the other. Historically, denigrating the other has been an effective way of asserting control, power, and identity. Rohlehr (1990) argued that, like so many other art forms, the *calypso* is probably best understood as part of a broader culture of a people struggling to retain their own uniqueness in a time of oppression and repression. The fertility dancers, the stick fighters, and the calypso singers were participants in the celebration of an ethic of manhood struggling to salvage some control even while still suffering the stigma of being descendants of slaves.

Like the *calypso*, the *corrido* and *romance* emerged as songs of a people in economic depression. The early stagecoach which ran to and from San Antonio at the turn of the century carried hundreds of Mexican emigrants to Texas in search of a better life. Once in Texas, they suffered or experienced what Peña (1985) described as a common occurrence in interethnic contact. Their culture underwent the changes of adaptation, syncretism, and reinterpretation. By the 1930s, Texan-Mexicans (Tejanos) were overwhelmingly poor. Over 63% were living in dire poverty. As with all immigrants, assimilation into the main stream did not take place without a great deal of "reinterpretation and syncretism." The harsh economic and psychological conditions that were imposed on the Mexicans in Texas forced them to adapt, but not without resistance. The resistance was a determined effort to counter American cultural hegemony by striving to maintain some of their old symbols or creating new ones.

Peña argued that border music, particularly the *corrido* and the *romance*, must be seen and understood as a countercultural symbol, "la musica de la gente pobre" (Peña, 1985). This music became symbolic expressions that exerted a kind of organizing principle for a people deprived of their cultural roots. They were a summarizing symbol that spoke primarily to the people's attitudes. The lyrics and the artists dwell on the Mexican past, and the spirit of nationalism was fostered and strengthened through the romanticization of life in the *haciendas* and in the qualities of the *ranchero*. Manliness, self-sufficiency, candor, simplicity, sincerity, and patriotism are themes of the corridos and are exalted as admirable and idealized characteristics of the Mexicano.

Like the *calypso*, the *corrido* and the *romance* are male dominated songs, having emerged out of a patriarchal system. The original *conjunto* musicians were raised in rural, proletarian settings, with parents who worked in the fields, and most of them received almost no schooling. Like the old calypsonians, many top singers died quite destitute, earning just enough to satisfy their economic needs, but not enough to make them rich. Again, like the calypsonians, the *conjunto* musicians rarely ever attained stardom. They saw themselves as entertainers, fulfilling a social function (Peña, 1985). Yet, even though the artists are from the margins, they are, in Gramscian terms, organic intellectuals, who assume the responsibility for protecting the interest of the groups (Gramsci, 1971). The artists, as Patterson (1975) argued, perform functions similar to those of the scholar and other men of letters, in that they serve as transmitters of ideas within their society, while expressing the conditions and resentments of the people. As such, they are marginalized by those of the dominant culture, but they dominate (occupy central positions in) the subculture.

Analysis of the Two Art Forms

Mexico and Trinidad maintained strong links with Spain throughout the colonial period. In the early 19th century in Trinidad, and in the late 19th century in Mexico, the musical forms were heavily influenced by European vogues. The music and dance in both countries included the polka, redowa, waltz, and quadrille, largely because of the European communities but also because of the low cost of the musical instruments. The bel canto, too, derived from European opera, also had a downward movement from upper class to the working class in both societies, influencing both the calypso and the tejano music, by placing emphasis and importance on the voice of the soloist, which continues to be an important feature in both art forms. The singer is the main artist who dominates the performance.

I will analyze the songs of the 1900–1960 period, for it was then that both art forms became a channel for social and political commentaries. It was also during this same period that both art forms emerged as ways of self-celebration of the artist as a "sweet man," a macho man, in control of several women. In both art forms, there are strong evidences of a relationship between social oppression and the denigration of woman.

From a sociohistorical perspective we can establish both calypso and tejano music as products of social and institutional systems. As institutional forms of discourses, according to Foucault (1980), they serve the function of regulating and differentiating the people in their communities. In both cases the artists are people in the margins, urban dwellers whose only capital is their labor, a socioeconomic factor that provides clear evidence of linkage between the male ego and economic earnings derived from work. But the artists are also part of the patriarchal system and are products of Spanish Catholic cultures. Their songs (via the lyrical content), beside documenting historical events, also reveal their relationships with and opinions of, women.

The Depiction of Woman

As predominantly male-dominated art forms, the *calypso*, the *corrido* and the *romance* speak of women from the position of the male patriarch. An analysis of over 140 Tejano songs collected and translated by Robb (1980) and a review of over 150 calypsos by Rohlehr (1990) reveal that, in general, references to and descriptions of women follow Biblical trends. Principally, she is the treacherous Eve responsible for the downfall of men. The following are the main categories that emerged from this analysis:

1. Woman is the cause of man's tragic situation;
2. Woman is unfaithful, cunning, and beguiling;
3. Woman is lascivious and greedy;
4. Woman needs to be controlled either by warnings, threats, and/ or physical abuse;
5. Old women are ugly hags to be distrusted;
6. The ideal woman performs roles of mother and home caretaker;
7. Woman is the embodiment of carnal pleasures and as seductress and temptress she must be resisted.

At the same time, the male heroes in the songs are painted as larger than life. They are strong, valiant, and aggressive. For example, the Mexican male is super macho and, of necessity, the antithetical woman is unfaithful and submissive. The ballad singers of *corridos*, in stark contrast to singing the praises of the heroes of the epic ballads, sing of the deeds of the common man, as in "The Ballad of Gregorio Cortés" (Robb, 1980, 189–192). Perhaps the most popular ballad in tejano musical history, it inspired the making of at least one film called *Ballad of Gregorio Cortés* and has led to several *corrido* versions of the same theme. In all the versions, the wrongly accused fugitive, Cortés, is elevated to the position of a folk hero who succeeds in defying and eluding gringo authority. He becomes a symbol for Mexican strength of resistance to American culture and ideology.

The macho image in the *corridos* and the *romances*, according to Moraga and Anzaldúa (1983) grew out of a traditional concept of pride and manliness. The term *machismo* was originally used to describe a man who was able to provide a living for his family. Mexican men were, and still are, socialized to believe that it is their duty to economically support their family. Because of the Depression of the 1930s, the men struggled to find jobs that could adequately help support their families. The family was the only site where working-class men could perform their patriarchal duties. It was the domain in which they could construct their identity as productive citizens and successful men. The inability to meet such societal demands can create a sense of disempowerment and self-loathing, according to Hodge (1974) and Moraga and Anzaldua (1983). The result is to transfer this loathing on the person who is perceived to create the hardships. In postcolonial Catholic societies this person is usually the submissive, subordinate woman.

Hodge (1974) expressed the belief that the macho behavior of many calypsonians goes back to the effects of slavery which created an utter devaluation of the manhood of the race, thus rendering the male powerless to carry out his traditional role of protector of the tribe. The long-lasting effect of the legacy of slavery was that his manhood was reduced to his brawn for the labor he could do for his master and to his reproductive function.

According to Peña (1985) and Rohlehr (1990), women and alcohol become scapegoats for social and economic oppression. Money, or rather the scarcity of it, became a popular theme in these songs. The singer either complains that without money there is little hope for a love relation to succeed, or that women are only interested in a man's financial status and their affection varies according to his financial earnings. Although the singer acknowledges that money is needed to buy food, that is to sustain life, he laments the fact that he is not appreciated for himself. In *Money Is King*, for example, (Rohlehr, 1990, p. 217) the singer sings:

If you have money and things going nice
Any woman will call you honey and spice
If you can't give her a dress, or a new pair of shoes
She'll say she have no uses for you.

In "Empty Belly" (Rohlehr, 1990, p. 220) the singer laments the fact that in spite of his struggles, the salary he receives is grossly inadequate to provide for his family. He believes that under the circumstance the woman should be understanding and supportive and should be prepared to undergo the necessary hardships and sacrifices. The woman who refuses to do so is greedy, materialistic, and unloving.

The lack of money is also the major reason for unrequited love in the corrido *El Abandonado* (Robb, 1980, p. 225). Here the singer, similar to the calypsonian, accuses the woman of not returning his love because he has no money.

You abandoned me, woman, because I'm very poor
And my misfortune is being a passionate man

The singers believe that sound economic resources and a steady financial income are important in keeping the family unit contented. They argue that they are important factors in creating a strong foundation for marriage and love. Yet, ironically, they extend little sympathy to women who, abandoned by the men who fathered her children, resort to forming alliances with other men.

Qualities of independence and industriousness so admirable in a man are, in a woman, seen as undesirable, destructive characteristics which could only lead to the breakup of a relationship. The singers, therefore, see it fit to mercilessly condemn single women who, having the responsibility to rear children during economic depression, aggressively seek other sources of income. Such behavior is empty and immoral, most unlike the women of olden days. "No Comparison" (Rohlehr, 1990, p. 222) depicts the new independent woman as ambitious and materialistic, and laments the passing of older values that supported the male identity and life-style:

> All the old-fashioned girl asked of life
> Was to be help-mate, mother and wife
> But the modern girl thinks more of sport
> Cigarettes, high balls and the divorce court

Men also must avoid relationships with the "pretty woman" who is fickle and unfaithful, mercenary and unreliable. They must also be wary of the woman who pursues professions that are traditionally male dominated. For example, in "Woman Will Rule the World" (Rohlehr, 1990, p. 223) the singer expresses a fear of losing power and control over the women. He laments:

> Long ago girls used to be schoolteachers
> And they became stenographers
> We next hear of them as lecturers
> Authors and engineers
> There is no limit to their ambition
> They're going in for aviation

The messages in the calypsoes are indeed similar to Biblical sermons in which women are urged to follow the Virgin Mary, the handmaid of the Lord, who is long-suffering, pure, and chaste. Attempts to control women and pressure them into living the traditional life begin when they are young. These sermons in songs act as a socializing force that teaches what is morally acceptable or not. They also define how women must behave. For example, young women are warned both against disobedience to their parents, and infidelity to their sweethearts and their husbands. The corrido "Rosita Alvarez" (Robb 1980, pp. 125–128), which has several versions, is believed to have to have gained widespread popularity because of the theme of tragedy that befalls the disobedient daughter. This song exemplifies the moral tight-rope that the woman must walk. On one hand she is warned not to dance with men other than her sweetheart. Yet when she refuses to dance with another man, in obedience to her sweetheart's wishes, her refusal is considered an insult to the male ego. In both cases death is her punishment. Paradoxically, the woman becomes both subject and object of the deed. The corrido ends with the words of the dying Rosita who begs other women not to be foolish like she was.

> Rosita said to Irene
> Do not forget my name;
> When you go to a dance
> Do not rebuff the men

Similarly, death is the punishment for treachery in "Jesus Cardenas" (Robb, 1980, p. 119). Believing himself dishonored by his sweetheart's dancing with other men, Jesus warns Chabela that she is not dealing with "little school boys now." He avenges his honor by killing her, and the corrido ends:

> Fair Chabela tried to say
> As she lay on the ground
> Be careful, all you young girls
> Don't give men the run around.

Ramirez (1970) provided the following explanation for the degradation of the feminine image and for the perpetuation of the belief in the intrinsically treacherous nature of woman as depicted in the corridos and romances. Seen as treacherous and fickle, the woman's avowed love is therefore always to be tested. If she is found to be unfaithful, she is killed. If she is loyal and true, she is also threatened with death as a form of deterrent, as in the romance "Las senas del esposo" (Robb, 1980, pp. 61–62). The song recounts how the husband disguises himself to test his wife's loyalty. He says:

> And I did it in order to know
> If you were good or bad

If you had come with me
I would have cut off your head

The significance of these "sermon songs" must be understood in their historical contexts. The songs emerged in the aftermath of World War II. Indiscriminate sexual relationships in war periods have always contributed to the increase of fatal diseases including venereal diseases. As yet another way of exerting control and power, the artist cleverly uses these socioeconomic reasons to instill fear of horrible death and damnation, very much bringing to mind the destruction of the biblical city of Sodom and Gomorrah. Women are given a clear code of behavior. They are urged to be patient, moral, chaste, and decent, and their reward will be marriage to a wholesome gentleman. Failure to keep these "commandments" is punishment either by death from a horrible disease or living a life of hell in a whorehouse.

The double standard of morality so typical of patriarchal society is clearly seen when we realize that many of the calypsonians themselves consorted with the very same women whose actions they condemn. The prostitutes are mercilessly condemned, but he who consorts with them receives neither blame nor punishment.

The macho image of the man as sweet man, Rohlehr (1990) suggested, is probably based on their own lack of self-confidence, a fear of being rejected, the shame of being cuckolded and/or of contracting venereal diseases. The Freudian analysis is helpful in explaining the fear of losing sexual power and control. Part of this fear, according to Rohlehr (1990) is the need to promote his own manhood, which is tied to his self-esteem. The singer therefore debases the woman in an attempt to build his own ego. But there seems to be a certain lack of logic in this theory. Why not debase a man of equal status, or another man of higher status in his attempts to redeem his manhood. Why should he be redeemed by denigrating one who is inferior? It is more logical to accept that these men are simply repeating the doctrines they learned from their Christian teachings that perpetuate traditional roles of women as inferior objects of possession and control.

Rohlehr (1990) stated that the assumption that woman is naturally fickle and unfaithful exists in many societies, but he says it has a particular rootage in colonial explantation societies. Unfortunately, he does not attempt to present any explanation for this rootage although he does admit that it was part of an "ideology of patriarchal control." Prusak (1974), on the other hand, traced the connection between Hebrew and Greek mythologies that place woman as the cause for evil in the world. He showed the similarity between Jewish and Christian myths that teach that woman is the origin of evil. The Pauline and Augustinian doctrines, on which present-day Christianity is guided, still teach that man alone was made in the image of God and woman was derived from the rib of Adam. Prusak concluded that the myths were created to buttress patriarchal culture and exclude women from public roles and so retain dominance over civil and religious society.

Ruether (1974) also provided convincing arguments for the male-female and the body-soul dualism in patristic theology. According to Ruether, woman is not only inferior, being derived from a rib, but she is also devoid of the spirit of God. The result of this assimilation of spirit-body, male-female, is that woman is not really seen as a self-sufficient whole person, as in the image of God, and her carnality must be made subject to the spirit. Although it is revolting on one hand, it is seductive on the other.

On the basis of this belief, men should avoid establishing liaisons with the free-spirited young woman known for her licentious behavior and voracious sexual appetite, and with the libidinous older women. When the singers do recommend relationships with older women, they do so because they believe that such relationships are safer since they present little threat to their ego. Older women are less inclined to be unfaithful, and more tolerant of the man's infidelity. Whether old or young, women become the bane of man's existence.

In the calypso, "I Don't Want No Young Girl" (Rohlehr 1990, p. 235), the artist clearly expresses the male sentiments about the "old lady." He describes her as "heaven." She is diligent in that she always has his meals prepared and on time, and she is understanding and wise to the ways of the world in that she knows that he cannot be late for his other dalliances. Yet the old woman is still not to be trusted completely, for she can be callous and capable of ruthlessly discarding and replacing her male partner, even at his deathbed, as in "Firo Liro Li" (Robb, 1980, p. 56):

> The poor widow was weeping
> The death of her husband.
> Under the bed
> She already had another man hidden.

The madonna/whore image is obvious in both art forms. Women are either idealized or are condemned. The ideal woman is presented as submissive and obedient, catering to the wishes of the man. She is to be the either the handmaid of the Lord, or if she is like Mary Magdalene, the prostitute, she is saved only by giving up the life of sin and following Jesus, the Savior. In both cases her only hope for redemption is submission to the "Lord."

The dichotomization of woman by Catholic morality (and, of course, Christian morality in general) facilitates the conversion from person to thing. Traditionally presented as not being made in the image of God and an unimportant part of Adam, a rib, she can easily be objectified and commodified. As objects of food or playthings she can be discarded, and/or trashed. As sexual sources of gratification for the man's appetite, she can to be used or abused. In the *corrido* and the *romance* she is an apple to be eaten, a jewel to be stolen, a pet to be fondled, or a flower to be plucked. In the *calypso* she is a vampire bat, a piece of terrain to traverse, a pussy, a rat or a lizard.

The woman, according to the artists, is both exploiter and exploited, active agent and passive recipient. On one hand, as a passive thing, objectified, she can be exploited, for she lacks human qualities. On the other hand, when, because of his weak will, the man is unable either to desist from criminal acts, or to provide financial support, the woman is seen as responsible for this disaster. She is depicted as selfish and insensitive, an exploiter of his misfortunes who unsympathetically discards him for another more fortunate one. The songs reveal very subtle and interesting relations in the morals presented and those of Christian doctrine that teach that the poor are blessed and "shall inherit the earth," and there is virtue in poverty. The virtuous woman is urged to embrace poverty, rather than seek out economic independence or self-sufficiency.

Rohlehr (1990) and Peña (1975) both referred to the harsh socioeconomic circumstances out of which the artist spits his venom on the woman, using her, as Peña suggested, as a scapegoat for these socioeconomic hardships. Such a theory probably provides possible expanations for the treatment of women. It, however, does not give an adequate explanation for the selection of the woman as the object of his frustration and anger. Why is it that these male artists do not perceive other men in other sectors of the community as the cause of their suffering and poor living conditions? Why is it that in communities where men are obviously in positions of power, the woman must be seen as aggressor and oppressor?

It is important to remember that these two art forms are male dominated. They are discourse patterns of men talking to men about "men" matters. The notion of "man among men" is built on the old Greek patriarchal society where only men were seen as intellectually fit to "speak" in public. Performance in verbal artistry was considered a male domain, a male prerogative. I suggest that by examining the art forms as linguistic discourses we can better understand why and how women are depicted. According to Worcester and Schaeffer (1970), although there was the rejection of colonialism in the third and fourth decades of the twentieth century, there was an assertion of the masses for a greater share in the national patrimony. There was the perpetuation of male domination. Local patriarchy replaced foreign patriarchy.

The male artists in their songs are merely continuing the discourse of Christian male leaders like Augustine and Paul, who have bequeathed to third-world Christian men their misogynist philosophy and patriarchal value systems. In "Los Diez Mandamientos" (Robb, 1980, pp. 65–66) and "Mandamientos de Amor," (pp. 67–68) the singer even elevates himself to the level of Divinity as he boasts that the Ten Commandments do not apply to him, since his own love commandments mandate that he serves his greater love, his sweetheart.

There are literary features of these art forms, as with written narratives, that also explain their survival, their increasing popularity, and their resilience to pressures over the years. One feature is that which Rohlehr (1990) and Peña (1985) referred to as the corpus of works (libraries) to which the younger artists can refer. Another is the variety of versions of many of the songs. This means that there is constant repetition of the themes, allowing for the moral teachings imbedded in these stories to be passed on orally, from generation to generation. Yet another feature lies in the tight structure of both art forms, ensuring that the story and the message be succinct, thereby facilitating easy retention and reproduction. Hill (1975) pointed out that the calypsoes of the period under review, were composed around a certain number of fixed tunes, and Robb (1980) presented evidence of many versions of the same *corridos* and *romances*.

A socioeconomic theory is useful in examining how class differences, like other hierarchical systems, allow those marked by difference to be the scapegoats for unnamed fears, as in the case of women depicted in the two oral art forms. But what are these fears? Cixous (1986) suggested that one fear is that of losing control. According to her, women in such societies are repressed to ensure the system's functioning. The weakness with Cixous' theory is that it supposes that the working-class male performer/artists are concerned with, or aware of the system (the bureaucratic/governmental agencies) and how it works and that they, as working-class poor people, have a vested interest in ensuring its smooth functioning.

A more useful theoretical framework by which to understand the treatment of women in popular art forms is one that allows for an examination of the history of the influences of these art forms, and the art forms themselves as textual bearers of moral teachings, as a perpetuation of colonial values, and a way of preserving and maintaining patriarchal domination. Research into another oral art form, the *piropo*, (Moore, 1996), has provided substantial evidence of the influence of Spanish courtly love poems, in form and content even after five centuries.

Conclusion

This chapter suggests that, at best, women in the *calypso* and the *corrido* are depicted as tenuous sources of love and happiness. At worst they are objects of pleasure to be exploited, or animals without soul to be brutalized and beaten into submission. I have argued that the sermons preached by these border musicians, marginalized artists, are no different from those preached in the Christian Bible thousands of years ago. Oral literature, like written literature, does serve to perpetuate patriarchal power.

I have also suggested that it is possible to understand the texts as genres of symbolic action, tools of resistance. Until this discourse is interrupted/broken by the woman's voice, the male will continue to "hold the floor." Signs of interrupting the discourse emerged as early as Lady Iere (1935) who sang:

> Love me or leave me
> Or live with Miss Dorothy
> The time is too hard
> For me to feed a man that is bad.

In "Run away" (1979), Singer Francine, preached directly to the women folk urging them to take their lives into their own hands:

> Dog does run away
> Cat does run away
> Child does run away when you treat them bad

Woman put two wheels on your heels
You should run away too.

Finally, Denyse Plummer (Sharpe, 1987) extends the discourse to
its limit by declaring that "Woman Is Boss." In this calypso, the discourse (and privilege) of the male-dominated art form is rudely interrupted by a strong declarative, and Plummer, ironically a Trinidadian
white woman who is not from the working class, claims not just equal
status but superiority over the male "preachers."

Probably because of its geographical proximity to the United States,
and the enormous increase in immigrant populations from Spanish-
speaking communities, *tejano* music no longer focuses on issues of
resistance and defiance. The former songs of resistance of the forties,
fifties and sixties have been replaced by American influenced pop songs.
The *canciones* (love songs) have grown in popularity and *corridos*
and *romances* are relegated to the past. The major challenge for Tejano
singers, and to a lesser degree for the calypsonian, is to compete for
American mainstream audiences. The artists must strive to create music
that is more "universally appealing" both in themes and melodies,
and the function of the music is primarily to entertain, not to teach.

References

Apple, M. (1990). *Ideology and curriculum.* New York. Routledge.

Blacking, J. (1969). *Venda's children's songs. A study in ethnomusicological analysis.* Johannesburg: Witwatersrand Univ. Press.

Bourdieu, P. (1984). *Distinction: A social critique of the judgment of taste.* Cambridge: Harvard University Press.

Brooks, N. (1976). The analysis of foreign language teaching. In R. La Fayette (Ed.), *The culture revolution in foreign language teaching* (pp.26–36). Skokie: National Textbook Co.

Cixous, H. (1986). *The* newly born woman: *Theory and history of literature.* (Trans. Betsy Wing). Minneapolis: University Minnesota Press.

Edwards, F. (1983). Run away. On *Run Away* [Audiocassette}. Port of Spain, Trinidad. Rhyner Records.

Foucault, M. (1980). *Power/knowledge.* New York: Pantheon.

Franco, Jean. (1982). What's in a name? Popular culture theories and their limitations. *Studies in Latin American Popular Culture, 1,* 5–14.

Garcia, R. (1982). *Teaching in a pluralistic society: Concepts, models and strategies.* New York: Harper and Row.

Gramsci, A. (1971/1929) *Selections from the prison notebooks .* In Q. Hoare and G. Howell-Smith (Eds. and Trans.). New York: International Publishers.

Herrera-Sobek, M. (1982). The acculturation process of the Chicana in the corrido. *De Colores Journal, 8,* 7–16.

Hill, E. (1975). The calypso. In M. Anthony and Andrew Carr (Eds.). *David Frost introduces Trinidad and Tobago* (pp. 73–83). London: Deutsch.

Hodge, M. (1974)). The shadow of the whip: A comment on male-female relationships in the Caribbean. In O. Coombs (Ed.). *Is massa day dead? Black moods in The Caribbean* (pp. 12–20). New York: Anchor Press/Doubleday.

hooks, b. (1984). *Feminist theory: From center to margin.* Boston: South End Press.

Lady Iere. (1935). Love me or leave me. On *Love me or Leave me.* [LP] Port of Spain, Trinidad: Rhyner Records.

Miller, A. and D. Coen. (1994, February). The Case for Music in the Schools. *Phi Delta Kappan,* 459–461.

Moore, Zena. (1996). Teaching culture: The Piropo. *Hispania, 79,* 113–120.

Moraga, C. and G. Anzaldúa, (Eds.) (1983). *This bridge called my back: Writings by radical women of color.* (2nd ed.). New York: Kitchen Table Women of Color Press.

Patterson, T. (1975). Notes on the historical application of Marxist cultural theory. *Science and Society, 34,* 257–291.

Peña, M. (1985). *The Texas-Mexican Conjunto: The history of a working-class music.* Austin: University of Texas Press.

Prusak, B. (1974). Woman: Seductive siren and source of sin? Pseudepigraphical Myth and Christian Origins. In R. Ruether (Ed.), *Religion and sexism: Images of woman in the Jewish and Christian traditions* (pp. 89–116). New York. Simon and Schuster.

Ramirez, S. (1970). *El Mexicano, psicología de sus motivaciones.* [The Mexican, psychology of his motivations] Mexico: Editorial Paz .

Robb, J. (1980). *Hispanic folk music of New Mexico and the Southwest.* Norman: University of Oklahoma Press.

Rohlehr, G. (1990). *Calypso and Society in pre-independence Trinidad.* Port of Spain, Trinidad: Gordon Rohlehr.

Ruether, R. (1974). Misogynism and virginal feminism in the fathers of the church. In R. Ruether (Ed.), *Religion and sexism: Images of woman in the Jewish and Christian traditions,* (pp. 150–183) New York: Simon and Schuster.

Sanchez, A. G. and A. Dominguéz. (1975). Women in Mexico. In R. Rohrlich-Leavitt (Ed.), *Women cross-culturally: Change and challenge* (pp. 95–110). The Hague, Mouton Publishers.

Sharpe, L. (1987) On woman is boss. [Recorded by D. Plummer.] On *Woman Is Boss.* [Audiocassette]. Port of Spain, Trinidad: Rhyner Records.

Worcester, D. & W. Schaeffer. (1971). *The growth and culture of Latin America.* New York: Oxford University Press.

Consuming Memories: The Record-Centered Salsa Scene in Cali

Lise Waxer

Introduction

In this paper, I explore links between recorded music, popular identity, consumption, and cultural memory in the rise of Latin American salsa music in Cali, Colombia. As both product and also vehicle of mass-mediated cultural expression, recordings have played a pivotal role in the forging of contemporary subjectivities in many parts of the globe, offering "new resources and new disciplines for the construction of imagined selves and imagined worlds" (Appadurai, 1995, p. 3). Salsa's adoption in Cali since the 1960s provides a particularly clear instance of this process. Indeed, by the 1980s, salsa permeated local life so strongly that local media began dubbing Cali "the world salsa capital." While I am not interested in proving or disproving this claim, the strength of this image in local popular identity is undeniable. In specific practices of reception and consumption, Caleños (natives of Cali) have actively incorporated a mass-mediated, transnational musical style into local cultural expression. Through repeated, quotidian activities of listening and dancing to salsa recordings, people have learned, embodied, and transmitted a certain cultural knowledge about what it means to be Caleño. "Cultural education," hence, has entailed organic processes of identification and memory flowing out of, and in turn reinforcing, popular cultural practice and everyday experience.

Salsa is a popular dance music that developed in the Latino barrios of New York in the 1960s, based on earlier Cuban styles and also incorporating elements from Afro-Puerto Rican traditions and North American jazz and rock. Recordings of the new sounds emanating from New York were rapidly taken up by working-class Caleño youth during the 1960s, soon spreading to leftist intellectual circles in the middle classes as well. This process parallels salsa's diffusion to many other parts of Latin America, especially Puerto Rico, Venezuela, and Panamá, and emerges from the strong transnational influence of salsa's Cuban antecedents in earlier decades. Rather than taking up musical instruments and developing a live local salsa scene, however, Caleños concentrated their expressive energies in dancing to recorded salsa music, creating a unique, local style of salsa dance. From the 1940s through the 1970s, "playing music" more often than not was literally a matter of sliding a nickel in the jukebox, or spinning records on the old home gramophone. Unlike music scenes in other parts of urban Latin America, where records have served mainly as an adjunct to or tool for musical creation and live performance, in Cali, recordings have constituted the focal point of musical activity, even after live music began to flourish in the early 1980s. As Charles Keil's study of *karaoke* in Japan (1984) and Peter Manuel's exploration of cassette cultures in India (1993) suggest, the appropriation of media technology to local musical practice and creativity is an area needing more attention than it has conventionally received. While an increasing number of scholars are investigating the relationship between live and mediated music, the privileging of live performance as more "real" or "authentic" than listening and dancing to records continues to dominate our perceptions of musical practice. In Cali, however, the predominance of records over local musicians until recently is a relatively unusual social phenomenon, requiring a different perspective. Recordings are objects of consumption, indeed, but practices of consumption must be seen as dynamic and meaningful systems (Douglas & Isherwood, 1979), tied to other domains of affect and experience. In the following pages I focus on Cali's *salsotecas* and *tabernas* (specialty bars for listening to salsa recordings) and examine the historical importance of recordings in local cultural practice.

Salsotecas and Tabernas

While conducting research in the field from late 1994 until summer 1996, I often spent Friday nights at the Taberna Latina (Latin Tavern). This was one of my favourite salsa hangouts in Cali, located on Calle Quinta, Fifth Street, just a few blocks south of the exclusive Club San Fernando. Affectionately known as "the Latina," the taberna is a cramped, intimate bar that caters to serious salsa aficionados, one of over sixty such establishments—also called *salsotecas*—for which Cali is renowned. Unlike typical salsa nightclubs in New York, Miami, San Juan, or Caracas, where you would expect to hear a live band, salsotecas and tabernas like the Latina center around recorded music. In particular, they focus on the recordings of *salsa dura* (hard/heavy salsa) that played a key role in consolidating this music as Cali's principal popular expression during the 1960s and 1970s—the sounds of the Fania All-Stars, Hector Lavoe, Eddie Palmieri, Ismael Rivera, and others. Nightclubs featuring live music also form part of Cali's current scene, having developed in conjunction with the rise of local bands and the increase of appearances by international *orquestas*. Salsotecas and nightclubs, in fact, are parallel offshoots of the 1960s and 1970s *grilles*, or discotheques, that used to feature recorded salsa dura when it was the main commercial style. Neither type of establishment charges entrance fees, depending primarily on liquor sales to generate a profit. In keeping with the times, however, nightclubs—like their Puerto Rican, U.S., and Venezuelan counterparts—now feature *salsa romántica* (romantic salsa), not the hard-driving rhythms of classic "roots" salsa. (As in other parts of Latin America, salsa romántica's fusion of sentimental pop *balada* with salsa rhythms has dominated local radio and dictated the style of local salsa bands since it emerged in the late 1980s.) What is unique in Cali's case, however, is the strong presence of places such as the tabernas and salsotecas—public spaces for maintaining salsa dura as a vital component of local popular culture.[1]

Gary Domínguez, owner of the Taberna Latina, often commented to me that Cali is "la ciudad de memoria musical" (the city of musical memory). His observation is based not only on the large community of record collectors in the city, but also on the prevalence of establishments in which the recorded music of Cali's yesteryears continues to animate weekend carousing. Recordings have long played a central role in local popular culture, being a prime source of music for the city's predominantly working-class population from the 1940s through the late 1970s. During this period Caleños developed a scene centered around dancing to records of *música antillana* (Cuban-based sounds) and salsa, as a response to multiple forces of social upheaval, rapid urban growth, and increased links to transnational influences, markets, and technologies.[2] Cuban, Mexican, and Hollywood films reinforced the effects of record discs, providing visible images to accompany the sound and serving as influential models for styles of dancing and dressing. I hold that the rise of this record-centred dance scene is central to salsa's predominance and continued vitality in the contemporary self-image of Caleños.

Salsa dura's current popularity is no mere holdover, but indeed, points to how physical expression, consumption, and nostalgia are braided into the core rhythm—the *clave*, if you will—of contemporary Caleño popular life.[3] Dancing and listening to records of música antillana and salsa can be seen as repetitive "techniques of the body" (Mauss, 1973) through which the consumption of this music has been literally incorporated into the grain of local expressive activity. In Cali, the repeated gestures of dancing and listening frame an erotics of local urban identity—they are potent, embodied pleasures that inscribe a certain cultural knowledge of what it means to be Caleño.

The formulation of an imagined link to Cuba, Puerto Rico, and New York, evoked in the significant and oft-heard phrase "somos caribeños, aunque no vivimos en el Caribe" (we are Caribbean, even though we don't live there), points to a simultaneously local and globalized cultural identification that emerged from this process. In these cultural practices, we can detect "the workings of the imagination in a deterritorialized world" (Appadurai, 1996, p. 63), through which Caleños have sought to reposition their sense of local identity at a particularly unstable point in recent history, a period when Cali metamorphosed from a small provincial town to a major regional and industrial center.

The Latina's engaging atmosphere certainly illustrates the imaginative, subjective possibilities borne through the local adoption of salsa. Several photos and posters of Puerto Rican salsa stars and old Cuban maestros adorn the walls, and the ceiling is covered with broadsides advertising past events held at the club. A virtual "hole in the wall" measuring only three meters wide and twelve meters long, the Latina is barely large enough to fit the fifteen small tables lining its perimeter. Two mammoth speakers are positioned at each end. Don't be surprised by the trombone bell jutting impudently over the speaker to the left as you enter—when you hear the dynamic horn choruses punching out from these salsa tunes, you'll understand why it was placed there. A disc jockey's booth by the right wall doubles as a bar that seats an extra five or six people. Behind this bar, over a thousand classic, out-of-print salsa LPs are stashed alongside the console and playback equipment; nearly a hundred compact discs and cassette tapes are kept in a drawer beneath the turntables. The two waiters on duty are kept busy running up and down the stairway next to this bar, where the beer keg and liquor bottles are kept behind a small counter located near (but not too near) the basement john. Meanwhile, owner Gary Domínguez, in pork-pie hat and tee-shirt, keeps records spinning from his booth. Gary, a bearded, reserved man in his late 30s, becomes extroverted and animated behind the turntables, flashing the house lights on and off to punctuate exciting percussion breaks and horn lines, and interjecting frenetic commentary over a microphone as if doing a live radio show.

The salsa featured at the Latina and other tabernas and salsotecas is *dura* indeed, marked by driving percussion and piano, emphatic bass, catchy *coros* (vocal choruses), aggressive horn lines, and dynamic musical arrangements. As fans put it, this is music that makes you want to dance! Yet, owing in part to the modest economic means in which the Latina (and most salsotecas) began, there's no dance floor here to speak of. Those who feel inspired to dance must do so in the tiny spaces between tables. While hard-core aficionados often prefer to sit and focus on listening to the music, Caleños in general like to dance, and many tabernas and salsotecas have expanded in recent years, adding a dance floor in order to satisfy public demand. The Latina, however, remains small and cramped. This is not to say that there's no movement—there's plenty, and it becomes more animated as the evening wears on and quantities of beer, rum, and *aguardiente*[4] are consumed. People sway back and forth, and some enthusiasts, particularly young men, play along with the music by slapping out rhythms on the table-tops. The mood is exuberant, and the crowd sings along with each song, emphasizing the lyrics with spirited gestures. Clients used to bring cowbells and maracas to play, but the club banned this practice, on the grounds that it disturbs other customers. I can appreciate this prohibition, having heard fans bang cowbells loudly and out-of-sync at various salsa events. (Indeed, a Puerto Rican salsa musician told me that back home, it's considered disrespectful to "play along" with the band, especially if you can't keep time.)[5] Once in awhile, however, Gary will let a friend take down one of the three *chekeres* (Afro-Cuban beaded calabash shakers) hanging on the left wall, to play along with the music.

To accommodate more customers, an additional twelve tables have been arranged on the outdoor patio by the club entrance. An awning and potted palms frame this outdoor area, marking it off from the sidewalk onto which people have parked their cars, and providing marginal cover from the curious stares of those headed towards El

Sandwich Cubano (The Cuban Sandwich), a late-night fast food joint next door. If you sit outside, you'll find it easier to converse without having to yell above the music. My favorite place, however, especially when I attended the Latina alone, was at the bar. Because most people come here to enjoy the music, not to make sexual conquests, I was usually safe from the advances of strange men, and here I also had a prime vantage point for viewing the slides and video clips that Gary usually features at regular intervals throughout the night, projected on the screen and TV monitor that are located directly above the entrance. Gary's antics are pretty entertaining, too, and he is always willing to let me look at album covers or answer my questions about the music being played. With the engaging musical selection, Gary's hospitality, the club's quality sound equipment, the photos and posters, the videos and slides, and the enthusiastic and participatory mood of the clientele, the Taberna Latina seems like salsa heaven for a (relatively) new fan from North America like myself.

I often got to the Latina at 10:30 p.m., still early. More people would arrive, peaking after midnight and stretching the Latina to its 80–100 person capacity, especially if was a night just after *quincena*, or payday (the 15th or 30th of each month). Despite the early hour, however, many clients had already shown up in eager anticipation of the night's *audición*, or special "listening," that highlights the musical career of a particular artist or group. Gary's audiciones have become an institution since the Latina opened in 1983. Providing more than just a nostalgic musical excursion for long-standing salsa aficionados, these events are also a rich opportunity for younger fans or newcomers to learn about salsa history and styles. Drawing from the over 8,000 records in his collection, Gary is able to present a comprehensive and exclusive selection of musical items that span the career of the artist or group featured in these audiciones. A xeroxed handout containing biographical information and additional background materials compiled from various sources is provided, along with a playlist of the evening's selections. Embellished with musicians' photos and an engaging montage of visuals and graphics, these handouts are artesanal products in themselves, collected by patrons through the years. Tonight's audición features Richie Ray and Bobby Cruz, early salsa stars whose appearance at the 1968 Feria is often cited as a watershed in the history of Cali's scene. Gary puts on their recording of "Amparo Arrebato," written in honor of a famous local salsa dancer, and the song, well known among Caleño salsa fans, gets an enthusiastic response, with people singing the lyrics and clapping along.

Among the large community of salsa fans and *melómanos* in Cali, Gary is a key figure, an organic intellectual who has long championed and disseminated knowledge about salsa and its Cuban and Puerto Rican roots, not only through events at the Taberna Latina, but also through regular radio programs, the organizing of monthly "open-air salsoteca" gatherings in city parks, and concert productions. Although fans, melómanos (aficionados) and record collectors were already well established by the time Gary became active in the early 1980s, one wonders how much Cali's current salsa scene owes to his own prominent efforts. More important, however, is to see how the practices centered around recordings of música antillana and salsa have evolved so as to produce such spaces as the Latina, and such persons as its owner.

Gary's catch-phrase about Cali as "the city of musical memory" raises central questions about salsa as a nexus of local identity. Exactly what music is being remembered? What larger cultural memory is indexed by reference to these sounds? Why has it been important to preserve and maintain this memory? Why recordings, instead of live salsa bands? How does Cali's musical memory serve to position Caleños within regional and national contexts, where issues of economic access and political representation come into play? In what ways is "musical memory" itself a contested terrain for negotiating social difference? Rather than treating the continued local passion for música antillana and salsa dura as "mere nostalgia" or fruitless yearning for the past, it is helpful to see how recordings of these musical styles serve to anchor local participatory activities and a sense of stability, community, and tradition. This is particularly important in a city that is still rapidly developing, bombarded by new influxes of economic capital, migration, and mounting urban violence.

Recordings of música antillana and salsa have been the primary vehicles not only in the adoption of salsa in popular life, but also in its maintenance as a local tradition. Requiring only basic playback equipment to reproduce a documented version of live performance, they have provided a relatively flexible and inexpensive avenue for the maintenance of a salsa scene, in comparison with live music. Recordings have provided the raw material for new popular subjectivities in Cali, influencing the creation of an imagined link to the Caribbean which has enabled Caleños to situate themselves with regards to the national context. Beyond this, however, recordings are imbricated at the center of a consumer culture—through buying, listening, dancing, collecting, disseminating—which forms the site of symbolic negotiations over social differences, lifestyles, and cultural positions. "Musical memory" itself, hence, becomes a contested site in which negotiations over present cultural identities are played out. The development of keen aficionados has emerged as a specialization of consumption practices within this sphere. The detailed knowledge that melómanos prize (e.g., artists, recording dates, and stylistic developments) represents an elaboration of cultural capital in the salsa scene, used to garner prestige and enhance social status.

Salsa dura lyrics, portraying scenes and daily struggles common to barrio life, still resonate with the experiences of many Caleños today, particularly in the lower classes, and this can be seen as one reason for its continued popularity and maintenance. Such an explanation, however, is superficial, since similar conditions prevail in other Latin American cities where salsa dura also once flourished, but where commercial spaces for maintaining this style are no longer viable. Rather, the prevalence of this style has to do with the importance of recordings of salsa and its Cuban-based antecedents in Caleño popular culture from the 1940s to 1970s. The emergence of recordings in local popular life, in turn, relates to the processes of diffusion through which salsa's Cuban-based antecedents arrived in Cali.

"Lo que trajo el barco" (What the Ship Brought)[6]

Cuban-based musical styles (música antillana) first entered Colombia's southwest region in the 1930s through the Pacific port of Buenaventura. The strains of Cuban son, guaracha and bolero were particularly well liked. Being Cali's only immediate connection to routes of international transport and communications, Buenaventura was an important port, the first South American stop for ships passing through the Panama Canal before moving on to Guayaquíl, Lima, and down around the cape to Buenos Aires. Until Cali's international airport was built in 1970, maritime transport was the principal mode of travel for both commerce and leisure. Not only did cargo ships dock in the port, but also luxury ocean liners such as those of the Graceline fleet, which ran regular South American cruises from San Francisco before it folded in the early 1970s. For the upper classes of Cali and the surrounding regions, trips to Europe or North America for study or pleasure were the norm, and the only route was out through Buenaventura and through the Panamá Canal. These passenger ships provided live music, usually a Cuban-style dance orquesta that performed the standard cosmopolitan fare of foxtrots and Cuban rhumbas. Similar bands performed for tourists at the lavish Hotel d'Estación, which was located next to the docks across from the train station that brought passengers to and from Cali.

From the 1930s through the early 1970s, Buenaventura was a lively, cosmopolitan port, much more so than it is today. The loading and unloading of cargo, the hustle of informal markets in the street, the arrival of glamorous cruisers and rich foreigners, the babble of tongues from around the world, the strains of dance music from the hotel, the sartorial elegance of sailors and ship captains, the innuendo of their cologne—all these combined to create a kaleidescopic ambience, set against the lush tropical rainforest surrounding the port. It seems only natural that the Cuban-based sounds of música antillana, with their wide diffusion and cosmopolitan associations, should have entered Buenaventura. Despite the presence of Cuban-style jazz bands in the port, however, it is through recordings, not live music, that these sounds reached the majority of the populace. For one, it is likely that these bands performed watered down versions of Cuban music, and in any case, the wealthy hotel and ship patrons who were the main public for these orquestas did not have substantial contact with the lower classes. Radio broadcasts from Cuban stations cannot be factored in as an influence either—although these emissions were key to the diffusion of Cuban music to Colombia's Atlantic Coast in the 1920s and 1930s, Buenaventura and Cali were too far for clear reception. (Also, although I do not have clear information on this, I presume that, in any case, most people would not have had easy access to shortwave radio sets.) Rather, it is recordings that were the main channel of diffusion, and it is the sailors who worked on ships that docked in the port who became pivotal actors in their dissemination.

The figure of the Caribbean or black American sailor had a particularly strong impact in Buenaventura. Referred to locally as *chombos*, these sailors were admired for their worldly ways, their manner of dress,[7] and their style of dancing. Not only did they bring their musical tastes and dance moves with them, they also brought recordings of these sounds. Medardo Arias, a native of the port, recalls:

> Yo alcanzo a recordar, como hacia mis nueve o diez años, veía llegar por las calles del puerto, verdaderos tropas de marineros de Jamaica, de Puerto Rico. Casi todos, marineros de la compañía Graceline, que era la compañía de pasajeros de entonces, que recalaba en Buenaventura. Y en aquel entonces, esos marineros, a quienes algunos llamaban chombos, protagonizaron uno de los fenómenos musicales más importantes de aquella época. No solamente

por su manera muy particular de versirse, sinón también por una forma de bailar que no se conocía entonces entre nosotros. Era una forma de bailar bastante Caribe, unos pasos que revolucionaban totalmente el concepto que se tenía del baile. Y entonces, la gente fue aprendiendo con ellos también, no solamente de bailar sinón también de la música que estaba iyendo del mar.

[I can remember back to when I was about nine or ten years old, I saw virtual troops of sailors arrive in the streets of the port, from Jamaica, from Puerto Rico. Almost all of them, from the Graceline Company, which was the passenger line at that time which docked in Buenaventura. And in those days, those sailors, who some referred to as chombos, instigated one of the most important musical phenomena of that time. Not only for their singular manner of dressing, but also for a style of dancing that wasn't then known among us. It was a very Caribbean way of dancing, with some steps that revolutionized the concept we had of dancing. And so the people learned from them too, not only how to dance, but also about the music that was arriving by sea.]

According to Cesar Machado, sailors began bringing 78 r.p.m. records to hawk from port to port in the late 1930s, and this informal traffic increased through the 1950s.[8] Says Machado, sailors also carried other items to sell, but records were their most viable commodity. Local residents of the port would often buy entire boxes of records from chombos, and then sell these in the street to individual buyers. Machado himself purchased his first 78 r.p.m. recording in 1953 from one such vendor, for the price of two Colombian pesos, a significant purchase for him at the time, since he was still a teenager and didn't have much money. Most working-class Caleños who travelled to the port during this period usually went for reasons of commerce; Machado, for instance, frequently accompanied a friend who sold trousers in the port.

Obviously, the mere fact of showing up with flat acetate discs for sale does not explain why they became such a hot commodity. The key link which led to popularizing the music recorded in their grooves lies in the bars and cabarets of Buenaventura's red-light district, La Pilota. This was the area frequented by the chombos, who went there to drink, dance, hang out, or find a woman for the night. According to Medardo Arias, La Pilota was the largest red-light district in all South America, and sailors saved up their money to spend in the bars and brothels there.[9] Most of the prostitutes working in La Pilota were not local women, but white and mestiza women from the interior, as well as Venezuelan, French, and even Japanese prostitutes from abroad (Arias says there was a geisha house in the district). By the 1940s, most of these bars had jukeboxes—called *traganiqueles* and later, *rockolas*—and because many of the sailors docking in the port favored música antillana, this is the music that was played. Popular spots that featured such music include El Bar de Prospero, a canteen opened by Prospero Lozano in 1962 and one of the first places to specialize in salsa. The Monterrey cabaret was another spot, and featured live music and floor shows in addition to the latest recorded sounds; Piper Pimienta, one of Cali's pioneer salsa musicians, fronted the Monterrey's house band during the early 1960s.

Since La Pilota was the center of port nightlife and entertainment, música antillana and salsa quickly caught on among locals. Although it is important not to essentialize racial identity when analyzing the transnational spread of música antillana, the fact that Buenaventura's population was (and remains) predominantly Afro-Colombian must be taken into account when considering why this music became so popular. The chombos who listened to música antillana and brought these recordings were also black or mulatto, and the lyrics of countless songs are filled with references to a black racial/ethnic identity: *eh, negro* (hey, black man), *mulata linda* (pretty mulatta), *el tambor/ritmo africano* (the African drum/rhythm) and so forth. Although distinct in specific instrumentation and musical form, the basic stylistic features of Afro-Cuban and Afro-Puerto Rican music are similar to those of the local Afro-Colombian *currulao* tradition, as both derive from musical elements found throughout sub-Saharan African music. These include: interlocking polyrhythms, call-and-response vocals, improvisation over a rhythmic/melodic ostinato, percussion, and a preference for dense or buzzy timbres and textures. Since their musical "habitus" was already oriented to a similar musical aesthetic, it was not a far stretch for *porteños* (natives of the port) to adopt música antillana and, later, salsa. Based on people's anecdotes and my own trips (accompanied) to the port's current red-light district, I assume that this happened first among porteño men, who hung out in La Pilota not so much for the prostitutes as for the drinks, music, and ambience. Young boys, attracted by the music, lights, and bustle of these clubs, also took to música antillana and salsa. Too young to be allowed into the bars, boys hung around on the streets outside, peeking in and imitating the dance moves of the sailors they admired. Some of these youngsters, such as Orlando Watussi, later became important figures in Cali's record-centered dance scene (see below). Local musicians, too, took up música antillana, and by the late 1960s there were over ten local bands performing in this style, also adapting the traditional currulao to this cosmopolitan sound.

The worldly, cosmopolitan associations of música antillana no doubt reinforced its local popularity. We tend to attach the term "cosmopolitan" to jet-set sophisticates, members of the urban middle and upper classes who have received a formal education, often in elite institutions, and who have the resources to travel widely, consume luxury items, and so forth. Yet, if we consider cosmopolitanism in its literal sense—being "of the world"—then sailors, too, must be included in this realm. Although certainly not from the elite socioeconomic ranks of those usually considered to be "cosmopolitan," sailors have shared a similar position of moving between different cultural spheres and different locations. By the very nature of their work, they have been central to processes of commodification, commerce, and the movement of international capital that has shaped contemporary globalization and cosmopolitan technologies. Since they have little economic power or status in relation to those who own the shipping companies or use them to transport their goods and services, however, perhaps it is most appropriate to think of sailors as "working-class cosmopolitans," a proletarian sector laboring within the transport operations of international capitalist expansion. Connected to multiple localities and distinguished through particular codes of dress, physical bearing, talk, musical taste, and manner of dancing—themselves adapted and resignified from other cosmopolitan styles—the chombos transmitted an alternative cosmopolitanism to the Colombian southwest, one accessible to the working classes of Buenaventura and Cali. For this populace, economic growth and technological developments were tying people increasingly to international markets and cultural flows, but they were blocked for reasons of socio-economic class and lack of resources from accessing the elite spheres of cosmopolitan culture. Música antillana, however, was an accessible signifier for "being in the world," adopted from the worldly chombos to become part of local cultural identity. The vogue for música antillana in the 1940s and 1950s became further reinforced through the many Mexican movie musicals that featured these sounds. Recordings, nonetheless, remained the most prominent vehicle for and index of "working-class cosmopolitanism," reflexively shaping a cultural identity among porteños that was simultaneously local and also connected to the larger world.

Through the 1950s and 60s, the image of the record-toting sailor became typical in Buenaventura, welcomed with open arms for the latest musical sounds he brought with him. Ivan Forbes explains:

Con la creación de la Flota Mercante Gran Colombia, muchos naturales de la región tuvieron oportunidad de embarcarse, y ésos traían los últimos éxitos musicales. Si nosotros pensamos en la época de los años '55 o los años 60, de pronto es un paisano de Buenaventura, un negro con su caballo achatado, con una camiseta muy bonita, unos bluyines, unos mocasines, de pronto con una cachucha, masticando chicle. En un lado, una bolsa con comestibles para su casa, y en otra bolsa del otro lado, los discos, 25 o 30 discos. Y comenzaba, eso duro, a trasegar entre el muelle y la casa porque en cada esquina le paraban: "¿Qué me traiste? Muestreme estos discos. "No, éste es de Cortijo, éste de Daniel Sanots, y éste, de Celia Cruz." Por fin, lo mismo llega a su casa, e iniciaba la fiesta.

[With the creation of the Grand Colombian Mechant Fleet, many natives of the region had the opportunity to travel, and these people brought back the latest musical hits. If we think about the epoch around 1955 or the 1960s, maybe it's a fellow Buenaventuran, a black man with his hair straightened, with a really nice shirt, blue jeans, loafers, maybe a cap, and he's chewing gum. He carries a bag with comestibles for his house on one side, and in the other bag on the other side, there's records, 25 or 30 records. And this guy starts to shuffle from the docks to his house, because on every corner they stop him to ask, "What did you bring me? Show me those records." "No, that's Cortijo, this is Daniel Santos, and this one, that's Celia Cruz." Finally, he arrives home, and the party starts.]

Medardo Arias, who grew up in the port, told me similar stories about sailors arriving home. He himself had an uncle who worked in the Gran Flota Mercante, and the family always looked forward to the times when this uncle came back to the port, since he always brought the latest salsa releases from New York City as well as posters of salsa concerts and related events. Given that many of the sailors working for the Colombian merchant fleet were from Buenaventura, it is not surprising that they should have brought their newly adopted musical preferences back to the port, serving as culture brokers in the local adoption of música antillana and salsa. This influence then spread to Cali.

By the late 1950s and through the 1960s, enterprising record dealers in Cali established a solid trade with sailors, travelling regularly to Buenaventura to purchase records. These dealers often placed special orders with sailors to bring bulk shipments of particular recordings, that they would then sell to salsa dance clubs and individual collectors in Cali. According to Lisímaco Paz, who became involved in this trade during the mid-1960s, this was the only way to obtain recordings of música antillana and salsa.[10] Those Caleños who were wealthy enough to travel to New York, where most of these recordings were produced and sold, still looked down on this music, considering it low-class and a *relajo* (scandalous), in Paz's words. Owing to Buenaventura's distance from Cali, there were relatively few record dealers who made routine trips to the coast, only some 15 to 20 individuals, according to Paz. (Although Buenaventura is now less than a 3-hour drive from Cali by the new highway, back then the trip involved a 12-hour journey by railway.) One usually placed orders with sailors, based on the samples they carried, or on local demand back in Cali, especially if it was already a hit among local salsa fans. Says Paz, the size of these orders varied, depending on whether it was a varied selection of albums or several copies of one particular recording (e.g., a hundred or more copies of an especially popular album). When the sailors with whom orders had been placed passed through the Panama Canal on their way back from New York, they contacted the record dealers in Cali to notify them of their arrival in Buenaventura within two or three days. These individuals would then travel out to the port to receive their musical cargo.

According to Lisímaco Paz, most of these dealers also offered deejay rental services for private functions (providing records, sound equipment, and the disc-jockeying), thus creating a market for their records. As Cali's record-centered dance scene blossomed through the 1960s and the craze for *pachanga* and *bugalú* (early salsa forms) seized the city's working classes, competition developed amongst record dealers and disc jockeys to obtain the most recent and exclusive recordings from New York. In order to preserve exclusivity, deejays began erasing the record labels so that the name of the artist and song could not be read, hence preventing competitors from ordering the album. Pacini observes a similar practice among deejays in the *picó* (large sound system) phenomenon of Cartagena and Barranquilla during the 1980s, when sailors were also the only means to obtain recordings of Afropop, Zairean *soukous*, and Caribbean *soca* (1993). By the mid-1990s, these genres had been adopted locally in the hybrid style referred to as *champeta* or *terapia*, and I was able to find recordings of these sounds when browsing through record stores in Cartagena in 1995. The parallel with Cali's early salsa scene is striking, however, and given the fact that the *picós* started in the late 1960s with salsa dura, it is likely that in those days Cartagena and Barranquilla deejays also erased the labels of their most exclusive salsa recordings, just as their Caleño counterparts did. In both cases, it is clear that the difficulty of obtaining recordings enhanced their desirability as commodities, since the amount of time, effort, and money invested in acquiring them was converted directly into symbolic capital and social prestige.

With the advent of Fania Records in the late 1960s and its aggressive push into South American markets during the 1970s, salsa recordings became easily available, as domestic distribution networks replaced the earlier trade through Buenaventura. The symbolic value attached to recordings persists, however, especially amongst collectors and melómanos. As indices of cosmopolitan connections and also markers of prestige, salsa recordings emerged as highly significant objects in local popular life during the 1960s, explaining in part why they have continued to be so important. Their use as a principal source of music for the creation of a vibrant and creative dance scene—much in the way that recordings were used for breakdancing during the rise of African American hip hop in the late 1970s (see Rose, 1994)—helps to fully understand why recordings have been so crucial to local popular culture.

Conclusion

In a sense, buying, listening, and dancing to records of música antillana and salsa have comprised an everyday, on-the-ground manifestation of larger economic and sociopolitical developments shaping Cali's recent growth. For Caleños, recordings—both as consumer objects and as sources of musical sound—have served as an index of new, cosmopolitan ties created through rapid urban expansion, industrial development, and increased international transportation, commerce, and communications links since the 1940s. The daily experiences and social practices of Caleños have been dialectically shaped by pleasurable bodily activities centered around records (e.g., dancing and listening). That dancing to such music was often (and still is) related to sexual conquest underscored its physical and affective impact. For certain aficionados, practices of buying and collecting records also reinforced this process. This process has framed the erotics of local urban identity and the formation of local cultural memory.

Despite the flowering of local live salsa bands during the 1980s and 1990s, recordings still occupy a central position in Cali's scene. This more recent scene, however, is associated with the surge of commercial salsa romántica into local nightclubs and radio airwaves, and is also tied to the strong influence of the Cali cocaine cartel on the local economy during this time. Recordings of música antillana and salsa dura, hence, have acquired additional value as an index of "the good old days" before the 1980s, when Cali was untroubled by urban violence and when people went out to dance nearly every night of the week. Cali's salsotecas and tabernas have arisen as particularly significant sites for recuperating and maintaining a cultural memory of these earlier times. One collector and salsoteca owner refers to the salsotecas and tabernas as "vinyl museums" that function to preserve salsa's legacy for future generations.[11]

Along with buying and collecting records, listening and dancing to salsa have emerged as quotidian but significant acts through which Caleños virtually re/member how they experienced and made sense of the city's transformation into a major urban and industrial center. In recent years the music industry has tied local bands and media to its own commercial project, hence ignoring the base that facilitated its entrance into the city's popular culture in the first place. Within this context, the recorded music central to Cali's earlier salsa scene continues to serve as the focal point of musical activity for working-class Caleños, shaping and reaffirming the experiences of their everyday lives.

References

Appadurai, A. (1996). *Modernity at large: Cultural dimensions of globalization.* Minneapolis: University of Minnesota Press.

Douglas, M. and B. Isherwood. (1996/1979). *The world of goods: Towards an anthropology of consumption.* New York: Routledge.

Keil, C. (1984). Music mediated and live in Japan, *Ethnomusicology 28*(1), 91–96. [Reprinted in C. Keil and S. Feld (Eds.), *Music Grooves.* (pp. 247–256) Chicago: University of Chicago Press, 1994].

Manuel, P. (1993). *Cassette culture: Popular music and technology in North India.* Chicago: University of Chicago Press.

Mauss, M. (1973). Techniques of the Body. *Economy and Society, 2*(1), 70–85.

Pacini Hernández, D. (1993). The *picó* phenomenon in Caragena, Colombia. *América Negra 6*, 69–115.

Rose, T. (1994). *Black noise: Rap music and black culture in contemporary America.* Wesleyan: Wesleyan University Press.

Waxer, L. (1994). Of Mambo kings and songs of love: Dance music in Havana and New York from the 1930s to the 1950s. *Latin American Music Review 15*(2), 139–176.

———. 1996. *Salsa* in Cali: Popular Identity and Local Style in a Hemispheric Musical Culture. Presented at the 41st Annual Meeting of the Society for Ethnomusicology, Toronto.

Author Note

I would like to thank Thomas Turino, Cameron McCarthy, Steven David and Greg Dimitriadis for comments made on earlier drafts and sections of this paper. Research in Cali was supported by grants from the Social Sciences and Humanities Research Council of Canada, the Wenner-Gren Foundation, the American Association of University Women, the Nellie Signor fund (University of Illinois International Studies), and the University of Illinois Graduate College, all of which I gratefully acknowledge. Portions of this paper were presented to the Society for Ethnomusicology (Waxer, 1996).

Notes

1. In Cali, the term *salsoteca* specifically refers to places that feature only salsa; *tabernas* such as the Latina, on the other hand, also feature other, related genres, such as traditional Cuban son, Latin jazz, and contemporary Cuban styles such as *songo* and *timba*.

2. Although Cuban styles form the basis of *música antillana*, the influence of these sounds beyond Cuban borders makes it difficult to conceive of such music in purely national terms (see Waxer, 1994). I prefer to use the term "música antillana" (literally, music from the Hispanic Caribbean) because of its fluid, transnational reference. In addition, this is the term most commonly used in Colombia to refer to salsa's musical antecedents.

3. *Clave* is the central rhythmic timeline or pattern around which all other rhythmic parts in salsa are organized.

4. A locally produced hard liquor made from sugar cane, and flavored with anise. *Aguardiente* is considered to be the national drink of Colombia, and varies in potency from region to region.

5. Ricky Rodríguez, salsa arranger and also pianist of Orquesta Mulenze, personal communication, 18 June 1995.

6. The title is adopted from a 1990 documentary (itself named after a well-known 1972 salsa recording by Ismael Rivera) produced for Imágenes TV by Medardo Arias about the entry of recordings of *música antillan* and salsa into southwest Colombia.

7. According to Medardo Arias, onshore dress was usually a tropical version of a Harlem zoot-suit, complete with Panamá hat, two-toned shoes, watch fob and chain, and walking stick, all swathed in a thin cloud of vetivert cologne (personal communication, 6 May 1996).

8. Personal communication, 20 February 1996.

9. Personal communication, 6 May 1996.

10. Personal communication, 19 February 1996. The following details about the record trade are based on the taped interview conducted with Lisímaco Paz on this date.

11. Luis Enrique "Kike" Escobar, personal communication, 11 April 1996.

MUSIC IN THE CONTESTED METROPOLIS: ROCK AND THE CONTRADICTORY POLITICS OF YOUTH

Live Through This: Music, Adolescence, and Autobiography

Chris Richards

Introduction

There are two main intentions guiding the discussion to be presented in this chapter. First of all, I want to consider the concept of taste and to engage with Pierre Bourdieu's argument that taste is an expression of an individual's objective location in systems of social classification and difference. Though I have derived fundamental aspects of my understanding of taste from the work of Bourdieu, and will clarify these in the following discussion, I want to argue for more emphasis on agency in the formation of taste. The second intention is to examine forms of school-based writing in the representation of popular cultural experience. In the research for this chapter in 1994–95, I explored an autobiographical mode of writing with twelfth year students (16–17 years old) in a selective high school in north London. The emphasis on an autobiographical form was intended to elicit evidence of how "adolescents" represent themselves, to themselves and to others. To call upon them to draw on music, as a symbolic resource, in their autobiographical self-accounts required some plausible model of self-representation. The BBC Radio 4 program, *Desert Island Discs*,[1] provided a starting point.

Some preliminary attempts to determine a viable approach to "music biographies" were made in the context of a media research seminar involving myself and a number of teachers of media studies in secondary, further, and higher education. The form in which members of the seminar were asked to report on their musical tastes replicated the flattery, and the fantasy, of being invited to select favored

records to play on *Desert Island Discs*. The session was interestingly
unnerving, personally revealing, and, to some extent, uncomfortable.
Thus, even among consenting adults of similar educational background,
and mostly already quite well known to each other, self-presentation
through musical tastes was perceived to be more risky than a discussion in which selections of books, films, television programs, and even
clothes might be the main concern.

These biographical games suggested several possibilities. Taste in
music appears to be constructed as revealing of "interiority" because
music is culturally positioned as a distinctively "expressive" and "affective" medium. Moreover, there is a broad, though culturally circumscribed, reading of the "physical" characteristics of music as mysteri-
ous: a medium which, because it cannot be seen, can be felt but not
touched, and which may be experienced as both filling the external
space around us and penetrating the boundaries of the body as well,
might thus be equated with religious concepts of spirituality and of
intersubjective communion. The histories of both European "classical" and of African-American music are significantly entwined with
traditions of religious assembly and of the various configurations of
intersubjectivity which they have aspired to achieve. For example, Jazzie
B's "Soul-II-Soul," though seemingly an entirely secular concept, nevertheless recovers the religious connotations of soul music.[2] Of course,
the religious modalities of intersubjectivity inscribed in soul performance are always also constantly reappropriated as metaphors of sexual
experience. This is perhaps further confirmation of the way in which
translation between the domains of religious, sexual, and musical experience is characterized by some convergence around concepts of
disconnection from the everyday and a dissolution of the enclosing
boundaries of the subject (see Bourdieu, 1986, pp. 79–80).

In this context, taste, as well as being a matter of locating the self in
a social classification, can also be understood as an element in the
discursive construction of relations between subjects. Thus, subjects
may position themselves in relations with others through a mapping
of such relations onto the allegiances and divisions available in discursively constructed taste categories: friends might, for example, register "friendship" through a common liking for rap and not pop. Equally,
the negotiation of boundaries may be, in fantasy, strictly around a
singular self, or may locate the self with numerous others (fans, perhaps) or, of course, may be dyadic—in the "sharing of tastes," as a
signifier of intimacy. Such boundaries can also be exclusions, some-

times vigorously insisted upon, by people for whom the intersubjective taste relation is more sharply defined by refusing to include others.

There are emotional dynamics involved in the formation of tastes and taste allegiances which, though no doubt informing responses which can be read in terms of public social self-positioning, are not thus exhausted by such a reading. Bourdieu's methodology (usually involving large-scale social surveys and "questionnaires") provides the means for mapping relations between cultural choices, objective social positions, and the distances between classes and class fractions within a national culture. The statistical production of such a map has a provisional validity—it allows plausible hypotheses about relations between culture and class on a macrosociological scale. However, it does not address questions of biographical specificity or, in thus neglecting such questions, conceive of social subjects as "divided" and complexly formed through many more social categories than class and as continuing to reform themselves in more fluid and variable sets of relations with others. To suggest how Bourdieu's work might inform teaching, I need to complement his own approach by attending to the subjective negotiation of the meanings given to tastes by people themselves.

In the context of a macrosociological model of social relationships and their reproduction (Bourdieu, 1986), individual subjects, their biographies, and their familial histories become illustrations of the structural order within which their tastes are located. I want to argue that teaching requires a more "situated" knowledge, informing and illuminating the more particular details of classroom exchanges. The practice of teaching demands more attention to agency and to the complexity of individual subjects' choices and self-understanding than the practice of (macro) sociological theory. Thus, though following much of Bourdieu's analysis of taste, its level and purpose cannot adequately inform the practice to which my own account relates.

Bourdieu does not eliminate agency from his theoretical system but he does quite carefully qualify what it might mean:

> Without subscribing to the interactionist—and typically petit-bourgeois—idealism which conceives the social world as will and representation, it would nevertheless be absurd to exclude from social reality the representation which agents form of that reality. The reality of the social world is in fact partly determined by the struggles between agents over the representation of their position in the social world and, consequently, of that world (Bourdieu, 1986, p. 253).

With this in mind, it is useful to turn to what Bourdieu has to say about youth:

> The "young" can accept the definition that their elders offer them, take advantage of the temporary license they are allowed in many societies ("Youth must have its fling"), do what is assigned to them, revel in the "specific virtues" of youth, *virtu*, virility, enthusiasm, and get on with their own business—knight-errantry for the scions of the mediaeval aristocracy, love and violence for the youth of Renaissance Florence, and every form of regulated, ludic wildness (sport, rock, etc.) for contemporary adolescents—in short, allow themselves to be kept in the state of "youth," that is, irresponsibility, enjoying the freedom of irresponsible behaviour in return for renouncing responsibility (Bourdieu, 1986, pp. 477–478).

"Youth" and "adolescence" are institutionally powerful categories to which young people are subject but which they also draw upon in contesting the social relations, particularly of schools, in which they are positioned. Thus, Bourdieu's reference to "struggles between agents over the representation of their position" should also qualify his suggestion that the young "allow themselves to be kept in the state of 'youth.'" For though this is one plausible reading of the social position "accepted" by young people, many other meanings and consequences of "irresponsibility" need to be considered. Otherwise, there is a risk of acquiescing in Bourdieu's construction of an historically enduring deception in which the differing possibilities of "youth" are blurred together. To the contrary, I want to emphasize that if tastes in youth are less constrained to fit into the prevailing order of (good) taste, then they can be less conforming to cultural boundaries, both those of "official" culture and of popular culture. They might be more promiscuous, more (dis)located and more unpredictable than Bourdieu appears to accept (see Bourdieu, 1986, pp. 466–7). "Youthful irresponsibility," however much a deferral of social power and responsible adult agency, can be productive of significant cultural innovation and not least through the mixing of perhaps otherwise disparate cultural elements which, confined to the young, are thus brought into relation with each other. Schools, for example, because they bring together disparate groups on the basis of their youth, provide one kind of context for such mixing (cf. Hewitt, 1986, p. 154). Thus while reconfirming the subordination of the young, they also contribute to the preconditions of cultural (re)combination.

The limitations of Bourdieu's descriptions, particularly when faced with historical specificity and change, with expanding cultural diversity, and with questions of political action and ethical choice, have been noted by many critics (Connell, 1983; Frow, 1987; Mander, 1987, pp. 427–453; Shiach, 1993). Despite this, the account developed in the rest of this chapter continues to engage with his approach to the logic of taste. My own emphasis, however, is upon taste both as public social category (which might therefore be the object of extensive discursive analysis) and, for social actors, a continuing relational strategy, drawing upon historically particular cultural repertoires, always provisionally fulfilling a variety of purposes in the lives of particular individuals. Some of these purposes I would expect to be available to subjects as strategies of which they can be conscious, and of which they can give accounts, if the need arises; other purposes are undoubtedly of the kind mapped into Bourdieu's elaboration of habitus. Still others may well be more intractably unconscious, in the psychoanalytic sense, and are thus, strictly speaking, beyond the scope of my research.

However, it is of some importance, at this point, to acknowledge the psychoanalytically informed approach adopted by Cohen:

> [T]he family romance in all its forms . . . potentially connects the child to sites of social aspiration outside both family *and* school . . . [working-class youth] construct out of materials to hand (friends, work-mates, the neighbourhood) those territories of desire (Freud's "other scenes") which make the oppressive circumstances of working-class life and labour seem just about bearable (Cohen, 1984, pp. 148–149).

He argues that the resources of popular media culture are incorporated into the fantasies constructed both within families and in the gender-divided self-presentations of adolescent peers. Thus, in delineating the family romance, he focuses on:

> those normative structures of projective identification through which parents and children, usually of the same sex, misrecognise in each other the social embodiment of developmental ideals constructed by the dominant culture . . . [thus] TV, or movie stars, rock stars, sporting personalities . . . furnish the models for "supermum" or "superdad" against which actual parents are often compared invidiously. They also provide all those "famous" first names (e.g. Elvis, Marilyn) whose symbolic function is to inscribe the child's history in a certain genealogy of parental desire (Cohen, 1984, p. 148).

Such fantastic transformations of the immediate facts of family relations and identities are not, of course, peculiar only to the working-class subjects of Cohen's research. The students discussed here are also caught up in transitions explored, in part, in terms of other places, other selves and a sexuality somewhat disembedded from real relations with others.

Autobiographies: Live Through This . . .

The following discussion centers on the way in which a selection of 22 twelfth year students represented themselves in response to this request:

> I would like everyone to work out a way of selecting six track titles which might be used to represent yourself—using music to structure a condensed autobiography—to other people. It is up to you to decide on the kind of audience you want to address and what the context might be; equally, the context might well suggest a particular persona. You could, for example, imagine a scenario in which you have been invited onto a radio programme to talk about yourself and the music that you like. So, in whatever terms you choose, you need to suggest why your tracks matter to you, when they did so, and what you can say about them now.

I had prepared this in advance of my meeting with the students but, in fact, I neither read it to them in exactly this form nor gave it to them on paper. To some extent, their response to the task might be judged as informed by a degree of respectful acquiescence and relative familiarity with the manner, and interests, of academics. These students, all studying for A-levels in a selective school, were themselves mostly organizing their present in terms of a future in, and beyond, study at the university level.

Virtually everyone present gave me what they had written. What remained unsaid was whether they should expect to see it returned to them and, if so, for what further purpose. The teacher[3] responsible for the A-Level course seemed to speak as if their writing was "for me," to be given without any expectation that it be returned. This tended to locate what they had done as more of a response to a research enquiry than a necessary piece of coursework. The A-Level students were addressed as willing and capable, and as familiar both with forms of writing about themselves and with being requested to produce them for teachers. My presence and my requests were accepted because of such preexisting expectations, shared by students and teachers alike. In effect, I assumed both the outcome of their particular experience of schooling and their complicity in the continuation of its demands even beyond the limit of compulsory attendance.

Indeed, to write about themselves, in some detail, must have seemed quite "natural" for students accustomed to believing their words, and their thoughts, to be of value. To be asked to provide writing for research, beyond the requirements of teachers, perhaps seemed further confirmation of what they "knew" about themselves. Despite this, there *were* also a few students whose writing subsequently suggested some ambivalence and I will discuss these examples in the course of this chapter.

Autobiography, as a classroom genre, is typically introduced by teachers as a means to recover early childhood experience and clearly also entails the prescription of subject positions distinct from, because enabling reflection upon, those located "in childhood" (see James, 1993). These students were very much accustomed to being positioned, by teachers, as mature, distanced, and reflective (cf. Moss, 1989). In fact, they were all likely to be very competent in this particular social practice of remembering and to have access to a variety of discursive forms in judging how to represent themselves on this particular occasion (see Middleton & Edwards, 1990).

Here, I suspect that I had invited a piece of writing with far more popular precedents than *Desert Island Discs*. In the wider cultural organization of long-term memory, popular music radio constantly "orders" the past through the recovery of "chart music," differentiating seasons and years and decades. Alongside such practices as photography, particularly in combination with holidays, music has been constructed as one of the primary means of recovering "memories," of "liminal moments" and particularly their associated "emotions." The construction of self-continuity, in the context of "time-space compression," draws upon the resources provided by commercial popular music (Harvey, 1989, p. 292). The task thus invited them to use a cultural resource with which, in these more general terms, all would be familiar. This may well be a further explanation for what was, on the whole, a relative subordination of school-orientated features in their writing. The discursive forms on which they drew in producing their notionally self-representational texts appeared mostly to derive from a popular rather than a "scholastic" repertoire.

On the particular occasion when I requested their writing, the group was composed of white students only, of whom perhaps two or three were Jewish. The past trajectories of these students were strongly convergent. At the age of 11, they had been selected from a large number of applicants by competitive examination and were therefore likely to be characterized by a significant commitment to educational achievement. The school has also favored those students who are accomplished in the performance of "classical" music and many were, in those terms, musically "literate."

In their writing, the range of musical references and the modes of self-representation suggest, to some extent, shared repertoires. Indeed, there is some evidence of "tastes," in Bourdieu's sense, which might be connected with their class and educational locations. However, it is important also to read these pieces of writing as self-representational in their forms of organization, rather than simply in terms of explicit evidence of musical preferences. Taste, as a feature of social position, does not disappear from my analysis but it is clearly more than an "objectifiable" quality of subjects and is more appropriately examined as a trope in the contextually variable discursive construction of the self.

David

In response to a brief "questionnaire," scantily completed, David, a Jewish boy, not yet seventeen, responded to "What do you expect to do when you leave (school)?" with "Go to the shop + buy a coke! Ho Ho Media Studies at a University" [spelling corrected]. The elaboration of his self-account extended to five A4 pages (lined, with a margin) of small hand-written reflection. It was presented with the title "Fish," his name, and signed and dated.

There are numerous spelling mistakes, words are crossed out, and the handwriting is sometimes awkward, occasionally difficult to read. The *formality* of presentation expected of "schoolwork" was not, it seemed, a significant priority. The narrative exceeds and defies the constraint contained within the invitation (six tracks), naming whole albums and entire genres and only reluctantly settling for less. He talked confidently to the whole group about his selection and played the cassette that accompanied the writing. Clearly, the organization of his self-account can be read as an accomplished act of synthesis between the forms of school writing and those of more informal practices. The ordered, linear narrative, appropriately paragraphed, demonstrates the competence of a student whose continuing formation is achieved, sustained, and confirmed in the production of essays. But the title defies school conventions, transitions are more representative of informal speech genres ("Lets jump a bit now. . ."; "Another Leap forward now. . ."), and, quite often, he produces lists of artists, as if detailing the extent of his collection and finding satisfaction in presenting more publicly a mostly private writing practice. Indeed, his private investment, a sustained gathering of music into himself, animated his display of informal knowledge, overwhelming the sanctioned generic artifice of selecting six tracks. It seemed as if the urgency of self-presentation as an expert exceeded any more disciplined self-positioning as strictly competent within the given terms of the task.

His writing combines introspection with an assertive attention to detail. He draws upon a discourse in which early childhood experience is equated with the fundamentally formative moments of individual subjectivity. He begins "From very young. . .," and positions music as "integrale" (sic), "key," able to "stick in my mind." He claims "My mother tells me I was able to clap to the rythm of records from about 6 months and I suppose that from then the influence realy was important" and, reiterating, continues "From very young I remember certain tracks specificly. . . ." His account, thus framed, becomes a display of interiority and of competence in its recovery and analysis:

> By the next couple of years my tastes had turned to PUNK ROCK, The Stranglers. My parents had one of their albums and I was in love with the song, 'Golden Brown'. Again just realy because of repetitive play and familiarity with the track. At the time when I heared the record it conjured up an Image of a long, tiled passage, curving. This must have been a passage at a tube station in my mind's eye probably because at the end of the track there was a kind of echoy effect which must have played on my mind.
>
> Perhaps this is cheating but for my third choice I am choosing all three Hit Factory albums the best from PWL, Stock Aitken + Waterman. I cringe at the thought now but at the time I was so proud to be like part of this whole thing. I by purchasing this record, was part of the Hit Factory!

Such a "confessional" and "personal" statement has a tactical value here: it is a condition of his claim to expert knowledge that such self-positioning be given depth and honesty and a history. The capacity to remember in detail, and to articulate such memory, also provides further confirmation of his scholastic credibility for, however "trivial" and ephemeral the recollected "tastes" might be, it is in his display of reflective self-distancing from them that his authority is constructed. Indeed, it is also likely that, in this highly competitive educational setting, he was willing to "reveal" so much because, in doing so, he positioned himself as that much more "knowing" than his fellow students.

A further tactic involved in sustaining his "position of knowledge" involved what may be a distinctly "masculine" relation to music. For example, he writes:

> As a Jew I had had my Bar Mitzvah and therefore gained a pretty lucrative sum of money. I spent nearly all over the next 2 years on cassette singles. . . I massed 119 cassette singles which I do pride myself on their diversity and variation.

I want to suggest, if tentatively, that it was the boys who collected music and appeared to enjoy opportunities to make public the quantity, and sometimes the range, of what they had accumulated. To have a collection may be a way of marking out a public, and individually differentiated, self in the context of family and friendship networks. It is also, plausibly, a support for a particular practice of remembering, strongly accented as "individual" by contrast with, for example, the practice of keeping a family photograph album (cf. Middleton & Edwards, 1990; Harvey, 1989). Thus, though there are many ways in which a collection connects the collector to more broadly shared social identities, for boys this practice may signify a tactical separation from familial others, and thus have some importance in claiming a particular kind of masculine identity (see Chodorow, 1978).

David also asserted that:

> I realy don't have any records that have Emotional connotations for me and the reason I buy a record is because of the sound and the quality not just because everyone else likes it or its a particular genre.

Again, this reaffirms his self-construction as an "expert" and it is possible to suggest that in relation to music, which is culturally constructed as "emotional," it was important for him, in this educational context, to define knowledge in terms which emphasize the achievement of rational discrimination, choice and control. In some circumstances, it may be more imperative for boys to position themselves within the terms of such a knowledge because they thus locate themselves as less vulnerable to the implication that they may be positioned by others. In a school where the achievement of "knowledge" has been highly regarded, and striven for, not to espouse mastery in elite forms of knowledge could be problematic for both boys and girls. Within media studies, where an overtly theoretical discourse can reassure those devoting their time to the study of popular forms, pop music is an awkward object, untheorized and immediately a part of current everyday life.

Distancing, by invoking "memory," for example, might thus become of some importance. For David, where distance is not claimed, the music is of a kind usually construed as hypermasculine and, in his account, is given a selective political credibility:

> Now I have one choice left. The only area I haven't touched is rap. I now consume more rap than anything else perhaps because of its alternativeness, its legendry qualities or perhaps the rebelios attitude that prevails. My diversity in this area is apparent too with like for Old-Skool (sic) so called Gangsta rap, Jazz rap, G-Funk, and newly created Horror rap. My final choice though is from none of these. It is British, anti-racism anti-homophobia anti-sexism yet still with a sharp rhyme and a unique quality leading to contravesy in the music press. The record's *Call it What You Want* by Credit to the Nation.

Once again, this achieves several purposes. It sustains his self-representation as mobile across taste boundaries, itself a feature of the "indeterminacy" of "adolescence," and confirms that he knows such hard, male music. However, it also displays an explicit act of choice which, in the same moment, reasserts a politics appropriate to his positioning as a serious student in a liberal educational domain. In his concluding comment, he explains that for several years

> I had no TV therefore was an avid listener to radio and listened to music no one else had heard of. When It comes to music I like to think I know what I'm talking about and this has been the case since my early teens. It is and I hope it continues to be an integrale part of my life.

In effect, he represents his own relation to music as both "personal" and "expert." The account, from early childhood through to his self-positioning within a continuing "adolescence," translates the layering together of several distinctive phases of his experience into an implicit guarantee of the cultural authority to which he lays claim (cf. Ross, 1989, pp. 81–2).

Caleb

Caleb's '*Media Studies. Most memorable music tracks,*' by its title, locates what follows as belonging both in the domain of popular discourse and in the subject of media studies. Memory and acts of remembering are of considerable importance here. In this case, the narrative is not that of the self as expert, but as emergent "adolescent." Like David, he presented much of his written account of himself to the whole group and was perhaps even more confident in doing so. There is also a similar tactical self-construction as the more mature, reflective self able to recall and retell emotionally accented events from an earlier period, almost as if the adolescent figure thus reconstructed was really a fiction. In fact, it would be plausible to suppose that these "memories" are not Caleb's at all but are rather contrived in accord with the columns of teenage magazines. His act of public self-positioning combined humor and self-mockery with an implicit emotional authenticity. The text became both a script for a performance and, carefully word-processed, copy ready for publication:

> When I was in junior school, I had mixed feelings about the school Christmas parties or discos. I would look forward to it because, there would always be that chance of dancing (or not!) with that girl I was madly and passionately in love with. However, there was the fact that my clothes were not the height of fashion, but worse then that was that I never knew the words of the songs. . .
> The song I remember the most from these discos was Michael Jackson's "Beat it." All the boys knew the words, the girls only seemed to like those boys that knew the words, and hey, I didn't. All except for "So beat it, beat it, beat it, beat it." I remember lots of times when my worst nightmare would seem to come true. After plucking up the courage to ask my favourite girl to dance, the song would come on, and not wishing to be humiliated I would pretend I needed the loo, and run and disappear there. However, trying to keep my street cred, I would come back out again at the chorus singing "Beat it, Beat it," as if I knew the song like the back of my hand. Realising, I couldn't go to the toilets again, I would last the remainder of the dance by either turning around a lot, or covering my mouth whilst in a coughing fit (naturally singing the words as well!)

The rest of his account is constituted through a similar "remembering" of particular songs in "typical situations" with parents, friends, and girls. Writing as a school student, sexuality is simultaneously claimed and disowned: an attribute of a self distanced by memory. In common with the talk of some radio deejays, music is represented as giving access to that self and the emotions otherwise forgotten:

> Overall the majority of the songs, seem to indicate the desire for a romance with a girl when I was younger. Most of the songs have some reflection on the feelings I used to have towards different girls. Music on the whole does invite feelings of love and similar emotions to surface. However the songs that really mean the most to me are songs that remind me of a friend or a friendship, or some important time in my childhood.

Caleb's appropriation of a discourse of "adolescent emotionality," though carefully contained by the framing of a male self, suggests a continuing self-location somewhat within "adolescence."

When I began this research, I expected to be able to make some clear connections between the choices of music students offered, features of their social position, and other aspects of their publicly displayed identities. In fact, it was difficult to conceive of mapping relationships between forms of music and social identities in any very "reliable" way.[4] Preferences could be very unstable and publicly declared preferences changed, tactically, with the circumstances. For some, distinct claims to musical knowledge were of some importance, but, for many others, preferences were represented as more contingent, and to attach much significance to particular choices would be unproductive. Again, then, the question of taste is better defined in terms of how these students represent their *relation to* music: "contingency" might thus be understood as one particular kind of "taste-relation," a matter of particular cultural practices of self-presentation—if, also, sometimes an instance of individual disavowal.

Unlike David, Caleb did not make his choice of music a tactical claim to authority in the domain of popular music. His list was brief, eclectic but broadly popular: "Beat It," "Living Doll," and "The Young Ones" (Cliff Richard), "Tears of Heaven" (Eric Clapton), *Die Zauberflöte* (Mozart), "End of the Road" (Boyz II Men), "I've Had the Time of my Life" (from *Dirty Dancing*), "Lady in Red" (Chris be Burgh) and "Love Shack" (B-52s). Of course, it would be possible to note what is not included here and to remark on its proximity to such "bland" categories as "easy listening" or "MOR" but, in the end, explanation would have to return to the details of the circumstances which have been recalled in Caleb's selection and representation of these tracks.

It is important to note at this point, that for both David and Caleb and many of those students discussed subsequently, biographical organization of their writing does not produce a sharply delimited "progression" from one music to another. There is often, if not always, an unwillingness to allow one music to entirely displace another. As I have suggested, to make equations between their choices and their identities, on the basis of such evidence, would be very difficult. Identities tend to be represented by many of the students as insistently undecided. Furthermore, it is important to acknowledge that the connections between musical choices and "identities" are not likely to be "simply" available within the conscious repertoires of discourse they deploy, and that such connections may prove intractably elusive.[5]

A further perspective on this is suggested by Roger Hewitt, who has argued that to visualize "identity" in a "polyculture" it may be helpful to compare urban graffiti with palaeolithic "cave paintings" (Hewitt, 1992). In each case, images are superimposed within the same physical space and thus coexist in relations of cumulative "de-stabilization." I want to suggest that, to some extent, though chronologically ordered, the effect of these "adolescent" students' statements of musical interest is to accumulate layers of cultural identification without there being a "core" identity beneath any one of them. It seems unhelpful, therefore, to select one layer and declare it to be unequivocally more fundamental than the others. To some extent this argument converges to confirm the case made by Cohen (1986) against the notion of simple "transitions" through childhood, adolescence, and into adulthood: the idea of singular, and clearly separated, *stages* is inadequate to the description of identities.[6]

Nicholas

So far, I have discussed the writing produced by two boys, and, of course, it is tempting to make generalizations about the gendering of the positions they adopt. To complicate this somewhat, I want to continue with further examples from the boys' writing before turning my attention to a selection of the girls' responses. Nicholas's *"6 Tracks"* presents an account of his musical preferences which oscillates between choices seemingly located in an autonomous self, choices located in his family history, and choices which are defined more by an occasion shared with friends. He produced a detailed and carefully handwritten account, adhering, even more closely than Caleb, to the prescribed instruction. The complexity of his response to the task is thus, remarkably, contained and ordered within three sides of A4. All six of his choices are represented in terms which draw upon a repertoire of distinctive "emotions" and, often, typically liminal experiences. Sometimes, it seems as if the encounter with a new and intensely "emotive" music is itself a liminal moment:

> (i) "Back to One" recorded by Obituary taken from the album *The End Complete* recorded in 1992 for Roadrunner. . . It really opened up my mind to a new form of music. At first I was shocked because I had never heard any music like this ('Death' metal) and it was such a departure from the music I'd heard before, it was much more brutal and extreme. Because of this album I went on to buy and become interested in more extreme forms of music and this has basically shaped my musical tastes of today and the other bands I used to listen to no longer interest me except maybe holding memories of when I was younger.

His interest in "death metal," and related forms, is further illustrated with "'Anaesthesia' Bass solo from the Album 'Kill Em All' recorded by Metallicas Bassist Cliff Burton. . ."; and "'World of Shit' Nailbomb from the album 'Point Blank' released on Roadrunner records 1994," on which he comments:

> This song as well as appealing to me musically being a hybrid cross between punk and death metal also appeals to me lyrically. Nailbombs lyrics are very social and political. . . Also is a very violent + aggressive song + is a good song to listen to when youre angry, it has an almost cathartic effect on me a good way of neutralising my anger.

This particular characterization of music as intensely affective will emerge as common to many of these students in discussion of subsequent examples. But here it is notable that the violence and apparent nihilism of the music is, on the whole, subordinated to a rationalist political discourse; thus "World of Shit" is:

> about the violence racism hate etc which is "bred" in the world by many of the worlds politicians + statesmen and how the earth as well as us is suffering consequences and how the solution lies with us as does the future. I prefer lyrics to be meaningful and to have a point + that is why this song appeals to me.

Like David, Nicholas achieves a mix of interests here. The aggressive masculinity of metal is celebrated but also, in school, assimilated to a discourse in which such music is both "cathartic" and politically "educational." This might suggest a quasi-heroic self-construction, locating himself in an implicit narrative of discovery, trauma, and subsequent development. Through the extremity of the metal domain, he has become a more mature and politically sophisticated person. At the same time, such a narrative doubles as an account of learning and, consistent with the explanatory mode of address, reconfirms both his present, and his future, as a student for whom "adolescent" experience has been explored and explained.

A further aspect of the construction of "adolescent" experience, in this case as an almost uniquely memorable biographical moment, is evident in many students' accounts of their summers, out of school.[7] Here, remembering, as one practice through which to sustain identity, clearly draws upon a broadly shared discursive repertoire, though there is also a distinctive individual inflection, an accenting of both remembered "contents" and of their retelling. In this case, Nicholas again, the evaluative emphasis on one track sustains the "rational" subject position, reviewing experience and selecting from it to allow an aspect to stand as a public statement of taste:

> "Fool to Cry" by the Rolling Stones originally recorded 1973 but rereleased on *Jump Back*. . . This song is another song I particularly like partially because of the memory and also because I think its a great song. The memory is of the first day of the Summer holidays after me and my friends finished our GCSEs. Met some of my old friends from primary school and some of my friends from this school all got together round one of my friends houses and decided to recreate Woodstock the festival in his bedroom seeing as we obviously didn't make it to the first one and it was summer of 35th [sic] anniversary. We just sat around listening to bands we would have liked to see play. (Rolling Stones, Doors, Pink Floyd, Jimi Hendrix etc.) It was a really nice sunny day and was a very 'mellow' experience. This song now always reminds me of that day and indeed the whole summer which was probably the best summer of my life. The song is possibly the best song I have ever heard memory aside.

A similar tactic is apparent in Nicholas's two remaining choices. Thus his account of Morricones "Good Bad + Ugly" [Ecstacy of Gold], taken from the soundtrack to the film, becomes a careful consideration of what part memory has played in forming a taste for such an apparently anomalous choice. The track is defined as enabling the recovery of an intense, "atmospheric and epic," experience which has, like his own "Woodstock," a distinct location in a liminal time: "Me and some friends went to see Metallica play at the Milton Keynes bowl. Before Metallica come on they always play this music . . . one of the highlights of 1993." Similarly "Feed the World"/"Do They Know It's Christmas?" (Band Aid), which has no musical connection with his other choices, is explained in terms of a distinctive biographical moment:

> At this time my mother was in hospital about to have my youngest sister Jessica. On the night Jessica was born me and my other two sisters spent the night at friends houses while my Dad went to see my sister. The next morning as we drove to the hospital to see our new sister we were listening to the radio . . . it reminds me of that day even now and I always associate it with my youngest sister.

"Taste" in this account is produced as the outcome of a particular practice of remembering, widely shared and culturally popular as I have suggested, but also inflected towards the inscription of a distinct, reflective, individual self, assessing what combinations of coincident circumstances have motivated the given selection. The rhetorical tactics of the account as a whole are to construct, not a "kind" of person, but himself as an individual.

To conclude this selective discussion of writing produced by boys, I want to turn now to a minority in whose accounts music was subordinated to sport. Given the biographical invitation, they responded with accounts in which they brought another variant of popular practices of remembering into what were carefully negotiated appropriations of the task. For these boys, a primary self-positioning through music was unwelcome, but they nevertheless produced self-accounts which were almost more committed to a repertoire of "personal," "liminal" and "emotive" moments than several of those who positioned themselves as "knowing" about music. It may be that, in the context of this largely middle-class group of students, and in a school where musical knowledge and skill, though not of the popular kind, have been given a high prestige, the inscription of the self in accounts centered in sport was an assertion of a continuing class position. The competitive and bodily forms of male sport were drawn into an implicit refusal of the musical repertoire more widely shared in the group as a whole. Indeed, some evidence of self-conscious class positioning emerged in these cases.

Paul

Paul's selection of tracks, untitled, undated, was handwritten. Paul writes of songs which recall "things that have happened to people or things that I can relate to." In fact, he names only five tracks: "Eye of the Tiger," from *Rocky III*, "because when watching the film the adrenalin starts flowing and now that song has the same effect"; "Simply the Best," "kind of related to boxing because Chris Eubank has used [it] as his anthem"; "Money for Nothing" by Dire Straits; "Go West" by the Pet Shop Boys, "it is not the song I like but the adaption of the song by the Arsenal supporters . . . it reminds me of when Arsenal won the European Cup Winners Cup last season and the happiness that went with it"; "Abide with me," "purely because of the fact that when they used to sing it in the FA cup final, the atmosphere must of been unbeli[e]vable with 120,000 people singing the song. . . I wish I could of been there."

If "Money for Nothing" seems incongruous among such explicitly sport-related celebrations of competition and victory, his explanation draws it firmly into a class-inflected discourse of individual aspiration: "When I listen to it it gives me some inspiration because I know that some working-class people have made something of their life, they are stars and have made plenty of money, in some ways it gives me a bit of hope for the future." Whatever other meanings, and other contexts, these songs may have becomes irrelevant to Paul's appropriation of them as emblematic of, and sustaining for, a class identity which is shared by only a very small minority of the group (see Walkerdine, 1986).

Spencer

One of two other boys to make significant reference to sport is worth quoting in full here. His self-positioning is particularly exact, counterposing the repetitive inscription of the indexical pronoun "I" to all who are not "I," "some people" (see Harré & Gillett, 1994, pp. 107–108):

> I would not say that I was a music lover and for this reason I have found it extremely difficult to find any songs that either describe or say something about me. Some people listen to music all the time but I am not one of those people. Some people only listen to one style of music that they love, I am not one of those people. I listen to the radio to keep up with the latest tunes and I occasionally buy singles, but I hardly ever buy albums because I normally only like the song and not the artist.

These unspecified others are plausibly a majority of those in the larger group to which, in the production of this self-account, he belonged. There is, in this context, also some effort to refuse the implication that his identity might be fixed in a relation to a specific "artist." He refuses the risk of being taste-classified by others. Nevertheless, he does record, in a sparsely word-processed script from which he had omitted his name, some distinct preferences:

> One record that I have always like[d] is "Chariots of Fire." From an early age I have been sports mad and extremely competitive and this tune always makes me want to go out and compete. It makes me think of the slow motion scene from the film, which sends a tingle down my spine every time. I did not particularly enjoy the film but the tune is brilliant and would probably be one of my "Desert island discs."
>
> Another song that inspires me is "World in Motion" by New Order which was made with the assistance of the 1990 England world cup squad. This makes me think about the great world cup that England had and how we came so close to winning it. The song itself is not that great but the memories are. David Platt's last minute goal against Belgium in the quarter final was magical and Gary Lineker's in the semi final was superb. I have probably never felt better than the moment that goal went in.

The progression in each of the descriptions presented here is through the "song" to its "effect": it "makes me want to go out," "makes me think about"—to compete and to win or to remember (almost) doing so. For Spencer, as for Paul, the emotional dynamic of self-positioning in such a discourse of competitive aspiration appears to arise out of the coincidence of coming from a working-class family and into an intensely competitive school—with upward mobility clearly on their horizons. Music, here, may serve to connect remembered contexts with the repertoire of emotions produced by such a competitive discourse, but it is not ever "in itself" the object of the emotions represented in this account. Music, for them, is not a primary symbolic resource in defining and representing their identities in this context and, to the contrary, some significant effort is apparent in their "embedding" of their chosen "songs" in other, "non-musical," scenes.

For example, in both of the following accounts, the "songs" are acknowledged as means to invoke or elicit particular fantasies or memories and to achieve a vicarious self-identification with male action scenarios. Despite listening to music, there is no self-positioning as a participant in music-orientated youth cultures:

> A more modern song that makes me think is Bon Jovi's "Blaze of Glory" and it talks about the exploits of Billy the Kid who is someone that I would have liked to have known, I admire his style and the song says how he would not just die peacefully but he would like to go out in a blaze of glory and that is what I would like to do.
>
> As football is my main hobby in life a song that I love to listen to is "Alive and Kicking" by Simple Minds. This has only become a song that I would think of since SKY television used it in their campaign to promote the new FA Premier League and in the adverts they had the song playing and the pictures were of great goals, saves and tackles from the Premier League. So now whenever I hear the song, great memories of football come flooding back.

Spencer's last choices are entirely consistent with his earlier construction of a bounded self, set apart from the liberal middle-class milieu inhabited by the majority of the school's students:

> My final two songs are the national anthems of both Great Britain and the United States of America. First that of the USA, the "Star Spangled Banner." I like it because I admire the way that although it is a national anthem they allow popular singers to adapt it their own way as if it were an ordinary song. The anthem sung by Whitney Houston at a Superbowl a few years back was great and made me think that I would like to be American. The words of the song are also significant to me, at the end when it talks about "the land of the free and the home of the brave" really inspires me. "God save the Queen" is

a song that will always make me feel proud to be British. Ever since I can remember I knew the words and I always stand when I hear it played. Perhaps the best rendition of the national anthem is heard at FA Cup Finals because football fans are mostly male and they all love there country so they sing loud. I am pleased to say I have been part of two FA Cup Finals and the singing of the anthem just before kick off was exhilarating and it gave me a real buzz. This also makes me think of representing my country in the Olympics and I imagine how great it must feel to be standing on the top of the rostrum with a gold medal around your neck, knowing that you have won for queen and country.

To choose the British and American national anthems, in this context, appears to be a double gesture, certainly of further separation from the culture of the students, but also of defiant subversion of teachers' assumptions about "young people." Here, the songs are drawn into a discourse in which he further positions himself as a subject of, and actor for, nationhood and monarchy. Furthermore, sport is represented as a medium for the expression of loyalty to nationhood, just as, earlier, he submerged himself in the unified "we" of England—". . . the great world cup . . . and how we came so close to winning it."

It is important, at this point, to recall that this piece of writing was a response to a specific and "teacher"-imposed task. As I have argued, the particular response has some relation to the student's social position and to his location within the context of the school and the group. But it is also an attempt to do what was asked. In producing his response, he confirms himself as a student and thus his acceptance of the position assigned to him in a continuing, unequal, dialogue with the teacher. He was asked to represent himself in terms which were defined with reference to *Desert Island Discs*. The radio program is open only to celebrities, to people who have achieved fame through sport, politics, music, theater, literature, and so forth. Here, the invitation to be positioned as a celebrity is engaged through a fantasy of ultimate victory in the Olympic Games, a fantasy identified realistically enough with the moment at which the British National Anthem is played. Read backwards from this achievement of celebrity, the rest of the account becomes a plausible fiction. This story of a sporting hero thus sustains his position as a student, responsive to the discursive regime imposed upon him, but also allows him to refuse some aspects of a liberal, middle-class culture.

So far, I have not examined the gendered features of these boys' self-accounts in any detail. However, before discussing examples of the girls' writing, some more expanded comments on the gender aspect need to be offered. For example, one feminist perspective on music, that of Susan McClary (1991; 1994), includes the argument that an important tendency in centuries of discourse around music is to characterize it as a threat to social order and particularly to the maintenance of such order through regimes of masculinity. Among Plato's anxieties about music was:

> the sensuous body as it can be aroused by the musics of women or ethnic groups noted for their "laxness," such as the Lydians. What remain suitable for the Republic, then, are genres of music dedicated either to the martial discipline of the Spartans or to the moderate exchange of ideas through rhetoric. (McClary, 1994, p. 30).

Quoting St. Augustine, John of Salisbury and John Calvin, McClary argues that:

> One of the themes running through these citations is the fear of emasculation. In a culture rigidly structured in terms of a mind-body split, music's appeal to the body predisposes it to be assigned to the "feminine" side of the axis . . . nothing less is at stake than masculinity itself and, by extension, the authority of church, state and patriarchy (McClary, 1994, p. 31).

It could be argued that the boys who distance themselves from any explicit self-positioning within music are refusing an identification which, in this patriarchal tradition, would be read as feminine. However, the construction of music as "bodily" and "emotional," though familiar, can also be contrasted with its construction as abstract, mathematical, and disembodied; either way, to pursue only one tendency in the cultural construction of music risks an essentialism (see Green, 1997). Thus when McClary proposes "that music is foremost among cultural 'technologies of the body,' that it is a site where we learn how to experience socially mediated patterns of kinetic energy, being in time, emotions, desire, pleasure" there is the possibility that she replicates the characterization of music central to "masculinity itself" (McClary, 1994, p. 33). It is possible that for these boys, rather than for others in the group, music may have a "feminine" connotation which they therefore overwhelm by subordinating music to male sport. But, as I have argued, that tactic does seem more motivated by class interests. The forms of "masculinity" which they claim may be as important for their "working-classness," in this context, as for their denial of "femininity."

In fact, there were many more boys in the group who did engage positively with music of various kinds. Rather than essentialize music as "feminine" or "physical," there is a need to consider "music" as a diverse phenomenon which, as a unified category, or as a collection of disparate genres, is remade with divergent meanings in its inscription within particular discourses. So, to conclude this discussion of the boys' writing I want to reaffirm that an understanding of their choices cannot be accomplished simply at the level of generalized cultural polarities but requires some specification of the social relations of the particular context and of how they act to sustain and reinflect those relations.

Autobiographies by Girls

I want to devote the remainder of this chapter to a consideration of the writing produced by several of the girls in the group. Like the boys, they were involved in a process of selective remembering which, in its presentation, involved them in constructing a public taste persona. As in the examples already cited, there is some degree of self-conscious construction of themselves as "adolescent" and as recalling liminal moments through the recovery of particular songs. However, it is apparent that these girls, to a greater extent than the majority of the boys, drew upon a discursive repertoire within which music seemed to be constructed as expressive of the self as interiority. Certainly, more evidence of self-positioning within discourses of sexuality was also present in their writing though, as already committed A-Level students, the projection of themselves into "educated futures" was hardly a matter of equivocation. Here, the writing could tactically unite the demands of various discourses, notably those of "femininity" and of a popular psychology, to offer "subjective depth," as itself the emblem of the "personhood" on which their futures turn. These middle-class girls are accustomed to expect to have a great deal to say about themselves and, in response to my request, it was quite "natural" for them to do so.

Angela
Angela's account, a corrected handwritten text, began with this:

"Summertime"—Fresh Prince and DJ Jazzy Jeff.
I can't remember when I first heard this song, but it was definitely on a sunny day. I managed to record it on to a compilation tape of summer songs, which

I played all day, every day, throughout the summer, every summer. So its a
very nostalgic song which I feel represents my "laid-back" self. Its also my
form of escapism during the colder seasons. Just listening to it creates the
feeling of warmth . . ."an air of love and of happiness. . ." that I associate
with summer. I like the beat, the lyrics and the continuity of the lyrics.

As I have suggested, the "summer" motif recurs across a high proportion of the accounts produced by this group. It is evidence of the
popularly circulated equation between the remembering of distinct
seasons and the particular music at one time coincident with them.
For the music radio audience positioned as "adolescent," "summers"
are constructed as a series of distinctive thresholds to be actively remembered, and to be self-consciously constructed as memorable as-
they-are-lived. Such a motif is not at all peculiar to the girls, but, in
Angela's account, it is used to represent a "section" of her "self."
Indeed, the assembly of her choices suggests the containment of difference and even contradiction "within" the depth of her subjectivity.
This is an engagement with the discourse of "adolescence" which
takes the implicit attributions of inconsistency and irresponsibility, of
emotionality and fantasy, and incorporates them into the self-construction of a reflective, developing, "interesting" person. In effect,
Angela achieves a tactical compliance with her educational location as
a successful female student. The next two choices exemplify this:

"Soul to Squeeze"—Red Hot Chilli Peppers.
I first heard this while I was crammed in the back of a car with 2 other guys.
We were on our way to an all-day rock festival with the last band being my
favourite band at the time, "Soundgarden." Only last summer (1994) this
happened during my holiday in Canada. The guy on my right was a close
friend of mine and had paid for my ticket and organised the drive up there. It
was his tape we were listening to, which he had made especially for the journey. The song came on, and immediately all the men in the car stopped
conversation and mimed along to the words (playing the instruments too). It
was the most perfect song in the world to be heard. The sun was shining, I
was travelling at 90 miles an hour on a freeway, I was on my way to see the
best concert of all time (fully paid for), no parents, no restrictions and lots of
men!

'Daughter'—Pearl Jam
Not particularly one of my favourite tracks of all time (that changes according
to mood and season), but it is a representation of a section of my personality
concerned with the relationship between me and my parents. Coming from a
close-knit, and often very protective, family I sometimes feel like wanting to
break away and become independent so that I can do what I want all the time

and not have to feel guilty or indebted towards my parents. Other times I am
so desperate to please them and make them proud so that they can see the
result of all their efforts. I also want them to see me as a "person" not just
their daughter, their possession, something they can control.

Angela's remaining tracks—"Anna Begins" by Counting Crows, "the
Reality Bites soundtrack" and "Slide Away" by Oasis—are accompanied by a similar mix of locating commentary with reflection on the
various "sections" of her "personality." The text, as a whole, juxta-
poses differently inflected self-representations:

1. summer, nostalgia, my "laid-back" self;
2 a teen-movie scenario—"no parents, no restrictions and lots of
   men!";
3. intra-familial adolescent angst;
4. "Anna Begins"—"I first heard it in my room when listening to
   the album". . . ."a beautiful song. . . I listen to it when I'm feeling in a sensitive mood";
5. "the 'Reality Bites' film . . . contains a character that I would
   like to be—a graduate with a job in the media, living with her 3
   best friends and making a documentary about them";
6. "Slide Away" . . . "the melody is surprisingly catchy and stays
   in my head throughout the school day—enabling me to get
   through it."

Thus, as I have suggested, each song appears to anchor a distinctive
way of representing herself, in part because of the particular lyrics
and musical genre of each track, but also because of the way in which
various desirable identities can be constructed around them—sometimes by recovering the memory of specific occasions, sometimes by
suggesting the circumstances in which the song might be literally heard
or remembered. As I will argue in the following discussion of Christina's
writing, there is some basis for suggesting that this self-account is also
an assertion that middle-class girls do have fun, that their identities
are not contained by their academic futures.

Christina
Though particular bands, even particular tracks, do recur in the girls'
accounts—Nirvana and Oasis for example—and can therefore be read
as evidence of a particular socially differentiated and generational experience, rather more extensive similarities can be identified at the

level of the shared categories through which their writing is organized: summer holidays, best friendships, relationships with boyfriends, relationships with parents, coping with intense emotions.

Christina's account, abbreviated here, usefully illustrates the typical repertoire of "emotional thresholds" and "relational contexts" drawn upon in the girls' production of their self accounts. Once again, "summer" emerges as a prominent motif, "remembered" in terms which seem derived from the common, informal, and conversational exchange of such memories rather than from any particular experience. Indeed, the elements of memory become combined with imagined settings, "a sandy beach late at night." To some extent, such generic consistency suggests self-positioning within quite general, and popularly disseminated, accounts of what the lived experience of youth should be:

> "Wild World" by Maxi Priest . . . a big hit in Cyprus while I was on holiday there a few years ago. Everywhere I went it was playing—in the bars and clubs and blaring from loud stereos on the beach. It reminds me of the people I met there and the great times we had together. Everytime I hear the song now it makes me feel as though I am back there—I can close my eyes and dream myself in Cyprus. It is also a song which epitomises the season of Summer. It is of the reggae genre, fresh and mellow, something you can really imagine dancing to on a sandy beach late at night.

This description, in common with several others,[8] while undoubtedly representing some actual experience, is also an appropriation of a public discourse, to be found in teenage magazines. By reconstructing memory through such discourse, the writer positions herself, in this context, as belonging to one popular, but also particular, construction of youth. Her choice of "Lithium" (by Nirvana) is similarly located, both geographically and discursively, and introduces the trope of friendship:

> This song reminds me of my holiday in Newquay last year. It was after my GCSE's and I was there with my friend Nici. The clubs in Newquay were quite grungey in their style of music and this song, a grunge anthem, was the favourite being played everywhere and reminds me of the fun Nici and I had.

Other choices more emphatically represent the intersection of friendships with liminal experience, and again, the effect is to position the writer as a girl "with friends," who has "a good time." To some extent, therefore, her account seems to sustain the kind of social identity which, through from earlier childhood, is of such intense and public importance in the lives of girls (see James, 1993; Hey, 1997) but does so, again, by appropriating the popular discourse of teenage magazines. Christina thus positions herself as more like other "ordinary" girls and less the "brainy" special case at this highly selective school. It may be that to write in the forms of popular teenage magazines is to seek "normalization." Valerie Hey has commented on this:

> For the middle class girls the working class girls "abnormality" centred upon their "excessive" heterosexuality—"jailbait" as one of them told me. Hence working class girls according to this discourse were *over-feminized*. Conversely, working class girls viewed middle class girls as *"under-feminized"* because their "brains" disqualified them from the feminine category altogether, and thus from claims upon the "really important" and central markers of (hetero)sexual self-identity (Hey, 1995, p. 19).

Here, several of the girls make a claim to a sexuality which, in the terms observed by Hey, they are not supposed to possess. So, in explaining her choice of "Gett Off" (by Prince) Christina writes:

> This song takes me back to the third year in senior school. My best friend at the time Cassie and I were very much into dancing and Prince. When Gett Off was released it was our dream come true—a dance track by Prince. We choreographed our own dance for it. Later on that year we went to see Prince perform at Earl's Court and this song was the highlight of the evening.

By choosing a notoriously sexually explicit song and, more generally, by adopting a discourse more broadly shared by other normal, sexual girls, a self-positioning resistant to the academic and nonsexual connotations of the school context is suggested. Similarly, in attaching a particular anecdote to "Always" (by Bon Jovi), she introduces a statement of her position as someone's "girlfriend":

> This is one of those songs which makes my spine tingle every time I hear it. It makes me think of my boyfriend Paul and has quite a romantic story behind it. . . A few days later he gave me the single of "Always" accompanied by a single red rose and it has been one of our songs ever since.

However, as I noted above, to both retain friendships with girls and to move on into distinctively new phases, and acquire new friends, is also an important feature of her self-representation. For example, her account of "Alive" (by Pearl Jam) is strongly marked as relocating her beyond earlier, more "childish," phases of "adolescence." She writes:

> This song signalled a new era in my life. It reminds me of new friends and a new style. This was the beginning of my love for indie music. . . My taste

changed from mainstream pop to indie, grunge, acid jazz. It also marked the beginning of a special friendship with a girl named Steph and it is a song we both adore.

Finally, her account of "Live Forever" (by Oasis) is further evidence of the importance in this context of being someone who goes out and participates in the public life of youth:

> This is one of my favourite songs off one of the best albums I have ever heard. It reminds me of the Oasis concert which I went to just before Christmas. This was the song everyone was waiting for and when Oasis performed it the entire audience erupted into verse in unison. It was an amazing atmosphere and experience marking a brilliant concert.

Thus, in this account of an "adolescence" by no means confined to the bedroom, she further confirms her public identity as more than a clever and conscientious student.

Emily

As I have suggested, other girls offered accounts in which much the same repertoire of elements is combined in explaining the selection of tracks. For both boys and girls, the request had involved asking them to represent themselves by selecting material from a cultural domain which is already heavily constructed as sexual, as "bodily" and as "affective." Many of the boys did choose to write about "songs" which they could assimilate to various discourses in which "bodily" and, sometimes, intensely emotive states were integral features (listening to death metal in one case, to the National Anthem in another). If a consistent difference between the girls' and the boys' self-positioning in relation to such a domain can be identified, it is evident in the tendency of the majority of the boys to rationalize the "states" they describe and thus to recover some distance from, and implicit control over, the experience they recall. The girls, though certainly also achieving distance through the act of writing itself, produced accounts in which self-positioning as emotional, sometimes as implicitly sexual, was not qualified by the more overt social and political recovery of emotion evident in, for example, the writing of David and Nicholas. Consistent with the argument that, here, middle-class girls lay claim to sexuality, it is also the case that they position themselves as "emotional" and "physically moved" in ways which, again, contradict the negative equation, in popular discourses, of academic success with emotional depletion.[9]

For example, this account translates the common attribution of "adolescent" emotional volatility into its affirmation:

> Manic St. Preachers—"Suicide is Painless" and Dame Kiri Te Kanawa—"O My beloved father"—Both are "mood" songs. MSP is more of when in a depressed mood to put the song on full volume and lie on your floor listening to the words is probably the most moving thing. Putting on Dame Kiri manages to make me so relaxed when in any mood. Especially in an incredibly angry and physically tensed time putting on this song, deep meaningful breathing and then moving your arms and then whole body to this song makes me feel so completely overcome with a "happiness of rage"—hard to put into words. . . . But one song that I do want to mention apart from the above [Nirvana—"All Apologies"] has to be Janis Joplin "Piece of my heart" because she sings it with so much feeling that you are just speechless after it. It is such a drive around on a hot day with windows open and music on full blast type of song.

Among her other selections, which she explained more publicly in her self-presentation to the group (her writing appeared to be primarily "rough notes" for such a presentation), Emily, like Christina, cited music which could represent the formation of a "best friendship" ["Bangles—Olivia + Me"]. She thus, again, claimed a social position for herself which, in its public visibility, has more importance for girls than for a majority of the boys. But, to reiterate, she did so by also demonstrating how at ease and how fluently self-confident she could be in front of almost thirty people in an educational setting. So, whatever the interests fulfilled by the choices she declared and the experiences to which she connected them, her position as an accomplished student was never compromised.

Conclusions

Bourdieu's incisive comment that the young "allow themselves to be kept in the state of 'youth,' that is, irresponsibility, enjoying the freedom of irresponsible behaviour in return for renouncing responsibility" should not, as I argued above, be given a transhistorical status (Bourdieu, 1986, p. 478). Even the belief that youth is a phase of life which should be both "pleasurable" and "memorable" has a particular historical inflection, though some elements of such a discourse on youth are undoubtedly enduring. Here, it is important to recognize how such a discourse is taken up by particular young people and what purposes they achieve in articulating it in preference to other possible, and available, discourses. I have suggested that, in every case, multiple interests are served by their self-accounts. Within this group, different discourses are invoked—some allowing a rhetorical self-positioning as political, others claiming an "expertise" in the domain of music, and others giving priority to "pleasure" and "emotionality." Some of the students combined elements of all of these tendencies. There is the potential in this to raise, with the students, questions around the meaning of "adolescence" and "youth" for them and to pursue, more explicitly, the political and historical context of their expectations. Such a priority, in teaching, might also inform further research.

A further important emphasis of this chapter has been upon the embedding of music in the domain of popular discourse and the need, therefore, to consider "tastes in music" as features of discourse rather than in terms of a more abstracted relationship between the formal characteristics of music and particular subjectivities. In this context, taste has been reviewed in terms of its tactical definition between situated social actors and thus as a complex rhetorical feature of self-positioning. I have argued, therefore, that the overdetermined enactment of social relations within specific educational contexts significantly complicates the more generalized classification of taste categories in relation to class affiliations for "adolescents" with access to a wide array of cultural forms.

To conclude, this chapter has shown that there are significant gender differences in the relation to popular music claimed by these students, but that such gender differences are also strongly inflected by processes of class positioning within a context defined by high levels of educational achievement. These A-Level students, advancing towards an educationally framed horizon, and alert to every opportunity to make cultural capital of their experience, took up my requests willingly. In this sense, they put so much of "themselves" into the *Desert Island Discs* project because they were accustomed to seeing that what they "give" would be, if not immediately and literally, returned with cultural and educational value inscribed upon it (Bourdieu, 1992, pp. 76–81).

Author Note

The title of this chapter is taken from the Hole/Courtney Love album, *Live Through This* (Geffen Records, 1994, EFA 04935-2). A longer version of this chapter appears in Richards (1998b). An earlier draft was presented to the Media, Culture and Curriculum Special Interest Group at the Annual Meeting of the American Educational Research Association in San Francisco, April 1995.

References

Bourdieu, P. (1986). *Distinction: A social critique of the judgement of taste.* London: RKP.

Bourdieu, P. (1992). Price formation and the anticipation of profits. *Language and symbolic power* (pp. 66–89). Cambridge: Polity Press.

Butler, J. (1990). *Gender trouble: Feminism and the subversion of identity.* London: Routledge.

Chodorow, N. (1978). *The reproduction of mothering: Psychoanalysis and the sociology of gender.* Berkeley: University of California Press.

Cohen, P. (1984). Against the new vocationalism. In I. Bates, J. Clarke, P. Cohen, D. Finn, R. Moore, & P. Willis (Eds.) *Schooling for the Dole?* (pp. 104–169). London: Macmillan.

Cohen, P. (1986). *Rethinking the youth question.* London: Institute of Education Post 16 Education Centre.

Connell, R.W. (1983). The black box of habit on the wings of history. *Which way Is up? Essays on class, sex and culture.* (pp. 427–453). Sydney: Allen and Unwin.

Fornas, J., Lindberg, U., & Sernhede, O. (1995). *In garageland: Rock, youth and modernity.* London: Routledge.

Frith, S. (1983). *Sound effects: Youth, leisure, and the politics of rock 'n roll.* London: Constable.

Frow, J. (1987, January). Accounting for tastes: Some problems in Bourdieu's sociology of culture. *Cultural Studies, 1*(1), 59–73.

Green, L. (1988). *Music on deaf ears: Musical meaning, ideology and education.* Manchester: University of Manchester Press.

Green, L. (1997). *Music, gender, education.* Cambridge: Cambridge University Press.

Griffin, C. (1993). *Representations of youth: The study of youth and adolescence in Britain and America.* Cambridge: Polity Press.

Harre, R. & Gillett, G. (1994). *The discursive mind.* London: Sage.

Harvey, D. (1989). *The condition of post-modernity.* Oxford: Blackwell.

Hewitt, R. (1986). *White talk black talk: Inter-racial friendship and communication amongst adolescents.* Cambridge: Cambridge University Press.

Hewitt, R. (1992). Language, youth and the destabilisation of ethnicity. In C. Palmgren, K. Lovgren, & G. Bolin (Eds.), *Ethnicity in youth culture.* Stockholm: Youth Culture at Stockholm University.

Hey, V. (1995). 'Bitching' and 'little bits of garbage': Re-situating ethnographic evidence of girls' friendships. CREG Seminar Paper, University of London Institute of Education.

Hey, V. (1997). *The company she keeps: An ethnography of girls' friendship.* Buckingham: Open University Press.

James, A. (1993). *Childhood identities: Self and social relationships in the experience of the child.* Edinburgh: University of Edinburgh.

James, A., & Prout, A. (1990). *Constructing and reconstructing childhood: Contemporary issues in the sociological study of childhood.* London: Falmer Press.

Lees, S. (1986). *Losing out: Sexuality and adolescent girls.* London: Hutchinson.

Leppert, R., & McClary, S. (Eds.). (1987). *Music and society.* Cambridge: Cambridge University Press.

Lutz, C. A., & Abu-Lughod, L. (1990). *Language and the politics of emotion.* Cambridge: Cambridge University Press.

Mander, M. S. (1987). Bourdieu, the sociology of culture and cultural studies: A critique. *European Journal of Communication, 2,* 427–453.

McClary, S. (1991). *Feminine endings: Music, gender and sexuality.* Minneapolis: University of Minnesota Press.

McClary, S. (1994). Same as it ever was: Youth culture and music. In T. Rose & A. Ross (Eds.), *Microphone fiends: Youth music and youth culture* (pp. 17–40). London: Routledge.

Middleton, D., & Edwards, D. (Eds.). (1990). *Collective remembering.* London: Sage.

Middleton, R. (1990). *Studying popular music.* Buckingham: Open University Press.

Moss, G. (1989). *Un/popular fictions.* London: Virago.

Murdock, G., & Phelps, G. (1973). *Mass media and the secondary school.* London: Macmillan/Schools Council.

Nava, M., & McRobbie, A. (Eds.). (1984). *Gender and generation.* London: Macmillan.

Richards, C. (1998a). Beyond classroom culture. In D. Buckingham, *Teaching Popular Culture: Beyond Radical Pedagogy* (pp. 132–152). London: UCL Press.

Richards, C. (1998b). *Teen spirits: Music and identity in media education.* London: UCL Press.

Roe, K. (1983). *Mass media and adolescent schooling: Conflict or coexistence?* Stockholm: Almqvist and Wiksell.

Roman, L. G., & Christian-Smith, L. K., with Ellsworth, E. (Eds.). (1988). *Becoming feminine: The politics of popular culture.* London: Falmer Press.

Rose, T. (1994). *Black noise: Rap music and black culture in contemporary America*. Hanover, NH: University Press of New England.

Rose, T., & Ross, A. (Eds.). (1994). *Microphone fiends: Youth music and youth culture*. London: Routledge.

Ross, A. (1989). *No respect: Intellectuals and popular culture*. London: Routledge.

Sanders, C. L. (1971, December). Aretha: A close-up look at Sister Superstar. *Ebony*, 126–134.

Shepherd, J., & Giles-Davis, J. (1991). Music, text and subjectivity. In J. Shepherd (Ed.), *Music as social text*. Cambridge: Polity Press.

Shiach, M. (1993, October). 'Cultural Studies' and the work of Pierre Bourdieu, *French Cultural Studies*, 4(3), 213–223.

Shotter, J., & Gergen, K. J. (Eds.). (1989). *Texts of identity*. London: Sage.

Walkerdine, V. (1986). Video replay: Families, films, and fantasy. In V. Burgin, J. Donald, and C. Kaplan (Eds.), *Formations of fantasy* (pp. 167–199). London: Routledge and Kegan Paul.

Widdicombe, S., & Wooffitt, R. (1995). *The language of youth subcultures*. Sussex: Harvester Wheatsheaf.

Notes

1. This long-running program invites a celebrity to talk about her or his life and to anchor the account through a choice of records. The style of interviewing has become, in recent years, quasi-therapeutic.

2. Speaking of his sister, Aretha Franklin, the Reverend Cecil Franklin describes the intersubjective character of her performance:

    It's a combination of electricity and empathy. She generates the electricity, and the empathy comes with her being able not only to feel what all those people are experiencing but able to really experience the same things they are experiencing. You listen to her and it's just like being in church. She does with her voice exactly what a preacher does with his when he **moans** to a congregation. That moan strikes a responsive chord in the congregation and somebody answers you back with their own moan, which means I know what you're moaning about because I feel the same way. So you have something sort of like a thread spinning out and touching and tying everybody together in a shared experience just like getting happy and shouting together in church (Sanders, 1971, p. 126).

3. Both of the media teachers involved with the class (Pete Fraser and Nikki Blackborow) acted as key "informants," providing me with specific contextual knowledge to which I would not otherwise have had access.

4. Some of the problems of trying to make formal connections between subjectivity and music are discussed in Shepherd and Giles-Davis (1991) and Middleton (1990).

5. Middleton (1990) suggests:

    We do not . . . choose our musical tastes freely; nor do they reflect our 'experience' in any simple way. The involvement of subjects in particular musical pleasures has to be constructed; indeed, such construction is part and parcel of the production of subjectivity. In this process, subjects themselves— however "decentred"—have a role to play (of recognition, assent, refusal, comparison, modification); but it is an *articulatory*, not a simplistically creative or responsive role. Subjects participate in an "interpellative dialectic," and this takes specific forms in specific areas of cultural practice (p. 249).

6. Cohen elaborates:

    In sociologies of youth . . . transition is seen as a one way process—the transition from school to work, or childhood to adulthood. Freud's concepts of regression, compulsion to repeat, and transference, show that model up for what it is, an example of retrospective wish fulfilment, a convenient adult myth. Psycho-analytical research properly requires us to abandon the notion of transition, in favour of the notion of transposition (pp. 33–34).

7. My nephew, also in twelfth year studying A levels, responded to my written request to him with the following:

    Oasis—Supersonic . . . It means a lot to me because it reminds me of last summer which was the best time I've ever had—I'd just finished my exams . . . and I spent 4 months just dossing about with me mates, every day we would hang about in town, then play footy and then get pissed—I can't think of anything else I'd rather do. . . This song reminds me of that summer because on the last day before I started at college, a busload of me and about 15 mates all went to watch Oasis at the Hacienda in Manchester there was something very special about the whole thing—the band, the venue, the City, the time. I will remember it forever.

8. Carrie, for example:

    No Woman, no cry—Bob Marley. This was my holiday song for this year. I went on tour to Israel for three weeks. A lot of the time was spent travelling around by coach. We played this song a lot as its very soothing and mellow. Most of the time we were extremely tired and we were travelling long distances at night. We played this song whilst looking at the stars etc and falling asleep travelling through the middle of the desert.

9. In the teen magazine *Just Seventeen*, for example, one problem page letter complained of a girl's problem with her "brainy" reputation. The advice (with some irony?) was to read school books concealed inside a copy of the magazine.

Going Public: Rock Aesthetics in the American Political Field

Jonathan Sterne

It is as though people who betray the hopes of their youth and come to terms
with the world, suffer the penalty of premature decay.
—Horkheimer and Adorno, *Dialectic of Enlightenment* (1972)

In the last two decades, Americans have witnessed a number of
major changes in the structure and organization of political spectacle—
the performance of politics—a change that is connected with shifts in
the political and cultural fields themselves. A new generation of politicians is ascending to power and with them, cultural practices that
were once anathema to the political field (at least its public presentation) are now a central part of political spectacle. I wish to consider
here one such practice—rock and roll[1]—as emblematic of this shift,
and in so doing reframe some of the questions about the relationship
between rock and politics that have been central to recent rock scholarship. Even as scholars have sought to outline the political potential
of rock music, rock has became more and more of an instrument of
mainstream political activity. It has become a tool of political persuasion, but not in the way that so many cultural critics have imagined.
By reexamining two key appearances of rock in mainstream American politics—Tipper Gore and the PMRC's (Parents' Music Resource
Center) quest to regulate rock music in the 1980s, and the use of rock
music and culture in the 1992 presidential election—this essay offers
an examination of how and on what terms rock itself became an instrument of mainstream electoral politics. Rock's affiliation with related concepts like youth was reshaped in the social context of mainstream politics, where it had traditionally been more legitimate to speak
of youth than *for* youth.

While there has been much discussion of rock and the politics of culture, there has been considerably less discussion of rock and the culture of politics. This proposition may sound a bit flip, but consider that the vast majority of recent scholarship on rock music in the United States has been preoccupied with questions of cultural resistance and recuperation.[2] Scholars addressing rock and other popular music have often attempted to find a politics in the music itself, or in the practices surrounding it.[3] This trend in scholarship says more about the scholars than the object itself: there is a strong collective desire among leftists (or left-sympathetic scholars) to find progressive politics in the cultural practices they themselves enjoy.

At the very moment that academics began to focus on the cultural politics of rock music, rock took on a new set of valences in the culture of mainstream politics. In addition to being the object of derision on the one hand and regulation on the other (tendencies that have a long history, see Bennett, Frith, Grossberg, Shepherd, & Turner, 1993; Martin, 1988), rock—and attendant categories such as youth—became a point of positive identification for politicians and political constituencies. One could argue that rock's presence in political life only makes sense since rock is a central part of American middle-class commercial culture, but this claim says little about the appearance of rock bands at Bill Clinton's inauguration ball or Lee Atwater jamming with blues greats—events that would have been inconceivable even a few years earlier. In other words, the scholarly focus on rock's cultural politics has said little about rock's place in political culture.

The term "politics" itself has taken on a rather ambiguous meaning in recent cultural scholarship. No doubt that movements like feminism, queer politics, and antiracism have shown the need to attend to the political aspects of everyday life. Yet at the same time, we mustn't forget the other, more narrow, more conventional definition of politics. My reference to politics throughout this piece will mostly connote this much narrower sphere of activity, what Pierre Bourdieu would call the political field. The political field is a relatively limited set of elite institutions: the government and the very large semiprivate, private, nonprofit and "public interest" sectors that together drive the economy of Washington D.C. (such as it is) and appear in "political" news coverage. It is "politics" in the narrow, colloquial sense of the term. Clearly, the political field has its endemic practices, its own rites of institution, its own hierarchy of positions, and a unique network of relations among its actors. The presence of rock and roll, both as an object of political discourse and as a form of political practice—often by politicians themselves and those close to them—is my object of study here.[4] My distinction between the broader notion of "politics" and a "political field" is at least as much heuristic as it is empirical, but the distinction is useful for the purposes of this analysis.[5]

My project here builds on some of the questions raised by Lawrence Grossberg's work on rock and the cultural politics of what he calls "the new conservatism." Grossberg claims that conservatives attack rock through three related strategies: the first demands a complete rejection of rock music and culture; the second attempts to police the boundaries between the acceptable and unacceptable; and the third attempts to appropriate rock and challenge "youth culture's claim of ownership" (Grossberg, 1992, pp. 4–9; see also Grossberg, 1993; Grossberg, 1997, pp. 253–270). This new conservatism is itself part of a larger trajectory in the political field, a generational shift—and by this I mean both a real change in terms of who occupies positions of power, and a representative-demographic change in who makes a "constituency" in American politics. While there is no definitive break between "generational" regimes in mainstream American politics, Bill Clinton's election and reelection, in addition to the 1994 election of the first Republican Congress in decades, were widely hailed as marking such a shift. Nowhere is the opposition between young and old, the discontinuity between generations, more significant than among political elites, precisely because generational struggles are struggles over who will occupy positions of power, and on what terms those successions will occur. For these same reasons, such struggles are particularly crucial in a political context (Bourdieu, 1984, p. 295).

Rock music's position within mainstream media culture—as a locus of affective investment and as a marker of distinction through taste—have on multiple occasions made it an object of impassioned political discourse, especially given that three of its primary social functions (as noted by Simon Frith, 1987, pp. 140–142) are: a) to aid in self-definition, b) as a tool used to manage the relations between public and private emotional lives, and c) to shape popular memory, specifically by organizing a sense of time. Yet these social functions are hardly unique to rock music; in fact, one could just as easily say that electoral campaigns have these functional aspects as well, at least for those who participate in the political process. Traditionally, rock and electoral politics performed these social functions for two different populations. When they did collide, it was through the kinds of processes Grossberg describes, where political actors have attempted to ban, regulate, or control rock music. Over the last two decades, these two spheres have slowly begun to intermingle; rock has become a means toward capturing a "new" social identity, youth, that is being converted into a mode of identification within the political field. Rock appears to have become part of the electoral process—there is a growing understanding that rock audiences are a specific part of the electorate. Rock music has moved from an object of political discourse (e.g., through regulation) to an instrumentality in political life.

This essay considers two moments of articulation within this larger shift I am positing. The first section rethinks the Parents' Music Resource Center's attempt to legislate rock music in the mid-1980s. The PMRC has largely been discussed as an attempt to regulate rock music; it has been placed in the history of attempts to "control" rock music and its purported effects on youth. Grossberg cites the PMRC as an example of the conservative tendency to demarcate acceptable and unacceptable forms of rock music. Although there's no doubt that the PMRC did draw its rhetoric from other attacks on rock and popular culture, we miss a lot if we simply read it as another attempt at censorship (after all, it was not, strictly speaking, a movement for the censorship of rock music). On the contrary, a close reading of Gore's rhetoric in historical context will show that its true success was not in regulating rock music, but precisely in helping to articulate a new position for rock and youth culture in the mainstream of American politics. Not only did it try to circumscribe youth culture (through promoting mechanisms of parental control), it also constructed a new position from which such a regulation would be possible. In other words, the PMRC was a peculiar attempt to construct an aesthetics of rock music within a political space, and then "teach" that aesthetic to a larger culture. My point here is simple: discussions of the PMRC's attempts to regulate rock have largely conceived of its exercise of power as repressive. I argue that the maneuvers of the 1980s were more about *producing* and shaping the intersection of rock culture and political culture than *restricting* rock culture as such. Power is productive as well as repressive (Foucault, 1978, pp. 92–102).

If Gore's work in the mid-1980s was about legitimating rock music in the political field, more recent developments concern the nature of its deployment. MTV's campaign to mobilize young voters and the appearance of rock and roll in mainstream presidential politics are both attempts to instrumentalize rock in the service of expressly political struggles. This is less about the politicization of rock (though it is a particular kind of politicization) than the emergence of rock in mainstream American politics.

First Moment: The PMRC, or
Forging Rock as a Political Instrument

Tipper Gore, the founding mother and spokeswoman of the PMRC, in her 1987 best-seller *Raising PG Kids in an X-Rated Society*, constructs for us the beginning of her crusade:

> I had become aware of the emergence of explicit and violent images in the world of music . . . through my children. In December 1984, I purchased Prince's best-selling album *Purple Rain* for my eleven year old daughter. I had seen Prince on the cover of magazines and I knew that he was the biggest pop idol in years. My daughter wanted the album because she had heard 'Let's Go Crazy' on the radio. But when we brought the album home, put it on the stereo, and listened to it together, we heard the words to a different song, 'Darling Nikki': I knew a girl named Nikki/Guess you could say she was a sex fiend/I met her in a hotel lobby masturbating to a magazine. The song went on and on, in a similar manner. I couldn't believe my ears (Gore, 1987, p. 17).

This, we are told, is the mythical moment when the PMRC was born. But there is more to this story than is readily apparent. Tipper Gore has identified herself as a rock fan, and in fact confessed a special liking for James Brown. The apparent irony in this formulation ("James Brown fan flips when she hears Prince song"), provides an excellent lens for looking at the entire PMRC project as articulated by Gore. It is a classic case of speaking about social difference through aesthetic distinctions; politics working in the language of taste culture (see, e.g., Bourdieu, 1984; Frow, 1995; Hebdige, 1979; Herrnstein-Smith, 1991).

Given rock's function of shaping popular memory, it is possible to see the difference between James Brown and Prince for Tipper Gore not so much as an absolute aesthetic difference, but as a difference in use-value. James Brown appears as *affectively useful* in Gore's accounts: she casts Brown as embodying a kind of authenticity which she can then claim for herself as well. Her language here casts her less as some kind of social reformer coming in from outside rock culture to control its influence, but rather someone who knows rock culture all too well:

I think you still had to use your imagination a little with him; he was within bounds. Look, there's nothing wrong with rock being very primal. It can unleash energy and even sexual feeling. It's a sexual, sensual form of music, but I don't think that's bad. In fact, I actually like it. I have nothing against the primeval appeal of music—I understand it, I feel it myself, I think it's fine (Chapple & Talbot, 1989, p. 56).

Several things can be said about her repeated application of sexual adjectives to James Brown's music. First, these are terms she reserved for James Brown, and not, say, Frank Zappa. Second, her discussions of Brown are always in terms of his sexuality—eliding at once the gendered and racial dimensions to Brown's popularity. Brown's significance as a symbol of black power—both through his identity as a self-made "Soul Brother #1" and as the author of songs like "Say It Loud—I'm Black and I'm Proud" (Brackett, 1992; Garofalo, 1992a; Gilroy, 1991, pp. 212–213; Gilroy, 1993, pp. 72–110; Guralnick, 1986; Hoare, 1975)—completely disappear under the weight of Gore's sexual identification.

Gore thus situates herself within a long history of white constructions of blackness. As Michael Rogin and many others have argued, whites in America have used blackness as an index of an emotive, expressive, or more "natural" state; its invocation by the nonblack is a gesture of cultural identification with the bourgeoisie (hooks, 1992; see also Lott, 1995; Rogin, 1992, p. 440; Saxton, 1990). Similarly, Simon Frith has noted the tendency in rock criticism to construct the African or Afro-American as "a figure of white fear and white desire": representing "the other of bourgeois respectability" and "nature" as opposed to "culture" (1992, p. 181). Whatever her actual feelings on the matter, Gore's representation of James Brown as a catalyst for her "primal" (i.e., sexual) feelings has to be understood as a manifestation and expression of her white privilege, and that at the very moment she claims to "understand" the primeval appeal of Brown's music, she is appropriating difference through a classic colonial trope.

Through these rhetorical maneuvers, Gore can claim to know youth culture precisely as she critiques it; her insider status becomes a trope of legitimation. James Brown's music thus "represents" sexuality in Gore's discourse less because of any sexual content in Brown's music than because of the conventions of middle-class white appropriations of black performance. It also authenticates her represented experience by repeating the common sense of much white rock criticism— her speaking position is "humanized," "legitimated," or, more accurately, "bourgeoified" by it. Her representation of her experience of James Brown becomes a contemporary kind of cultural capital she can use, along with her other rock music experience (like playing in a Beatles cover band, and listening to Frank Zappa in college) that constructs her as occupying an "insider" position with respect to rock music and mainstream culture.

Prince has an entirely different although equally important function in Gore's discourse. If James Brown is the metaphor for her own pleasure and desire, then Prince is, to use Frith again, "the shocking other of bourgeois respectability"—the exemplar of that which must be contained. Prince is something of an easy target: a black male gender-bending performer who occasionally uses explicit lyrics.[6] Though Gore carefully avoids explicitly attacking Prince on the grounds of sexual deviance, that current flows just beneath the surface of her language. Prince has often been attacked on homophobic grounds or simply through insults to his masculinity,[7] and that was certainly part of the popular awareness of Prince at the time Gore was writing. In this way her language could appeal to already existing sentiment without directly speaking to it.

Although one could try to trace out all the chains of influence and lines of similarity and difference between James Brown and Prince and try to map them out on some kind of balance sheet, formal, textual and stylistic differences alone will not explain the absolute difference between the two artists in Gore's rhetoric: it is *time* that marks this difference. Gore represents James Brown as part of her experience of youth, her own sexuality and "primal" tendencies. Prince, on the other hand, appears to address the sexuality of her children. Gore's pleasures and displeasures, especially her representation of them, construct absolute differences between taste communities. In Gore's musicopolitical vision, Prince becomes the pervert and Brown the sexual athlete—as if Prince were such a far leap from James Brown in the first place.

The construction of a generational difference—marking a hypothetical endpoint to baby boomer youth culture somewhere after James Brown but before Prince—thus feeds into a larger generational move. The PMRC's move to "expose" rock music to parents, its infantilization of teenagers, and its vulgar media-effects theory were in fact parts of a double articulation for the baby boom generation in the political field. It was an attempt to consolidate a generational authority—simultaneously as parents and as "former" youth who wished to retain something of the label. As parents who'd "been there," the PMRC and its constituency (mostly white, middle-class identified parents then in their 30s and 40s) not only knew better the experience of youth than those people who were chronologically young, they also had the right and duty to police youth culture: in Gore's words, to "reassert some control over the cultural environment in which our children are raised" (1987, p. 13). This statement requires or invokes a position from which control of one's cultural environment is possible. The PMRC was about constructing a discourse of parental authority, specifically with respect to youth culture, that had been more or less in recess since the mid-1960s (Males, 1996).[8]

Gore's rhetoric was emblematic of the tension present in this strategy. She was a member of a social formation that had, to a great degree, authorized itself through discourses of youth. Now, in the 1980s, that social formation which had purported to test the boundaries of cultural institutions like the family suddenly found itself about to take control of them, and it could no longer simply authorize its position in terms of its youthfulness. Still, youth was an inextricable part of baby boom identity. The result, as Grossberg has noted, was that youth became a "battlefield on which generations of adolescents, baby boomers, parents and corporate media" fought to articulate it in a way beneficial to their interests (Grossberg, 1992, pp. 181–200). Gore's rhetoric was part of a larger canonization of the 1960s. This move was twofold: it disarticulated the definition of youth from the physically young, allowing an aging baby boom to hold onto its idealized experience, while at the same time temporally bounding that experience in such a way as to make it inaccessible to those who were born too late. Ironically, the very concept of youth became a way of constituting a boundary between the physically young and the forever young.

A temporally bounded youth also laid the groundwork for other articulatory moves. By virtue of being members of the dominant class who were growing older, the baby boom moved into durable institutions—most importantly, the state—that had their own peculiar rites of entrance that were not necessarily amenable to discourses of youthfulness. (That this *could* have been a moment of immense social transformation—at least based on the political claims of the youth culture from which these people emerged—should not be lost on the reader.) Some of the dominant *dispositions* within the so-called baby boom social formation were not necessarily congruent with the political *po-*

sitions that they were moving into within the political field. Attitudes such as a general mistrust of authority, a tendency toward informality, the fetishization of youth and youthfulness as a mode of experience, and pleasure in postwar popular culture such as television and rock and roll were poorly matched to the traditional codes of political performance and affectation—both for the politicians themselves and those surrounding them. Since the problem was one of legitimation, the solution was an enunciatory move (or rather a series of them). It required the founding of a *representative* position from which a constituency, or an identification, could be garnered—*and more importantly, spoken for*. It required a new kind of speaking position from within mainstream politics. The political field relies on this kind of representational logic: to act in the political field, one must be acting *as* or *for* somebody. Actors (and I mean either individuals or groups) in the political field function as proxies for a larger social group (for whom access to this field is relatively circumscribed). In doing so, the political actor becomes the substitute for the absent larger group, at least in the political field, so that the group is thereby politically constituted through its representation. In the political field, then, the representative literally embodies those for whom she speaks. To paraphrase Bourdieu, "As the personification . . . of a social fiction [she] raises those whom [she] represents out of their existence as separate individuals, enabling them to act and speak through [her] as a single person" (Bourdieu, 1991, p. 248). In return, she gains the power to speak and act as if the group *were* a single person.

Gore made this move through constructing a homology of authority. By continually deploying the term "parent" she founds her credibility and also opens up a network of possible identifications: she speaks as a parent to all parents. Both in founding the Parents' Music Resource Center (with other wives of Washington politicians), and in writing her book, she based her credibility on her "parentness," and relied on a pop psychology of adolescence and parenting to back up her arguments about mass culture and the relations of parents and youth. She constructed a simple one-to-one link between relations in the family unit and the subjects covered in her book: childhood development, violence, sex, suicide, Satanism, alcohol and drugs, and finally, rock concerts. This move constructed a position of "parent" as caretaker and authority figure within the family, conveniently addressing the popular anxiety over parenting at the time by grounding and stabilizing that parental position within a very traditional psychological and political discourse.[9] It also consolidated a privileged class position by using the white middle-class family ideal as a normative index.

The PMRC's program was a traditional middle-class cultural strategy of containment. Specifically, it was a move to articulate a generation of younger parents to very traditional middle-class practices and dispositions. Gore referred to drugs and violence, a reality for many inner-city residents, as a "fantasy world." She argued for the need to maintain children's innocence—an innocence that can only be constructed in a space free from physical danger and want of essentials—but she never took on the conditions of poverty that disallow such innocence at any age. Instead she called for parents to take a stand on media images that might disrupt her idealized family space. The middle class speaks as if it were the universal class.

This middle-class orientation was also manifested in the PMRC's distinctive approach to a "solution" to the problem of objectionable rock lyrics. The battle for cultural hegemony became a form of consumer advocacy:

> Our approach was the direct opposite of censorship. We called for more information, not less. We did not advocate a ban of even the most offensive records or tapes. We simply urged that the consumer be forewarned through the use of warning labels and/or printed lyrics visible on the outside packaging of music products (Gore, 1987, p. 26).

This remarkably Foucauldian strategy operates on the assumption that if rock music would simply offer up its "truth" through closer examination, it could be regulated and contained. Although other writers have argued that Gore's program amounted to censorship (Harrington, 1992),[10] it very deliberately marks a distance between itself and other attacks on rock. The goal was not to keep rock and youth culture outside the middle-class home, but rather to provide a means for navigating youth culture. Clearly, "the consumer" in Gore's account is the rational adult parent, who is able to adjudicate between appropriate and inappropriate music for his or her child if only the industry would offer a little help. The question of youth—either children or teenagers—as consumers of rock is entirely elided. Even though Gore used the rhetoric of control, the PMRC was less about the containment of rock as such than providing the tools for parents to use it within the dominant middle-class culture; it transformed the regulation of rock from a Moral Majority issue to a problem of consumer rights. The PMRC rhetoric used the familiar construct of the middle-class home as a frontier to be protected from external dangers, leaving parents as the sentinels standing guard. Called to action as parents, the middle class was once again the agent and guardian of civilization, except this time rock and rollers were on both sides of the gates.

Gore's rhetoric of protection is not a new thing, nor is it somehow specific to rock. The postwar culture in which rock emerged saw other struggles over the legitimate boundaries between children's culture and adults' culture. As Lynn Spigel writes, "the particular battles fought over childhood were linked to power struggles in the adult culture" (Spigel, 1993, p. 261). This kind of postwar political rhetoric draws on a half-century-old discourse that endowed youth with a particular kind of political *objectivity:* child-labor laws, the clean water movement, and the movement for pasteurization of milk and dairy products all took youth as their political object—something to be protected through legislation and political activity.[11] The difference between Gore's rhetoric and other attacks on rock, however, is that she also had to negotiate youth as an ambiguous category of political *subjectivity.* The boom in postwar youth culture did carry with it political valences, ranging from integration on the dance floor to the various student movements and the development of political consciousness (however temporary) in media outlets of youth culture such as *Rolling Stone.* Gore does little with this subjectivity except to assert it: she had her wild youth, she made some mistakes, and now she's all grown up. Gore elaborates a speaking voice that at once "knows better" than the youth culture even as it derives credibility from the language of youth culture.

Tipper Gore and the PMRC constructed their own cultural saliency through asserting their parenthood while reasserting their claim to youth. Through this gesture, they constructed a speaking position within the political field which appeared as though it could be mobilized almost indefinitely. They also successfully divided, bounded, and rearticulated youth culture for a generation coming to terms with its growing responsibility and political power. Thus, just as rock music was one basis of founding community in youth culture, so was it a point of identification and distinction (among several) for constructing an emergent political class and its constituency. The boundary between the physically young and the forever young—fostered by the entrance of rock and the trappings of youth culture into an arena where even the hint of rebellion had to be carefully tempered—helped create new possibilities for affective investments in mainstream politics and new modes of address for political actors to approach their constituencies. It is to the question of youth and rock as a form of political subjectivity that I now turn.

Second Moment: The Public Gets Down

Eight years after Tipper Gore first heard "Darling Nikki," her husband was half of a presidential ticket, and the ten-year-olds she was protecting in 1984 could now cast their votes. The generational struggle which was just beginning to materialize in 1984 had become old news by 1992. It had become more of a demographic issue than any other.

Baby boomers were about to assume power in the political field, while a new generation of youth had been successfully constituted as a demographic group—a political constituency as well as a target audience for cultural products like movies, music, and fashion. Yet in speaking of generations in this fashion, one must take care to avoid a simple correspondence theory, a realist fallacy where the language used to describe a group becomes the group itself:

> Many businesses ignore young adults because they are different than baby boomers. Despite their relatively small numbers, baby busters are the best market for cosmetics, movies, and many other products. Businesses can reach young adults if they understand that every generation follows new rules. For example, young adults are more conservative than boomers in some ways and more liberal in others (Mitchell, 1993, p. 50).

This kind of language, taken from an article in *American Demographics*, suggests a strictly realist definition of generations: they are there, and the corporate world simply has to go out and find them. But as with the political field, the marketing field also functions through a logic of transubstantiation: groups are represented through surveys and other research tools. The representation then becomes the group as far as marketers are concerned; the result is that a particular image comes to stand in for the actual group. Eileen Meehan (1990) has shown the skewedness of audience research in radio and television, and the same critique is relevant here. The concept of a "generation" of people is notoriously fuzzy—one cannot simply mark off a beginning and ending for a generation, whether we're talking about baby boomers, or the generations preceding and following them. While people who are roughly the same age *can* share a set of historically related and age-based experiences, it does not logically follow that they are *necessarily* of a shared consciousness or social position. As Richard Du Boff and Edward Herman point out, even reading something so self-evidently age-based as child poverty through the lens of generational politics alone risks effacing more fundamental axes of social difference: "The high rates of child poverty here don't prove generational mistreatment; they show that racism, sexism, and a ruthless elite and class system are taking a heavy toll of traditional victims" (DuBoff & Herman, 1996).[12]

But to dispense with a strictly realist conception of generations does not invalidate age as an analytical concept. On the contrary, the category of youth and the splitting of generations continue to exert tremendous influence in politics and public discourse, not to mention the broader media culture. Age remains a significant demographic category for marketing and for politics, and so it is no surprise that the politics of youth played a significant role in the construction of the 1992 presidential campaign. If Gore has sought to draw a boundary around a certain experience of youth during the mid-1980s, MTV and other media outlets were revitalizing and redefining the concept in popular culture at large. Thus, the prominence of rock music, youth culture, and young voters in the 1992 campaign was a result of a cultural collision of sorts. A number of factors contributed to this, but I want to focus here on the role of rock culture in the campaign.

Despite its commercial viability, this younger generation had not been particularly well constructed within a more explicitly political context prior to 1992. There was very little voter turnout in the under-30 range throughout the 1980s, although those who did turn out voted overwhelmingly conservative (Howe & Strauss, 1993, p. 13). But this group was one of Clinton's strongest constituencies in the 1992 election—he did much better among younger voters than he did among his own age group (Shriver, 1993).

Clinton's use of rock and popular culture more generally synergized with changes in the media field. While Clinton instrumentalized rock music and popular culture in an effort to gain the youth vote, MTV— perhaps *the* major media outlet claiming to represent youth and rock culture at this point in time—sought the legitimacy, power, and revenue that comes with being a major media outlet for political campaigns. The two developments—MTV's entrance into politics and Clinton's use of rock culture—marked a shift in the nature and tenor of political spectacle.

Clinton's use of popular culture can be understood as an authenticating move, very much in keeping with the strategy the PMRC used in the 1980s: dance to Little Richard, but dis Sistah Souljah. Even attacks on Clinton turned around when the terrain was popular culture. As Gilbert Rodman has pointed out, George Bush's strategy of associating Clinton with Elvis through attacks on "Elvis economics" and the like not only alienated a number of potential voters but also allowed Clinton to benefit from that association. In response to Bush's accusations, Clinton shot back with "I don't think Bush would have liked Elvis very much, and that's just another thing that's wrong with him" (Rodman, 1996, p. 90). This populist appeal *through* rock and roll exemplifies Clinton's basic strategy: rock becomes a point of political identification and difference. While for Clinton, this was a rhetorical strategy, for MTV it was a marketing fact.

MTV pitches itself to advertisers in both the United States and Europe as the primary way to reach the "16–34 crowd," as this age range constitutes the majority of its viewing share (Frith, 1993, p. 72). So it is significant that political content took up more and more of its news reporting in years preceding the 1992 election. Though not noticeably different in ideological tenor than other media outlets, MTV became increasingly willing to engage its audience politically. This trend developed slowly over time: MTV first organized voter registration drives in 1984. By 1990, it was airing prime-time "rock-the-vote" spots in which American rock stars encouraged MTV's youth audience to vote (Goodwin, 1992, pp. 148–155).

The 1992 campaign marked MTV's coming out as a political player. It conducted a million dollar "Choose or Lose" ad campaign encouraging youth voter participation. For the first time in its history, it covered both the Democratic and Republican national conventions. It invited all three presidential candidates to appear on live televised "youth forums," although only the Clinton-Gore ticket accepted. Clinton's interview on MTV garnered national attention; *Rolling Stone* claimed that "many of the questions posed were tough enough to put even the seasoned political reporters to shame" (Neely, 1992). After seeing Clinton's success on the channel, George Bush agreed to be interviewed by a MTV reporter.

MTV continued to push for its own inclusion in the campaigns by conducting a sort of press campaign of its own. MTV veejay Tabitha Soren, for instance, claimed that younger voters were not apathetic, but uninspired by the candidates. In a *Los Angeles Times* article whose titular pun was not lost on candidates or reporters ("Inspiration Requires New Channels"), Soren suggested this lack of inspiration might be cured by an appearance on MTV (1992). MTV's participation in the election received wide coverage during and after the fact; and this coverage was completely favorable, simultaneously lauding MTV's "serious" political participation and noting its importance to turning out the youth vote (DuBrow, 1992b; Mason, 1992; Mosely, 1992; Rosenberg, 1992; Suro, 1992). In fact, MTV became a synecdoche of the youth vote—in press coverage, the youth constituency became the "MTV vote" (Chapman, 1993). One commentator went so far as to claim that MTV and other media outlets such as talk shows had displaced network news as the primary means for candidates to reach a television audience (DuBrow, 1992a; Ostrow, 1992).

MTV's involvement in presidential politics did not stop with the election. It threw its own inaugural ball, perhaps the most popular in Washington, D.C. Backstage at the inaugural ball, Little Richard was quoted as saying "Bill and Al was havin' a ball, doin' it all. That man loves my music, he loves 'Good Golly Miss Molly.' He knows I'm the architect of rock n' roll" (Smith, 1993). Clinton clearly intended that message to get out, although he was careful in choosing the rock and pop acts to affiliate himself with. He managed to stay within the bounds of taste that Tipper Gore had fleshed out in the 1980s—more mainstream acts that had either outlived their controversial nature or had none to begin with: Chuck Berry, Little Richard, Fleetwood Mac, Barbara Streisand, even Barry Manilow. He picked one of the safest rap acts he could have—L.L. Cool J. Of course, Clinton had already established himself as within rock culture prior to his election. In addition to his widely noted saxophone playing appearances, he had bands like R.E.M and U2 entertaining the crowds in Little Rock on election night.

Although any "insider" to current rock culture would likely question Clinton's particular choices (lots of soft rock acts at the inaugural ball, for instance), the institutions did the work for him: Carole Robinson, senior vice-president of MTV, said "we thought it was a wonderful opportunity to celebrate the fact that young people got involved this year in the political process." The previous month, MTV's chairman, Tom Freston, was invited to Clinton's economic summit in Little Rock, Arkansas (Shriver, 1993).

The events of 1992 certainly mark MTV's advancement as a player in the political field, but more importantly, they mark the fruition of the work on rock and politics that began in the 1980s. The PMRC produced a sphere of acceptable rock culture for the political field into which politicians could later move. The Clinton campaign's use of rock culture was deliberate and careful, and it yielded positive and clear results. In fact, Clinton's use of rock culture became a model campaign strategy.

This history is now taking on a new shape, as the appearance of rock music in politics proliferates across the globe. While rock may have different valences in other national contexts, the mere repetition of the phenomenon suggests that the shift in political spectacle is not a purely American phenomenon. Since Clinton's success on MTV, other would-be heads of state have followed suit. MTV Asia recently offered guest-veejay slots to Taiwan's four presidential candidates during a special "Choose or Lose" slot on its local Mandarin-language channel. Lee Teng Hui—the incumbent—was the only one to refuse the offer, and MTV claimed his refusal was only because he didn't want to alienate other media outlets he'd already turned down. Even mainland Chinese officials had no problem with the feature, which contained no overtly political content. MTV Taiwan communications manager Gerund Wu claimed MTV was central to the political campaign: "Political PR departments in Taiwan arrange media in categories A, B, and C. We were A because they said the candidates cannot afford to ignore the power of youthful voters" (Burpee, 1996). A few months later, Boris Yeltsin also appeared on MTV to try to garner the Russian youth vote (Kelley, 1996). Reggae is once again playing a part in Jamaican electoral politics (Oumano, 1997). In the United States, Vaclav Havel, Lou Reed, Madeline Albright, and Laurie Anderson recently showed up at a John Zorn gig in New York. Reed commented that "In our culture, we think it's such a big deal that [Albright] showed up. In a really cool culture it would have been lame if she didn't. One little sign of humanity and we fall all over ourselves" (Panahpour, 1997). The connection between rock and humanity is hardly the sole province of democratic party members; former deejay Rush Limbaugh searched for the "hardest-pounding bassline" he could find to open his show, and settled on Chrissy Hynde's song "My City Was Gone." Limbaugh was not the least troubled by the song's ostensibly progressive lyrics (which are not heard on the show): "Here I am going to take a liberal song and make fun of liberals at the same time" (Munger, 1997).[13]

Rock Culture and Political Culture

For all of Clinton's success at mobilizing youth as a category of identification and as a voter demographic, his use of the category is hardly consistent. After seeking the youth vote through MTV appearances and rock and roll affiliations, the Clinton administration and the 103rd and 104th congresses continued the long tradition of youth bashing in the service of other political goals:

> Increasingly, Clinton's health and welfare policy has consisted of blaming teen-agers for nearly all major social ills: Poverty, welfare dependence, crime, gun violence, suicide, sexual promiscuity, unwed motherhood, AIDS, school fail-ure, broken families, child abuse, drug abuse, drunken driving, smoking, and the breakdown of "family values," the latest count as of this writing (Males, 1996, pp. 6–7).

No doubt the language of "teen pregnancy," "unwed mothers" and "violent gangs" is in part code for more direct class- and race-based attacks contained in welfare reform and related legislative programs. But that the very term "youth" can stand in for these other vilified categories suggests that it is not simply an otherwise innocuous term. On the contrary, its very ability to do some of the rhetorical dirty work in place of other more inflammatory language suggests that it, too, has acquired a special status in political rhetoric. The political objec-tivity of youth as a category results in the concept shuttling between positive and negative poles at a frenetic pace. In this logic, there are "the children" (white, middle class) who must be protected; and there are the youth who are perceived as threats to the white, middle-class ways of life—children of the poor, youth of color, white kids "gone bad."

These are not new images in American political discourse; they have had remarkable durability and utility throughout the 20th cen-tury (Acland, 1995). The new development, and the one that marks Clinton's difference from his predecessors, is the utilization of youth as a category of political subjectivity. Here, rock culture becomes a means to an end, a kind of instrument that can be wielded by either party: it is as open to Republicans as it is to Democrats. This instru-mentality stems from rock's unacknowledged ideological affinity with the political field as well as its adaptability to the history of political spectacle.

Rock culture and political culture have more in common than writ-ers on either subject would like to admit. Rock culture, often through its investment in the category of youth, retains a strong affiliation with notions of authenticity. As Theodore Graczyk has convincingly ar-gued, even the ironic "postmodern" stances of many current fans and musicians only exist in relation to this larger ideology of authenticity. This authenticity, in turn, provides a kind of endless loop into and out of bourgeois life:

> Twenty five years ago the protagonist of Lou Reed's "Rock and Roll" rejected her parents' material comforts and felt that her life was saved by rock and roll. It does not follow that she abandoned bourgeois attitudes. Instead, she was moved by the freshness with which rock gives public expression to their underlying values (Graczyk, 1996, p. 226).

Other writers, such as Lawrence Grossberg and Katrina Irving, have emphasized rock culture's roots in middle-class life and middle-class values. While Irving (1988, p. 170) describes rock counterculture as "a protest against the middle class by the middle class"—a kind of inauthentic rebellion—Grossberg sees rock as an essential part of middle-class life, a response to boredom and alienation that does not have any essential political character: "Rock's ideology was squarely located within the commitment to mobility and consumerism, although these may have been constructed as necessary paths to a life of fun rather than ends in themselves" (Grossberg, 1992, p. 145). Rock ideology may provide a critique of bourgeois culture, but it is also part of the mechanism of its reproduction. The ideology of rock is thus not so much a question of "left" or "right," but rather a set of beliefs about individuality, affect, the care of the self. Put simply, rock ideology is a species of liberalism. Rock emphasizes a kind of authentic individualism, both in the musician as artist and in the fan as a self-fashioning person. It is an ideology of "freely chosen" self-empowerment through identification:

> The unifying thread [of rock ideology] is an assumption that the unique individual is basic to authenticity. In a word, liberalism: there is no essential, common good beyond whatever autonomous individuals seek and choose as most worthy for themselves (Graczyk, 1996, p. 220).

This kind of thinking permeates rock ideology, and rock's individualism and populism are values quite sympathetic with the political field. As with Clinton's Elvis reference, rock ideology offers a language full of references to individual freedom, voluntary associations, emotional intensity, and personal authenticity without requiring any specific commitment to a political program or set of beliefs. As Graczyk puts it, rock ideology is big enough to encompass Rock-Against-Racism *and* Neil Young supporting Ronald Reagan; Fugazi and Skid Row. If it displays this kind of ideological coherence—a coherence around the nature of people rather than any kind of programmatic politics, then there is nothing about the ideology of rock that would prevent its use in political life.

Similarly, rock's appearance on the political scene is not any kind of carnivalesque rupture of political discourse. As a number of writers on the "public sphere" have noted, even if American political discourse exists with reference to an ideal of rational-critical debate, the practice of American politics has at least as much to do with the manufacture of public spectacle and personal identification as it does with voters making rational choices based purely on "the issues." Michael Schudson, summarizing the work of a number of historians, has argued that political spectacle has been central to the conduct of American politics, *especially* during periods of high voter turnout. During the late nineteenth and early twentieth centuries, political discourse was fused with popular culture: politics was more about popular songs and parades than it was about "issues"; Democratic and Republican party clubs doubled as dance halls (Schudson, 1992). Today, that tradition continues, as the media of entertainment are also the media of news and political discourse. While the youth of today don't hang out at dances sponsored by the various parties, it is certainly the case that political spectacle is organized according to the generic and media structures of popular culture at any given time. To become popular, politicians must *act* popular (Warner, 1992, p. 391).

Given the mutual affinities of rock culture and political culture, all that the political field required for rock to enter was a gesture of legitimation—a chance to bring rock and roll and its attendant appeal to youth as a form of political subjectivity into political culture at large. Tipper Gore's rise to national prominence through the PMRC represents such a moment of legitimation, where politicians found a way to "say yes" to rock culture, even as they retained the language of containment and middle-class respectability. The PMRC's discourse on rock music produced new possibilities for speaking and acting in political life, even as it appeared to be "about" the regulation of rock.

Concluding Questions

I have used the language of instrumentalization here because I want to move away from questions of authenticity and co-optation in the cultural politics of rock music. Authenticity and co-optation are both internal to rock culture; as a result, scholars who wish to talk about the political uses of rock music may have to reconsider their own analytical frameworks (Bourdieu & Wacquant, 1993, p. 251).[14] My original point in writing this essay was not to get rockers more involved in mainstream politics—nor to decry their existing involvement—but simply to suggest that the culture of rock does not naturally contradict the culture of politics. More importantly, I have shown here that the political uses of rock extend beyond questions of agency for the disempowered or the repression of that agency through efforts to regulate rock music: the PMRC's agitation for the regulation of rock in the 1980s should be read as producing rock as a useful tool in politics, and not simply as yet another attempt to put the kids down. There is nothing in rock or rock ideology that makes it somehow resistant to or contrary to political culture. If the disempowered and alienated may under some circumstances be able to find a voice through rock culture, the powerful are also able to use rock and roll as a way of shaping their identities, their political expression and activity.

In demonstrating that simple fact, this essay raises another, deeper question. I could easily end with a call for the left to take back the terrain of youth and popular culture—to instrumentalize rock to our own ends. "We must find a way to use rock to persuade people of our position," the conclusion would say, "so that the left, too, can appeal broadly to the people." But this line of thinking already assumes that the "strategic deployment" of rock is the fundamental cultural-political question. A prior question is whether leftists should automatically and actively pursue—in theory or in practice—the instrumentalization of rock culture, given what that instrumentalization has been shown to entail.

Author Note

This essay is expanded from the text of a talk given at "Rock*IN*Theory: An Interdisciplinary Conference on Rock Music and Critical Theory," University of Illinois at Urbana-Champaign, 19 February 1994. I would like to thank Greg Dimitriadis, Lawrence Grossberg, Richard Leppert, Carrie Rentschler, Carol Stabile and Mike Willard for comments on earlier versions of this essay, and Rob Sloane for some helpful references.

References

Acland, C. (1995). *Youth, murder, spectacle: The cultural politics of 'youth in crisis.'* Boulder, CO.: Westview Press.

Bennett, T., Frith, S., Grossberg, L., Shepherd, J., & Turner, G. (Eds.). (1993). *Rock and popular music: Politics, policies, institutions.* New York: Routledge.

Bourdieu, P. (1984). *Distinction: A social critique of the judgement of taste* (R. Nice, Trans.). Cambridge: Harvard University Press.

Bourdieu, P. (1988). *Homo academicus* (P. Collier, Trans.). Stanford: Stanford University Press.

Bourdieu, P. (1991). *Language and symbolic power* (G. Raymond & M. Anderson, Trans.). Cambridge: Harvard University Press.

Bourdieu, P., & Wacquant, L. J. D. (1993). *An invitation to reflexive sociology.* Chicago: University of Chicago Press.

Brackett, D. (1992). James Brown's 'Superbad' and the double voiced utterance. *Popular Music, 11*(3), 309–324.

Burpee, G. (1996, 23 March). Presidential candidates guest as MTV VJs. *Billboard,* 6–7.

Chambers, I. (1985). *Urban rhythms: Popular music and popular culture.* Basingstoke: Macmillan.

Chapman, S. (1993, 28 January). Baby boomers and Bill Clinton's generation gap. *Chicago Tribune,* p. A19.

Chapple, S., & Talbot, D. (1989). *Burning desires: Sex in America.* New York: Doubleday.

Cowan, R. S. (1983). *More work for mother: The ironies of household technology from the open hearth to the microwave.* New York: Basic Books.

DuBoff, R., & Herman, E. (1996, December). Review of *The scapegoat generation,* by Mike Males. *Z Magazine, 57.*

DuBrow, R. (1992a, 31 October). A revolution, pure and simple. *Los Angeles Times* p. F1.

DuBrow, R. (1992b, 28 August). Surprising answers in an MTV poll. *Los Angeles Times,* p. F9.

Fairchild, C. (1995). 'Alternative' music and the politics of cultural autonomy: The case of Fugazi and the D.C. scene. *Popular Music and Society, 19*(1), 17–35.

Fiske, J. (1989). *Reading the popular.* Boston: Unwin Hyman.

Foucault, M. (1978). *The history of sexuality, vol. I: An introduction* (R. Hurley, Trans.). New York: Vintage Press.

Foucault, M. (1979). On governmentality. *Ideology and consciousness* (6), 5–22.

Frank, L., & Smith, P. (Eds.). (1993). *Madonnarama: Essays on sex and popular culture.* Pittsburgh: Cleis Press.

Frith, S. (1987). Toward an aesthetic of popular music. In R. Leppert & S. McClary (Eds.), *Music and society: The politics of composition, performance and reception* (pp.133–150). New York: Cambridge University Press.

Frith, S. (Ed.). (1989). *World music, politics and social change: Papers from the International Association for the Study of Popular Music.* New York: Manchester University Press.

Frith, S. (1992). The cultural study of popular music. In L. Grossberg, C. Nelson, P. Treichler, L. Baughman, & J. M. Wise (Eds.), *Cultural studies* (pp. 174–186). New York: Routledge.

Frith, S. (1993). Youth/music/television. In S. Frith, A. Goodwin, & L. Grossberg (Eds.), *Sound and vision: The music video reader* (pp. 67–84). New York: Routledge.

Frow, J. (1995). *Cultural studies and cultural value.* New York: Oxford University Press.

Garofalo, R. (1992a). Popular music and the civil rights movement. In R. Garofalo (Ed.), *Rockin' the boat: Mass music and mass movements* (pp. 231–240). Boston: South End Press.

Garofalo, R. (Ed.). (1992b). *Rockin' the boat: Mass music and mass movements.* Boston: South End Press.

Gilroy, P. (1991). *There ain't no black in the Union Jack: The cultural politics of race and nation.* Chicago: University of Chicago Press.

Gilroy, P. (1993). *The black Atlantic: Modernity and double consciousness.* Cambridge: Harvard University Press.

Goodwin, A. (1992). *Dancing in the distraction factory: Music television and popular culture.* Minneapolis: University of Minnesota Press.

Gore, T. (1987). *Raising PG kids in an X-Rated society.* Nashville: Abington Press.

Graczyk, T. (1996). *Rhythm and noise: An aesthetics of rock.* Durham: Duke University Press.

Grossberg, L. (1992). *We gotta get out of this place: Popular conservatism and postmodern culture.* New York: Routledge.

Grossberg, L. (1993). The framing of rock: Rock and the new conservatism. In T. Bennett, S. Frith, L. Grossberg, J. Shepherd, & G. Turner (Eds.), *Rock and popular music: Politics, policies, institutions* (pp. 193–209). New York: Routledge.

Grossberg, L. (1997). *Dancing in spite of myself: Essays on popular culture.* Durham, NC: Duke University Press.

Gualnick, P. (1986). *Sweet soul music: Rhythm and blues and the southern dream of freedom.* New York: Harper and Row.

Hall, S., & Jefferson, T. (Eds.). (1976). *Resistance through rituals: Youth subcultures in postwar Britain.* London: HarperCollins Academic.

Harrington, R. (1992, 22 July). Is Tipper changing her tune? *Washington Post,* p. G7.

Harris, D. (1992). *From class struggle to the politics of pleasure: The effects of gramscianism on cultural studies.* New York: Routledge.

Hebdige, D. (1979). *Subculture: The meaning of style.* New York: Routledge.

Herrnstein-Smith, B. (1991). *Contingencies of value: Alternative perspectives for critical theory.* Cambridge: Harvard University Press.

Hoare, I. (Ed.). (1975). *The soul book.* London: Methuen.

Holland, N. (1988). Purple passion: Images of female desire in "when doves cry." *Cultural Critique* (10), 89–99.

hooks, b. (1992). *Black looks: Race and representation.* Boston: South End Press.

Horkheimer, M., & Adorno, T. (1972). *Dialectic of enlightenment* (J. Cummings, Trans.). New York: Continuum.

Howe, N., & Strauss, B. (1993). *13th gen: America's 13th generation, born 1961–1981.* New York: Vintage Books.

Irving, K. (1988). Rock music and the state: Dissonance or counterpoint? *Cultural Critique* (10), 151–170.

Kelley, J. (1996, 13 June). Rock wraps up the votes for Yeltsin. *USA Today,* p. A9.

Lott, E. (1995). *Love and theft: Blackface minstrelsy and the American working class.* New York: Oxford University Press.

Males, M. (1996). *Scapegoat generation: America's war on adolescents.* Monroe. Maine: Common Courage Press.

Martin, L. (1988). *Anti-rock: The opposition to rock and roll.* Hamden, Conn.: Archon Books.

Mason, M. S. (1992, 28 August). MTV aims to rock youth vote. *Christian Science Monitor,* 12.

McGuigan, J. (1992). *Cultural populism.* New York: Routledge.

McRobbie, A. (1991). *Feminism and youth culture: From "Jackie" to "Just seventeen."* Boston: Unwin Hyman.

Meehan, E. (1990). Why we don't count: The commodity audience. In P. Mellencamp (Ed.), *Logics of television* (pp. 117–137). Bloomington: Indiana University Press.

Middleton, R. (1990). *Studying popular music.* Philadelphia: Open Univerity Press.

Miller, R. (1991). Selling Mrs. Consumer. *Antipode: A Journal of Radical Geography, 23*(3), 263–306.

Mitchell, S. (1993, April). How to talk to young adults. *American Demographics, 15,* 50.

Mosely, M. (1992, 10 February). Where will the youth vote go?: The sleeping giant could re-elect Clinton. *Denver Post,* p. B7.

Munger, S. (1997, 25 August–1 September). Rockin' Rush: Radio pirate. *Nation, 265,* 26.

Murphy, R. (1989, 6 September). Warning labels contribute to climate of censorship. *Boston Globe,* p. 75.

Neely, K. (1992, 6 August). Clinton: I want the MTV vote. *Rolling Stone,* 22.

Negus, K. (1996). *Popular music in theory: An introduction.* Cambridge: Polity Press.

Ostrow, J. (1992, 4 November). Suspenseless night caps unusual year. *Denver Post,* p. A13.

Oumano, E. (1997, 25 August–1 September). Reggae says no to "politricks." *Nation, 265, 24,* 33–34.

Panahpour, N. (1997, 10–24 July). Random notes. *Rolling Stone,* 23.

Pateman, C. (1988). *The sexual contract.* Palo Alto, CA: Stanford University Press.

Rodman, G. (1996). *Elvis after Elvis: The posthumous career of a living legend.* New York: Routledge.

Rogin, M. (1992). Blackface, white noise: The Jewish jazz singer finds his voice. *Critical Inquiry* (18), 417–453.

Rosenberg, H. (1992, 2 November). Media coverage: The vote is in. *Los Angeles Times,* p. F1.

Saxton, A. (1990). *The rise and fall of the white republic: Class politics and mass culture in ninetennth-century America.* New York: Verso.

Schalit, J. (1996, September). Just say no to rock and roll. *Bad Subjects* (27).

Schudson, M. (1992). Was there ever a public sphere? If so, when? Reflections on the American case. In C. Calhoun (Ed.), *Habermas and the public sphere* (pp. 143–163). Cambridge: MIT Press.

Schudson, M. (1997, August). Paper tigers: a sociologist follows cultural studies into the wilderness. *Lingua Franca, 7*, 49–56.

Schwichtenberg, C. (Ed.). (1993). *The Madonna connection: Representational politics, subcultural identities, and cultural theory.* Boulder, CO: Westview Press.

Shriver, J. (1993, 13 January). MTV ball becomes "hottest ticket in town." *Los Angeles Times*, p. F1.

Smith, P. (1993, 20 January). The inaugural gala: A night to face the music and the masses. *Boston Globe*, p. 31.

Soren, T. (1992, 28 June). Inspiration requires new channels. *Los Angeles Times*, p. M5.

Spigel, L. (1993). Seducing the innocent: Childhood and television in postwar America. In W. Solomon & R. McChesney (Eds.), *Ruthless criticism: New perspectives in U.S. media history* (pp. 259–290). Minneapolis: University of Minnesota Press.

Suro, R. (1992, 30 October). Democrats count youngest voters. *New York Times*, p. A18.

Warner, M. (1992). The mass public and the mass subject. In C. Calhoun (Ed.), *Habermas and the public sphere* (pp. 377–401). Cambridge: M.I.T. Press.

Notes

1. Rock and roll can mean many things—here I am simply using the term to define a broadly and commonly understood area of popular music, with a bias toward mainstream rock culture (and its attendant white, middle-class, and male biases). Rather than offering a precise conceptual definition of the music and practices connected with it, I am more interested in the social definitions put into play by the people and institutions I consider in this essay—mainly politicians and MTV. At this level, then, I reproduce the vague "common sense" definition of rock because that is the definition operative in the contexts I consider.

2. These questions have tended to dominate recent writing on rock music in particular and popular music in general. Most of these studies descend from or are influenced by work done at the Birmingham Centre for Cultural Studies in the 1970s. For a classic formulation of the subcultural resistance paradigm, see Hall and Jefferson, 1976. The work of John Fiske and other cultural populists extended this position through the 1980s (see Chambers, 1985; Fiske, 1989, especially pp. 95–132; McRobbie, 1991, especially pp. 1–34 and 189–219). Most recently, there has been a backlash against this position, but most of these critiques tend to critique cultural populism as a way to attack cultural studies as such. Moreover, these attacks on cultural populism tend to leave intact the hegemony-resistance paradigm by critiquing the excesses of populism without effectively critiquing the ideology of authenticity that underlies the larger paradigm (in both its pessimistic and populist moments); see, for example, Harris, 1992; McGuigan, 1992; and Schudson, 1997. For a general overview of theoretical approaches to popular music, see Middleton (1990) and Negus (1996).

3. Perhaps the most elaborate attempt to demonstrate this approach is Reebee Garofalo (1992b). While the pieces provide some interesting analyses of rock and roll and other popular musics in various mass movements, it tends toward the assumption, or, perhaps more accurately, is structured by the desire to locate in rock some kind of essentially progressive politics (see also Frith, 1989).

4. Note that I am not making any particular claims about the legitimacy or illegitimacy of mainstream politics as an arena for political action, nor am I suggesting a program for engagement or nonengagement with the political field. I am simply arguing that an analysis of the political field ought to inform such programmatic issues, and that to date, scholarship that has attempted to provide "political" analyses of rock has tended to neglect such questions.

5. The relation of rock culture to specifically leftist politics is beyond the scope of this essay. In addition to some of the other sources cited below, see Fairchild (1995) and Schalit (1996).

6. Given the attention paid to Madonna's music several years ago (Frank & Smith, 1993; Schwichtenberg, 1993), it's surprising how little attention has been paid to Prince's work from the same period. Apart from a few formal musical analyses, little has been said about Prince's use of gender codes or his more problematic position for white understandings of black masculinity. Nancy J. Holland offers a brief musicological analysis of Prince's "When Doves Cry," though her analysis tends to abstract the song from any kind of musical history (Holland, 1988).

7. Even a black-positive band like Living Colour could not resist a slight on Prince's masculinity when they came through Minneapolis, asking "where's the midget?" as they stood on the First Avenue stage.

8. Neil Howe and Bill Strauss, in an otherwise reactionary book, also catalogue shifts in attitudes toward the generation after the baby boom. For their discussion of shifts in attitudes toward children, see Part One of Howe and Strauss (1993).

9. The analogy between family and state is a fundamental gesture of classical liberalism (Foucault, 1979); for a feminist critique of the family/state analogy, see Carole Pateman (1988, especially pp. 77–188).

10. Both sides of the "censorship" position ignore the fundamental differences between the PMRC and other antirock efforts. For an example of the "climate of censorship" position, see Richard Harrington (1992); for the opposing position, see Ryan Murphy (1989).

11. Nor was this strictly a political phenomenon, as appeals to motherhood and the protection of children also drove advertising for household products like refrigerators (see Cowan, 1983; Miller, 1991).

12. Du Boff and Herman's critique of Males takes a strictly realist view of generational politics and proceeds to debunk it. Males' response to their critique is interesting because he maintains an ambiguous position, somewhere between the realism he's accused of and a more careful conceptual framework that would not *presume* an identity between representations of youth and the experiences of young people.

13. A critical issue of *The Nation* appeared too late to be included substantively in this article, but it contains useful discussions of rock music and politics, as well as an excellent analysis of the political economy of the music industry (see, e.g., Munger, 1997; Oumano, 1997, as well as the entire issue).

14. The cited passage: "The force of the preconstructed resides in the fact that, being inscribed both in things and in minds, it presents itself under the cloak of the self-evident which goes unnoticed because it is by definition taken for granted." See also Bourdieu (1988, pp. 1–35) on the necessity of an "epistemic break" when studying the social world of which one is a part.

The "Chicano" Dance Hall: Remapping Public Space in Post-World War II Greater Los Angeles

matt garcia

Introduction

For the most part, the Mexicans in and around Los Angeles were economically and socially closest to blacks. As soon as we understood English, it was usually the Black English we first tried to master. Later in the youth authority camps and prisons, blacks used Mexican slang and the *cholo* style; Mexicans imitated the Southside swagger and style—although this didn't mean at times we didn't war with one another, such being the state of affairs at the bottom. For Chicanos this influence lay particularly deep in music: Mexican rhythms syncopated with blues and ghetto beats.

—Luis J. Rodriguez, *Always Running* (1993)

The dance hall and its music have become a popular referent for authors and film directors interested in representing Chicano youth culture in Southern California. In his book *Always Running*, Luis Rodriguez describes dances as sites where ethnic groups mingled, young men and women kindled romance, and youth gangs settled conflicts. Similarly, in his 1995 film *Mi Familia*, Gregory Nava sets a battle between his protagonist Chucho Sánchez (played by Esai Morales) and a rival gang member within a mythical Los Angeles concert hall. Other films, such as Allison Anders' *Mi Vida Loca* (1993) and Luis Valdez's *Zoot Suit* (1981) and *La Bamba* (1987) depict the dance hall as an important public space where Chicanos and Chicanas negotiated their gender, generational, and ethnic identities. The image projected in these films, especially *Mi Familia* and *La Bamba*, serves as a corrective to mainstream popular media depictions of American youth culture during the 1950s and early 60s. Television programs and movies such as *Ozzie and Harriet, Happy Days, Grease,* and *American Graffiti* suggest that most participants were white. In greater Los Angeles, on the other hand, ethnic minorities composed many of the bands and audiences that formed the basis of this youth culture.

Although recent popular media depictions revise and expand our understanding of 1950s and early 1960s youth culture, they also misrepresent the multifaceted social dynamics extant in the dance halls. First, they do not accurately reflect the truly multicultural world that existed at many of these concerts. Patrons came from a variety of ethnic backgrounds, which manifested themselves in the music and social relations prevalent on the dance floors and in the parking lots. Contrary to popular media depictions—old and new—teenage dance hall audiences were neither all-white, nor all-Chicano. However, since many of these halls were situated in predominantly Mexican American neighborhoods, Chicano youths significantly shaped this world.

Second, recent literary and film treatments of the dance halls focus attention on the potential violence at rock 'n roll concerts. Prior to the mid-1960s, the dance halls were not the gang war zones depicted in the film *Mi Familia* and the novel *Always Running.* Although physical confrontations threatened some, during the relatively prosperous years of the 1950s, patrons mostly experienced peaceful and friendly relations with their peers. These integrated public facilities were some of the first institutions where Angelenos from a variety of ethnic/racial backgrounds transcended Jim Crow-style laws and de facto segregation.[1] Intercultural dating, sharing of fads and fashions, and the formation of a culturally hybridized genre of rock 'n roll known as the "Eastside Sound" demonstrate the level of intercultural exchange prevalent at these shows.

This article concerns two Southern California dance halls, Pomona's Rainbow Gardens and El Monte's American Legion Stadium. Understanding how these dance halls came to be explains the Mexican influence in rock 'n roll and youth culture during this period. Although Mexican American teens comprised much of the dance hall audiences and bands, many African Americans, Asian/Pacific Islanders, and whites also contributed to the formation of this interethnic world. Through their engagement in this multiethnic youth culture, young Angelenos offered an alternative vision of race relations in the United States. For musicians, especially African Americans and Mexican Americans, the stage provided an opportunity to expand their knowledge of rhythms and musical instruments, and to apply their own cultural influences to the highly adaptable genre of music known as rock 'n roll (Lipsitz, 1990, 1994; Loza, 1995; Hamm, 1979). Equally important, audience members frequently commuted from segregated communities to intercultural dance halls and learned to accept and even embrace cultural pluralism.

Rainbow Gardens

Prior to 1950, Rainbow Gardens had an established reputation as one of the few premier venues for big band music in Southern California. Situated in the far eastern corner of Los Angeles County, the hall became a major stopping point for Euro-American bandleaders and personalities such as Harry James, Les Brown, Perry Como, Lou Costello, and Pat O'Brien who frequently travelled between Las Vegas and Los Angeles. Although rarely a black or brown face appeared in the audience, the great Count Basie transcended barriers of racial discrimination and exhibited his talents as one of the most revered bandleaders of the period. Latinos, although experiencing a significant musical renaissance of their own, did not appear at Rainbow Gardens as either audience members or performers.[2] In fact, when asked whether Mexican Americans attended Rainbow Garden's dances in the 1940s, former local disc jockey Candelario ("Cande") Mendoza commented:

> Oh, no. Absolutely not. In fact, and I hesitate to say this, but I think that even before then a Mexican American had to be **extremely** well dressed and not even look too much like a Mexican in order to get into Rainbow Gardens on a Saturday night [with the white bands] (C. Mendoza, interviewed by the author, 17 February 1995).

In spite of this discrimination, Latin American music from both sides of the border emanated throughout the citrus *colonias* and work camps via radio. Corresponding with the least valuable air time, and coincidentally, with the time many Mexican agricultural laborers went to work, Mexican disc jockeys inhabited the early morning hours of predominantly English-language radio stations with Latin American music programs. This allowed many Mexican Americans to stay abreast of the various trends in Latin American music coming from Mexico, Cuba, Puerto Rico, and the American Southwest. Exposure to *folk, conjunto, norteño,* and *orquesta* music established continuity with the past, while familiarizing local populations with contemporary Latin American music played throughout the Americas.[3]

Many Mexican Americans of the citrus belt recognized Cande Mendoza as the central figure in promoting this music. His presence on the radio made him a household name in the *colonias* throughout the San Gabriel and Pomona Valleys east of Los Angeles. And, as Pomona's first Chicano elementary school teacher by day, people came to know Mendoza not as a distant radio personality, but rather as an approachable role model for the community.

In 1950 Mendoza approached Rainbow Garden's owners, Gertie and Ray Thomas, about hosting a Latin American music concert on a weekday night. Gertie Thomas told him "you're gonna lose your shirt," but took pity on Mendoza and gave him use of the facilities without charge. He proved them wrong. Mendoza contracted Beto Villa, the popular Tejano bandleader to be Rainbow's first Latin American act. The concert drew over 750 people that evening, prompting Gertie to say: "How can this be? Who is this guy? He must be the greatest around. I cannot get that many people to come in and see Les Brown, Harry James, or even Count Basie on a Saturday night" (C. Mendoza, interviewed by the author, 17 February, 1995).

Soon after Villa's appearance at Rainbow Gardens the Thomases made Mendoza the permanent music consultant, booking manager, and emcee at the club. Although Mendoza mixed Anglo acts with Latin American bands, once Mexican Americans began to frequent the dance hall, whites ceased to patronize Rainbow Gardens. According to Cande Mendoza, "[Latin American] music should have had a cross-cultural appeal," especially since many Latin American recording artists garnered Anglo favor through their exposure on the national weekly radio show "The Lucky Strike Hit Parade" (C. Mendoza, interviewed by the author, 17 February, 1995).

After its incarnation as a predominantly Latino club, Mendoza reflected: "I don't think the Anglo population knew or cared about Rainbow Gardens—they ignored it, but didn't fight it." The Thomases' "careful" handling of the business probably had much to do with its marginal acceptance into the community. For example, in order to avoid any reasons for public opposition, the Thomases employed an army of predawn workers to clean up within a radius of several blocks of the ballroom's downtown location. Such "rituals" successfully averted any problems with a white-run city government.

Each Saturday night, Mexican American patrons came from all over Southern California for a memorable night of dance and entertainment. A predominantly Latino audience enjoyed performances by such varied and famous entertainers as Les Brown, María Victoria, Harry James, Luis Arcaráz, Lola Beltrán, Tín Tan, Lou Costello, Ray Touzet, Tito Puente, and Dámaso Pérez Prado. Local groups also appeared on the Rainbow stage as intermission bands. While most headline acts consisted of the twelve to fourteen piece orquesta bands, intermission bands often were much smaller, and represented the more working-class genre of music known as "conjunto." Consequently, a trip to Rainbow Gardens on Saturday nights exposed patrons to a full range of Latin American music: small, local working-class bands, to large, internationally known orquestas.[4]

Although Mendoza began his tenure at Rainbow Gardens as a champion of the Latin American big band sound, he also recognized the generational cleavages within the Latino community. In response to the growing popularity of rock 'n roll in the mid-1950s, Mendoza began Friday night dances at Rainbow Gardens to accommodate large numbers of Mexican American teens interested in the "new" American popular music. As with his big band shows, Mendoza successfully attracted notable recording stars, including Little Richard and a young, Mexican American rock 'n roller, Ritchie Valens.

Inspired by Valens and other Los Angeles bands, many local Mexican American youths formed rock 'n roll groups to emulate their heroes, play music, and create homespun sounds. Mendoza encouraged such experimentation by providing young Mexican American rock 'n roll acts a venue for their performances. Whether on his afternoon radio program for teens which began in the mid-1950s, or his Friday night dances at Rainbow Gardens, Mendoza's support of their music contributed to the formation of a regional rock 'n roll aesthetic known as the "Eastside Sound" made popular by groups such as *Thee Midnighters, Tierra, El Chicano, Malo,* and *Los Lobos.* Pomona Valley bands such as *The Velveteens, Ronnie and the Casuals,* and Rainbow Gardens' house band *The Mixtures* recorded many local hits, while drawing substantial audiences at clubs throughout Southern California.[5]

The emergence of rock 'n roll represented an important change in the direction of Mexican American/Chicano music. Although young people of the late 1950s and early 1960s shared an appreciation for mambo, conjunto, and orquesta, many viewed these forms as the music of their parents. According to Jerry Castellano, a veteran of the music scene and founding member of two Pomona bands *The Velveteens* and *The Royals,*"we appreciated it [Latin American music], but we were into another bag" (J. Castellano, interviewed by the author, 11 May, 1995). For him and his peers, Mexican music occupied a space on the kitchen table in the form of a transistor radio:

> Like any other person, all [Mexican] families did this—the father would get up early and eat breakfast before going to work, and the wife would get up and make breakfast for him—and they had a little radio with a *soft* Mexican station on so it wouldn't wake up the kids. That was the only time we heard Mexican music. . . . But, it wasn't the "in" thing to listen to Mexican music, because [Spanish] was a second language (J. Castellano, interviewed by the author, 11 May, 1995).

In addition to the language barriers, generational gaps also played a part in separating young Chicanos from music of a previous generation. For example, although Pérez Prado's popularity reached its highest level in the mid-1950s across a very diverse audience, a young, new generation of Latinos with a growing interest in rock 'n roll mostly regarded him as an elder icon of the Latin American big band scene. Jerry Castellano explains his generation's impressions of Prado:

> Everybody had their own taste, but mainly all the groups—the Latin groups and the big band groups—they were much older, much much older than us. Pérez Prado, when he was popular, he wasn't a young man. He was already— and I'm guessing—he was already mid-30s or 40s already. And the reason for this was because it took so long for them to get exposure. You know, TV wasn't in that much, and you couldn't get into radio [Latin American musicians on English-speaking radio]. It was very difficult to get the word out. So they had to travel a lot to get exposure (J. Castellano, interviewed by the author, 11 May, 1995).

Rainbow Gardens served as an important venue for bands such as Prado's and helped disseminate and popularize the music among the Mexican population of Southern California. However, for a younger generation of Mexican Americans (many second and third generation), born if not raised in a predominantly English-speaking, mass-culture-based society, this music did not have the same appeal. These youths increasingly validated artists' fame with their appearances at teen-oriented concerts, and on mainstream radio stations and television programs, while Rainbow Garden's Saturday night dances and entertainers became associated with an older crowd.

For Castellano and other young aspiring rock 'n rollers, generational as well as ethnic/racial affinity represented an equally important factor in encouraging young Mexican Americans to take up music as an expression of their culture. For example, Castellano recalls the importance of seeing Ricky Nelson weekly: "We grew up with him on TV. And I remember every time he sang or played, it was like 'if he can do it, so can we!'" (J. Castellano, interviewed by the author, 11 May, 1995). Such enthusiasm translated into increased record sales for rock 'n roll artists and encouraged record companies to focus more attention on the emerging youth market. When Ricky Nelson's 1958 hit, "Poor Little Fool," unseated Pérez Prado's "Patricia" for the number one spot on the America's Top 100, it represented just one example of a move on the part of the greater listening public toward rock 'n roll-oriented music during the late 1950s (Grendysa, 1995, p. 13).

Many Chicanos acknowledged the African American origins of rock 'n roll, and identified black artists as the inspiration for much of their own musical experimentation. For young Mexican American musicians who had also experienced the pain of ethnic/racial discrimination and segregation, the success of African American artists inspired Chicanos to express themselves musically, and engage in an industry that held remote, but not impossible, possibilities for acceptance and achievement. The success of Ritchie Valens, a local artist from Pacoima in the San Fernando Valley, galvanized other Mexican American youths. As Castellano remembered: "Especially when we saw someone like Ritchie Valens make it to the top—Wow! That means that we can do it, we can do it. . . . Chicanos that made it!" (J. Castellano, interviewed by the author, 11 May, 1995).

Although Valens had the good fortune of succeeding on a national level early in his career, the rock 'n roll music culture of Southern California mostly developed in the dance halls and small auditoriums throughout the Southland. Music groups, whose proliferation easily surpassed the number of recording companies willing to sign them, depended mostly on exposure at local venues such as Rainbow Gardens. By the mid-1950s, Cande Mendoza filled Rainbow's weekend schedule with rock 'n roll on Fridays, Latin American orquesta and conjunto on Saturdays, and *tardeadas* (afternoon dances featuring conjunto music) on Sundays.

Architects and planners, however, designed venues like Rainbow Gardens primarily for big band dances which catered to a more intimate ballroom experience.[6] The decor and acoustics complemented the big band musical aesthetic and inspired patrons to dress in their finest attire. The dress, demeanor, and formal presentation style of the performers evoked from their audiences attitudes and behavior that reflected the refined image of big band music (Lipsitz, 1990; Gilroy, 1993).[7]

Mexican Americans' rising interest in rock 'n roll necessitated a correlative aesthetic shift in the ways in which people experienced this music. While Cande Mendoza adjusted his focus to incorporate rock 'n roll music into Rainbow's weekend repertoire, the change did not (and could not) include spatial and structural alterations in the physical appearance of the building, inside and out. In spite of the many rock 'n roll concerts held at the dance hall, the aesthetics of Rainbow Gardens reflected the tastes of an older generation which had firmly established its reputation as a site for Latin American big band music.

El Monte's American Legion Stadium

El Monte's American Legion Stadium, on the other hand, developed directly out of the youth subculture which seized the mainstream during the 1950s. Located in the heart of the San Gabriel Valley, approximately 15 miles east of downtown Los Angeles, Legion Stadium drew a diverse, multicultural audience from all ends of the Southland. Art Laboe, a popular local radio disc jockey and concert promoter, remembered: "White kids from Beverly Hills, black kids from Compton, and local Chicano kids used to come out to our shows every weekend" (A. Laboe, interviewed by the author, 15 May, 1995).

Legion Stadium, a cavernous auditorium which was the site of wrestling for the 1932 Olympics and roller derby matches for the Los Angeles Thunderbirds, proved to be the perfect place for rock 'n roll concerts. Initially, Laboe and other concert promoters attempted to organize these shows within Los Angeles's city limits; however a city ordinance restricted gatherings of people under the age of 18. According to Laboe, "Concerts started at El Monte because the laws were different in the county than they were in the city [of Los Angeles]" (A. Laboe, interviewed by the author, 15 May, 1995).[8] These relaxed county laws also benefited other venues situated in Los Angeles's hinterlands, including Rainbow Gardens and the Long Beach Municipal Auditorium—the latter competing with Legion Stadium in size and reputation.

Angelenos' experience of life in greater Los Angeles—a network of suburbs connected by freeways and parkways—encouraged young people to drive from their homes to county dance hall sites. One scholar has referred to the Southern California metropolis as "polynuclear" because Los Angeles is composed of a subsystem of regions rather than one centralized city (Preston, 1971, 1972, p. 5). Although towns such as El Monte, Long Beach, and Pomona technically existed out-side of Los Angeles, most residents of greater Los Angeles considered them part of the metropolitan area.

Media also contributed to the formation of this "postmodern geography" (Soja, 1989).[9] Radio facilitated the creation of an "imagined community" among youths in Los Angeles based on equal access to programing and generational affinity. Although young people may have lived in a particular geographical region segregated by race and class, the common experience of listening to music broadcast across the Southland on KRLA and other radio stations prefigured the interethnic popularity of the halls. When Laboe and other disc jockeys assembled an array of popular performers aimed at attracting a teen audience, fans flocked to the halls.

The commute gave rise to an emergent car culture. According to one faithful El Monte patron, Richard Rodríguez, "lowriders were early fifties, and everybody was lowriding." To lower their cars, teens would either heat the suspension springs underneath their wheel base or load their trunks with sand or cement bags. Often, lowriders played music from *within* their cars as a way to prepare for the night's entertainment. According to Rodríguez, "You had your record player that was made by Craig. The actual 45rpm record inside the car! If you hit a bump in the street, there went the record" (R. Rodríguez, interviewed by the author, 20 May, 1995).[10]

In addition to the cars, clothes shaped the world of the teen dance halls. Unlike Rainbow Gardens, which maintained a dress code, Legion Stadium allowed young patrons to wear whatever they desired. This condition led to an eclectic, nonconformist fashion at El Monte, reflective of the cultural diversity extant in rock 'n roll audiences. Although a uniform style of dress did not predominate, young men and women had their favorite attire. Khaki pants and a "Sir Guy" brand, Pendelton-style, plaid shirt were particularly common among many local Chicanos, while Chicanas frequently wore a short sleeved blouse with a tight-fitting, short skirt, usually cut about six inches above the knee. These fashion statements expressed subtle acts of rebellion on the part of Mexican American youths who consciously broke with the "classy" suit-and-gown look of their parents. (R. Rodríguez, interviewed by the author, 26 May, 1995).

The multiethnic composition of El Monte's audiences affected teen fashion, as many white, Mexican American, black, and Asian/Pacific Islander youths shared styles and influenced one another. Often, the varying styles led to the development of "fads." For example, Jerry

Castellano recalls adopting the "collegiate" look of a cardigan-style, letterman's sweater worn by many white teens as a way of distinguishing himself from other Chicanos (J. Castellano, interviewed by the author, 11 May, 1995). Richard Rodríguez remembered that "the black guys—those guys would *dress* all the time! Those guys wore suits or sports coats." Many African American men dressed in suits that imitated the look of popular black performers such as Don Julian, Brenton Woods, and Richard Berry. Wearing tailored suits trimmed with velvet or satin along the sleeves and lapels, audiences adapted these fashions to their material means and aesthetic tastes to create "the Continental" look: "That would be narrow lapels, narrow pant legs, [and] Continental pockets meaning . . . kind of your western cut. But, it was a tapered pant or slack" (R. Rodríguez, interviewed by the author, 6 May, 1995).

Often, these fashions would make their way back to the stage as performers tried to adapt to the changing tastes of their audiences. White performers such as Fabian and Jerry Lee Lewis simultaneously influenced and incorporated changes in fashion by contributing their own regional tastes in clothing and appropriating styles worn by audiences and African American performers. These styles also informed the themes of songs, as represented in Hank Ballard's tune "Continental Walk." Similarly, the car culture inspired many songs such as *Thee Midnighters'* "Whittier Blvd." or, for a later generation, *War's* classic 1975 hit "Lowrider."[11]

The music and groups best represented the degree of intercultural exchange and ethnic/racial diversity present at rock 'n roll shows. Several bands consisted of musicians from a variety of cultural backgrounds, including African American, Mexican, white, and Asian/Pacific Islander. The racial/ethnic intermixing facilitated a blending of cultural influences within a musical genre already distinguished by its hybridized origins of African American rhythm and blues, jazz, gospel, and white country and rockabilly (Lipsitz, 1989, pp. 267–284). Created within the context of the ethnically diverse environment of Southern California dance halls, music emerging from this scene possessed a broad-based, cross-cultural appeal, which facilitated understanding among the racially diverse audience. Recalling how music affected his life, and the lives of people of his generation, Jerry Castellano remembered:

> The music of the fifties kind of helped because everybody got into it . . . the blacks were popular entertainers, the whites were popular entertainers. . . .

It helped bring generations—not generations—but cultures together and understand. We took that same road, and we tried to do the same thing as far as bringing people together. That's all we did in our music (J. Castellano, interviewed by the author, 11 May, 1995).

Castellano recalled adding a Jewish pianist with a "classical" background to his group, The Royals, as much for his musical contributions as for the message it delivered to audiences. "We did not want to keep it just a Chicano band" (J. Castellano, interviewed by the author, 11 May, 1995).

Such was the case with Rainbow Gardens's house band, The Mixtures. The self-conscious iconographic title of the group epitomized the intentions of many bands and artists who sought to reflect the multicultural world of Southern California's dance halls. Led by Mexican American pianist Steve Mendoza and African American saxophonist Delbert Franklin, the group also included a Chicano drummer (Eddie de Robles) and a Puerto Rican bass player (Zag Soto), a black horn player (Autry Johnson), a white guitarist (Dan Pollock) and an American Indian/West Indian percussionist (Johnny Wells). Although never achieving national fame, The Mixtures possessed an aural and visual appeal that garnered favor from Southern California's diverse audiences and radio personalities such as Bob Eubanks and Dick Moreland (Moreland, 1962).

That The Mixtures gained popularity as a live band but never as recording artists illustrates the importance of place in the formation of Los Angeles's interethnic music culture. Although many teens respected the "commercial" success of Ritchie Valens or Ricky Nelson, Southern California bands could also achieve significant notoriety from their live performances. Noting the unique qualities possessed by The Mixtures on their only record album (not surprisingly a live album recorded at Rainbow Gardens), Dick Moreland wrote, "California has discovered them to be the most exciting act which has ever provided in-person entertainment in their area" (Moreland, 1962). Although disc jockeys and promoters often used such hyperbole to sell records and tickets and increase their own fame, the emphasis on the live, or "in-person" quality of the band accurately reflects the significant connection between audience and performer and between music and dance, which made the dance halls the center of an emerging youth culture. Moreover, it demonstrates the egalitarian or democratic nature of musical production during this period. Although recording deals came to precious few bands, aspiring musicians could seek affirmation and acceptance outside the recording industry in the dance halls.

Most importantly, live music and dance in Southern California provided youths with the unique opportunity to dispose of the racial/ethnic prejudices prevalent among the larger society and a previous generation. Throughout the 1940s and 1950s, many African Americans, Mexican Americans, Jewish Americans, and Asian Americans mingled with one another in Southern California neighborhoods and experienced incidents of intercultural cooperation. George Lipsitz provides an optimistic appraisal of interethnic relations when he writes:

> On the factory floor, on public transportation, and on the streets of thriving commercial districts, diverse groups mixed with each other as never before. Wherever one traveled in the city's barrios, ghettos, and mixed neighborhoods, one could easily find the potential for intergroup conflicts and rivalries. . . . But there also existed a vibrant street life built upon communication and cooperation in community organizations and in neighborhood life (Lipsitz, 1989, p. 270).

The early success of such multiethnic groups as the Industrial Areas Foundation/Community Service Organization and coalitions to elect Edward Roybal facilitated productive interethnic, intergender relationships which occasionally resulted in romance and marriage.[12]

Nevertheless, prejudices against intercultural courtship and dating, particularly between nonblacks and African Americans, persisted in the minds of many parents of the 1950s. Richard Rodríguez recalls his experience living in Duarte during the early fifties:

> You see, back in the fifties, if you dated a black girl, your parents would probably move out of the area. If you were even seen walking with a black girl, [and you were] Mexican, your old man would probably take a switch [blade] to you (R. Rodríguez, interviewed by the author, 26 May, 1995).

These attitudes competed with experiences of intercultural cooperation in multiethnic communities. Living next to African American families in a community segregated because of racial restrictions in housing, Rodríguez recalled: "[My parents] rented a house to black people, [but] I was not allowed to date a black girl. My mother didn't want it, my uncles and aunts didn't want it. . . . And it was like I better not do this" (R. Rodríguez, interviewed by the author, 26 May, 1995).

The experience of growing up in a racially mixed community provided a basis of familiarity that presented the potential for breaking down color and cultural barriers. Through exposure to multiethnic music and contact with a racially diverse audience in the dance halls, a new generation realized some of this potential. As Rodríguez recalled:

> When I went to El Monte, I felt that I could date anybody I wanted to; I could
> dance with anybody I wanted to. But, I was a little shy yet at El Monte be-
> cause I was trying to understand the crowd, and why the girls would dance
> with black guys, and nobody's fighting over it (R. Rodríguez, interviewed by
> the author, 26 May, 1995)!

Eventually, such interethnic mixing on the dance floors and in the parking lots at rock 'n roll shows broke down youths' ambivalence towards intercultural romance. During the late 1950s, Rodríguez remembered seeing "more blacks dating white girls and Chicana girls." He added, "Every now and then you might see a white man with a black girl or a white man with a Mexican girl, or vice versa. . . . El Monte was a melting pot!" (R. Rodríguez, interviewed by the author, 26 May, 1995).

Political decisions and demographic realities in the citrus belt facilitated the blossoming of intercultural cooperation among youths in the 1950s. The combination of a growing youth population and the failure of the educational infrastructure to address such growth led to a high degree of cross-cultural mixing in local schools. Although communities were segregated by race and class, many students attended the same school. For example, in the heart of the San Gabriel Valley, the cities of Monrovia, Arcadia, and Duarte maintained just one high school for the three townships. Arcadia contained a white affluent and middle-class population, while Monrovia and Duarte had a cross section of black, white, and Mexican working-class families. Although this clash of cultures initially resulted in conflict, administrators, out of necessity, actively sought ways of facilitating understanding and tolerance by holding "get-acquainted dances," and naming the school mascot the "M.A.D. [Monrovia, Arcadia, and Duarte] Wildcats." Rodríguez recalls that

> they had a lot of problems. And then, on the other hand, when they straight-
> ened it all out it was a very strong and tight school. . . . They stuck to-
> gether to build and make the M.A.D. Wildcats a symbol . . . make it proud
> of [being] all together (R. Rodríguez, interviewed by the author, 26 May, 1995).

Music and dance served as a bridge between cultures and helped to ameliorate racial tensions on campus. Playing at a similar high school function in Pasadena, Castellano recalls how music forged a link between him and a mostly white audience:

> We went thinking we were going to be playing to a lot of Latinos. Wrong!
> They were all white. So we thought, "What are we going to do, what are we
> going to play?" So we decided we'll mix it up. We'll play their music, and we'll
> throw in ours once in a while. And, as it turned out, we played our own stuff
> and they loved it! (J. Castellano, interviewed by the author, 11 May, 1995).

Although Castellano and other Mexican Americans played a hybridized music composed of a variety of cultural influences, many still
acknowledged distinctions between mainstream rock 'n roll and "their"
music. Much of this can be attributed to the regional development of a
unique "Eastside Sound" characterized by the presence of Mexican/
Latin American influences. Although African American rhythm and
blues formed the basis of this music, Chicanos had their own variation
of R&B. Mexican teens emphasized a more "intense" rhythmic pattern. According to Castellano, "We didn't use a bass player; we used
rhythm guitar." In addition, the presence of a brass section, particularly a saxophone, often set Southern California, Mexican-influenced
bands apart from other rock'n roll groups. According to Castellano,
"We always had a saxophone, a rhythm section, and a brass section—
it was part of the makeup of our music" (J. Castellano, interviewed by
the author, 11 May, 1995).

Frequently, bands maintained contact with their audiences throughout a show so that patrons could call out to the performers, "play that
song" or "we want to do this dance" (J. Castellano, interviewed by the
author, 11 May, 1995). This made for a particularly "raw" or "primitive" quality, in which audiences' hoots and hollers figured promi-
nently in the Southern California musical aesthetic (Guevara, quoted
in Lipsitz, 1989, p. 280). Audience "contributions" were recorded on
many albums such as The Mixtures' "Stompin' At the Rainbow," or
the more popular hits of the period such as Thee Midnighters'
"Whittier Blvd.," and Handsome Jim Balcolm's "Corrido Rock."

The popularity of the latter song (which also served as El Monte's
theme song) demonstrates the important influence of Mexican/Latin
American rhythms on Southern California bands and the acceptance
of this music by a multiethnic community. Although the traditional
corrido typically contains words and a distinguishable rhyme scheme,
rock musicians probably used the title "corrido" not as a literal description of the song, but rather as a reference to the Latin American
origins of its musical arrangement.[13] "Corrido Rock" contains all of
the above-mentioned influences, such as a strong rhythmic guitar beat
with a saxophone lead that harkens back to a previous generation.

This dance hall "standard" represents an adaptation of the instrumental music enjoyed by a mostly Latino audience at places like Rainbow Gardens on a Saturday night. Moreover, the recording of this song by a white artist exemplifies the cross-cultural appeal of this music.

Music from a previous generation, however, was not as remote as the separation of these two worlds might suggest. For example, Latin American big band venues continued serving adult audiences through the 1960s. At Rainbow Gardens, where rock 'n roll and Latin American big band "shared" the stage, though on different nights, teens could keep up with the popular trends in Latin American music. Youths commonly began their musical education at home. Castellano recalled:

> I learned [music] from [home]. . . . My dad taught me or my uncle had taught me. . . . They were all Mexican chords. Then I used them in rock 'n roll and then as the years went by, I learned the seventh chord . . . the jazz chords . . . but, they all came from the Mexican chords that my dad used (P. Castellano, interviewed by the author, 11 May, 1995).

The experience of performing in church, at family functions, and in the community also shaped the tastes and attitudes of many young musical artists. María Elena Adams-González, for example, recalls how she got her start in music by singing at the Fiesta held every year in the Arbol Verde barrio in Claremont: "It was right next to grandma's [house] at the hall of the Sacred Heart Church in the community. Cecilia [her younger sister] and I would sing every year there" (M. Adams-González, interviewed by the author, 28 August, 1995). "Discovered" by Frank Zappa who lived in the Pomona Valley during the late 1950s and early 1960s, Adams-González went on to perform with the popular local band *Ronnie and the Casuals*, and later recorded and performed as a solo artist under the name Gina Terry.

Frequently, the origins of artists' music and the inspiration for their participation conflicted with the emerging "commercial" mentality of the industry. Ultimately, record producers and promoters came to dominate the rock 'n roll scene and soured many musicians' interest in pursuing a professional career in popular music. For example, Adams-González remembers singing for pleasure and to express her culture and feelings through song; however, "when Frank [Zappa] heard me for the first time at the Ontario Music Center, all I remember is him telling me he saw dollar signs." Adams-González commented that "Frank was a very nice man" but added that she did not view her talents as a vehicle to fame and fortune. After a short teen career recording and performing at local venues, Adams-González chose to leave the profession and pursue music in less commercial venues (M. Adams-González, interviewed by the author, 28 August, 1995).[14]

Similarly, Jerry Castellano recalled that "we didn't do it for money. It was something else to do, to stay out of drugs, to stay out of trouble." For Castellano and his partners forming a band represented another option for gathering with friends. Their popularity, however, attracted an agent, who imposed a new mode of relating to their music and to one another:

> When the agent came in, he did get us a lot more interest and bookings and stuff like that. But, what we later found out was that he was doing it for his own purposes. Things were beginning to happen, like little small arguments between us because of him. . . . To make a long story short, he took over the whole thing and we had no say so in it anymore (J. Castellano, interviewed by the author, 11 May, 1995).

Despite achieving some local success, Castellano and two original members eventually broke off from their first band *The Velveteens* and formed new groups.

Ultimately, the infiltration of the music industry by self-interested recording executives and predatory music promoters changed the complexion of the rock 'n roll. Although the "Eastside Sound" created in the 1950s and early 1960s continued in the music of some groups and is present today, the number of bands and the interest in live performances at small, intimate venues waned towards the end of the sixties and the early seventies.[15] Frequently artists would record original material and send it to a recording company for consideration. Often, the band or artist would never receive a reply; however, the music, or some portion of it, would manifest itself in the sounds of groups already signed by the label (J. Castellano, interviewed by the author, 11 May, 1995; R. Rodríguez, interviewed by the author, 26 May, 1995).[16] Even those artists who secured contracts with recording companies did not always profit from their creative endeavors. For example, Rosalie Mendez Hamlin, lead singer of *Rosie and the Originals*, signed an illegal contract with Highland Records in 1960 to produce her hit record "Angel Baby." Although the song became a megahit and propelled her career, Hamlin earned few royalties on the song until she won a copyright infringement lawsuit in 1988 (R. M. Hamlin, interviewed by the author, 26 June, 1997).[17]

By the early seventies, a small number of large recording companies had bought out many of the over 400 local recording labels of the 1950s and significantly consolidated the industry. This consolidation resulted in a concentration of varied musical expressions into the music of select groups and artists. Although musicians such as Jerry Castellano continued to perform and create music, access to radio airwaves and dance hall stages became increasingly difficult. By the late 1960s, radio stations and recording companies attempted to ensure their profits and market share by highlighting particular artists or "supergroups."[18]

The world of the dance halls and the message of the music also changed during the late 1960s and early 1970s as a result of the social, political, and economic turmoil of the period. In addition to the Vietnam War and its dramatic effects on teenaged populations, material inequalities, and persistent social injustice contributed to a fracturing of Southern California society. As the 1950s boom economy slowed, and industries began to relocate in right-to-work states, black and Latino communities were the first to be hurt by growing unemployment.[19] Although the intercultural mingling at places like Legion Stadium and Rainbow Gardens familiarized blacks, Latinos, and whites with one another, it also tended to accent the growing material inequalities among Southern California's residents. Moreover, as rebellions developed in Latino and black communities in response to the deepening economic and social crises, whites tended to recoil from the intercultural understanding of another age, back to their secure white, middle class neighborhoods. The construction of new schools and the further development of Homeowners' Associations, which supported de facto segregation along racial and class lines, facilitated such retrenchment.[20] With the "refinement" of commercial radio and the promotion of particular popular music stars and supergroups, a local music scene lost its appeal for many teens, including blacks and Latinos.

Conclusion

By the early 1960s, the mambo craze that swept the United States in the fifties had subsided and Rainbow Gardens' Saturday night audiences shrank. Although the Pomona dance hall remained a viable and profitable business, both the Thomases and Cande Mendoza chose to leave the music business. Gertie and Ray Thomas retired, while Cande, inspired by his involvement in community organizing and journalism, pursued a successful career in education and politics. In 1963 the Thomases sold Rainbow to the owners of Virginia's, another Latin American venue operating in downtown Los Angeles. Somewhat mysteriously, the facility burned down the following year, never to be rebuilt.

El Monte's American Legion Stadium continued to host dances through the 1960s on the weight of rock 'n roll's popularity. Initially, as the industry grew, so did El Monte's stature among fans. Towards the end of the 1960s, however, changes in both the music business and society made El Monte a less suitable place for live shows. Richard Rodríguez, who referred to the early concerts as a "melting pot," acknowledged that something had changed midway through the sixties. In a recent retrospective article he commented: "The shows inside the place reflected the changes going on outside. Stabbings, beatings, and riots were commonplace. Rival gangs fought each other as the music provided them with a soundtrack" (Rodríguez, 1996, p. 8). Ultimately, promoters moved performances elsewhere as laws changed and demographic, geographic, and economic circumstances shaped the location of entertainment. El Monte's American Legion Stadium was demolished by the city in 1974.

Compilation albums of that period, retrospective collections recently assembled, reunions such as the annual Memories of El Monte show, and the many "oldies" radio stations throughout the Southland preserve some of the memories of the music culture extant in greater Los Angeles between the end of World War II and the tumult of the 1960s. Throughout roughly two decades, the music and the atmosphere that pervaded its production offered an alternative vision of shared public space and intercultural understanding.

Latin American big band artists and radio personalities contributed significantly to the development of Southern California's music culture by their appearances on the radio and in dance halls like Rainbow Gardens. Both the presence of migratory and permanent Mexican workers, and the historical precedence of California and its Mexican cultural roots prefigured the development of this ethnically specific music culture. As Américo Paredes and more recently Rubén Martínez have argued, places such as the San Gabriel Valley and the entire Southwest represent a cultural area of Greater Mexico which transcends geopolitical boundaries (Paredes, 1993, pp. 129–142).[21] Mexican immigrants brought with them not only their labor but also customs and entertainment interests that affirmed and strengthened the cultural, economic, historical, and geographical ties to Mexico in particular and Latin America in general. These conditions contributed to Mendoza's fame as a radio personality and permitted him to successfully stage Latin American concerts at Rainbow Gardens.

Gradually, Latin American music and dance influenced the dominant culture. The rise in popularity of the mambo and the cha-cha-chá, as well as the significant fame of film and music stars such as Xavier Cugat, Carmen Miranda, and Pérez Prado stand as a testament to the cross-cultural appeal of Latin American music. However, whites did not dramatically alter their popular perceptions of Latinos, nor did they reconceptualize or reorganize public space. As Cande Mendoza discovered, whites may have listened to the music and performed the dances, but places like Rainbow Gardens on a Saturday night remained mostly Latino.

The creation of a shared, multiethnic public space, and crossfertilization among diverse musical traditions depended on a new generation of Angelenos. Although de facto segregation and material inequalities persisted, young people of various cultural backgrounds voluntarily chose to enter the multicultural environment of the dance halls and enjoyed the culturally hybridized sounds of Southern California rock 'n roll. Shaped by radio, television, freeways and parkways, the "postmodern" social geography of greater Los Angeles facilitated the convergence of Southland youths in a place like El Monte's American Legion Stadium.

The intentional blending of cultural forms, the use of symbolic iconography, and the incorporation of environmental influences in the music and dance hall culture suggest that many youths had more on their minds than just "good time" rock 'n roll. The music and experiences of these teens represent what Paul Gilroy calls a "politics of transfiguration." Communicating through nontraditional means, using nonlinguistic communicatory mediums such as rhythms, body motion, and fashion, these youths projected "an alternative body of cultural and political expression that considers the world critically from a point of view of its emancipatory transformation" (Gilroy, 1993, p. 39). Although their exchanges were often restricted to the dance halls, youths, nevertheless, quieted the dissenting voices implanted in their heads by a larger society to forge relationships across racial, ethnic, and class lines. The intentional blending of R&B, jazz, country, rockabilly, and Latin American rhythms; the purposeful cultural diversity in bands such as *The Mixtures*; the cross-cultural exchanges that took place on the dance floors and in the parking lots; and the sharing of fads and fashions across ethnic and racial lines all provide evidence of young Angelenos' alternative vision of human relation (Kelley, 1994, p. 47; Williams, 1980, pp. 41–42).

Historian Robin D.G. Kelley makes the important point, however, that, "alternative" does not necessarily mean "oppositional." Youth congregated to escape rather than to protest some of the prejudices extant in mainstream society. Still, their actions had "transfiguring" and "political" implications. Rather than challenge "ancient blue laws" or racial discrimination with direct protest, patrons chose to project an "alternative" reality by overcoming legal and geographic barriers, playing "their" music, and getting "into another bag." The desegregation of public space immediately affected local Chicanos living in communities where many of these dance halls existed, but the music and culture increasingly became the collective "bag" of all Angelenos. The history of Rainbow Gardens and El Monte's American Legion Stadium, therefore demonstrates that this intercultural exchange influenced not only music but also social relations in greater Los Angeles.

References

Davis, E. (1996). Liner notes to *The East Side sound, 1959–1968*. Dionysus Records.

Davis, M. (1986). *Prisoners of the American dream*. London: Verso Press.

Davis, M. (1990). *City of quartz: Excavating the future in Los Angeles*. London: Verso Press.

García, M. T. (1994). *Memories of Chicano history: The life and narrative of Bert Corona*. Berkeley: University of California Press.

Gilroy, P. (1993). *The black atlantic: Modernity and double consciousness*. Cambridge: Harvard University Press.

Grendysa, P. (1995) [LP] Liner notes to *Mondo Mambo*. Rhino Records: Los Angeles, CA.

Guevara, R. (1985). The view from the Sixth Street Bridge: The history of Chicano rock. In D. Marsh (Ed.), *The first rock & roll confidential report* (pp. 120–121). New York: Pantheon Books.

Haas, L. (1995). *Conquests and historical identities in California, 1769–1936*. Berkeley: University of California Press.

Hamm, C. (1979). *Yesterdays: Popular song in America*. New York: Norton.

Herrera-Sobek, M. (1990). *The Mexican corrido: A feminist analysis*. Bloomington: Indiana University Press.

Herrera-Sobek, M. (1993). *Northward bound: The Mexican immigrant experience in ballad and song*. Bloomington: Indiana University Press.

Kelley, R.D.G. (1994). *Race rebels: Culture, politics, and the black working class*. New York: Free Press.

Lipsitz, G. (1989). Land of a thousand dances: Youth, minorities, and the rise of rock and roll. In L. May (Ed.), *Recasting America: Culture and politics in the age of cold war* (pp. 267–284). Chicago: The University of Chicago Press.

Lipsitz, G. (1990). *Time passages: Collective memory and American popular culture*. Minneapolis, MN: University of Minnesota Press.

Lipsitz, G. (1994). *Rainbow at midnight: Labor and culture in the 1940s*. Urbana: University of Illinois Press.

Lipsitz, G. (1995). *Dangerous crossroads: Popular music, postmodernism and the poetics of place*. London and New York: Verso.

Loza, S. (1993). *Barrio rhythm: Mexican American music in Los Angeles*. Urbana: University of Illinois Press.

Martínez, R. *El otro lado, the other side* London: Verso.

Moreland, D. (1962). Liner notes to *The Mixtures'* album, *Stompin' at the Rainbow*. Los Angeles: Linda Records.

Otis, J. (1983). *Upside your head! Rhythm and blues on Central Avenue*. Middletown, CT: Wesleyan University Press.

Paredes, A. (1993). *Folklore and culture on the Texas-Mexican border*. R. Bauman (Ed.). Austin: Center for Mexican American Studies.

Pascoe, P. (1991). Race, gender, and intercultural relations: The case of interracial marriage. *Frontiers: A Journal of Women Studies*, Vol XII(1), 5–18.

Peña, M. (1985). *The Texas-Mexican conjunto: History of a working-class music*. Austin: University of Texas Press.

Preston, R. (1971,1972). The changing form and structure of the Southern California metropolis. *The California Geographer (Part 1 and 2), Vol XII and XIII.*

Roberts, J. S. (1979). The 1940s: The watershed. In *The Latin tinge: The impact of Latin American music on the United States* (pp. 100–126). New York: Oxford University Press.

Rodríguez, R. (1993). *Always running: La vida loca: Gang days in L.A.* CT: Clubstone Press.

Rodríguez, R. (1996). El Monte Legion Stadium. *The doowop society newsletter*. Copies provided to me by Rosalie Mendez Hamlin.

Rose, M. (1994). Gender and civic activism in Mexican American barrios in California: The community service organization, 1947–1962. In J. Meyerowitz, (Ed.), *Not June Cleaver: Women and Gender in Postwar America, 1945–1960* (pp. 177–200). Philadelphia, PA: Temple University Press.

Soja, E. (1989). *Postmodern geographies: The reassertion of space in critical social theory*. London: Verso.

Wicke, P. (1987). 'We're only in it for the money': The rock business. In (R. Fogg, Trans.) *Rock music: Culture, aesthetics and sociology* (pp. 113–134). Cambridge: Cambridge University Press.

Williams, R. (1980). Base and superstructure in marxist cultural theory. In *Problems in materialism and culture: Selected essays* (pp. 31–44). London: NLB.

Notes

1. I use the word "public" to describe the function of these halls, but not owner-ship status. Both municipal and privately owned facilities were used to host "public" concerts. Of the two dance halls discussed in this article, Rainbow Gardens was privately owned, while El Monte's American Legion Stadium was a publicly constructed and owned building.

2. For an understanding of the significant development of Latin American music in the 1940s see J. S. Roberts (1979), pp. 100–126.

3. For distinctions among Latin American musical forms, see J. S. Roberts (1979). Also, Steven Loza (1993) lists the various Latin American influences on music of Los Angeles during the twentieth century. Manuel Peña (1985) has written the most thorough analysis of Latin American music in the American Southwest. *Norteño* was a type of music developed in Monterrey, Mexico during the nineteenth century, which combined the accordion-based sound brought to the country by Eastern European immigrants with the indigenous music of Mexico. Later, this music migrated with Mexican immigrants to Texas, and became known as *conjunto*: a working-class music reflective of the socio-economic status of Tejanos (Mexican Texans). *Orquesta* was a merging of the big band sounds popular in the United States during the 1930s and 1940s with the Latin American rhythms of Puerto Rico, Cuba, Mexico, and the American Southwest. Peña (1985) argues that this was a "status" music cre-ated for the Mexican middle-class to differentiate themselves and their tastes from the Mexican working class.

4. Although Manuel Peña argues that orquesta and conjunto music appealed to two different classes of Mexican Americans, both forms were accepted and appreciated by Rainbow Garden audiences. According to Mendoza, most Rain-bow patrons favored the orquesta style of music (C. Mendoza, interviewed by the author, February 17, 1995).

5. *The Mixtures* were actually from Oxnard on the northern side of Los Ange-les, but gained popularity in the Pomona Valley.

6. According to John and Peter Setlich, two brothers, entrepreneurs and musi-cians who converted the structure before the Thomases bought the business, the ballroom was designed specifically to house big band music. They used the latest in dance hall architecture, running up a bill that ultimately forced them out of business (J. and P. Setlich, interviewed by the author, July 21, 1995).

7. Gilroy writes: "The particular aesthetic which the continuity of expressive culture preserves derives not from dispassionate and rational evaluation of the artistic object but from an inescapably subjective contemplation of the mimetic functions of artistic performance in the processes of struggles to-

wards emancipation, citizenship, and eventually autonomy" (1993, p. 57, 53).

8. Two other concert promoters, Johnny Otis and Eddie Davis, confirmed that laws were more lax in the county than in the city when it came to shows for youths. On liner notes to *The East Side Sound, 1959–1968*, Davis recounted his troubles with the law: "I gave a dance at the Shrine Exposition Hall [in Los Angeles]. 80% of the attendance was under 18. The police stopped the dance. I paid a fine and nothing ever happened." As a result, Davis moved his concerts to Rainbow Gardens in 1962 to avoid the harassment. Similarly, Johnny Otis moved his R&B shows to El Monte's American Legion Stadium to avoid "ancient blue laws" enforced by Los Angeles police officers to break up interracial, youth-oriented concerts. Otis claims he eventually had to pay off "El Monte city fathers" to allow him to continue his shows. See Davis (1996) and Otis (1983, p. 61).

9. In chapters eight and nine, Soja explains why Los Angeles possesses the archetypal postmodern geography.

10. Rodríguez attended shows regularly at El Monte's American Legion Stadium throughout its existence, and helped Art Laboe with the production of El Monte's reissued compilation album entitled *Art Laboe's Memories of El Monte: The Roots of L.A.'s Rock and Roll.* Today, Mr. Rodríguez serves on the board of directors for the Doo Wop Society, and is a part-time organizer of concerts and music events.

11. George Lipsitz explains how Southern California fashion and youth culture influenced the themes of rock 'n roll songs. The "pachuco" style and subculture in particular had an early effect on Southland music, manifested in Don Tosti's 1948 hit "Pachuco Boogie." Chuck Higgins's 1952 hit "Pachuko Hop" (popular with El Monte's audiences) demonstrated a continuing influence of the pachuco in the fifties. According to Rodríguez, Castellano, Mendoza, and Lipsitz, however, the pachuco subculture gave way to what Lipsitz called a "cholo" style in the 1950s. See Lipsitz (1989, pp. 271–272), and author interviews with Richard Rodríguez, Candelario Mendoza, and Jerry Castellano.

12. The experiences of labor and community organizers like Bert Corona and Hope Mendoza Schechter, who both married non-Mexican spouses, demonstrates the effect that activism had on breaking down cultural barriers in courtship and dating of this period. See interview with Bert Corona, M. García (1994), and M. Rose (1994). For issues concerning interracial marriage, see Pascoe (1991).

13. For a description of the corrido and its importance in Mexican/Mexican immigrant culture see, Herrera-Sobek (1993, pp. xxii–xxv) and Herrera-Sobek (1990).

14. Adams-González chose to sing for her local Catholic Church parish. She still participates in the church choir.

15. *Los Lobos* is perhaps the most prolific and commercially successful band currently representing the "Eastside Sound."

16. Castellano mentioned that the appropriation of artists' material by record executives was a common occurrence in the 1950s and 1960s. For example, he composed a song entitled "Jerry's Jump" with his first group *The Velveteens*. After Castellano left the band, however, the agent had the bandleader record the song under a new title "Johnny's Jump." Bobby Freeman's popular hit "Do You Wanna Dance" was derived from a song by Chick Carlton & The Majestics' song "So You Wanna Rock." See Davis, Eddie, *The East Side Sound, 1959–1968*. Special thanks to Hector González for sharing this information and directing my attention to important sources. Hector González inherited the Rampart record company from Eddie Davis when he passed away on October 6, 1994.

17. Hamlin's original contract with Highland Records paid her a penny per each record sale. This contract was voided because she was under-aged (15) when she signed it; however, she did not earn royalties on the song until two lawyers, Chuck Rubins and Steven Brown, helped her in 1988. "Angel Baby" has been described as the "Chicano anthem," and Hamlin is known to many in Los Angeles as the "First Lady of Rock 'n Roll." Hamlin lives in Albuquerque, New Mexico and still performs today.

18. For a thorough analysis of how commercial motives transformed the rock "business" during the late 1960s and early 1970s, see Wicke (1987, pp. 113–134). Rubén Guevara describes how this process took place in Southern California. See Guevara (1985, pp. 120–121).

19. Mike Davis explains how many corporations in the 1960s adopted General Electric's 1950s strategy of moving production to the "Sunbelt" (i.e. Arizona) where labor organizing was discouraged and legislated against. See Davis (1986, pp. 127–138). In his book, *City of Quartz* (1990), Davis examines how the white Los Angeles power structure directed redevelopment money into ventures that benefit white Angelenos while abandoning black and Latino communities. The 1965 Watts Rebellion and the 1970 Chicano Moratorium in East Los Angeles represented just two climactic events in an ongoing struggle to protest against such civic neglect. See Davis (1990, pp. 101–149).

20. For a history of how Homeowners' Associations helped sculpt the segregated landscape of greater Los Angeles, see Davis (1990, pp. 152–219).

21. Lisabeth Haas applies this concept to her study of Mexican American culture in Orange County, California. See Haas (1995, p. 11). Rubén Martínez's suggests that this Greater Mexico could be widened and redefined as a Greater Latin America. See Martínez (1993).

The Organization of Affect: Popular Music, Youth, and Intellectual and Political Life (An Interview with Larry Grossberg)

Carrie Wilson-Brown and Cameron McCarthy

> The Right is repoliticizing youth not as an active agent but as a passive victim in much the same way that they are repoliticizing and revictimizing all of the groups that are traditionally seen as oppressed.
>
> —Larry Grossberg

McCarthy: Larry, I would like you to comment on the following observation Simon Frith made in his essay, "The Cultural Study of Popular Music" [published in Grossberg, Nelson and Treichler, *Cultural Studies*]: "From my sociological perspective," says Frith, "popular music is a solution, a ritualized resistance, not to the problems of being young and poor and proletarian, but to the problems of being an intellectual . . . pop music [is] a site for the fantasies and anxieties of the intellectual" (p. 179). I wonder what is your response to this definition of popular music? How would you define popular music?

Grossberg: I think Simon left out a word or two. The study of popular music may be a response to the anxieties of the intellectual, but I think, it is extraordinarily conceited to assume that the field of popular music is defined by the intellectual. I think Simon is right to the extent that the ways in which we study popular music and the forms of popular music that we study are often as much related to our own fantasies and anxieties as they are to what's going on in the world, but I think this is true in any intellectual work. This is true with people who study anything. Their [intellectuals] own fantasies, desires, and anxieties are implicated in the ways they construct the object [of pop music] and the ways they attempt to make sense of that object.

McCarthy: I was wondering if one implication of what Frith was saying is that historically there was some kind of an impact of the intellectual on the production of music and music's role in everyday life in England. That somehow the intellectual had a role in the actual production of a discourse around popular music to which musicians might, in some ways, respond or, in which there is some mediation of the needs, desires, and interests of audiences.

Grossberg: That is probably more true in England than it is in the United States for two reasons. The intellectual discourse around popular music in England has filtered from the academy into the popular press and because of the important role of art schools in the production of British pop. A lot of work by intellectuals around popular music has been taught to the people who are then going to make the popular music. Back in the 70s, I remember, there was a song called, "I'm in Love with Jacques Derrida." There was an exchange between the intellectuals, the music press, the musicians, the industry people and even the audience in England. The discursive exchange is very different in England than in this country. I think we get very little, in fact, intellectual discourse in the popular press. There is some. And it may be growing with the importance of alternative music and the college music scene. You are getting bands formed out of students who are influenced, if not by people studying music, then by people studying media and cultural criticism. So it may be changing here a little, but it is very different in England. In this context I think Simon is probably more correct. You know Simon sits on award committees. He sits on the industry's award committees. There is no academic in the U.S. who sits on the Grammies or even sits on the Rock-n-Roll Hall of Fame board.

McCarthy: So you are saying the discursive economies of the production of popular music are very different in the two countries?

Grossberg: Yes.

McCarthy: Could it be the case that there is a more elaborated culture industry [in the United States]? In other words, can the different arguments that are made about media and broadcasting in England, relative to their historical development in the United States, be mapped onto popular music? Those arguments being that the system of broadcasting was more rapidly and thoroughly commercialized and commodified in the United States than in England. Would a similar argument be relevant to music in the sense that there is more of a culture industry in the United States and [ultimately] less of a role for the intellectual?

Grossberg: Yes. Those are some of the conditions that define the differences. I think the fact that England is such a small geographical culture means that it is much more visible. It means that any particular event can have a much wider impact. Think if all of the United States were shoved into New York City or into New York State. The networking would be much easier. Part of it has to do with, maybe, Britain's Europeanness. There certainly is more, or traditionally has been more, of a public forum for intelligent cultural criticism in England. When Simon Frith was writing as the rock critic for the [London] *Times* or even if you look at magazines like *New Musical Express* and *Melody Maker*, a much more academically oriented discourse is apparent. It was not a sin to start talking about poststructuralism and deconstruction or [Jean] Baudrillard and Derrida. Whereas here if you were ever to do that, say in the *New York Times*, you would get it back and they would say, no one knows what this is about. Those are different climates. Maybe it's Richard Hofstadter's *Anti-Intellectualism in American Life*.

McCarthy: Right, anti-intellectualism returning with a vengeance. One line tracing the distinction could be youth and age. A mainstream approach to the issue is that intellectuals are people writing in the university outside the sphere in which music really happens, outside of the sphere in which music is produced, consumed, felt. This sphere is a sphere of youth and somehow this can be stated as an opposition or in terms of a generational gap.

Grossberg: I like to assume people writing about music in the academy are still a part of the culture of its production and consumption. There are probably people writing about rock music, for example, or rap who don't like it. But usually you can tell who they are. People living in the academy are also people who live outside of the academy. I know some who have never been out, actually I know a lot who don't get out . . . but I think those of us in cultural criticism are [people who live outside]. I think you're right. Age has something to do with it. Simon [Frith] is right that a lot of the academic work on rock music is defined generationally. If you think of people from Simon's generation or my generation, they are fairly similar. We were the first generation to grow up on pop and define ourselves by it and bring it into the academy and think we should and could legitimize it as a subject. In part, Simon is right that by doing that we were in a way legitimizing our lives and legitimizing our sense of what matters and what shapes our lives in the world. In the past 20 years a generation gap has developed so that increasingly it's still the case that the trends within pop music are the terms that were defined by my generation. I'm not sure why that's the case. But, the generations since feel a certain frustration with that: in a sense we still are the ones who lay the framework within which youth is studied, analyzed, comprehended, and made sense of. There is quite a distinction in the way youth is experienced in the 90s and the way it was experienced in the 50s and 60s when Simon and I grew up.

McCarthy: Could you talk a little bit about that distinction.

Grossberg: There is all the trivial stuff. Oh yes they are exposed to AIDS, and the media hype has gotten worse, and the commercialization of their culture has gotten worse, and they're cynical etc., etc. . . . but I think youth has been repoliticized and that's what I think is more interesting. Its repoliticization is partly intentional. The Right is repoliticizing youth not as an active agent but as a passive victim in much the same way that they are repoliticizing and revictimizing all of the groups that are traditionally seen as oppressed. The struggles intellectually have been to move from victimization to some sense of active participation both in one's own oppression and one's own resistance. I think the Right is pushing against that. The Right is treating youth as helpless . . . the victim of media messages or what have you. And at the same time the generation of the 50s and 60s refuses to give up its youth or its power to define youth and the experience of youth.

Wilson-Brown: On that point, you have stated that cultural studies has lost its way by constantly looking for the resistance and agency of the subject. How does this belief shape some of your arguments in *We Gotta Get Out of This Place* on "rock formation" or rock in general? You just described youth as generational or temporal, but your book outlines a spatial model. Is your model of cultural analysis working against a cultural studies obsessed with resistance and agency?

Grossberg: I need to separate a number of lines to answer that. One, I think cultural studies and cultural criticism, more generally, was right to recognize that audiences are not passive, that they do things with what they are given, that they do at some times resist the intended consequences, and that they sometimes do resist the political consequences of their environment. But part of me says, well if everyone's going around resisting all the time, why are we losing. And we are losing fairly rapidly. It seems to me cultural studies gave up in that process what I thought its original task was: to find a better description of what's happening in order to imagine better ways of transforming that. Work on resistance, while I still think it's important, was only part of a description of what was happening. The question then became, how do you describe what's happening and why did it seem so reasonable and inevitable for cultural studies to move down the path it did. So, second, it seemed to me the models it [cultural studies] had of culture and power were not up to the task of describing the nature of struggles taking place today. If you constructed the struggles solely in terms of domination and resistance or solely in terms of struggles over subjectification and identity, then you miss the ways in which, behind our backs, we were all being pushed into positions that we never wanted to occupy. That's why I started to ask questions about power as a spatial organization rather than a temporal one.

Wilson-Brown: Can space be redeployed in oppressive ways? Specifically in the description of the body in your book—if space is taken up and the metaphors of geography become remapped upon the body—isn't that reproducing a discourse of colonialism and positions of domination?

Grossberg: It could . . . I'm looking for a description of what's going on. Given a description of what's going on there is always the possibility that those people who are winning the battle can say, you know that is a pretty good description of what we are doing, and maybe if we are more self-conscious we could do it better. That is the risk of any kind of critical analysis. The normative dimension, while woven throughout, is also capable of being disarticulated and rearticulated. In fact, I happen to know there are people in advertising and public relations who read cultural criticism in order to do a better job of creating the very kind of postmodernist statements that many of us want to contest. You could read [Dick] Hebdige and [Jean] Baudrillard and [Stuart] Hall and Cornel West and have a better understanding of what the world is like and use that. If we are right that people don't have to use things the way they are intended, then we have to accept that about our own work and take the risk that we can't control the consequences of our own work. Which is not to say we should not do what we can to struggle against such (mis-) appropriations.

McCarthy: One of the implications of what you just said is confronting the level at which intellectual work is incorporated. We like to think of ourselves as relatively autonomous [beings] reflecting on a world, marking out certain forms of critique. One of the suggestions arising from your statement, that there is a sophisticated appropriation of intellectual work within advertising, is that we are severely incorporated. I don't know that there is much reflection on this point and I don't know what exactly the implications are for intellectual work, particularly with respect to politics. Your making that statement raises that question in a very significant way.

Grossberg: Yes. I don't think academics are relatively autonomous. In fact, I am generally now suspicious of the notion of relative autonomy as a way of not looking at where you're not autonomous. The real interesting question is how are you implicated? Relative autonomy is a way of avoiding seeing one's own imbrication in the relations of power and one's own determination in a larger context. I think the problem is we are very much incorporated and implicated in the larger context of American culture and economics. Any claim that the university is now autonomous, given the increasing role of business and increasing regulation of state government, is just holding onto dreams that probably weren't real to begin with. The problem is, you're right, we aren't reflecting on it and, therefore, we're leaving it up to other people to define how we are incorporated. I think one of the interesting things about the Right is that they are very conscious about the lines by which the academy connects up to the world outside, both in terms of mechanisms of translation from the academy into the popular press and in terms of lines by which the popular press is fed images of the academy. For instance, the whole PC debate is a wonderful way by which the Right has implicated the academy with very little resistance from the academy. The success the Right has had popularizing people like Allan Bloom or Dinesh D'Souza is an example of the latter. We are very bad at public relations as a whole. We are also very bad at what [Antonio] Gramsci defined as the second function of the political intellectual, communicating our work to a larger audience who may find ways of using that work. I believe we are very bad because we do, in part, see ourselves as relatively autonomous. Therefore it's kind of silly to worry about that boundary . . . whereas boundaries are always porous and reconstituted and part of what constitutes the term is related around the boundary.

McCarthy: In *We Gotta Get Out of This Place*, one implication of what you were saying is that the Left is overtaken by events. In summarizing these developments you use the term the "organization of affect"—the sense that there is a social mobilization of energies that do not constitute a simple homology with class, gender, race and so forth. I don't know that this insight has been taken up related to the concept and ideas [surrounding affect] . . . could you talk a little bit about the organization of affect.

Grossberg: In the particular of contemporary America or as a concept?

McCarthy: As a concept and then in the particular.

Grossberg: I don't think I invented it. Walter Benjamin's notion of an organization of pessimism, used to describe Europe in the early part of this century, was a crucial idea for me. The concept has a theoretical resonance. This has a lot to do with the fact that I started studying culture by studying music, not literature or visual media. This also influenced my sense of the importance of space and affect. Theoretically, I came to the argument that said we had to recognize, as I think Michel Foucault argues, that discourse could have a wide range of effects and that while there were people studying semantic/cognitive/signifying/representational effects, there really wasn't much work studying the other kinds of effects. I used the term affect to describe not all of those effects but a certain range of effects which can be described in terms of intensities. Now there is a little ambiguity because on the one hand someone like Jean-François Lyotard or Gilles Deleuze uses intensities to describe all effects, including meaning effects and I agree with that, but I think there is also a kind of narrower range of effects for which intensity is the primary characteristic. There are things like emotions and passions and investments. That something matters to me is, first, a question of the intensity of the relationship, it's not a question of the quality (although there are different qualities of mattering). It could matter for a variety of different reasons, but what I'm saying, when I say it matters, is that my relationship to this tape recorder [used in the interview] is more intense than to that stapler [on the table], so it matters more. This notion, of course, exists in a wide range of discourses. It's much like Sigmund Freud's notion of "catechresis" or Julia Kristeva's notion of "the unconscious." Many of those discourses or many of the attempts to speak about it assumed that affect was some kind of unorganizable chaos, the only effect of which was either to be repressed or to erupt, explode, and therefore disrupt.

I wanted to think about this as comparable to the plane of meaning. If ideology is a kind of map of meaning and we struggle over ideologies, in the sense of mapping the world according to meaning, why couldn't we struggle over affect in terms of the maps of the ways we relate to the world emotionally, passionately, in terms of what we can and cannot invest in, what can and cannot matter? If you look at contemporary culture and at popular culture in general, that seemed to me a crucial dimension of what popular culture was about. It was not only about the meanings it offered but the ways in which people invested in it and the world, and about the ways in which [popular culture] affected their moods and emotions. I've always felt Bob Pittman, so-called inventor of MTV, was right. MTV is a mood enhancer. That's what pop music has always been. You ask kids what they do with music they will say, well, it depends on my mood. If I'm in a bad mood and I want to stay in a bad mood I put X on. If I'm in a bad mood and I need to get psyched up I put Y on. Consumers of popular culture are extraordinarily good in knowing how to fine tune the map of affect and where they're located in it.

If you take that and begin to ask what happens if there is a political and social struggle over the possibilities of those kinds of manipulations and activities, over the range of sites where one can invest, and over the ways in which investments can be organized and begin to matter, then I think you begin to have a way of understanding the kind of politics that has been going on in America since Reagan. Whether one could trace this process back to its formation in Nixonian conservatism, I'm not sure. I don't mean to say that politicians have consciously chosen this—although sometimes I think it is a deliberate strategy—it's partly the fact that the nature of politics has changed. Politics has become, quite willingly, the art of the possible. What do people think? You go with the polls. Well, the polls are not a major source of intellectual meaning or intellectual commitment. Polls are a measure of where people are invested at the moment. What matters to them. Where their emotional beliefs are invested. The sense of cynicism that politicians, journalists, and academics have observed in their [the peoples'] politics seems to suggest that the real struggles today are over non-ideological matters.

This was my attempt to rethink Stuart Hall's initial observation, when he described Thatcherism as the new conservatism, when he said that what you were beginning to get is a formation in which people did not necessarily agree with the ideological position that they supported. They *consented* to conservative leadership. I was trying to figure out how that was possible without contesting Stuart's analysis of Thatcherism, because I don't know Thatcherism or England well enough. The kind of ideological explanation he was offering did not fit the United States. Really what was happening was an enormous effort to reorganize the field of where peoples' passions were located, defined, and organized. It is quite interesting that in the 60s and 70s if you spoke about an abortion demonstration, what you meant was the pro-abortionists were out in force, and in the 80s and 90s what it meant to say there is an abortion demonstration is the anti-abortionists are out in force. Why was it in the 60s and 70s that the Right wasn't protesting and in the 80s and 90s the Left isn't protesting? (Obviously, an exaggeration, but nevertheless true, despite my use of such an abstract notion as *the* Left.) Where is the activity on the Left? It's not that there are no Leftists, it is just that they seem disconnected or maybe not anchored into what they believe in, and I include myself. We [the Left] believe in the protest. We believe in the positions. The sense of frustration that these [protests] aren't going to accomplish anything is a naturally manufactured part of that affective organization. I think the sense that there are so many issues which the media proliferates is part of that [affective] organization. There aren't so many issues because *they are all connected.*

McCarthy: Is there a possibility that the issue of the organization of affect, relative to mainstream political life, has to do with a closer mobilization of the energies developed in the media, the Hollywood industry, and advertising? There is almost a science, of say, focus groups and the deployment of focus groups research, which was very much a part of Reagan campaigning strategy and philosophy. These distinctions have always been a problem for the Left, specifically in the area of pleasures, and consumerism. I think there is a sense of a disconnectedness from the things that motivate people in contemporary political life.

Grossberg: Again, there are two issues. First, yes, this is connected to what I would probably try to describe as a kind of increasingly prevalent popular media logic. I don't think it's inherent in popular culture or the media, but I think it is the emerging dominant logic of popular culture since the Second World War—to put more and more force into the affective side, to privilege the construction of the affective rather than the cognitive side or rather than the play between them—which popular culture has done before. This isn't a criticism, because to put the emphasis on the intellectual side rather than the affective side is just as bad. Nor is there some kind of ideal dialectic. There are always struggles among competing kinds of effects and I think the media, television, popular music, and advertising are leading the way towards the domination of affective discourses. It becomes more and more powerful as a presence in our lives and more and more comes to define the dimension within which we think of ourselves as responding to the discursive world. Consider the change in polling—from public opinion polling, which at least ostensibly tried to measure what people believed in, to a new kind of polling, which is what they use now in the campaigns which tests out slogans and tries to measure people's emotional responses to the slogans. I have read some articles about it [new polling techniques] and the interviewer [in one article] pointed out that the slogans were incredibly vague, like "A New Morning in America" or "Let a Thousand Lights Shine," and one of the people who designed it pointed out that's just the point, because in this kind of research, meaning just gets in the way! What we are measuring is emotional response. "A Thousand Points of Light" registered real high, so they went with it. One of the analyses of the problems of the last [presidential] election was that the Republicans couldn't find a slogan that measured high enough on this affective scale. So there is an extraordinary understanding of the logic of the media and popular media as it has developed over the last 30 or 40 years, coming together with capitalist and political discourses to define an extraordinarily, rapidly expanding machine of discourse which imprisons us within a particular affective organization.

McCarthy: But this is a contradictory field. For instance, the conflict now over heavy metal or gangster rap, with respect to Bob Dole and elements within the Republican party, and interestingly, within the Democratic party, suggests that certain forms of affect or affective responses are seen as intolerable.

Grossberg: Yes, there are certain kinds of affects that now have to be policed. Rap is the best example because the affect of Rap is extraordinarily angry. Rap is: we're getting fucked and we know it and we know who's doing it. This is most explicit in Gangster Rap. It is the state, the law, the capitalists who are fucking us. That kind of anger has to be policed in America. Part of the problem is that I have this feeling, it's a guess, that if white kids weren't listening to Rap it wouldn't matter. But the problem is white kids are [listening to Rap] and that's what you can't tolerate. [According to the dominant logic] if it were black kids, we could keep it in the ghetto, isolate it, make it invisible and unable to travel. But this music has a kind of mobile expanding field that is particularly dangerous.

McCarthy: Now why hasn't the Left been able to capitalize, relate to that logic, or even defend that [position on Rap]?

Grossberg: Part of it is because the Left in America has never been comfortable with popular culture. Along with that, it's never been comfortable with consumerism, it's never been comfortable with pleasure, it's never been comfortable with affect. The Left has traditionally believed itself rational and if you look at the most powerful statements in Marx, like *The Communist Manifesto*, they are the least rational of Marx's statements. The *Grundrisse* had little impact on history. *The Communist Manifesto*—"workers of the world, unite"—now that's what had an impact. But, I think we were very nervous about it [affect] and we are very nervous about the media discourses that use it and that use fantasy, desire, and pleasure as ways of mobilizing affective commitments.

Wilson-Brown: In your description of affect you carefully distinguish between libidinal and nonlibidinal pleasure. Do you privilege the nonlibidinal or do you mediate between the two? Feminist theory, traditionally, has used psychoanalysis to get at sexual, gender, and racial issues. How would you address these issues, mediating around psychoanalysis or the libidinal?

Grossberg: I privilege the nonlibidinal primarily because I think there's a lot of people writing about the libidinal. Just as Foucault says, there are lots of people writing about meaning so I'm going to write about something else; I want to say, well there are a lot of people writing about desire in a libidinal way, but no one is talking, or few are talking, about the broader domains of affect. How it relates to issues of race, gender, etcetera, is a really good question and very difficult. What I want to say at the moment, and I am still trying to figure this out, is that the way in which the Left's map of affect has been constructed, not necessarily by the Left, has been around issues of identity. The question is how and why. I think we need to step back and say: obviously it's quite true that for people living in our society issues of race, gender, sexuality, etcetera, have become extraordinarily powerful political sites on their mattering maps. The question is why. It's not inevitable or natural and the question is how has that come about. Is it the best way for the Left to try to organize the mattering map of politics? My intuition is, well, no. No one has made a good argument, for me, that we ought to accept that map as it is. If you think of affect as somehow unorganized and random then you say, we've got no choice, this is where it is and this is what we are struggling with.

These commitments entail a political struggle and organization in which we are not necessarily the primary agents. It's partly constructed by the necessities or the conditions of people's lives, it's partly constructed by the Right's discourse, it's partly constructed by capitalism, it's constructed by a whole set of determinations. The question is, is it the best construction? Can we understand it? Do we need to say, well this is where people are but we need to move them somewhere else? We are too stuck saying, this is where people are so what we need to do is come up with better theories of where they are, instead of saying we need to understand how they got where they are and where we might imagine they could move.

It's not that I think race, gender, sexuality, or ethnicity don't matter. It's that I want to say, so far, the only ways we can think of them mattering or we can even theorize them is within the existing mattering maps. There is good evidence that there are serious political problems with that organization. Can we image another organization? This is why I have a critique of alliances. If the map is the way it is, I don't see how alliances can be formed. That is not to say we go back to a map that says these don't matter. Again, if you think in those terms what you're saying is affect isn't organized. Things either matter or don't matter. I want to make a map in which they matter in different ways at different sites. We construct a different map in which they matter and in which politics could be reconceived. Not to eliminate race and gender but to rearticulate race, gender, ethnicity, and sexuality into alternative political strategies. The struggle isn't over race, but the struggle is over something. Race is the way in which the system of power has constructed one line of distribution. If you're black, the statistical odds are you won't have—and then name whatever value you want—you won't have money, you won't have education, you won't have language. So the struggle is over the distribution, not over the line. And then we need to look at what the system of distribution of value is and beyond that, I don't know how to proceed yet.

Wilson-Brown: For instance, the Left's response to the PC debate was to parlay onto the Right's discourse instead of constructing a new discourse.

Grossberg: And that's exactly why we [the Left] are losing and will almost inevitably lose the battle over affirmative action. You cannot, in fact, justify affirmative action unless you challenge the system itself, the system of distribution itself. Unless you say the distribution itself is problematic, the typical person out there looks out and says, well the distribution is random, it's just statistical chance. It's not my fault that black people don't get to college. There are some black people who do [go to college]. So it can't be the line that's at issue. Affirmative action, as we've defended it, is a defense of tearing down the line rather than saying, well no, what we want to tear down is the whole system of distribution of value in which we define value as inevitably and inequitably distributed. We are systematically losing the battle. While I can't explain it exactly, it's perfectly reasonable to me that we are losing. I just look at the alternative discourses and say, obviously, given those alternatives and given the map, as it were, of where we are, this is the only direction that the country can move in.

McCarthy: One of the things that occurs to me as we talk here about this issue of organization around politics is where the Leftist intellectual is located in the new discursive political field. Since you raise the question of affirmative action, how do we understand the organization and mobilization of feeling and affect, on the one hand, as constituting a new possibility for politics and, on the other, questions of political economy which you seem to be getting into? They sound like two disconnected discourses. When we talk about inequality we talk about it as a structural meaning, we talk about it almost infrastructurally. When we talk about issues of affect we seem to be talking about something that's not distributed in the same way. Hence we seem to be talking about two different economies that cannot be linked.

Grossberg: The problem is how to link them. I think the problem is how to understand reality or human lives at least as multiplaned, constructed of different economies which have influences on one another. Pierre Bourdieu's idea that there are economies of value in process (economic value, symbolic value, cultural value, and, I would add, affective value) is right. Unfortunately, Bourdieu assumes too much of a homology between the economies. Understand that part of the struggle is to link various economies. This itself is part of the political struggle: the ways in which you link an affective economy to an economy of capital. For example, I do not understand why the liberal Left is afraid to attack capitalism and the radical (political economic) Left can only dream of overthrowing it. Both of those positions seem absurd to me. I don't think you're going to overthrow capitalism; I don't think you would mobilize much popular support. On the other hand, there is an enormous amount of popular affective hatred of capitalism. If one struggled to find ways to link those, you could begin to mobilize a significant Left. Why the Left was so quiet over, for example, health insurance and failed to become a public voice that could have said obviously the bad guys are the insurance companies. We all know that everyone knows that. Why isn't anyone attacking the insurance companies? Well, look, they give $5 billion, or whatever the amount is, to politicians. That's popular knowledge. There is a lot of affect invested in a map that says, big business is bad. But it is organized in a way that this part of our affective map has been protected from any articulation into politics. This is why I say I don't think that politics is so fragmented today because issues are linked. But they are fragmented on our affective map.

McCarthy: One of the points to support what you are saying about the instance of health care being connected to the organization of affect is the crucial role that advertising played in the selling of the anti-universal health care position in the 1994 elections. The Harry and Elaine ads, for instance, that showed a middle-class couple being afraid of what was going to be the change to come. There was no counter to that position at all.

Grossberg: There is no counter to any of the Right's combative rhetoric [such as] the anti-abortion ads, the antidrug ads, all of which are purely affective. Imagine a counter-ad in which Harry or Elaine turned out to be an insurance executive. Those ads that show you pictures of wonderfully healthy little boys and girls and talks about the "right choice." Where are the pictures of the starving kids dying of disease in America and saying, "Is this the right choice?" Is it better to let a child live in poverty? Part of what the Left learned in the 60s, it didn't learn it but it sort of knew it, was that affect mattered. It mattered in the way the war in Vietnam was contested. It mattered in the mistaken assumption that politics was lifestyle. The insight that politics is lifestyle suggests that affect mattered. You couldn't change the world by giving a soldier a flower; nevertheless, the insight is that emotional life does matter in politics. It seems to me the Right has learned that. Remember that wonderful antiwar poster with the baby that was napalmed and it said, "and babies too." That's no different from the anti-abortion ads. The Right has learned the lessons that the Left gained in its break from the traditional Left, but now, it seems to have renounced them.

McCarthy: What do you think of Edward Said's work in *Representations of the Intellectual*? He takes a kind of Adornian position. He is very attracted to Theodor Adorno. The interesting commonality between Said and Adorno is that they are and were both critics of music. Said seems to take the position that an intellectual really is defined as someone who goes against the grain. The commitment to mobilize politics around, say, the organization of affect would be a short-term strategy, [signalling] incorporation and compromise, and what is needed is in fact a little bit more—courage is a bad word—let's say, a more unyielding attack from the Left. A more systematic critique that doesn't skirt around what might be seen as the difficult issues, for example, the implication of the major countries of the West in oppression in the Third World and so forth. How do you reconcile that position with the one you seem to be taking which, in some ways, states that [Said and Adorno's] position on intellectual work is obsolete?

Grossberg: There are a number of different points Said is making. Some of them I agree with and some I don't. One is that I am very reluctant to define "an intellectual" but let's say Left-wing political intellectual in the contemporary North Atlantic world. Of course, they should look at the implication of the United States in global relations. You can't deal with simple isolated locales anymore. I think he is absolutely right about that. I think to understand the complex interpenetration of economies—economic, affective, ideological, etcetera—in the United States today you have to understand that many of these economies transcend local and even international boundaries. I don't think you can understand what's happening in capitalism today unless you start with a global view. I don't think you can understand some of the politics of race in America today unless you understand the economics of Third World labor. At that level he is correct. And it is certainly useful to have long-term visions and to have a systematic and coherent critique, although I am suspicious of utopias except as strategies. You can have a systematic critique of capitalism that would call for its abolition. Although I don't think we have that, one could have and should have a systematic critique. But I don't think that's all we can have. You also have to have a strategic critique because the cost of putting off a strategic critique in the name of visionary critique is too high. It's just too high and I'm not willing to pay the price. Second, and related to this issue, I am influenced enough by Foucault to think that it's good to have visions, but they have limited effects. Again, visions are things that are deployed for affective purposes. Wouldn't you like to live in a world where all people were equal . . . it's a wonderful affective appeal. Yes, we should be making that more. We should be making appeals to utopian visions based on critiques, not as the necessary condition of our political analysis, but as a strategic maneuver in a war of power. The third point is, one always has to negotiate strategically what the battles are that have to be fought in the short run and in the long run. Given the fact that I think the United States has an enormous implication in global relations—power, economy, etcetera—I, therefore, think it's quite critical that we fight some local battles over the politics of the United States. If that means compromising and sacrificing the utopian visions in order to make a slightly better choice for the short term, then I think that's quite necessary. Hell, Said has made a lot of compromises in his life. I don't think they're wrong. That's what life, power, and politics are about.

Wilson-Brown: Related to the intellectual and the object, when Lynn Spigel was here [Unit for Criticism and Interpretive Theory's Cultural Studies lecture series at the University of Illinois-Urbana] she said something interesting at the tail end of her lecture. She said that popular culture is not only radically intertextual but radically self-reflexive and critical. For example, she confronted this phenomena when her work and arguments relating to the debate over Barbie were summed up in a 30-minute episode of *The Simpsons*. Do you also see this phenomenon or is this a naive notion of what's occurring in the cultural field.

Grossberg: Is popular culture increasingly reflexive? Obviously! But the issue is why does that become our focus? I see that as the logical consequence of the directions cultural studies has made and I see it as somewhat limiting. It has led me to numerous conclusions. One is that I increasingly do not think of myself as someone who studies popular music. Cultural studies still operates too much within a textual model. . . . I am going to text A or text B or text C. Inevitably, the text becomes a metaphor or a metonym of a larger whole, and then you end up finding the larger whole in other metonyms. So it is not surprising that this would occur if you look at the world's relation to Barbie and Barbie's relationship to the world. Barbie is taken as a metonym for gender relations which you can find somewhere else. It's OK, I have nothing against it. It is not what I want to do, and that's not all I think cultural studies should be doing. The second thing is because we assumed cultural studies was supposed to be self-reflexive, we now occupy the position that cultural studies ends up being about us. I always thought it was supposed to be about the world and not about us. Self-reflexivity is a model of limitation. It was supposed to be about the *limits* of what I could and could not do or say or understand, not about "I." As a result of both of these points I increasingly want to agree with someone like Meaghan Morris, that the object of cultural studies is not *texts* but *contexts*. It is not about me but about everyday life. What we are studying are contexts and whether or not one finds it convenient to enter into a context through a certain set of texts is a tactical choice influenced, for example, by one's own critical strengths. But if all we end up doing is constantly interpreting new kinds of texts (because literary critics weren't doing it), I wonder what will become of cultural studies: it will constantly rediscover what we already knew.

Wilson-Brown: This is really endemic to a practice of analytically locating good and bad images or winning and losing cultural footing, within a simple model.

Grossberg: If you start with a model of text and then you have production and consumption or encoding and decoding or whatever model, you are going to end up with the same bivalent choices. Well you're mystified or you're resisting, instead of understanding that this is not really the issue. The issue is how those texts operate as discursive events which are constituting relations of power. In some instances it may be necessary to figure out how the texts are being used, not because that's what you want to know but because it is a piece of the puzzle. You want to know what the effectivity of those relationships are informing in larger contexts and organizations of power.

McCarthy: Finally, Larry, one of the criticisms arising out of people like Allan Bloom, William Bennett, and others is that cultural studies and the study of popular music represent a Left intellectual excess. These theories of investigation don't belong to academic life. How would you begin to make the case for the study of popular music and its role in teaching and pedagogy?

Grossberg: I'm sure if you looked at the medieval university and the expansion of fields like biology or sociology, they were met with objections. The objection to the novel was that literature wasn't suppose to be about ordinary people. What happened to the Greek classics? Bennett's critique is very similar. My answer is, the function of the university is to produce knowledge, to understand the world, and to teach people how to understand and live in the world in more critical, intelligent, and rational ways. If we simply ignore the major aspects of people's lives, then we are not fulfilling our function. That isn't to argue that we should be teaching *only* popular music or television but that we have to teach them [students] how to be critical about the environment that they have grown up in—critical in the sense, simply, that they understand what is going on and can develop better ways of navigating their ways through it.

THE PEDAGOGY OF
MUSICAL AFFECT

"No Guarantees":
Pedagogical Implications of Music
in the Films of Isaac Julien

Warren E. Crichlow

Music is the memory bank for finding one's way about the world.
—*Songlines* (October 1991)

The record and the cassette is more powerful than television or the newspaper as far as youth are concerned.
—Bulldog in *Diary of a Young Soul Rebel* (1991)

The point I am trying to make is that the study of music can be more, not less interesting if we situate music as taking place, so to speak, in a social and cultural setting.
—Edward Said, *Musical Elaborations* (1991)

One has to work within and against the grain of fetishism to draw them [audiences/students] in to hear questions they might not want to hear.
—Isaac Julien, interview with bell hooks (1991)

Introduction

Black popular music engages contemporary life with powerful yet contradictory narratives about race, sexuality, class, and religion. Its youthful vitality, innovation, and transgression give voice to counter-narratives of inclusive national and transnational identities. Yet black popular music also expresses broader feelings of social nihilism, at times retreating into conservative doctrine, sometimes in an audible disdain for difference. Indeed, the most commodified forms of hardcore music popular among working-class youth contain a hideous lyrical text of fear, violence, misogyny, and homophobia. As we will see, Isaac

Julien's[1] two recent films, *Young Soul Rebels* (Julien, 1991) (winner of the Critics' Prize at the Cannes Film Festival) and *The Darker Side of Black* (with Black Audio film collective) (1994) evocatively demonstrate this tension. The contradictions discussed throughout this chapter spring from black popular music's verve and the limits of how such verve can be expressed. I consider how black music might be listened to and learned from if its contradictions can be engaged.

Grounded in historical and contemporary music, Julien's two films, while straddling distinct genres—the narrative feature and the documentary film form, respectively—examine vividly the shifting nature and possible implications of the politics of black popular culture. The 1970s setting of *Young Soul Rebels* excavates the diasporic crossing of black American funk and soul music. That seminal connective moment helped to inspire the formation of an incipient black British youth culture in search of identity, representation, and social change. *Young Soul Rebels* offers a reflective narrative about young black people asserting the music they found personally pleasurable in the midst of heightened political, cultural, and sexual divisions within their generation and nation.[2]

The documentary *The Darker Side of Black* provides a cultural critique of the early 1990s, when tendencies within dancehall music in Jamaica and gangsta rap in urban U. S. hip-hop culture achieved mass-culture prominence. Both forms of black popular music express resistance to reversals of decolonization struggles within the "new world order" and to the decline of civil rights within the domestic United States. Simultaneously, dancehall and gangsta rap articulate nationalist and essentialist paradigms of intolerance toward difference. Such cultural fluctuations mark dynamic contradictions in the music. Sometimes, an insistent rhythm turns inward towards the cultural policing of what it means to be a black male or female, heterosexual or homosexual. At other times, lyrical boundaries give way to improvised possibilities that permit more open-ended questions about self and other. Through both a critical deployment of cultural critique and a commitment to disrupting rigid cultural politics of race, identity, and representation, Julien's two films provide exemplary means for considering popular music as curriculum text and pedagogical context.

Popular Music, Curriculum, Pedagogy

As curriculum text we may understand popular music to be something more than individual expression, style, and the formalism of performance. Buckingham and Sefton-Green (1994) call popular music "pop as industrial product" (p. 62), music as a productive process of technology, commercialization, and reception. Popular music may also be considered in terms of what Edward Said identifies as the space between "the ideal purity of the individual experience . . . and . . . its public setting" (1991, p. xiv). Said reminds us that music emerges from and is situated in social, cultural, and historical geography. His interrogation of classical traditions of Western culture directs attention to both the varied roles music plays in society, and how music is deeply implicated in relations of power and knowledge.

The socially reproductive and politically transgressive possibilities of music, suggests Said, can be examined with fruitful results by asking contextual and relational questions about, for example, "the affiliation between music and social privilege; or between music and nation; or between music and religious veneration" (1991, p. xvi).[3] These are not exhaustive queries. They do, however, open curricular inquiry to the question of music as social construction, as aural representation and, in Brotzman, Hopkins, and Ali's (1991) phrase, as a "memory bank" for negotiating a world of beauty and contradiction. Musical forms drift, travel, and intermingle between other spaces and times of civil society, their meanings become transformed in the process, and these hybrid formations can be understood as aural and oral histories connecting the past to the present in ways that anticipate possibilities for the future. Isaac Julien heightens this tension, visually interrogating black music as oral history. His filmic canvas is a space where memories of slavery circulate, where musical creativity connects with traditions of survival and resistance but can abruptly shift to its "darker" side, displaying the rigid neoconservatism of religious fundamentalisms.

If music provides a text to decode cultural production and representation, then it can also help to create a pedagogical context for "teaching about difference differently" (Britzman, D., Santiago-Vállez, K., Jímenez-Múñoz, G., & Lamash, L. 1993, p. 188). As a filmmaker and cultural activist, Julien's pedagogy works through an "invitational mode of address" to create a context in which culturally restricted questions about difference and otherness are freed for open inquiry. By transgressing representational convention, Julien aims to foster debate on race, gender, and sexuality where it has been closed down. He is particularly interested in disrupting staid conceptions of black masculinity and problematizing the cultural politics of representing the black body. Like novelist Toni Morrison (e.g., 1992) who writes to raise complex questions about race, community, and gender that have not been satisfactorily addressed, or painter Gordon Bennett, whose visual practices are precisely meant to disturb and disrupt a closed racial field of "pictorial reproduction" (1995, p. 7), Julien makes films to both contest and to defamiliarize dominant regimes of representation and their strategies of image-making. His project is rooted in a counter-strategy that he calls "representational ambivalence": the creation of "gaps or lacks in the representations" (Julien quoted in hooks, 1991, pp. 131–132) that invite consideration of unstated, repressed ways of looking (or listening) that are masked or appear as threatening. As he explained in an interview with bell hooks, the study of ambivalence is essential to investigating black masculinity:

> In black popular culture, of course, hard representation is what's important in articulating polemics against racism and institutionalised racism. But if we're actually trying to create a discussion amongst ourselves or trying to show another kind of representation, it's important to portray a kind of construction of masculinity which is something very fragile and vulnerable (p. 132).

Julien's work can be the beginning of a pedagogical encounter. Indeed, while students' pleasures, desires, and consumer preferences in music are, as Said noted, part of individual experience, that experience is also formed and practiced in social and cultural settings.[4] Music can serve as a beginning point or occasion for asking broader, more difficult questions about the dynamics of cultural setting, identity, and politics that articulate social context. To paraphrase Julien, questions that might begin to get at music as a cultural relation are: What does the music do? How does it perform? What does it articulate politically, sexually, culturally? "Where does this leave you?" (Julien quoted in hooks, 1991, p. 131). Such questions may move the study of music toward a more critical discourse which negotiates the space in between private pleasure and public performance, where issues of representation, popular culture, and individual and collective identity dynamically reside. In both Julien films discussed in this essay, music is offered as a space where the most slippery contradictions of contemporary culture, politics, and society erupt in visual and kinesthetic forms. From sound systems to dance floors in moments where rhythms and "structures of feeling" (Williams, 1958) are expressed bodily, music can be heard as a question of pedagogical encounters.

Young Soul Rebels

Part coming-of-age memoir and part fictional narrative pushed by a murder mystery plot, *Young Soul Rebels* dramatizes an emergent moment in black British popular culture. Julien depicts this period as one rife with what bell hooks (1991) observes as "identities in collision, and collusion" (p. 126). The film richly considers where these slippery oppositions—black/white, gay/straight, radical chic/conservative reactionary—clash but also shows how these oppositions touch each other to the sensuous backbeats of punk, disco, and soul musics in neighborhoods and on the dance floor. Set in 1977, the year of the Queen's Jubilee (the celebration of Queen Elizabeth's fiftieth year on the throne), the film explores the cultural stakes in the tensions between national insecurities about "Englishness" and the energetic counter-narrative of young black people growing up asserting, "I am British, but. . . ."

Music is integral to this story, circulating through the film by the medium of radio and the icons of cassette and radio-recorder boom box. Of his own youth, Julien recalls how important listening to music—records, radio, and cassettes—was to the formation of identities and life-styles. The film is set at a time in Britain when representations not only of black people but black music were absent from the media and the airwaves. As Julien explains:

> Listening to Funkadelic, Parliament and all that kind of "new jazz" if you like—funk jazz—was very important to young black people. . . . So they started to broadcast illegally and to form their own radio stations. And this is part of the narrative of Young Soul Rebels . . . the first younger black people to start playing music that they wanted to hear (Julien quoted hooks, 1991, p. 137).

Chris (Valentine Nonyela) and Caz (Mo Sesay), two older teen deejays who operate their own pirate radio station, called "Soul Patrol, 107 FM," are the central characters of Young Soul Rebels. Illicitly the two friends broadcast black American soul and funk music from a makeshift studio hidden in the back of an auto repair garage. Chris and Caz's collaborative breach of East London airwaves presents double cultural transgressions: the two are not merely unlicensed interlopers. More importantly, the duo's programmatic transatlantic link with black American music marks a self-conscious intervention into dominant white youth cultural forms of the time, and a generational break with older yet narrowly construed black British cultural forms.[5] Their underground musical project engages in "funkin' up" a relatively homogeneous space of culture and style. These "soul bwoys" use music to help reinvent a distinct yet inclusive black working-class youth popular culture. They move against and beyond the historical context of racial marginalization and stigmatization of color and lifestyle.

The pulsating sound track of Soul Patrol and the dance club provide aural and visual cultural sites, but these musical moments also serve as pretext for thematics of transgressive politics, pleasure, and desire at play in the film. The opening scenes begin with a soundtrack juxtaposition of punk rock and soul from 1977: X-Ray Spex's "Identity," Parliament's "P. Funk Wants to Get You Funked Up," and The Blackbyrds' "Rock Creek Park." This incongruous/intertwining music sets the stage for hybrid and taboo images. From a darkened street, a young black man, TJ (Shyro Chung), climbs over a fence into a closed park. He turns on his large boombox to tune in the voices of Chris and Caz introducing Roy Ayer's "Running Away":

> We don't love each other/like we used to do. . .
> Running away . . . Running away
> You don't do the things you used to do
> Running away (Ayer quoted in Julien, 1991).

Nodding approvingly to the sounds, the young man hits the record button to bootleg onto his own cassette the unauthorized transmission of this new and exciting music. But the dark, secretive shadows of the wooded park reveal other transgressions: sexual movements and murmurs of different masculinities, dangerous and marginalized desires. Suddenly, TJ's hand is tenderly, then roughly, touched by another hand, male and white; the upbeat radio rhythms are silenced and replaced by intimate talk. What appears to be a sexual liaison gives way to violent struggle, theft and murder. TJ is left dead, in an act witnessed only as muffled sounds captured unsuspectingly on the still-rolling-cassette in the boom box. By the film's chaotic conclusion, the crime's mystery has unfolded. In its course we gradually come to learn as much about fears of unstable masculine identities and envious desires distorted by racialized anxiety as we do about those utopian possibilities that find articulation in the music.

Young Soul Rebels is dense in the range of social antagonisms and pleasures it examines. It resists abstracting the music from life problems, a commitment perhaps best announced in the film with Roy Ayer's lyrics to "Running Away." In the film narrative there are the expected apprehensions about police harassment, employment, steady money, aspirations, and competitiveness that do pervade late adolescent transitions and friendships. However, ordinary friendship strains are rendered more complicated, partly because Chris is biracial and Caz darker skinned. Furthermore, the sensitive relationship they share forces the viewer to interrogate his/her conscious or unconscious quickness to peg the straight and the gay "looking" male body. At work here is an "ambivalent playoff" as Julien (Julien quoted in hooks, 1991, pp. 134–135) calls it, one that problematizes representations of black heterosexual and homosexual men. In the film, straight/gay definitions are disrupted (but never with any certainty) by the hetero-erotic relationship between the young Chris and Tracy (Sophie Okonedo) and the homoerotic, interracial relationship between Caz and punk socialist-worker Billibud (Jason Durr).

The investigation of TJ's murder draws attention to a wider context of police harassment of young black men and youth's homophobia and violence against lesbians and gays. The reactionary extremes of the skinheads, New Right nationalist sloganeering, and swastika symbols on urban walls are opposed by the Left's less-than-adequate cultural strategy of a counter-Jubilee protest concert: "Fuck"—or later in a more soulful twist, "Funk"—"the Jubilee." This political reality is made concrete through the portrayal of young people—black, white, mixed race—who share the neighborhood space, who grew up together going to school and listening to the same music, but who now occupy opposing political positions.

The vivid tension here is that despite socially constructed differences, choices, and subjectivities young people create, an emotional link binds them together in shared history and personal knowledge. Similar contradictions are also played out in the intrafamilial strife between Caz and his otherwise supportive auto mechanic brother, Carlton (Eamon Walker), over masculinity, race, and music. For example, in a heated argument about who murdered TJ, the two brothers almost come to blows over differing views on biracialness, whiteness, and sexuality:

Carlton: Can't trust dem 'alf caste bwoy ye no. Ye don't know which side them on. I could well believe it was one of them that kill that black bwoy. . . .

Caz: Now what ya sayin'? What, 'cos Chris my mate? Or 'cos I mix with white people. . . So that's wot it's about, yeah? I mix with white men. . . I *fuck* with white men! (Julien, 1991)

In tensions of family and friendship, race relations and homosexuality are connected through the musical conflicts between politics and pleasure, and between progressive activist organizing and lifestyle.

Another scene particularly revealing of this latter tension occurs at the entrance of a tube (subway) station where Chris walks into the

middle of a group of punk politicos distributing Socialist Worker newspapers and "Fuck the Jubilee Concert" flyers:

Chris: So disco sucks, does it?
Billibud: Mindless, capitalist crap!
Chris: And Punk's not?
Billibud: Depends on how you use it. Don't it? (Julien, 1991)

Humor and social critique mark this scene, framing the comical but
not irreconcilable difference between Chris's cool soul boy "look" and
the outlandish clothes, dyed hair, and anarchic semiotics of the punks.
Evoked in a more important way, however, are the questions of how
music is to be used politically and for whom? These queries provide
openings for possible dialogue across difference, which does indeed
eventually occur. "Don't it?" has no immediate answer. This seemingly simple question exposes a reality that music is already marked by
differences that require negotiation and where points of agreement
may be, at best, temporary. This realization forces an accounting of
the way music is received and enjoyed by different publics. We might
consider music's relation to the body and to "structures of feeling"
brought about through dance movement, the way rhythm and sound
in space and time actually express narratives of identity, desire, and
politics.

From Billibud's idealistic perspective, music, pure and simple, is
the draw that will mobilize diverse segments of the working class in
unity to oppose racist, xenophobic, and absolutist nationalism. Billibud's
romantic stereotyping leads him to assume that including roots reggae
(as if this is the only music black people relate to) will provide the
means to mobilize unity in the protest concert/rally. Chris assumes
that any music organized by white anarchist youth will provide few
danceable pleasures for black-working class youth relate. Billibud se-
ductively presses Chris to attend the concert: "Should be something
there you could dance to. . . . Look, Misty and Roots [reggae band],
you'd like that, wouldn't yer?" Chris's mocking response to what he
perceives as Billibud's simplistic reductionism is, "Oh wow! Look . . .
I'm in a rush. . . ." But real issues remain that straddle the tensions
between musical pleasures and activism. An Asian punk girl inter-
venes in the dispute between the two young men, proffering a leaflet
listing recent racist attacks in the area, which exhorts all to "picket
'bout police indifference." Chris is drawn back to TJ's murder and in
this poignant common ground is fashioned through his decision to
help with leafleting.

Perhaps George Clinton and Funkadelic's funk-unity anthem, "One Nation Under a Groove" (1978), centers the hopefulness and inclusive mood regarding the achievability of common ground across race, class, gender, sexuality, and other "differences." Appropriated from black America by black British youth culture, the one-nation metaphor had its earliest manifestations in a new hybridity engendered in underground dance clubs. Soul boys and girls, punks, gays, straight females and males mingled under the transatlantic grooves, but with an extraordinary specificity that made the underground dance club scene part of what was "*really* happening" within rebellious East London youth culture in the late 1970s.

Young Soul Rebels visualizes this historical moment through a night scene at the Crypt, an old church tomb converted into a small bohemian dance club. Here Chris and Caz continue their spirited soul interventions, *working* the sound system and the young masses from the deejay rostrum. As the changing of the deejay guard takes place, there is a corresponding yet uneasy transition in the music: from the punk band X-Ray Spex doing "Oh Bondage Up Yours," to the U.S. Soul Players Association's upbeat "I Like It." A different crowd—darker skinned, more colorful, more lesbian and gay—moves onto the dance floor in a slightly tense exchange with the mostly white, mostly male punks, as slamming "pogo" movements give way to exuberant, stylized soul dancing that celebrates the body and sexuality. But this shift of the margins to the center of the dance floor also empowers music and dance to produce—at least temporarily—a kind of transcendent atmosphere of potentiality: an instant in which a space is won for differences to coalesce around common desires. As the scene closes out to the "fast and funky sound of War: 'Me and My Baby Brother,'" Caz and another male friend are in the center of the crowd doing the "bump"[6] in triumphant fashionable abandon, as if to shake from their bodies the immediate residues of everyday oppressions that might otherwise leave them feeling defeated and unable to face the next day's challenges.

The tenuousness of this victory on the dance floor shows how triumph-or-defeat is one binary this film challenges. For if we take seriously Stuart Hall's oft-repeated phrase "no guarantees," then we must admit that in the struggle for social change there are never total defeats or total victories. From the point view of what Hall (1992) calls "the struggle over cultural hegemony, which is these days waged as much in popular culture as anywhere else" (p. 24), then the more-or-less commodified music that inspires the bodies on the dance floor is not simply "capitalist crap." As Parliament Funkadelic (Clinton, 1978) declares, "Here's a chance to dance our way out of our constrictions. Gonna be freakin'!" By the same token, neither can this grooving victory in/over syncopated time and space be at all equated with full-fledged political or material transformation.

Yet these small victories are part of the dialectic of cultural change, where cultural hegemony is constantly shifting. As Hall pointedly reminds us, cultural struggles are "always about shifting the balance of power in the relations of culture; it is about changing the dispositions and the configurations of cultural power, not getting out of it" (Hall, 1992, p. 24). Hall's point is illuminated in the park riot scene at the conclusion of *Young Soul Rebels* where, even as the murder of young TJ is solved and avenged, the more organized right-wing and skinhead forces completely trash the left "Funk the Jubilee Concert" rally. In what may be seen as a bittersweet conclusion, Chris and Caz emotionally recapture their friendship. Together with Billibud, Tracy, and her girlfriend, Jill, the friends retreat to the radio station hideout, where they busily work to salvage records damaged in the melee.

The film's finale belies a perhaps overly optimistic spirit that collective starting over is possible and necessary, since there is no getting out of the cultural politics. Here there is no mopish, immobilizing retreat into a "'nothing ever changes, the system always wins' attitude" (Hall, 1992, p. 24). While the cultural strategies that might make a difference are not prescribed, these young soul rebels take performative advantage of Charles Erland's "Let's Play the Music," to engage a new formation soul dance that suggests the beat will go on.

Groove in Transformation

If the Funkadelic's refrain, "one nation under a groove getting down just for the funk of it," was a universal signature of youthful hopefulness at the end of the 1970s, then developments in black popular culture and its music in the 1990s reflect a retreat into more local concerns. This shift in some forms of black music is highlighted in the central controversy of *The Darker Side of Black*: the ties between some black music and homophobia, specifically the homophobic lyrics of Jamaican dancehall deejay Buju Banton's infamous recording, "Boom Bye Bye."[7] The transatlantic circulation of Banton's song from dancehalls in Jamaica to the streets and clubs of London and New York City, as the film's narration explains, symbolize[s] recent changes in black popular culture, in particular the shut-down of its political hopes. Eleven years after the death of Bob Marley the desire to change the world nurtured in the fateful meeting of reggae music—the Rastafari belief—has been abandoned (Julien, 1994).

Released three years after *Young Soul Rebels*, *The Darker Side of Black* interrogates similar themes of identity through music, race, sexuality, and homophobic violence—but with a significant difference. Whereas *Young Soul Rebels* presents a rather linear yet highly stylized narrative accessible to mass cinema audiences, *The Darker Side of Black* intercuts televisual documentary with promos from music videos and interview-style commentaries by various dancehall and rap artists, cultural critics, and activists (including a candid interview sequence with the late Michael Manley, the former prime minister of Jamaica). In addition, "stylized mise-en-scene," as Ken Feil writes, "contextualize phenomena and commentary in terms of the unrepresentable existential 'absurdity' . . . of the colonial past" (1994, pp. 7–8). These subversive strategies add passionate yet ironic effect to the film's pedagogical interventions into race, identity, and representation.

Politically, *The Darker Side of Black* eschews didacticism while unabashedly asserting a counter-discourse that provokes the viewer to confront difficult questions about homophobia in the black music industry and the antigay violence it may inspire. But this is a story whose dynamics go further back than musical memory alone may wish to venture.

The Darker Side of Black

The Darker Side of Black opens with a dramatic long shot sweeping down from a clifftop home, over the rural landscape and finally dwelling on the urban density of Kingston, Jamaica. The smooth, firm voiceover, by cultural critic and writer Paul Gilroy, describes this locale as both the "capital of reggae music" and a "place where the memory of slavery remains close to the surface of life." Past and present, music and history come into dynamic play. A quick succession of formalized scenes anticipate the film's recurring themes of sex, oppression, religion, and redemption: a close-up shot frames a black man's manacled ankles against surf on white beach sand—white hands hover above him holding a Bible; sun reflects the calm ripple of still waters reminding us of a time of slave ships in the harbor; the distant figure of a black man in long robes solemnly roams the beach carrying an ancient Bible; a long shot gazes on resplendent sea at dusk from a bridge bringing traffic into present-day Kingston as Bob Marley and the Wailers's (1974) slow spiritual refrain, "revelations," gradually increases volume in the sound track.

By juxtaposing realist documentary and formalist visual strategies the film challenges the viewer to reflect upon shadowy complexities of history and their relation to the present. These images leave memory traces of black popular music's historical linkages to African dance and song traditions. The sea caressing the island shore engenders music as central to slaves' creative will to survive the middle passage and their collective resistance to Christianity's justifications for racial hierarchies. Traversing time and space we enter a present where these "same embattled forms are being worked on," as Gilroy's narration reminds, in a context of new technological possibilities but also enduring oppressive forces. Here, the tension between past and present, signified in music now "circulat[ing] globally thanks to new technologies that dissolve distance" (Julien, 1994), also reflect contemporary diasporic experiences of migration, displacement and mass suffering in center and periphery black inner cities.

In this film the body becomes the local concern to which music in black popular culture refers. Against deepening levels of social, political, and economic marginalization, the body is a last stand. It is celebrated, violated, and defended, marking the principal site over which the powerless seek to reclaim power, particularly in the arenas of sexuality, masculinity, and racial identity. In *The Darker Side of Black* this reclamation of the body is played out in the bodies of black male artists who perform competitively within but also transgress the transnational mass-culture industry, where recognition is meted out and lucrative recording/distribution contracts are solidified. The film mentions such record industry phenomena as Jamaican deejay Shabba Ranks' two Grammy Awards and how, outside the industrial circuit, U.S. gangsta rapper Ice Cube's album *Death Certificate* defied protocol by topping sales charts without the benefit of commercially controlled airplay. To the rhythm of the narration, the camera moves to the streets of inner-city Kingston where men and women assert the individual power of their bodies "in a world indifferent to their suffering" (Julien, 1994). In a recording studio, dub reggae artists combine cutting-edge technology, bass, and drum to create a dense new sound to accompany the body's attitude of resistance. In a crowded dancehall club, the zoom focus follows a lone male dancer who—brimmed hat, open jacket revealing a colorful dress tie on a shirtless chest—performs this attitude in ritualized pelvic gyrations, and with shoulder/arm/hand gestures, and ecstatic facial expressions.

But Julien also examines what is perhaps the underside of a return to the body. Against rampant social indifference, control over the body is also asserted violently in music lyrics and images in music videos; their "realism" is difficult to distinguish from the real violence in the streets. In *The Darker Side of Black*, hardcore dancehall and hip hop's collusion in the marketing of violence as popular culture commodity and "the gun" as signifier of physical control are shown to have both their justifications and their critics.

On location at the street level in a Harlem, New York, record shop, an off-camera interviewer discusses gangsta rap with two young black women. They say gangsta rap is "cool," but also implicate it in the protean violence they witness, as well as in the changing attitudes they observe in young children in their community. In interview commentaries, rappers Ice Cube and Bushwick Bill locate the tropes of the gun and "gangsterism" in rap as part of the larger-scale violence they perceive today, for example, in U.S. imperialism on a global dimension and in the violent history of the "discovery" of America. "We see the gun so much," Shabba Ranks adds from a studio in Jamaica, "so, we talk about the gun. What else can we do?" (Ranks quoted in Julien, 1994).

Writer and cultural critic Cornel West, who provides commentary throughout the film, argues that the nihilistic representation of death and violence in gangsta rap lyrics should not be surprising, given the levels of personal and material misery among poor and working-poor people. Internally destructive dynamics may account for the pull of nihilism in a black community feeling increasing "hopelessness, lovelessness, and meaninglessness"; but, as West analyzes, there is also a contradictory push:

> As you can imagine, the market reinforces a certain theatricalizing of nihilism . . . that . . . puts a kind of premium on a certain kind of posing and posturing. . . . But it takes on a life of its own, and by taking on a life of its own, it does produce certain kind of effects and consequences beyond the market (West quoted in Julien, 1994).

In one music video extract, Ice Cube raps with chilled resignation, "I guess it was a good day. I didn't even have to use my AK," while in another promo, the visceral rap ensemble Onyx roars with hardcore in-your-face intensity, "Just throw your guns in the air. Pump pump like you just don't care."

These representations cut both ways, writer and cultural critic Tricia Rose argues in her perceptive interview commentaries. To paraphrase Rose, hardcore gangsta rap reflects real suffering and the violent oppressions of black life on the margins while it simultaneously mocks stereotypical figures—the dark, secretive, sexual, violent gangster—so central in American popular culture. "I think we need not take rap so literally," Rose concludes; its power and visibility "does not mean that everything that comes out of this genre is real—it's about representation, a play on those figures" (Rose quoted in Julien, 1994).

Pinpointing the effects of violence in the music beyond the market is complex. Commenting on camera, distinguished University of the West Indies professor Rex Nettleford dismisses the advocacy of violence found in certain forms of dancehall as simply youthful voices speaking as youth: "When I am a child," Nettleford muses, "I speak as a child. Well, you know what follows" (Nettleford, quoted in Julien, 1994); while from New York City, Donald Suggs, Gay and Lesbian Alliance Against Defamation activist, argues that the real issue is that the ideas some adolescent boys espouse about violence, women and gays have such prominence that they seem "to speak for an entire community" (Suggs, quoted in Julien, 1994).

Suggs's point about who speaks "for" whom opens the central analytic question Julien raises implicitly through the dialogic sequences the film presents; that it is not only who speaks, but how—those who speak through access to commercial music have more power. West's focus on market forces is key because the "how" has to do with who has accessibility to the technologies of mass cultural saturation through the music industry. In a recent interview with New York writer Bruce Morrow (1995) about *The Darker Side of Black*, Julien articulates this dilemma:

> Young, black, straight men do have the space to voice their anxiety, frustrations, and their phobias . . . that has to be looked at for what it is. It's only one section of the Black working class voice. But it makes a lot of money, and I guess that's what counts in the commodification of Black popular culture (p. 20).

The film points out that despite the claimed affront to mainstream culture sensibilities, hardcore rap has risen to the top of the charts.

Rose's explanation for this reality is that these forms of popular culture have a certain resonance or performative value within "patriarchal narratives which are more accepted in American culture" (Rose quoted in Julien, 1994).[8]

As suggested by several commentators in the film, musical forms do have a semiautonomy that may lead to effects that have a "life of their own." However, the dancehall and gangsta rap's initial entry into the public sphere—its marketability—may have as much to do with the pleasurable catchiness of the rhythms as with an implicit acceptability within patriarchal power relations. This is particularly true of content that is masculinist, homophobic, patriarchal, and misogynist. Such tensions in lyrical representation, conscious or unconscious, have pervaded insurgent music in popular culture from the early days of rock and roll to the current forms of hardcore rap and dancehall. And there are few viable alternatives to the dominance of these music styles in the market place or on the air ways, although even within popular culture dominant gendered and sexual definitions are ironized, too, through such artists as Little Richard, James Brown, Sly Stone and George Clinton, to name but a few innovative figures in funk and soul music.

Against the Grain of Popular Music

The issue of rap lyrics' literalness around violence and guns is given greater urgency in *The Darker Side of Black* as the camera turns to what the voiceover announces, "The lyrical gun has now identified a new enemy target. Queers!" The film excerpts from Buju Banton's "Boom Bye Bye" music video:

> Two men hitch up and a hug up an a lay down in a bed
> Hug one another an a feel up leg
> Send for the 'matic and the uzi instead
> Shoot them now, come on now make we shot them
> [sudden sound effect of a gun shot] (Banton quoted in Julien, 1994).

Banton appears on camera unabashed in his opposition to homosexuality. In his interview commentary he claims to be only one of the many voices in Jamaica talking to the people, simply issuing a warning "as straight as we talk." Speaking in a husky patois, he denies that his song intentionally advocates violence toward gay men (or presumably lesbians):

> I've heard a number of songs which have incited violence . . . not only against
> that section of the gay people them[selves], but to even black people we selves,

you know, and people never did go out and . . . really and truly go carry out
the actions. . . . But everything is blown out of proportion still, and God
know why, but who, there's no way the wicked can ever prosper (Banton
quoted in Julien, 1994).[9]

Moving within the urban space of Kingston and transatlantically to
London and New York, the camera brings together many voices to
discuss whether "Boom Bye Bye" encourages violence against and
disparity toward homosexuals.

Speaking from her office in the Kingston Legal Aid Clinic, Florizelle
O'Connor argues that "Boom Bye Bye" records faithfully the majority
Jamaican attitudes toward homosexuality, but it also faithfully records
the gunshots heard as part of rampant violence in Banton's impover-
ished Kingston neighborhood. She resists the view, however, that the
song "consciously or unconsciously" directs anyone into violent actions against a homosexual person, known or unknown (O'Connor
quoted in Julien, 1994). From Jamaican musician Karl Frazier's perspective, however, Buju Banton may not be fully conscious of his impact within the culture, but the point of the song is clear: "If I don't
like what somebody else does, whether I know it or perceive it, I can
go and kill that person" (Frazier quoted in Julien, 1994).

Frazier's interpretation is echoed in London by black British writer
David Dibosa who, looking straight into the camera, states: "In terms
of my own personal experience, music such as 'Boom Bye Bye' shouted
homophobia from the roof tops" (Dibosa quoted in Julien, 1994).
Dibosa, a gay man, recounts in vivid terms—"from the sharp end"—
his own experiences of anti-gay assault. Jamaican Tourist Board official Aston Cook dismisses the controversy over the song, saying its
impact was limited to dancehall culture and that the controversy really
took place in "the gay movements abroad" (Cook quoted in Julien,
1994). Back in Greenwich Village, New York, a group of young gay
men outside a night spot tell the off-camera interviewer that the song
has heightened conflict and violence between gays and straight Jamaicans and African Americans in some New York neighborhoods.

The Darker Side of Black affirms that in an already homophobic
environment, "Boom Bye Bye" and other songs containing similar
lyrics do encourage violence against gays. The film makes its intervention not to censor any music but to open up the space for discussion
of masculinity and sexuality which the music, intentionally or not,
closes down. Rather than permit the dissenting voices critical of Banton
to dominate, the film's nonlinear approach of juxtaposing opposing

voices and perspectives effectively challenges any commonsense, totalizing right/wrong response to this dilemma. In this way, the film's
invitational mode of address achieves a critique that privileges what
Ken Feil (1994, p. 10) terms "decentering . . . without dissing." For
example, gay activist Donald Suggs reports that the goal of proactively
opening a dialogue with black-oriented radio stations in New York
City who played "Boom Bye Bye" was not to pull the song from the
air but to have stations examine the song and take responsibility for
the message they broadcast into the public sphere. Part of taking responsibility, Suggs argues, is ensuring that homophobic lyrics are "not
the only message that young people, particularly young black people
in the black community get about lesbians and gay men" (Suggs quoted
in Julien, 1994).

Pedagogically, the intent of this film is to move the viewer to engage in a broader interrogation of the ways a song like "Boom Bye
Bye," as Julien puts it, "tries to enlist from its audience" a very specific position on black masculine identity and gender roles (Julien quoted
in Morrow, 1995, p. 20). Julien challenges representations that insist
that homosexuality is antithetical to black masculinity, that black masculine integrity must be preserved at the cost of brutalizing any man
who is gay, and that the roles and identities admissible within black
masculinity are identifiable in their homogeneity, particularly with regard to self-presentation (machismo), politics (nationalist), and sexuality (heterosexual).

Yet it is always possible to read these representations, or what Julien
calls popular culture music's "verbal articulations," complexly against
the grain. For example, while the film shows there is a strong antigay
tendency in dancehall, we also see that a visible yet outlawed gay
culture (homosexuality is literally illegal in Jamaica) has had the contradictory effect of freeing up latent possibilities for safely feminizing
the male body through adornment. The camera pans a dance club
where men are seen dancing, posing, and profiling admiringly in shim-
mering, colorful outfits that seem to cross the borders between men's
and women's wear. In his interview commentary, musician Karl Frazier
observes this phenomenon:

> Gay culture, I suppose, has influenced the [male] style of dress in dancehall
> . . . the sequins, the diaphanous material that you'd think that women would
> wear, the hair styles, the ornaments that they wear in their hair, the coloring
> that is used, all of these have been adopted and they [men] can adopt them
> because there is strength in numbers, so everybody is doing it (Frazier quoted
> in Julien, 1994).[10]

Gender roles and homophobia are most clearly linked in the film's examination of the controversy around the New York City based rap group Brand Nubian's hit song, "Punks Jump Up to Get Beat Down." This segment provides interview commentary by the group's members, Lord Jamar, Sadat X, and Sincere, defending their views on women, which are articulated in their song "Love Me or Leave Me Alone." Women should either "live according to their nature," the young men say or "y'know, [they] could get dissed." The screen flashes to a dreamy mise-en-scene of three women dressed in white, heads veiled, sitting at the feet of a religious man; the organic setting and brightness of the shot seem to naturalize the passive position of the women. The implication is that women who are not subservient to (Afrocentric) patriarchal desire are subject to be "dissed." As Brand Nubian spokesman Lord Jamar put it, "If you [women] really want to be with brothers like us, y'know, that I'm saying has knowledge of self, then you have to get knowledge of yourself too, or else you gotta be out of here, y'know what I'm saying" (Jamar quoted in Julien, 1994). A short time later Brand Nubian reappears in the film asserting that "Punks Jump Up. . . " was not a gay-bashing song, although they do feel homosexuality "is wrong." A music-video extract shows a young man, his nose bloodied, sprawled on a subway platform; the band hovers tauntingly above him, rapping against a funky jazz rhythm:

> . . . to the jaw and you won't pop that junk no more
> Explain to your punk friends as you're lying on the floor
> Did you want some more, I didn't think so
> Just got whipped like a sissy in the clinch so (Brand Nubian quoted in Julien, 1994).

Unlike the requirement of female subservience to black working-class male patriarchal desire, the threat of violence implied in the term "dissed" is made real toward the purported gay male—the "sissy" on the floor. This figure of the less-than-masculine male so threatens patriarchal desire and heterosexual stability that it requires eradication: "you won't pop that junk no more." And music rhythmically carries Brand Nubian's demand for adherence to their version of knowledge of the masculine "self" quickly "before I punch you in the face with the goddamn bass" (Brand Nubian quoted in Julien, 1994). Within the discourse of male hard-core rap and dancehall, these ideas and their attendant desires for stable, powerful identity, have taken on particularly macho, antigay, and misogynistic forms. Sexual difference is denied, and positions of vulnerability and victimization—figured both as feminine and gay—are viciously policed. Women are dismissed as bitches and whores, or evaluated with respect to their willingness to subordinate themselves to men; gay men, real or imagined, are subject to outright violence.

As the film shows, Buju Banton, Brand Nubian, and Shabba Ranks find rationalizations for these positions in their selective appropriations of scriptural writings, Christian and Islamic (members of Brand Nubian are identified in the film as adherents of the 5% Nation, a splinter group from the Nation of Islam). In an extremely defiant interview comment, Ranks makes his position on gender roles perfectly clear: "I live by the words of Bible, and this say I must multiply, and another to another is an abomination of this" (Ranks quoted in Julien, 1994). The camera hold Ranks in an unflinching pose of moral righteousness that evokes the sentinel-like figure seen patrolling the beachfront at the beginning of the film.

The Darker Side of Black refuses linear answers to difficult questions about representation and masculinity in black popular culture music. Certain representational tendencies within the music require cultural intervention because, the film implies, their hardcore articulations circulate globally through market forces that allow them to appear—without counter-narrative alternatives—as the "cultural dominant," speaking for all and saying everything. While music and its effects, the film insists, are more difficult to pin down, there is still the ethical question of the cost of such expressions of fear and violence.

Resistance

The Darker Side of Black also illustrates the dynamic play of what Hall terms "the mark of difference *inside* popular culture" (Hall, 1992, p. 28). For example, British female deejay Monie Love does not merely contest male rappers' reduction of women to the signifier "bitch"; in her commentary she actually negates it, through her self-assured critical agency and strong personal-is-political posture. On camera, Jamaican deejay Lady Saw and dancehall models like Queen Carlene articulate provocative but nonetheless ironic forms of gender role transgression through what Carolyn Cooper, a professor at the University of the West Indies, analyzes as a centering of the female body in the space of dancehall.[11] British female film director Inge Blackman argues that black lesbians appropriate dancehall as a site to celebrate black women's sexuality and bonding. Expressions of sexuality and lust among women, "not really allowed in any other kind of black popular culture" (Blackman quoted in Julien), can be directly signified in dancehall *ragga*—a term for Jamaican-derived dancehall music, risque attire and erotic dance movement fashionable in the viibrant black London dance club scene.

Finally, *The Darker Side of Black* demonstrates how hardcore masculinist rap and dancehall are themselves contradictory. Shabba Ranks, Buju Banton, and Brand Nubian, among others, police "the borders between masculine/feminine and heterosexual/homosexual," as Ken Feil contends. But, he adds, they also "transgress the material suffering of racist, classist hierarchies through music, stardom and the transformative space of the dancehall" (1994, p. 8). Hardcore rappers and deejays, therefore, engage in cultural strategies of transgression and resistance to cultural hegemony that are simultaneously contradicted by the conservative role they play in containing and policing difference inside black popular culture. Taking into account the ambivalent tensions in this dynamic context of popular music is central to developing pedagogical interventions.

Interview commentaries in the film directly address strategies to disrupt forms of representation and power in popular culture. However, the politics of pedagogies that challenge dominant representational processes are shown to be difficult, and they are also subject to their own contradictions. Like the defeat of the "Funk the Jubilee Concert" in *Young Soul Rebels*, cultural strategies of resistance can act back on themselves in unintended ways and often divide communities that should pragmatically find something in common. One vivid example of this dilemma portrayed in *The Darker Side of Black* is the condemnation and criticism of homophobic rap and dancehall lyrics that emerged from the mostly white gay press. Important as their journalistic intervention was, it had the one-dimensionalizing effect of inscribing—othering—the whole of black popular culture as homophobic and misogynist. Resistance, in this case, became just another "cultural dominant" which not only could not hear but also silenced the complexity of responses to the songs that emerged from black communities. As Blackman charges, "most of the prominence has been given to black people who are homophobic . . . what you don't hear are the more complex issues raised by black people who are not homophobic and who are also avid fans of *ragga*" (Blackman quoted in Julien, 1994).

Some counter-strategies, as New York City gay activist Suggs describes, work too well, thus undermining and limiting the intended political effect. In this case, activists intervened in a scheduled appearance of Shabba Ranks on the popular *Tonight* talk show. Their intent was to make Ranks take responsibility for a homophobic comment that "lesbians and gay men ought to be crucified" (see e.g., Noel, 1993). The *Tonight* show canceled his appearance, but, Suggs says retrospectively, "That was unfortunate in a way. I would have much rather seen him go on and have to explain in front of an audience of millions of people."

Other interventions represented in the film suggest the possibilities of strategic practice within hip-hop and dancehall cultures. In an interview, musician and writer Michael Franti of the rap ensemble Disposable Heroes of Hiphoprisy describes his song "The Language of Violence" as an example of a counter-narrative in the context of homophobic rap. Using rap's advanced technologies and catchy rhythms, Franti's lyrics tell the story of violence acting back on kids who beat up on someone they suspect is gay; later, in prison, one of the victimizers is himself a victim of rape. Franti thoughtfully adds that the song is not a statement simply about homophobia but

> a statement on the use of language to degrade people. . . . [Y]ou could replace any victim in there, somebody who is black, somebody who is Asian, somebody who is woman and still have the same effect. . . . I think that's the importance of the song, and I think that's the importance of speaking out on . . . homophobia" (Franti quoted in Julien, 1994).

Critical clergy also engage in counter-narratives which resist selective appropriation of biblical texts to justify homophobia in dancehall and elsewhere. At the Jamaican Council of Churches, Reverend Neville Callam finds the fragmentary way young musicians evoke the Old Testament to formulate positions on homosexuality to be "completely without foundation" (Callan quoted in Julien, 1994). Cornel West and Reverend Jones of Unity Fellowship Church in New York City argue that Levitical law sanctions many everyday activities that we have come to take for granted. The challenge, Rev. Jones asserts, is to press the mainstream church on how much of Levitical Law it is "going to exclude or choose to include in order to oppress lesbian and gay people" (Jones quoted in Julien, 1994). He later revises and reverses Buju Banton's "bye bye" metaphor to urge collective efforts to say "bye bye" to a host of social ills and inequalities like violence, poverty, and unemployment.

The Darker Side of Black attempts an intervention into the difficult terrain of black popular music, where issues of black masculinity, sexuality, and gender roles are struggled over, policed, and transgressed. The film critiques but also highlights the "difference" inside black popular culture and within the ranks of music producers and audiences. Pedagogically, the important contribution of *The Darker Side of Black* is its success in resisting didactic solutions while providing multiple perspectives that may inform debates and dialogues on cultural strategies that might make a difference. But like the successes, failures, tensions, and resolutions portrayed in the youthful engagement of music in *Young Soul Rebels*, this film provides no once-and-for-all guarantee for effective intervention into the ever-shifting forms of cultural hegemony. The ambivalent final narration argues against simple analysis but also understands contemporary musical forms as providing no more than "perverse remedies to today's miseries" (Julien, 1994). Such a conclusion echoes Stuart Hall (1992), whose analysis anticipates the long cultural and pedagogical struggle ahead:

> By definition, black popular culture is a contradictory space. It is a site of strategic contestation . . . it never can be simplified or explained in terms of simple binary oppositions. . . : high and low; . . . opposition versus subordination. There are always positions to be won in popular culture, but no struggle can capture popular culture itself for our side or theirs (pp. 26–27).

Postscript: "Teaching Difference Differently": Worrying the Guarantees of Reception

This essay makes the central claim that the two films under discussion provide a rich curriculum text for interrogating ambivalent and contradictory tensions of difference surrounding black popular music. Like any critical textual practice, the counter-strategies employed by Julien— such as mixing forms and ideas to make hybrid images and representations, the utilization of Brechtian distancing techniques, and, of course, the contesting subject matter—subvert dominant representational processes.[12] These practices aim to confront and throw into question sedimented commonsense-held positions by viewers.

The question remains: Do these strategies necessarily assure that audiences will automatically open up to new forms of dialogue on culturally restricted questions? In other words, does their employment guarantee that the open, interrogative nature of the films will be echoed by considered responses from its audience? The pedagogical context, the classroom in particular, occupied by students with diverse biographies, desires, and political outlooks, offers a unique site to examine the possibility for dialogue within this larger conundrum of audience reception. Yet this site can generate additional tensions of its own, unleashing specific yearnings, fantasies, and defenses that react to exhibited texts. The continuous sliding between plurality and sameness in the classroom works against knowing in advance how knowledge incited by musical and visual forms might "worry" the identities of students. The machinations of "how knowledge of identities and cultures is produced, encountered and dismissed in classrooms as homogeneous and hetereogeneous" (Britzman et al. 1993, p. 189) are at issue here.

Can the representational counter-strategies offered by Julien's films be extracted to help construct a pedagogical context for teaching about popular music and difference "differently"? Given that Julien's representations accept and work with the unstable nature of meaning, we are left with no tangible road map, no clear signposts. In the struggle over representation there is always a danger that students will repeat the closing down of critical inquiry that the film's deconstructive strategy attempts to open up. Teachers must be prepared to understand that their students' interpretations derive from identifications which may refuse any ambivalent play with conceptions of difference and "otherness"; identifications may claw back to staid definitions that the film's pedagogy is aiming to subvert.

If these films engage the complex ambivalences and tensions, loves and hatreds that slip and slide within and around popular music, then teachers might take their pedagogical cues from the films themselves. First, an openness to and familiarity with the practices of cultural critique that Julien actively employs. Second, a willingness to engage with the conflicting knowledges students may bring to an encounter with representations that contest dominant definitions of race, gender, and sexuality. Such a pedagogical stance provides no secure outcomes but may afford fertile ground for asking questions about how contradictions within black popular music might be listened to and learned from.

Teachers willing to work with difficult knowledge know full well that screening contentious "close to the bone" material can engender chaotic moments in the classroom. These are the risks encountered when opening the Pandora's box of difference (Hall, 1981). Such reception dynamics become manifest in a fascinating ethnographic study conducted by Dan Yon (forthcoming) on showing *A Darker Side of Black* in two Greater Toronto high schools "where concerns with race, ethnicity and class converge." In one school a group of students found the film irrelevant to their needs for "essential truths and fixed meanings" about race, community, and sexuality in particular. While sharing similar concerns for more "pressing problems," such as racism and social inequities, a group from the second school found the film rich in opening debate about violence and sexual difference *within* their community. Yon's reading of students' responses to *A Darker Side of Black* highlights the complex and contradictory ways young audiences negotiate representation and produce meanings unanticipated by pedagogical intent.

Julien's films offer catalysts to "teach about difference differently." Such an encounter will open up spaces of ideological struggle, the right of any worthwhile pedagogical context. As teachers, we must be prepared for the pedagogical challenge or duty of working through such struggles with students, recognizing with Hall that there are no guarantees, no simple answers or expectations, that no side can fully win or assume the stability of final victory.

References

Bennett, G. (1995). The non-sovereign self (diaspora identities). *Left Curve, 19*, 4–9.

Britzman, D., Santiago-Váles, K., Jímenez-Múñoz, G. & Lamash, L. (1993). Slips that show and tell: Fashioning multiculture as a problem of representation. In C. McCarthy & W. Crichlow (Eds.), *Race, identity and representation in education* (pp.188–200). New York: Routledge.

Brotzman, P., Hopkins, F. & Ali, R. (1991, October). *Songlines*. Berlin: Free Music Production CD # 53.

Buckingham, D. & J. Sefton-Green. (1994). *Cultural studies goes to school: Reading and teaching popular media*. London: Taylor & Francis.

Clinton, G. (1978). *Funkadelic: One nation under a groove*. New York: Warner Bros.

Cooper, C. (1995). *Noises in the blood: Orality, Gender, and the "Vulgar" Body of Jamaican popular culture*. Durham, NC: Duke University Press.

Feil, K. (1994). "Inappropriate others": Queer theory's documentary agency and *The darker side of black*. University of Texas, Austin. Unpublished manuscript.

Gates, H. L., Jr. (1997, April/May). Black London: The rise of Afro-Saxon culture. *New Yorker (Special Europe Issue)*, pp. 194–205.

Gilroy, P. (1993). *The black Atlantic: Modernity and double consciousness*. Cambridge: Harvard University Press.

Givanni, J. (Ed.). (1995). *Remote control: Dilemmas of black intervention in British TV & film*. London: British Film Institute.

Hall, S. (1981). Teaching race. In A. James & R. Jeffcoate (Eds.), *The school in the multicultural society* (pp. 58–69). London: Harper.

Hall, S. (1992). What is this "Black" in black popular culture. In G. Dent (Ed.), *Black popular culture* (pp. 21–33). Seattle, WA: Bay Press).

hooks, b. (1991). States of desire: Isaac Julien in conversation with bell hooks. In Julien, I. & MacCabe, C. (Eds.), *Diary of a Young Soul Rebel* (pp. 125–140). London: British Film Institute Publishing.

Julien, I. (Director). (1991). *Young soul rebels* [Film]. Available from London: The British Film Institute.

Julien, I. (Director). (1994). *The Darker Side of Black* [Film]. Available from New York: Filmakers Library.

Julien, I. & Mercer, K. (1988). Introduction: De margin and de Centre. *Screen* 29(4).

Leger, D. (1995, September). Buju Banton: One God! *TRUE, 20*, 63.

Lipsitz, G. (1994). *Dangerous crossroads: Popular music, postmodernism and the poetics of place*. London: Verso.

Marley, B. & The Wailers. (1974). *Natty Dred* [LP]. Jamaica: Island Records.

Mercer, K. (1994). Introduction: Black Britain and the cultural politics of diaspora. In K. Mercer, *Welcome to the jungle: New positions in black cultural studies* (pp. 1–31). New York: Routledge.

Morrison, T. (1992). *Playing in the dark: Whiteness and the literary imagination*. Cambridge: Harvard University Press.

Morrow, B. (1995, Summer). Interview with Isaac Julien. *Fuse Magazine, 18* (3), 15–23.

Noel, P. (1993, January 12). Batty boys in Babylon: Can gay West Indians survive the "Boom Bye Bye" posses? *Village Voice*, pp. 29–36.

Phillips, C. (1997, Winter). Interview with Stuart Hall. *Bomb*, 38–42.

Said, E. (1991). *Musical elaborations*. New York: Columbia University Press.

Walcott, R. (1997, March). Sounds/Songs of black postmodernity: History, music youth. *Educational Researcher, 26* (2), 35–38.

Williams, R. (1958). *Culture and Society*. London: Chatto and Windus.

Willis, P., with Jones, S., Canaan, J., & Hurd, G. (1990). *Common culture: Symbolic work at play in everyday cultures of the young*. Boulder, CO: Westview.

Wimsatt, W. U. (1994a). *Bomb the suburbs: Graffiti, freight-hopping, race and the search for hip-hop's moral center*. Chicago: The Subway and Elevated Press.

Wimsatt, W. U. (1994b, September 9). In defense of wiggers. *In These Times, 18* (22), 39–40.

Yon, D. (forthcoming). Pedagogy and the 'problem' of difference: On reading community in 'The darker side of black.' *International Journal of Qualitate Studies in Education*.

Notes

1. Isaac Julien is a London-based director and founding member in the 1980s of the Sankofa Film and Video Collective. For more than a decade he has made films in collaboration with fellow independents, including *The Passion of Remembrance* (1986); *This Is Not an AIDS Video* (1987); *Looking for Langston* (1989); and *The Attendant* (1991); *The Question of Equality* (1995) (a four-part series made-for-television); and with Mark Nash, *Frantz Fanon: Black Skin, White Mask* (1996). As a critic and writer in debates about visual theory and representation, especially theory around contemporary black popular culture, Julien has held numerous teaching posts and residences in the United States and in Europe.

2. It also provides insights into the historical roots of black British identity and the setting for a generational renaissance in black British cultural and expressive production that is prominent today. See for example, Julien & Mercer, 1988; Mercer, 1994; Givanni, 1995; Phillips, 1997; Gates, 1997.

3. For example, without submitting to crude reductionism or denigration of individual pleasure, Said (1991) shows how music can perform in a wider cultural field as a social activity in relation to ideological formations such as imperialism or fascism—how it can adapt to or transgress "worldly situations" (pp. 34–72).

4. For an ethnographic account of young peoples' experience with and symbolic work on popular music, see P. Willis (1990), especially pp. 59–83.

5. For extended analyses of diasporic linkages between music and youth cultures see, for example, Gilroy, 1993; Lipsitz, 1994; and Walcott, 1997.

6. Is the bump a refined pogo or is the pogo an aggressive bump? This is a playful question but one that should be considered in light of the various ways in which cultural signs are never stable in the film. (Rinaldo Walcott, personal communication.)

7. Banton, whose international media spotlight stalled after the outcry over "Boom Bye Bye," has since refashioned himself through conversion to Rastafarianism, trading in his former gangsta-style toasts for a new "roots reggae" commitment to community and family. See, for example, Leger, 1995.

8. Although not mentioned in the film, patriarchal narratives may also account for the large young white male consumer audience for gangsta rap. See, for example, Wimsatt, 1994a & b; also films such as Larry Clark's recent film *Kids* [Excalibar Films] which capitalizes on uncritical representations of white adolescents acting-out (hetero)sexuality through appropriation and sterotypical imitations of black male hip-hop posture.

9. Ironically, in arguing that his song is benign, Bantun overlooks the relationship between language and slavery, racialized terror, and violence, as well as the effectivity of discursive justifications across the chronicle of human holocaust.

10. I thank Rinalo Walcott for pointing out that much of the finery observed in dancehall is abstracted and reconstituted from disco culture, a popular music and dance form of the seventies in which gay men played a major formative role. Masculinist and homophobic tendencies within popular music and dance have drawn from this history in creative though visibly ironic ways.

11. For an extended analysis of the female body and erotic play in dancehall, see Carolyn Cooper, 1995.

12. For example, ideas such as the notion that form is political and could radically effect viewers' responses, that the adoption of particular forms could elicit certain affective responses from the spectator, were espoused and became popular in late 1970s reception theory, in Britain's influential journal *Screen*. No doubt Julien was both exposed to and contributed to this seminal theory/practice debate. See, for example, Julien and Mercer (1988).

Learning from the Blues: Beyond Essentialist Readings of Cultural Texts

Ruth Vinz

Then I heard Bolden's cornet. . . . I thought I had heard Bolden play the blues before, and play the hymns at funerals, but what he is playing now is real strange and I listen carefully, because he's playing something that, for a while sounds like the blues, then like a hymn. . . . He is mixing up the blues with the hymns. He plays the blues real sad and the hymn sadder than the blues and then the blues sadder than the hymn. That is the first time that I ever heard hymns and blues cooked up together. Strange cold feeling comes over me: I get sort of scared because I know the Lord don't like that mixing the Devil's music with his music. . . . I close my eyes, and when he blows the blues I picture Lincoln Park with all them sinners and whores shaking and belly rubbing. Then, as he blows the hymn, I picture my mother's church on Sunday, and everybody humming with the choir (Dude Botley, quoted in Neal, 1989, pp. 108–109).

Improvisation. Contradiction. Confrontation. Affirmation. The music throbs with meaning—rueful and glum and disconcerting. But, who makes it "feel" and "mean"? Who beclouds the performance with botheration? Dude Botley describes his experience listening to Bolden as if it were the blues coming on—a portending dark and cold where sinners and belly rubbing vie for position with the radiating light, hymn, and mother's church. The message of the blues is fulfilled in this musical moment, emphasizing, in yet another version, the never-ending struggle of living. The situation illustrates how emotionally charged, what sheer exhilaration comes from participating in the musical possibility offered as Buddy Bolden blurs boundaries that are often perceived as contradictory forms and content in the African American musical tradition (Cone, 1972). Botley's response contains its own contradictions—a pull toward both the secular and sacred. The music and the response are a complex blending of Botley and Bolden's cultural knowledge of blues and hymns, the evocation of aesthetic, affective, and intellectual responses, and the near paradoxical valuing of both the secular and sacred. And, Bolden's "hymns and blues cooked up together" suggest the dynamic in art, an example of how forms keep changing with each reinterpretation or re-creation as we humans imagine and value and live and represent the flux of our living in multi-identities of our experiences and imaginings.

In stating that there is a dynamic in art and that its forms keep changing, I am conscious of a long history of those who struggle to define how, when, and if this should happen. Dewey (1980) examined and attempted to delineate what is authentic and essential in aesthetic objects and experiences in *Art as Experience*. His project was to determine the features of the aesthetic that change and those that are permanent in order to determine "the relation between permanence and change" (p. 322). In a sense, he declared that there are acceptable and not-so-acceptable ways to break with "the crust of conventionalized and routine consciousness" (Dewey, 1934, p. 183). However, he didn't account for the impulse of the covert and the implicit as forces that keep art dynamic. It is Bakhtin who examines continuity and change from this perspective. Bakhtin's (1968) understanding of the degrees of parody and travesty in performance in popular art forms leads me to liken Bolden's blurring to an alternative speech form which liberates "norms, hierarchies, and prohibitions of established idiom" (p. 188).

Of course, intentions are hard to pin down, but attempts to name the principles of permanence and change have been the philosophical project of many. From this view, the Bolden/Botley incident could be understood through Foucault's (1980) delineation of the relationship between power and sanctioned truth—as, in this case, what might be "true" blues:

> Each society has its régime of truth, its 'general politics' of truth: that is, the types of discourse which it accepts and makes function as true; the mechanisms and instances which enable one to distinguish true and false statements, the means by which each is sanctioned; the techniques and procedures accorded value in the acquisition of truth; the status of those who are charged with saying what counts as true (p. 131).

When Botley creates an extension, distortion, parody, or improvisation on an accepted blues discourse (or whatever the intention of spontaneous creation), there is always the possibility that he will help constitute some new politics of truth. More likely he will create dissonance
or, less satisfactorily, will find his music blown into the dissipating air.

Recognizing the confluence of continuity and change, Bolden's
improvisation may show the constant struggle against claims of certainty in the message and medium of the blues. More fully, however, it
can be explained through the act itself, as Deleuze (1993) has chosen
to interrogate:

> There is no act of creation that is not transhistorical and does not come up
> from behind or proceed by way of a liberated line. . . . Creations are like
> mutant abstract lines that have detached themselves from the task of repre-
> senting a world, precisely because they assemble a new type of reality that
> history can only recontain or relocate in punctual systems (p. 50).

For Kristeva (1984), there is an identifiable process in understanding
change in the text/act production:

> the path completed by the *text* is not a simple return, as in the Hegelian
> dialectic, from the "predicate" to the "subject". . . Instead it involves both
> shattering and maintaining *position* within the heterogeneous *process*: the
> proof can be found in the phonetic, lexical, and syntactic disturbance visible
> in the *semiotic device* of the text (p. 56).

This web of interpretive positions from Dewey to Kristeva is intended
to illustrate how the meaning from this one Bolden/Botley musical
moment cannot be easily tamed.

What I wanted to demonstrate by pushing the lines of interpretation on this one incident (Bolden/Botley) in so many directions is how
difficult it is to construct meaning. Each moment is constituted by the
present and the past and by the contingency of positions from which
it could be understood. To write a clean line of interpretation about
the meaning of the Botley/Bolden story, to tie it in neatly with the
points I hope to make in this chapter, to structure an analysis that can
lead to my declaration of meaning, and maybe, just maybe, to sum up
with a moral to the story—these acts of representing meaning are
ingrained in us through much of the educational enterprises in which
we have been a part. Some of us work hard to re-member through
collective and conflicted means, to make plural what may appear singular. But, it isn't easy to work in such ambiguous spaces, and I have

found in my work with prospective as well as in-service teachers that as much as they recognize that cultural studies and issues of diversity should be central in their curricular and pedagogical work, they, as we, find it difficult to imagine ways to keep the texts of culture open and alive and beyond essentialized versions.

This article describes how I, along with student teachers and in-service teachers in a course that focused on issues of diversity, began to engage in curricular and pedagogical theorizing about the study of cultural texts. Through our study, we attempted to understand how our own ways of learning "texts" informed us about practices that encourage readings beyond essentialism. In what follows, I describe what prompted the choice of the blues as the site of study, and I examine some of my own and the teachers' reflections on the relevance of this experience to our understanding of curricular and pedagogical issues. Further, I explain how we came to recognize the complexities and contradictions found within the blues as a cultural text and the questions this raised about teaching and learning.

We attempted to read beyond the contestations, many of which arose because individuals with very different ideologies, politics, life experiences, and other sites of difference were brought together in this diversity class and expected to learn together. As Bakhtin (1984) indicated, "The single adequate form for *verbally expressing* authentic human life is the *open-ended dialogue*. . . . To live means to participate in dialogue: to ask questions, to heed, to respond, to agree, and so forth" (p. 293). Dialogic interaction competes with monologism, which, as Bakhtin pointed out,

> denies the existence outside itself of another consciousness with equal rights and equal responsibilities, another *I* with equal rights *(thou)*. . . . Monologue is finalized and deaf to the other's response, does not expect it and does not acknowledge in it any *decisive* force (pp. 292–293).

Our first challenge was to learn to listen to each other—really listen and hear.

Working Against Monologue

To begin, many of us in the class began to make that common and not very helpful "rush to judgment." Some class members were quickly labelled by the sympathies they expressed for certain positions, and what became perceived, in some cases, as their consistent positions

on issues. In a sense, these teachers essentialized the texts of themselves. This was not always a conscious and deliberate positioning,
but was the result, as one of the teachers said, "of all of us being a
little crazy with our own themes and issues." For example, Eliza identified herself as a feminist and was first to point out sexist language,
gender inequities, and male domination during class discussions. Sandra
informed the class during our first session that any issue, "whether it
be sexual orientation, class, gender, or whatever doesn't count until
the race issue is taken care of." Paul responded adamantly that Sandra's
position excluded him from consideration:

> As a gay man, I can't support Sandra's position. I understand race is impor-
> tant, but I had rocks thrown at me in the parking lot of the high school I
> attended, so I see discrimination as an issue that varies in kind and sub-
> stance. I can't accept prioritizing by type.

Sandra responded that while his issue was "important, it just isn't as
central to the problems in this country as race is." Seeing that such
naming and essentializing could occur with "dynamic" (living) texts in
our very classroom gave me pause to wonder how we could avoid
essentializing the cultural texts that we would teach and learn.

The tensions that arose during the first weeks seemed to result
from an underlying assumption that there is only so much privilege to
go around and that those folks who consider themselves on the margins will need to fight for their share. Joanne reminded her classmates
of this at the end of the second week of class:

> As a Latino woman who was educated in New York City public schools, I
> learned quickly that the issue of race only counted for African Americans.
> When I'd bring up the idea of discrimination against my people, it was blown
> off by my classmates who thought race was only about being black. As I've
> thought about that over the years, I think it's a natural reaction to protect our
> own causes first.

In other words, public utterances made during class began to "name"
various identities and locations of individuals. By coming to see each
other in a representational scheme, the students and in-service teachers created a form of essentialism as they began to label themselves
and others around the issues. In doing so, they began to read the
"texts" of themselves and each other in nearly essentialist ways.
Bakhtin's (1986) conception of text is useful here as it is best "understood in the broad sense—as any coherent complex of signs" (p. 103).

However, the concept of "coherent" is part of what I think needs to be challenged if we are able to move beyond essentialized readings of people or culture.

Narratives of experience, rational argumentation, deferral to authorities, and silence were all discourses used to advance, contest, or subvert knowledge of self and others as we attempted to carry on conversations and establish some operational principles for ourselves as a class. Although the teachers were learning to talk to one another, there was unequal power located in their various positions in relation to issues of race, gender, sexual orientation, class, age, and teaching experience. Depending on any individual's relationship to a particular issue, a form of marginalization occurred. For example, the more distant any given teacher might be from issues of sexual orientation, the more marginalized was he or she in a discussion on gay issues. The same was true in discussions that turned to gender issues. Some males moved toward silence as these discussions ensued. At times, class members examined the dynamics in the room that were related to who had knowledge on a particular topic, who was the accepted or stated authority, and who had an acknowledged right to speak. As Quame suggested, "It's like we deliberately take a stance and plant ourselves firmly in that place. Then, we get labeled from that position and wonder why." With this pattern developing, most of us were motivated to deal with it directly. The chance to do so revealed itself in quite an unexpected way.

The blues became a site for study of cultural texts because of a particular incident that occurred in class. During the fifth week, the student teachers and in-service teachers introduced their course project topics to their classmates. My purpose for assigning these projects was to engage the teachers in a study of a cultural text or texts of their choosing, hopeful that such a project might help them problematize issues of curriculum and pedagogy that they might find useful as they facilitated their students' study of cultural texts. One female teacher, Lisa, found herself criticized for deciding to study the blues. Twelve out of approximately twenty-eight teachers in the class, in varying degrees of confirmation, informed her that a 22-year-old Jewish woman from Park Slope could not understand, as one teacher phrased it, "diddly squat" about the blues, "either its messages, forms, or the white appropriation of blues production."

Broadly speaking, the teachers contesting her choice of cultural text were staking a claim for authenticity of a black musical genre that they believed could not be understood by a white person. As the discussion became more heated, one teacher informed her that she "couldn't understand the suffering. You're white, so your people don't know suffering like what's expressed." I found the comment ironic, considering Lisa had shared with the class in one of the earlier sessions that both of her grandparents on her mother's side of the family were victims of the Holocaust. Of course, another teacher in the class was quick to point this out.

The discussion was a particularly productive moment in helping all of us see beyond the essentialized versions that we were creating of each other. As several of the African American teachers shared their feelings about the blues, it became clear that their opinions did not reflect a unitary or official version of the art form. Robert, one of the first-year teachers, suggested that "it doesn't much matter anyway because the blues is a dead form. That's about slave days, times past. Nobody in my family listens to the blues anymore." Quame disagreed. "Anyways, man, the blues is still alive in rap cause signifying is new and old." Regina remembered that her grandfather "would enter sort of a trance-like state, sort of transported beyond suffering" when he listened to the blues. That brought a response from Raymond. "Listening to these guys moanin' about their lives must have been a peak experience when you were suffering yourself. They knew what it means to be black." Robert, Quame, Regina, and Raymond's very different readings of the blues became the first example that showed concretely how any one response might essentialize what is obviously a complex system of signs and meanings. The class discussion reminded me that Toni Morrison (1992) had warned that we should be "mindful of the places where imagination sabotages itself, locks its own gates, pollutes its vision" (p. xi). And I wondered, as the debate continued about whether or not Lisa should study the blues, how I might help these teachers and myself be more vigilant about our assumptions and expectations. How might we develop curriculum and pedagogy that help us distance ourselves occasionally from the known in order to teach ourselves about the complexities of various race, class, gender, or other socially inflected identities in order to think and see and experience differently? Then, of course, I wondered if this was even the question to be asking.

The teachers enrolled in this class came with various understandings about the cultural certainties and confusions in their own lives as well as with agendas and questions about how these issues might be important to their lives and their students' lives in school. In this class—made up of African American, Latino, Asian American and white teachers from a variety of economic backgrounds, ages, sexual orientations, and a near equal gender split, I found a lively and disparate group. One of the main difficulties in dealing with issues of difference could be read as symptomatic of the incongruence between (a) what any person might take on as a learned rhetoric to challenge oppressive social and political formations and (b) their individual acts of collusion that perpetuate the oppressive social and political formations. The rift between the discourse and the act was foremost in the minds of all of us because we were spending our days in inner-city classrooms as student teachers, teachers, or supervisors. Time and time again, members of the class expressed how the experience strained their sense of balance and certainty.

Part of the dissonance was related to the issue of the uncomplicated rhetoric about "doing" multicultural education that seems pervasive in many schools. Most of the in-service teachers in this class had participated in various staff development projects where various types of proposals for multiculural curriculum had been described. Many had participated in school-wide projects to promote multicultural curriculum across disciplines. The prospective teachers had almost no knowledge of the issue. Most had not been exposed to the concept or manifestations of multicultural work in their own educational experience and were just beginning to hear discussions in the schools where they were student teaching and in their coursework at the college. In New York City, attempts to educate students into issues of race, sexual orientation, class, and ethnicity produced angry rhetoric on all sides and led to the dissolution of a multicultural curriculum as well as to the firing of the superintendent of schools. But, multicultural education lumbers along in benign ways. For example, students in New York City schools have the museums, the concerts, the diverse populations at their fingertips, and many teachers use these resources as a central part of their curriculum. Of course, the question is: What messages do students construct from their visits and their study around those visits?

Too often, not only in this city but elsewhere, cultural studies have relied on a shopping mall approach. On Monday of a given week, students begin their unit on Native Americans. They learn that Native Americans lived in tepees, used tomahawks to scalp white folks, wore headdresses, and danced around a fire before eating their meal of blue corn and buffalo meat. By Wednesday of the same week, literature is added as an important cultural artifact; therefore, one or two poems (sometimes including Longfellow's "Hiawatha") represent tribal life of the past and present. By Friday, students take a trip to The Museum of the American Indian with its unsurpassed collection of artifacts and carry home their own renditions of tepees, tomahawks, or headdresses that they made during the art period. During the second week, students study Latinos. They commit one or two phrases of Spanish to memory, eat tacos and enchiladas on Wednesday, read excerpts from *Barrio Boy* on Thursday, and their trip to El Museo del Barrio ends with a festival where the piñatas they have made on Monday are broken open. The events, as I have outlined them, are exaggerated, but I am certain that the messages students carry away from their multicultural studies may not be much different from what is portrayed here. So, in some ways the project with the blues led the focus away from, yet closer toward, experiencing the bewildering disjunctures between what was happening in schools and what the teachers in this diversity class wanted to happen in their classrooms and schools. The teachers knew that something was missing from these ways of studying but determining what wasn't easy.

Confounding the Blues

One of the great challenges in studying cultural texts is how to confront and confound the overt and latent structures, themes, and ideologies embedded in our ways of thinking, living, and imagining them. It's probably obvious to say that through sustained rather than short-lived encounters with various cultural *texts* we might have a better chance of promoting multiple rather than essentialist readings. But in the need for coverage, we may hurry our way in practice toward a less than careful reading of these texts. We make too easy what is hard. In a way, I am attempting pedagogically to represent some version of the concept of *heteroglossia* which Bakhtin (1981) has described as

> specific points of view of the world, forms for conceptualizing the world in words, specific world views, each characterized by its own objects, meanings, and values. As such they all may be juxtaposed to one another, mutually supplement one another, contradict one another and be interrelated dialogically (pp. 291–292).

The web of understanding remains incomplete but spun more intricately through multiple viewpoints. This, of course, is what I think the study of cultural text in multicultural education needs to be about—transcending one-dimensional, objectified histories, art forms, or human beings. Obviously, the blues is not the only text which has the potential for transcendence through multiple interpretations, but I offer this as an example.

As a class, then, we agreed it would be productive to engage in an extended examination of the blues as a racial, musical, and cultural manifestation of more than individual performers, particular songs, political or ideological discourses, and arguments about who can learn the blues and who can't. Through such a sustained encounter, we hoped to ground our questions, confront our tensions, and construct meaningful discourses about the issues of our cultural confusions and comfortable trust in the Janus head of binary opposition. For me, it became an opportunity to examine a concrete form of the complex processes of articulation, negotiation, and invention that characterize the dialogics of culture that I was attempting to work out theoretically and pedagogically. We devoted the next several weeks in this course to the study of ourselves as we studied the blues.

In the earlier part of the semester we had discussed and read examples of injustice and inequality in schools and classrooms. We'd interrogated autobiographical accounts and considered how classroom practices affirm or deny difference. We'd even described our own political agenda and agreed heartily to disagree. When the blues overtook us, we began again. Reading Houston Baker (1984) got us started. For him, a study of the blues involved

> a willingness on my own part to do more than merely hear, read or see the blues. I must also play (with and on) them. Since the explanatory possibilities of a blues matrix—like analytical possibilities of a delimited set of forces in unified field theory—are hypothetically unbounded, the blues challenge investigative understanding to an unlimited play (pp. 10–11).

We took ourselves less seriously when we thought of unlimited play. In some ways Baker set the tone of our exploration. Once we stood back to see what was happening, we made an attempt to understand the space of difference through our willingness to do more than hear, read, or see the blues. We learned to play (with and on) them.

The implications for me as a teacher were multiple, but I'd suggest at least two facets of particular promise. First, I learned to focus on moments when it is worthwhile to stop the flow of rhetoric and forward movement and to read, meditate on, write about and keep the dialogic between the perennial text and its ever changing readings. Second, this study of the blues became a discursive space in which I set aside my predetermined curricular agenda to create real curriculum from the very flow and demands of what was happening in the classroom. Pedagogically, we tried to imagine how to structure a study that would illustrate how layer on layer of meaning, as multiple readings were produced, might create an ever-varying text. Through the search itself, through the ever-changing narrative of what we were learning and questioning, we examined our ideologies and challenged our common and differing experiences, beliefs, and interpretations. None of this proved easy to implement nor is it particularly easy to explain.

Narratives of Partiality

The working title of this section is meant to suggest that a study of the blues or of any cultural text is both partial to aspects of the text under consideration and represents only limited aspects of the possible content or approaches that are available. Obviously what texts were studied and how these were analyzed, as well as what I've chosen to report here, represent only my interpretation of what transpired. The students would have some twenty-eight other narratives of the experience to tell.

The class divided into four groups, and each group selected particular aspects of the blues that they chose to study. They did not reveal the particular focus of their study to other class members until they began presenting. Each week, during five subsequent class sessions, *every* group presented some facet of their study. It was the job of each group to represent the complexities of their learning for their classmates. During each class meeting, multifaceted aspects of blues-as-a-text within and between groups, layer overlapping layers, offered multiple perspectives and linked various aspects of the blues into a web of meaning. The hope, at least, was to create a representation of the differential play of how knowledge of the blues was being constructed.

Readings from Group 1: Beyond Sacralized Origins

This group began with a question: What are the varying explanations of blues' origins? They discovered that many anthropologists and folklorists give partial answers to this question but have not come to a singular understanding. Their examination revealed a profusion of regional styles, a gradual absorption of one style into other performance styles, and a reassertion of specific folk practices into new locales. In their first presentation to the class, they described how context shapes explanations of origins. As Bakhtin (1986) suggests, "Even *past* meanings, that is, those born in the dialogue of past centuries, can never be stable (finalized, ended once and for all)—they will always change (be renewed) in the process of subsequent, future development of the dialogue" (p. 170). The group divided their original seven members into subgroups to present the positions from various disciplines. To make the idea of context clear, the group presented explanations of origins from various perspectives—that is, from a black music historian's search for beginnings, a cultural critic who concentrated on the role of record label production, a sociologist's view of the "need" for blues, and a music theorist's discussion of innovation. They gave us layer on layer of explanation to demonstrate contradictory, complementary, and diverse interpretations. In each of their weekly presentations, the group provided one explanation after another of origins. As Robert suggested during their first presentation:

> First, we just wanted to find out where the blues had come from. Many of us had our own agendas. Clyde, for example, wanted to show the influence of white southerners on the blues. I wanted to say it was really a black form co-opted by whites, and some people didn't have an opinion. When we got into the study, we realized that we had things we wanted to prove, so we're reminding each other of that as we go along. It's hard though. It's easier to remind someone else than be reminded yourself.

As they worked together, they helped each other look for multiple interpretations to complicate their habit of searching for answers and certainty. As Anika, one of the student teachers in the class, wrote in her journal:

> Learning through reading or listening to other group members, trying to keep an open mind—these are things I'm thinking are obligations that I have to really learn about a subject deeply. Teaching entails handling cultural products with integrity and making a dialogue out of more rather than less. This experience helps me think about how I might teach.

The group did not engage in a genealogical reading in the Nietzschean (1883–91/1961) sense of origins—mapping roots and main shifts (pp. 142–144). Rather, their reading focused on the multiple perspectives of the blues' genesis and mutability. Although this reading contained sociohistorical components as part of the meaning implied by roots, it extended such an examination to include the ideological functions in the generative as well as interpretive practices. For example, they reported more than a singular search for origins (for some of these students, the idea of origin is equivalent to ownership) to a more diffused search for the cultural and material forces that sustain or nourish the perpetuation and mutation of blues (i.e. using definitions of *root* in Webster's to include: to plant, impress, establish, uncover, rummage or be a vital part of).

One subgroup examined folk blues, concentrating on interpretation of melody lines, instrumental figures, and song lyrics from local traditions (Evans, 1982; Ferris, 1978; Dixon, 1989; Palmer, 1981). They studied written accounts of rural or small town folk blues as well as compiled oral histories with musicians or fans who lived in New York City. They listened to retrospective collections and examined explanations of folk processes—how the folk blues were learned, transmitted, and recomposed. They shared various versions of this material with the class each week and concentrated on pointing out the complicated configurations within the word *origin* itself.

Another subgroup looked more closely at the form and content of the blues as it has been influenced by the urban context (Keil, 1991). They examined prevailing conventions in popular taste to determine how dependence on radio stations, clubs, and record companies control issues of production. During their presentations to the class, they shared various interpretations on these issues as well as their own reactions and what they were understanding about their own site of study in comparison with what other groups were sharing with them.

Another subgroup considered roots of a different kind. They examined source material for the lyrics. Eddie House (1965), a Mississippi blues singer, states:

> People wonder a lot about where the blues came from. Well, when I was coming up, people did more singing in the fields than they did anywhere else. Time they got to the field, they'd start singing some kind of old song. Tell his ol' mule, "Giddup there!" and he'd go off behind the mule, start plowing and start a song (p. 45).

Origins in this version were interpreted as an artistic outlet, a cathartic moment meant to ease the burden. What this subgroup discovered was an age-old explanation of art as a form of emotional release. They shared evidence to support how influential the Delta blues were on the Rolling Stones, Bob Dylan, Eric Clapton down to the metal or glass slides on their fingers (Ferris, 1978). Behind the overt connections, themes such as lamentation, survival in the struggles of daily life, and hopes for a better future paved the way for rhythm and blues.

This group's many readings over a five-week period did not provide a definitive answer to origins, but each of their versions on origins jarred an essentialist reading. During the weeks of this study, it became increasingly clear that one of the major difficulties in understanding the blues is the sheer quantity and variety of the expressions within shifting situational contexts. Group members articulated aspects of controversies—the paths and meaning of development, the psyche and referents behind the lyrics, and the contested borders musically, artistically, and economically. In their last presentation, Jewel reflected on what she had learned through the group's work. "I see why it becomes simplified—it takes so much time to make issues complex and to present multiple perspectives." Carrie, one of the first year teachers in the class, suggested, "Students rebel at uncertainty. They want answers. I think it will take re-educating them and me. We need to unlearn much of the learning process we've been involved in."

One subgroup who examined African roots found the lessons learned by one researcher appropriate to the search they were undertaking. Samuel Charters traveled to West Africa to find the roots of the blues. Although he believed that the blues sprang from the complex cultural period of slavery in the United States along with harmonic forms and instrumental styles derived from the European context, he suggested that certain elements in the singing style and rhythmic structures might have their genesis in the distantly remembered African background. He speculated that the West African griots were the closest to the blues singers. The subsequent journey, beginning in February 1974, is described in *The Roots of the Blues*. Charters (1981) attempted "to find traces of an *experience*, and not only that, I was looking for traces of an experience that had occurred hundreds of years before" (p. 2). As with any search, his was a complicated one. When he first heard the music of Jali Nyama (*nayama*, the singer) in the city of Banjul, Charters was surprised how little the music sounded like the blues in rhythm, harmony, melodic figures, and the lyrics (sung in Mandingo). Yet, Charters heard overtones of mood and style that seemed related to the blues.

The subgroup demonstrated the complexity of his search. Charters became interested in a small, 5-string banjo, the halam. The instrument had the "bright jangling sound of the southern banjo" (p. 60). Charters noted that the player, Camara, used a finger pick and placed it on the top of the nail and used it on the downstroke, just as the banjo players do today in Kentucky and Virginia. I was seeing something that had a clear connection with the United States, but this time, ironically, it was something associated now with white musicians in the South. The instrument had been adopted by whites as part of their impersonations of blacks in the minstrel shows, and in the rural areas whites had learned much of the early banjo techniques . . . from their black neighbors (p. 60).

Through the entire journey Charters found elusive little fragments—similarities in the style of singing, of rhythmic figures, of texturing of voice and accompanying rhythm. At the end what Charters described is inherently interesting to a study of cultural texts:

I had come to Africa to find a kind of song, to find a kind of music and the people who performed it. But nothing can be taken from a culture without considering its context. . . . The journey I'd begun had taken me to places I hadn't expected, and the ideas and attitudes I had at the end of it were different from where I'd started. . . . It was these things I had to carry along with me, along with the tapes and notes in my bag (p. 150).

Layers upon layers of what all of the groups were discovering about the blues led us to recognize, as had Charters before us, that our study was a rudimentary and preliminary investigation with much left unexplored and unexplained. What was centrally important for me was that we had begun to see the strenuous effort it takes to examine a cultural text. Bakhtin's (1986) conception of unconstrained dialogism has important implications for such study:

At any moment in the development of the dialogue there are immense, boundless masses of forgotten contextual meanings, but at certain moments of the dialogue's subsequent development along the way they are recalled and invigorated in renewed form (in a new context). Nothing is absolutely dead: every new meaning will have its homecoming festival (p. 170).

This group, then, began to unearth the contextual meanings and the invigorated forms of the blues for the rest of us.

Reading #2: Living in the Landscape of Multiple Consciousness

The second group set out to fathom the complexities of those who created the music. They began by sharing excerpts from Du Bois's (1903/1961) description of double consciousness:

It is a peculiar sensation, this double-consciousness, this sense of always looking at one's self through the eyes of others, of measuring one's soul by the tape of a world that looks on in amused contempt and pity. One ever feels his two-ness,—an American, a Negro; two souls, two thoughts, two unreconciled strivings; two warring ideals in one dark body . . . to merge his double self into a better and truer self. In this merging he wishes neither of the older selves to be lost (pp. 16–17).

The group described how they began their examination using the concept of alterity as a point of entry into the alternative visions not only between the inner and outer world or among diverse people, but also the contours of difference within a person. This group examined how the lyrics of blues disclose the paradoxes of living in landscapes of divergent needs and of recognizing passions and contradictions that exist for individuals.

One subgroup presented versions of the purposes and techniques through which blues singers shape their multivocal identities. During their series of presentations they demonstrated various forms of alterity, that is, in the form of seeing oneself seeing. One subgroup examined the trope of doubleness as an exemplification of displacement—in effect, a shuttling between center and margins. From the Delta jump-ups to Mager Johnson's songs, lyrics contained expressions of leaving: "I'm a traveling man," and because life is difficult, the singer laments, he has traveling on his mind. He plans to buy a train ticket and follow the tracks to a place that may promise a better future (Evans, 1982, p. 229). As James McPherson (1976) writes, the train was an image of promise that

> might have been loud and frightening, but its whistle and its wheels promised movement. And since a commitment to both freedom and movement was the basic promise of democracy, it was probable that such people would view the locomotive as a challenge to the integrative powers of their imaginations (p. 6).

This subgroup played a variety of blues songs each week and asked class members for their readings of the lyrics. As Eliza wrote in her journal:

> I began hearing what Gates defines as signifying practices in these songs—particularly the figure of the double-voice. In the songs there is a blurring or reconfiguation of prior and subsequent meaning. I can't explain it yet, but the tropes shift and change, reminding me that what happens in a blues song is a manifestation of the contradictory consciousness that is buried deep within each of us.

The effects of displacement as detailed in blues lyrics was noted by another subgroup who saw conflict between lovers or spouses, separation from a religious life, or lack of hope for a better future. Students discovered persistent acknowledgment of oppositional and contradictory worlds in lyrics. They presented lyrics of many songs that forecast the break up of relationships: "I'm goin' away sweet mama," the singer announces to get his woman off his mind and end his worries (Oliver, 1968, p. 90). As they played various songs, class members identified a variety of tensions between the secular and sacred life, ranging from mild cynicism to rage about the ineffectiveness of the preacher or church to alleviate the suffering encountered in life. The subgroup shared lyrics that suggest that the temptations for the secular life are too great to be ignored: "I bow down to pray," but, the singer counters, the blues overtook that mood as did women and whiskey (Oliver, 1968, p. 47). Some class members suggested, however, that the blues are not solely about the lack of hope. As Grace suggested: "Within the lyrics is a love of life, an energy of living. I see a powerful presence of joy and a passion for living." David, on the other hand, found themes of contradiction, such as "leaving and returning and the tensions between wanting to feel joy and the fear that feeling that joy will lead to its loss."

An equally compelling argument was made for continuity—the desire to reestablish relationship, and the impulse to return home. The subgroup began one presentation with a song recorded by Bumble Bee Slim: "I had so much trouble" that, the singer suggested, his nerves were wearing down. He considers hitching a ride on the train to escape but expresses his fear of leaving. He revels in his indecisiveness (Oliver, 1990, p. 60). The subgroup demonstrated through several songs the many contours of meaning told in blues lyrics—singers aware of the possibilities and limitations, of rewards and liabilities, and of leavings and homecomings. As this subgroup acknowledged, variety and dissonance are not necessarily contradictory. This was what I couldn't have expected but was hoping for—a reading of cultural texts that provoked students to reach beyond their assumptions and their experiences and to take heed of others' constructed lives. As Sarah, a first year teacher, acknowledged,

> I am feeling a commitment to remind my students of the mystery below the surface of what other people create. It isn't just the song, the novel, or the painting, it's the beliefs, the yearnings, the numerous frailties that are some of what lie beneath.

As this group proceeded with their study of lyrics, they discovered submerged themes that masked or signified political activism and hostility. What they were reading, buried within many of the same lyrics they had studied earlier, were messages of resistance. The group shared a recording of the song "Strange Fruit." The singer introduces a contention that southern poplar trees bear a strange fruit, a fruit composed of black bodies hanging in trees whose leaves and roots are blood-soaked (White, 1966, p. 55). The group suggested that the song contains a powerful protest image that is not uncommon in the lyrics of blues. Messages housed in many such songs are reminders of the repression and subsequent resistance. These messages need to be taken into account and studied for what they reveal about past as well as current oppression. There were some uncomfortable silences as this song was discussed with the entire class although three people in the group recognized the image of lynching. As Larry Neal (1989) stated, "Behind the lyrics of the blues and the shuffling porter loom visions of white throats being cut and cities burning" (p. 72). The class did not venture into this area for discussion, possibly holding in abeyance their unspoken or contradictory feelings about the deep injustices and seething hatred that somehow they felt implicated in. Whatever the motivations, the class was not ready to tackle this particular aspect of what had been uncovered. I do think that when Bakhtin, living in the Stalinist period with its own versions of appropriation and politicization of cultural texts, described verbal subterfuge and masking as forms of resistance, he understood a version of how cultural production finds ways to cover up purposes and identities while probing beneath the surface appearances in the subterranean edges (Gardiner, 1992). After an uneasy silence, the subgroup presented several examples of songs that served as a reminder of the hope for a better future and the impossibility of better times, of defiance or endurance, of concealment and discretion—all the paradoxes and complexities that reflect what is at work in a cultural text. As one singer warns: "You better be smart," you better make the right moves, and not protest loudly or you will surely have trouble with those in power (Nash, 1969, p. 44).

This group stated that they hoped to help other members of the class read the messages in the lyrics more carefully and confront examples that demonstrate how multiple texts can rupture our retreat into a singular reading. They shared excerpts from some of Cone's work (1972) in which he suggests that it is necessary to view the blues from the perspective of black people's attempt to survive in a very hostile white society. The blues are not political treatises, and neither are they radical statements on social revolution. . . . The blues are statements of and for black people who are condemned to live in a extreme situation of oppression without any political leverage for defining their existence (p. 119).

Margarita, one of the veteran teachers, added,

> I am moved by the metaphors and images in blues to recognize the brutal savagery of marginalization and create a metaphor for myself. The silence of marginalization is a low moan, an interrupted howl, and a long note of yearning. I have examples of this from my own culture that I could add to this, but I wonder how other people in the class would react to me making an assumption that the cultures are somehow similar.

The problem with what Margarita suggested is that it could be viewed as a strategy of containment, a way of minimizing cultural difference although this, of course, was not her intention. But, she said, for the first time she understood how someone else might interpret it to be that.

This group found it important to emphasize the dialogic between experience and expression. For example, one subgroup presented how the trope of dualism may have contributed to stereotyping as the blues became popularized and distributed in mass media through records and live performances with large audiences. They suggested that a blues singer's message can, both explicitly and implicitly, create a metonymic displacement wherein the message represents the reality, in beliefs and actions, of black people's motivations and lives. The lyric as expression blurs with the lived life of people. One group member suggested that not only whites but blacks may be taken in by such stereotyping. The lyrics often contain messages that represent people who are driven by drink, promiscuity, and anger. Charlie Patton, for example, in "Elder Green Blues," sings that he likes to fight, get sloppy drunk, "ball" and "walk the streets all night" (Palmer, 1981, p. 70). Song after song reinforced the message. The artistic and idiosyncratic yearnings get dangerously muddled in a representational ground that blurs artistic expression with the lived experience of blacks. Whether to forget their troubles, create distance for catharsis, or to mask complaint, the blues singers communicate a representation of black identity.

The subgroup grappled with the concept of the double voice that is evident in the signifying practices within the lyrics as well as the music. They distributed excerpts from Gates (1988) who defines it: "Signifyin(g) is the figure of the double-voiced" (p. xxv). He identifies four types of double-voiced relation: a trope repeated with differences, oral narration, talk between one black text and another(s), and refiguration (pp. xxv-xxvii). These types reminded the group that we had read earlier in the semester a similar idea in Bakhtin (1986), who described the double-voiced utterance (both word and discourse) of signification as the process of inserting new meaning into an utterance that carries prior meaning. Margarita shared Geneva Smitherman's (1977) delineation of the rhetorical strategies in signification. Among them are: indirection, metaphorical/imagistic/rhythmic language, humor, and irony, often in the form of puns (p. 121). Themes work in contrasting pairs: leaving and returning; self-pity and boasting; abuse and praise. The dialogic between contrasting pairs has its effect. Take a song like "Baby, You Sho' Lookin' Warm" (Evans, 1982, p. 50). The woman's pleasant appearance is contrasted with the condition of the singer, who is shabby, feeling tired and fearful that he will fail. The singer's intention of leaving to improve his lot in life contrasts with the woman who has already left. Form, style, and content serve to create contrasts and tensions. Rhythmic tensions and uncertainties emphasize the underlying ambiguity and compactness that is supported by the call-and-response pattern and contrasting images.

In this particular segment of their discussion, they played various songs in class, noting how in the blues, signifying turns audience expectation on itself. Some of the music they shared led others in the class to note the following principles in blues:

(1) Incongruence exists between what the listener expects and what the singer or instrumentalist delivers.

(2) The upbeat is played into the downbeat. The downbeat exists in the silence rather than the sound, working oppositionally to expectation. Expectations in form and key are made elastic, stretched nearly beyond recognition.

(3) Ambiguity exists between major and minor harmonies.

(4) Structural regularities are easily identified—three call-and-response sections in common time, twelve bars, and regular rhyme schemes.

(5) There is a near double dialogic at play—every sung or spoken phrase is balanced or connected by an instrumental response.

(6) Blue notes sound misleading, flatted on the third and seventh, not quite where our expectations would lead us. It's like playing the notes on a piano in the cracks of the keys.

(7) The relentless repetition of phrases in novel combinations reinforces the statements and counter-statements.

As they ended, this subgroup reminded the rest of the class that signifying disappoints expectations. Pointing to the seven principles they had just listed on the board, Rachael reminded us all that this was a partial rendering and not always an accurate one. She described her own reading as one where tension is the overall effect achieved. She stated that she'd discovered that underlying rhythm and harmonic structures result in a counter-tension produced by indirection. She discovered some devices used to distort or mirror expectations: the use of caesuras (breaks), talking the story, repetition of melody or lyric with variation, refiguration or blending of one piece with others, and use of rhetorical tropes (metaphor, metonymy, and irony). When the expectations are thwarted, Rachael questioned, "Are signifying practices going on? I can't always tell and I feel like I'm supposed to know. Maybe it's something I can't experience from this particular music. I'm not sure." Sean, a member of another group, jumped into the conversation:

> I was reading last night about signifying. We're looking at it in literature but it seems connected. I started to think about signifying as a veiled persuasion. I understand that in terms of what you are saying about tension and not understanding fully what lurks underneath. I don't think that is about being from a different culture. I would think that might be true even if you know the blues well. It seems to be the point.

Another subgroup interviewed blues singers, and listened to song after song now recorded on shiny silver CDs that belie the origins of these folk songs. Throughout this group's study, they tried to represent the range in moods, themes, and aesthetic practices that spoke to them across cultural, racial, ideological, and musical distances. Although multiple readings cause confusion by the innumerable variants, as with the bending and flattening of notes in a blues song, these can help portray the complexities of entering another's world. This group's readings presented the rest of the class with a concrete enactment of how ideology shapes and influences both the production and reading of cultural texts, of the processes that support or thwart that production and reading.

Reading #3: On Men and Women

The third group grappled with what the lyrics suggest about sexual explicitness and the politics of gender. Group members questioned from the beginning whether or not the songs perpetuated representations of gender in negative ways. Many group members reacted angrily to what they perceived as violence toward women. "How," Patrice asked, "can there be a normal, respectful relationship when women are fantasized about through violent acts?" Others felt their sensibilities were challenged. As Jim suggested, "I get put off by all the explicit sex, I've always thought sex was a private act, not for public display. In these songs, it's like a celebration sometimes and then I see denigration as well. It's confusing." A few questioned whether or not such lyrics promote and perpetuate inequality and in some cases brutality toward women. One young woman informed us that she was

> offended. How could women listen let alone sing some of this garbage? It belittles women and men too. There's no real feeling. I guess it's like this is the alternative if you're frightened to give anything of yourself for fear of getting hurt.

Group members tried to name some of the assumptions that may have caused their classmates' reactions.

The group found that the subject matter of the blues often deals with the frustrations as well as the exhilaration of love. The lyrics contain imagery rich in the erotic, boastful accounts of sexual prowess, and laments about the misunderstandings associated with infidelity and disintegrating relationships. There is a female singer lamenting about always being kicked and dogged by her man, but she goes on to lament that she can't get him off her mind (Smith, 1928). And a male singer boasting that he "roots everywhere I go" (Williams, 1937). Often the lyrics have been interpreted as a pornographic boasting about sexual exploits. For example, in the song "Spike Driver Blues," the singer boasts that his "spike it never bent" and of his prowess in conquest, technique, and frequency (Darby, 1937). The group presented several examples of these songs and described how they thought the overt sexual casualness encouraged representations of women as sex kittens or victims. However, some members of the group interpreted this differently. They shared lyrics which they believed may portray some preoccupations with sexual acts and male/female relationships, but these, they suggested, represent an imagined rather than a lived life. "Possibly," Yolanda suggested, "representations of mating and lovemaking may suggest stereotypes rather than reality." However, this was an issue that did not elicit agreement. Many group members and other classmates felt that such images do inform or construct reality.

Some of the questions that this group brought to the entire class were: What is the relationship between reality and representation? How do our ideological and moral stances influence our readings? How have these issues been dealt with in the textual criticism on the blues? What are the reactions of contemporary black feminists to the lyrics of the blues? They undertook a reading of the discourse on gender represented in the lyrics and critical commentary written about the lyrics.

One subgroup compiled material that suggested how the conditions black males faced resulted in a powerlessness that may have influenced what the students described as sexist behavior. Unemployment, low paying jobs, and racism may have encouraged violence toward women. As Oliver (1968) suggests,

> This projection of the self-image in the blues is sexual fantasy which has its parallels in pornographic invention. In blues songs the dream world of sexual mastery is realized and the realities of racial oppression are side-stepped. The power-seeking manifestations of masculinity in an Adlerian sense are denied most Negroes and are expressed instead through aggressive sexual fantasies. . . . Such expressions of unreasoning violence are sung as humorous songs, but the humour is chillingly grim (p. 255).

This group examined images of sexual oppression. They found expressions of women from slave days that encouraged stereotypical images of black women as concubines, conjurers, breeders, and property. While a black male-defined ethos equated manhood to sexual prowess, the male was powerless in most areas of his life, leading him to seek out ways to feel in control.

Black women became a cultural construct through which that power was exerted. As civil rights activist Septima Clark stated: "I found all over the South that whatever the man said had to be right. They had the whole say. The woman couldn't say a thing" (Clark as quoted in Brown, 1986, p. 79). Several of these teachers felt that this particular argument decenters females, undermining their identity and allowing their identities and bodies to be usurped because of the sympathy for the male's struggle for power. Yolanda quoted bell hooks (1990) to support this perspective:

Feeling as though they are constantly on edge, their lives always in jeopardy, many black men truly cannot understand that this condition of "powerlessness" does not negate their capacity to assert power over black females in a way that is dominating and oppressive; nor does it justify and condone sexist behavior (p. 74).

Another subgroup found that the women singers perpetuate sexual explicitness themselves. In many versions of "Kitchen Man Blues," appreciation for a man's jelly roll received several stanzas of elaboration that conclude with the singer's recognition that she just can't live without her man (Martin, 1928). Other renderings of the woman's pleasure with a man's prowess can be found in various versions of "My Man O' War." Images of big artillery, bullets, and hitting the mark figuratively describe the sexual act (Miles, 1930). Group members grappled with this new information and questioned again whether or not the tensions between men and women that might be distorted in the *expression* are true to the *actual experience* of black men and women. They focused for a time on what women blues singers revealed about their feelings toward males in the images created and in the relationships described. Was such sexual play an adopted stance, a male way of seeing and believing? Was it necessary for women who were to have a voice as blues singers to adopt this stance as well? They described the social and cultural codes through which gender has been interrogated, suggesting that part of the reactions to the gender politics might be anachronistic. But Thelma, one of the student teachers, objected to this idea, indicating that in the class where she was teaching, "these adolescents need to get in touch with their histories and see how those histories have changed and need to change. It isn't right to say anything like this was acceptable in another time and place." The debate continued and various class members continued to challenge one another on this point. Much to the frustration of some, they came to realize that there was no institutional authority, no definitive text that could *give* them answers.

Attempting to look at the issues more closely, members of one subgroup interviewed blues singers and presented their findings to the class. One male singer suggested: "So many songs are about escape from pain. And that's primarily a male thing. Women, well, they take a beatin' because of male impotence in the career area." Another said: "The blues are the way out and a way into identity. It's mostly messing around with a feeling and not to be taken seriously. It's the performance that counts." A third, the only woman, reflected: "Maybe it's just playfulness, these songs. That's the way I feel about it when I'm singing. It's not real life—just like movies—it's playful and sexy." Maybe, some members of this subgroup suggested, there is a common understanding between men and women about the vivid ways of describing sexual politics.

Some group members focused on how standard verses and phrases were passed from singer to singer and singer to audience. Blues singers possessed a large reservoir of traditional blues verses that they used for improvisation. Do such representations of sexuality get passed along in the verses and phrases? The history of the form grows within and outside of the community, carrying with it messages that are continuously reshaped and reformed. Do the lyrics exaggerate fantasies as a way to regulate behavior, release tension, or bring catharsis? The lyrics might be considered outlets that channel expressions that would otherwise remain unspoken. As group members explored this with the rest of the class, they asked: Is it possible that the lyrics focus not only on another person but on the identification of otherness in self? Consciousness of a gendered self as well as a gendered other constructed in society forms a dialogic link between self and society. Bakhtin suggested that the "processes that basically define the content of the psyche occur not inside but outside the individual organism" (Voloshinov, 1973, p. 39). Bakhtin explains further the "internalization of the voices a person has heard, and each of these voices is saturated with social ideological values . . . retaining the full register of conflicting social values" (Bakhtin as quoted in Morson, 1986, p. 85). As a class, we interpreted the lyrics as one example of gendered representation within a social dialectic existing as part of a complex historical, social, and cultural text of sexual politics. The group engaged other class members in various explorations of this theme in each successive presentation over the five weeks.

The group discovered that no simple representation or answers exist. While they found women oppressed in some ways, they also discovered that the social function of blues, whether to cope with or transcend the conditions, served to solidify black women. Black women singers achieved a central place in the blues tradition. As Michele Russell (1982) pointed out, the "blues, first and last, are a familiar idiom for Black women, even a staple of life" (p. 130). For some feminists, these women singers defined their identities, analyzed their lives, and took possession of their future through the music (Collins, 1990). Viewed in this way, many of the lyrics suggest acceptance of womanhood and a spirit of independence. Consider, for example, Bessie Smith's "Cadillac Man." She laments that her man, once a Cadillac and now a worn out Ford, has never supported her. Although she gave him room and board for fifteen years, she plans to change things (Russell, 1982, p. 133). As Jamal, a second year teacher, commented,

> The black females in my eleventh grade class have great trust in themselves as shapers of tradition and art. They've read Morrison, Walker, McMillan, and Hurston. They take pride in the strength of these women. My adolescent girls have models now because we "allow" black women writer's voices to be heard.

These perspectives on gendered relations demonstrate the instability of meaning and interpretation. Analyzing the specifics, as we did in our study, allowed us to examine the controlling images and ways of interpreting the complex relationships, as represented in the lyrics, between men and women. Some songs objectified women as Other; other lyrics illustrated the fierce independence and control that women exerted over their lives. We discovered that each interpretation revealed other angles of vision through which to examine the meaning of the lyrics. Each partial perspective represents one aspect of multiple and competing understandings. Working in this way, members of the class suggested that they were learning to, as Regina stated, "listen and hear. I am more tolerant of learning from the experience rather than trying to judge or validate it based on my needs to judge or compare someone's beliefs and assumptions with mine." Jamal added, "It's just difficult to accept that there isn't an answer. No matter how many perspectives we study, these don't make a whole." Jamal and his classmates reminded me of what Alice Walker (1983) had to say about how we might open our minds to really listen:

> What is always needed in the appreciation of art or life, is the larger perspective. Connections made, or at least attempted, where none existed before, the straining to encompass in one's glance at the varied world the common thread, the unifying theme through immense diversity (p. 5).

Reading #4: "Your Blues Ain't Like Mine"

Lily woke up when the singing began. She lay quiet and still in her bed until her head was full of songs and the strong voices of the fieldworkers from the Pinochet Plantation seemed to be inside her. Part of the song was soft like a hymn; then it would rise to the full force of vibrant gospel and change again to something loud and searing, almost violent. The music was rich, like the alluvial soil that nourished everything and everyone in the Delta. Lily began

to feel strong and hopeful, as if she was being healed. Colored people's singing always made her feel so good (Campbell, 1992, p. 9).

The fourth group read African American literature as a way of studying the blues and brought to their class presentations various excerpts
demonstrating how blues form and themes penetrate African American literature in very individual and distinct ways. They read Ellison's
Invisible Man or Hurston's *Their Eyes Were Watching God*, mixed
in Arthur Flowers's *De Mojo Blues* and *Another Good Loving Blues*,
added Campbell's *Your Blues Ain't Like Mine*, poems, and short
stories that demonstrate the interpenetration of cultural texts across
genre and form. They illustrated through their presentations how the
blues provided technique, story, and structure for many black writers.
Sherley Williams's poetry shows the influence of blues improvisation.
Jean Toomer's incremental use of repetition functions in ways that
emphasize the contradictory world in which Kabnis will achieve manhood. And who can forget Ann Petry's (1966) "Solo on the Drums"?
When Kid Jones looks at the marquee and sees his name, it is a
moment that clarifies the blues theme of naming as an assertion of
identity:

> His name was picked out in lights on the marquee. The name of the orchestra
> and then his name underneath by itself. There would have been a time when
> he would have been excited by it. And stopped to let his mind and his eyes
> linger over it lovingly. Kid Jones. The name—his name—up there in lights that
> danced and winked in the brassy sunlight (p. 165).

The group reminded us that Ralph Ellison (1966) valued folk culture as a powerful vehicle for understanding the character of a group.
He believed that folklore illustrated "the first drawing of any group's
character" in which we see the "boundaries of feeling, thought and
action which that particular group has found to be the limitation of
the human condition" (p. 172). And there was the black poet Sterling
Brown, who travelled throughout the South to discover the folk. He
studied the traditional as a repository of historical, social, and psychological portrayals of the contemporary. Add to the list Langston
Hughes's poetry for its reliance on the meter and the irony of the
blues. Or, Wright's Bigger Thomas as a characterization from black
folk balladry and the physical and spiritual violence that is acknowledged. The recurrent themes, tropes, and practices come back to sound
again in contemporary cultural texts. And so it is that the material of
triumphs of the human spirit, tragedies of the most sinister kind, love

and loss, catastrophe and bounty continue to be themes growing into a network that preserves and extends itself.

This group presented to the class examples of the intertextuality in theme and the transformation of technique from music into language. The list goes on, but as a class we began to recognize the intertextuality in theme and the transformation of technique from music into language. As Houston Baker (1984) suggests:

> By writing experience in native (read: blues) as opposed to literary language, Afro-American writers have accomplished the American task of journeying from mastered existence to independent, national form. The subtle, parodic, inversive, complexly reflexive blues texts of black writers testify to the vitality of an Afro-American matrix as they fulfill the longstanding dream of an American Form (p. 114).

This fourth group highlighted an interdependent set of practices and discourses within the blues (related to historical, social, or political contexts) as an example of the larger formation of cultural texts of black identity.

The purpose of this group's presentations was to illustrate to their classmates examples of how to decenter the blues from the musical text and to gain some understanding of technique linked to other cultural aesthetic practices. They brought a quote from Toni Morrison (1984) to frame their last presentation. The quote highlighted what many of us had struggled to understand and to say:

> One of the major characteristics of black art is the ability to be both print and oral literature: to combine those two aspects so that the stories can be read in silence, of course, but one should be able to hear them as well. It should try deliberately to make you stand up and make you feel something profoundly in the same way that a Black preacher requires his congregation to speak, to join him in the sermon, to behave in a certain way, to stand up and to weep and to cry and to accede or to change and to modify—to expand on the sermon that is being delivered. In the same way that a musician's music is enhanced when there is a response from the audience. . . . Because it is the affective and participatory relationship between the artist or the speaker and the audience that is of primary importance (p. 341).

This group suggested that as teachers they were interested in involving their students in cultural studies, decentering (moving from genre to genre) reading to demonstrate the complexities.

For the teachers and prospective teachers in this class, experiencing multiplicity across genre extended the learning. In coming to recognize that while "your blues ain't like mine" (Campbell, 1992), each of us, with the help of the musicians as well as writers, learned that the versions of blues are part of a building dialogue. As the group presented, I was reminded of what Maxine Greene (1993) has taught us:

> There can only be an ongoing, collaborative decoding of many texts. There can only be a conversation drawing in voices kept inaudible over generations, a dialogue involving more and more living persons. There can only be—there ought to be—a wider and deeper sharing of beliefs, an enhanced capacity to articulate them, to justify them, to persuade others, as the heteroglossic conversation moves on, never reaching a final conclusion, always incomplete, but richer and more densely woven, even as it moves through time (p. 213).

I believe that considering how the blues informed African American literature opened new perspectives on the interplay among cultural texts for all of us. And, behind the intellectualizing of cultural studies, the group who brought the literature to us helped us pay heed to what it means to be human and humane in ways that rupture essentialist understandings.

And I wonder whether the curricula we can create can be of a kind that will help us care for and wonder about the music we sing and the stories we write? This brings me back to where I began this last reading—to Bebe Campbell's (1992) *Your Blues Ain't Like Mine*. Beginning as it does with Lily's longing for song and the vanishing echo of its presence in the Mississippi morning, so it ends. Confronting the contradictions of death and new life, celebration and revulsion of the past, and the desire to touch again and to share the meaning of his origins, Wydell takes his young son back to where he was raised and where in many ways this story began and was played out:

> Wydell stopped the car in front of a settlement of run-down shacks, most of which appeared to be empty. He said, "This is where me and your mother is from. This is where your brother got killed. I thought you ought to see it one time in your life, just so you'd know. . . . You see all that water? Well, it used to be nothing but cotton, and before the machines come, black folks picked that cotton. Me and your mama and your grandparents, your aunties and uncles, we all picked that cotton. We picked that cotton until our fingers bled. And sometimes when it would get bad—and boy, it could get real bad—we'd be in them fields just a-singing, you know. 'Cause them songs, them songs could get you right. . . ." W. T. hesitated for a moment, and then he reached across to his father and wrapped his fingers around his thick wrist. He said, "Dad. What did you useta sing?" (Campbell, 1992, pp. 331–332).

The impulse to share culture and the equal impulse to learn it.

Antagonizing the Discursive Boundaries

And back to the original question: Can a young Jewish woman from Park Slope understand the blues? An answer to this question became less important as we continued our study. However, as Joel Rudinow (1994) has suggested, this tradition of claiming expressive authenticity goes "to the heart of the contemporary debate over multi-culturalism, the canon, and the curriculum" (p. 127). New readings unsettle and sustain traditions. What I learned was how difficult it is in writing to adequately represent the complexity of both the themes of the groups' readings, the interactions that occurred between and among groups, or to effectively model in the text anything other than the linear version.

The pedagogical practice of juxtaposing or layering required that the entire class hear other "versions" of the text as these evolved over several weeks. Within the groups, a creative tension existed between producing a group text and representing the focus issue in six or seven individual perspectives. The subgroups were both a deliberate attempt to reflect multiple perspectives within the chosen topic as well as a reaction to some group members' feelings that they were not being "heard" in their group. I believe the intimate involvement with a few classmates over several weeks broke down some of the essentialist versions of each other that they had scripted during the initial class discussions, although I suspect it created other essentialist versions as well. The elusiveness of outcomes cannot be gathered up in one place and evaluated. I do know this: The class sessions for me could be likened to a good blues piece. Expectations turned on themselves. The upbeat was played into the downbeat. The downbeat was heard in the silence rather than the sound, working oppositionally to expectation. Ambiguity lurked between major and minor harmonies. Notes flattened on the third and seventh, not quite leading where expectations might suggest. It was like playing the notes on a piano between the cracks of the keys. I will improvise future versions from this attempt, but in the end I felt some satisfaction that expectations about how to engage in cultural studies might be different for these teachers than when they entered through the door of our classroom for the first time.

You and I, the teachers in this class, Toni Morrison, and Muddy Waters, my whiteness and someone's blackness, the signifying and the signified, differ in the contexts and the content that make up the fabric of our lives. Bakhtin (1990) cautioned:

> Creative understanding does not renounce itself, its own place in time, its
> own culture; and it forgets nothing. In order to understand, it is immensely
> important for the person who understands to be located outside the object of
> his or her creative understanding—in time, in space, in culture (p. 99).

I can only say once more that we did not create a tidy or efficient
moment of learning; I didn't learn five principles for designing curriculum (Sleeter & Grant, 1988); I continue to ask how to create a place in
the classroom for students, and most particularly teachers, to continue their work of becoming, imagining, questioning, and transcending. I continue to ask: How might pedagogy address the complex process of transcending space and provide strategies for critique of
representations?

I've told something of my beliefs about a cultural education and
strategies for reading cultural texts. I've suggested how in one class we
worked together toward some further understanding. I haven't told
completely why this particular study was important to me or where it
really began. I suspect that my original reaction to the teachers who
questioned whether or not Lisa could study the blues has something
to do with my own experiences with the blues. I'd like to end with
that.

For me, the story of the blues began before I was in school. For
years I heard Blind Lemon Jefferson, Bessie Smith, Lowell Fulson,
and Booker White well into the dark of night. The voices came strong
and true. I began learning the blues. I didn't much understand what
was being sung, but I understood it was blue and that my uncles, rural
Idaho farmers who had spent the day in the fields and evenings in the
barns, found some connection. I could tell by the contemplative yearning
of their eyes and the way my Uncle Ned breathed in and let out the
smoke from his pipe. I could tell because this was a time when I could
stretch out across his lap, lost in blues. He stared off and moved into
someplace else. I mostly did the same. I cannot date these memories
back with exactness. Most nights for several years I watched my uncle
wrap himself into his own thinking, claiming a time and space for
himself in the music. Mostly he allowed me to be an eavesdropper. I
knew enough not to interrupt this time with chatter, so I just took in
what the records sang. I still hear phrases and voices. "Peach Orchard
Mama," "hitch me to your buggy, mama; drive me like a mule," "She
ain't so good luckin', and her teeth don't shine like pearls." I can hear
the small click from a scratch crisscrossing the grooves. I still see the
78 platter wobbling as the arm with its needle brought voices from

some great expanse. I didn't know the distance then. Couldn't imagine the separation.

This music was associated with the well-being of our house. During storms or nights when a mare was about to foal or an animal was sick and Uncle Ned stayed long hours in the barn, the house groaned in its own quietness. The women were darning stockings, patching shirts and overalls, or stacking the last of the dishes back into the cupboards. Or, grandmother would be bathing my brother in the tin tub on the side porch. Later, my mother would finish the night braid in grandmother's long hair. These activities separated them from the night music of the uncles who sat smoking and listening and staring off. Never do I remember the women listening to the music or suggesting that it wasn't music fit for a small girl. Never do I remember my uncles suggesting that I shouldn't be on the screened porch listening to Muddy Waters slide his thirds and sevenths into blue notes that signified more than sexual desires, the loss of love, or the need to move on down the line. I don't remember when I quit listening, but it must have been sometime after I was well into the rhythm of school, when homework caught up and carried me on a linear progression from one year to the next.

But I can still hear a man singing mournfully about "the woman that I'm loving done been here and gone." I can still hear the harmonica of Johnny Shines, cupped in his hand to make a fluttering sound much like the moan of a human voice, like the voice of my uncle the time he was kicked in the stomach by a wild mustang he'd taken off the range. I can still feel the rhythm of my uncle's fingers as he kept time on my shoulder or arm. And the voices of women, seductive in their lowness, calling for things that I didn't believe the women in our house ever longed for. Once in a great while, Uncle Ned would begin humming and his voice sounded less blue than the one growling from the speaker. Phrases of the women's conversations from the kitchen would mingle with the song. The dog would drowse on the mat near the screen door. The music would linger late into the evening and my uncle Ned would listen, absorbed in some sensations that I couldn't understand.

I don't know, for my uncles have been dead some years now, how or why they were led to the blues. I only know that they listened, that the music touched them somehow, and that they collected hundreds of platters that were stored carefully in trunks, each separated by green felt swatches when 45s and 33⅓ s modernized their collection. The trunks were shipped to me a year or two before Uncle Ned died. A handwritten note: "You were always the blues kid. Listen and have a good cry for all those nights we'll miss." On the other hand, I'm not certain that the motivation matters. They were not attempting to co-opt anyone's artistic expression, but there was some complex relation between space and time, manners and matters of living, social acceptance and alienation, and some moment of dwelling in an aesthetic space that had power over them, a longing that they brought to me. Something was ringing true for them.

References

Abrahams, R. D. (1970). *Deep down in the jungle: Negro narrative folklore from the streets of Philadelphia.* Chicago: Aldine Publishing.

Amselle, J. L. (1990). *Logiques métisse.* Paris: Payot.

Baker, H. (1984). *Blues, ideology, and Afro-American literature.* Chicago: University of Chicago Press.

Bakhtin, M. M. (1968). *Rabelais and his world.* (H. Isowolsky, Trans.) Cambridge, MA: MIT Press.

Bakhtin, M. M. (1981). *The dialogic imagination.* (M. Holquist, Ed. & C. Emerson & M. Holquist, Trans.). Austin: University of Texas Press.

Bakhtin, M. M. (1984). *Problems of Dostoyevsky's poetics.* (C. Emerson, Ed. and Trans.). Manchester: Manchester University Press.

Bakhtin, M. M. (1986). *Speech genres & other late essays.* (V. McGee, Trans.). Austin: University of Texas Press.

Bakhtin, M. M. (1990). Response to a question from the *Novyi Mir* editorial staff. In G. Morson & C. Emerson (Trans.). *Mikhail Bakhtin: Creation of a prosaics* (pp. 94–101). Stanford: Stanford University Press.

Banks, J. (1988). *Multiethnic education: Theory and practice.* Boston: Allyn & Bacon.

Bloom, A. (1987). *The closing of the American mind.* New York: Simon & Schuster.

Brown, C. (Ed.). (1986). *Ready from within: Septima Clark and the civil rights movement.* Navarro, CA: Wild Trees Press.

Campbell, B. (1992). *Your blues ain't like mine.* New York: Ballantine.

Carby, H. (1980). Multi-culture. *Screen, 34,* 64–65.

Charters, S. (1981). *The roots of the blues.* Boston: Marion Boyars.

Collins, P. (1990). *Black feminist thought.* New York: Routledge.

Cone, J. (1972). *The spirituals and the blues.* New York: Orbis Books.

Darby, B. B. (1937, April 30). Spike driver blues [78 rpm]. Decca 7816.

Deleuze, G. (1993). *The Deleuze reader.* (C. V. Boundas, Ed.). New York: Columbia University Press.

Dewey, J. (1954). *The public and its problems.* Ohio: Swallow Press.

Dewey, J. (1934/1980). *Art as experience.* New York: Perigee.

Dixon, W. with Snowden, D. (1989). *I am the blues: The Willie Dixon story.* New York: DaCapo.

Du Bois, W. E. B. (1903/1961). *The souls of black folk: Essays and sketches.* New York: Avon.

Ellison, R. (1966). The art of fiction: An interview. In *Shadow and act* (pp. 169–178). New York: New American Library.

Evans, D. (1982). *Big road blues.* New York: DaCapo.

Ferris, W. (1978). *Blues from the delta.* New York: DaCapo.

Flowers, A. (1993). *Another good loving blues.* New York: Viking.

Foucault, M. (1980). *Power/Knowledge: Selected interviews and other writings.* (C. Gordon, Ed. & C. Gordon, L. Marshall, J. Mepham, & K. Soper, Trans.). New York: Pantheon Books.

Gardiner, M. (1992). *The dialogues of critique: M. M. Bakhtin and the theory of ideology.* New York: Routledge.

Gates, H. L., Jr. (1988). *The signifying monkey: A theory of African-American literary criticism.* New York: Oxford University Press.

Gay, G. (1977). Curriculum for multicultural teacher education. In F. J. Klassen & D. M. Gollnick (Eds.), *Pluralism and the American teacher: Issues and case studies* (pp. 31–62). Washington, DC: American Association of Colleges for Teacher Education.

Gay, G. (1983). Multiethnic education: Historical developments and future prospects. *Phi Delta Kappan, 64,* 560–563.

Greene, M. (Winter, 1993). Diversity and inclusion: Toward a curriculum for human beings. *Teachers College Record, 95*(2), 211–221.

Henry, W. A. (1990, April 9). Beyond the melting pot. *Time, 135,* 28–31.

Higham, J. (1993). *Cultural capital: The problem of literary canon formation.* Chicago: University of Chicago Press.

Hirsch, E. D. (1987). *Cultural literacy: What every American needs to know.* Boston: Houghton Mifflin.

hooks, b. (1990). *Yearning: Race, gender, and cultural politics.* Boston: South End Press.

Hoover, K. R. (1987). *Ideology and political life.* Monterey, CA: Brooks/Cole.

House, E. (1965, July). I can make my own songs. *Sing Out, 15* (3), 45.

Keil, C. (1991). *Urban blues.* Chicago: University of Chicago Press.

Kristeva, J. (1984). *Revolution in poetic language.* (M. Waller, Trans.). New York: Columbia University Press.

Martin, S. (1928, December). Kitchen man blues [78 rpm]. QRS R-7043.

McCarthy, C. (1993). After the canon. In C. McCarthy & W. Crichlow (Eds.), *Race, identity, and representations in education* (pp. 289–305). New York: Routledge.

McPherson, J. (1976). *Railroad: Trains and train people in American culture.* New York: Random House.

Miles, L. (1930, January). My man o' war [78 rpm]. RCA RD-7840.

Morrison, T. (1984). Rootedness: The ancestor as foundation. In M. Evans (Ed.), *Black women writers (1950–1980): A critical evaluation* (pp. 340–349). Garden City, N.Y.: Anchor Press/Doubleday.

Morrison, T. (1992). *Playing in the dark: Whiteness and the literary imagination.* New York: Vintage.

Morson, G. S. (Ed.). (1986). Dialogue, monologue and the social. In *Bakhtin: Essays and dialogues on his work* (pp. 83–88). Chicago: University of Chicago Press.

Nash, L. (1969). Early in the mornin'. In B. Oster (Ed.), *Living country blues* (pp. 43–44). Detroit: Folklore Associates.

Neal, L. (1989). *Visions of a liberated future.* New York: Thunder's Mouth Press.

Nietzsche, F. (1883–91/1961). *Thus spake Zarathustra.* New York: Penguin.

Oliver, P. (1990). *Blues fell this morning.* Cambridge: Cambridge University Press.

Oliver, P. (1968). *Screening the blues.* New York: DaCapo.

Palmer, R. (1981). *Deep blues.* New York: Penguin.

Petry, A. (1966). Solo on the drums. In J. H. Clarke (Ed.), *American Negro short stories* (pp. 161–175). New York: Hill and Wang.

Ravitch, D. (1990). Multiculturalism e plurbis plures. *The American Scholar, 59,* 337–354.

Rudinow, J. (1994). Race, ethnicity, expressive authenticity: Can white people sing the blues? *The Journal of Aesthetics and Art Criticism, 52*(1), 127–137.

Russell, M. (1982). Slave codes and liner notes. In G. Hull, P. Scott, & B. Smith (Eds.), *But some of us are brave.* Old Westbury, NY: Feminist Press.

Schlesinger, A. (1992). *The disuniting of America.* New York: Norton.

Sleeter, C. & Grant, C. (1988). *Making choices for multicultural education: Five approaches to race, class and gender.* Cleveland, OH: Merrill.

Smith, B. (1928, August 25). Please help me get him off my mind [78 rpm]. Columbia 14375-D.

Smitherman, G. (1977). *Talkin and testifyin: The language of black America.* Boston: Houghton Mifflin.

Taubman, P. (1993). Separate identities, separate lives. In L. Castenell, Jr. & W. Pinar (Eds.), *Understanding curriculum as racial text* (pp. 287–306). New York: State University of New York Press.

Taylor, C. (1992). *Multiculturalism and the politics of recognition.* Princeton: Princeton University Press.

Tiedt, I. & Tiedt, P. (1986). *Multicultural teaching: A handbook of activities, information, and resources.* Boston: Allyn & Bacon.

Voloshinov. V. N. (1973). *Marxism and the philosophy of language.* (L. Matejka & I. R. Titunik, Trans.). New York: Seminar Press.

Walker, A. (1983). *In search of our mothers' gardens.* New York: Harcourt Brace Jovanovich.

White, J. (1966). Strange fruit. In T. Lehmann (Ed.), *Blues and trouble* (pp. 55-59). Berlin: Neuwied Books.

Williams, J. (1937). Rootin' ground-hog [78 rpm]. Aurora 7065.

Gender, Generation, Space and Popular Music

Angharad N. Valdivia
with Rhiannon S. Bettivia

It's 8:12 a.m. The feminist mom, who looks like she just got shot out of a wind turbine and has a cheap chardonnay hangover, is making pancakes for four 8-year-old girls having a sleep over party. Let's just say she is not in the most festive mood. Then, blasting from the other room, she hears the now-familiar faux-rap riff, "I'll tell ya what I want, what I really really want. . ." She peeks around the corner to see the four girls singing and dancing with wild abandon, sucking in "girl power" with every pore. Should she be happy that they're listening to bustier feminism instead of watching Barbie commercials on Saturday morning TV?

—Susan Douglas, 1997

Actually I just don't like the Spice Girls because I find them obnoxious and silly. They are like Barbies!

—Rhiannon, 1997

Introduction

Feminist moms, their daughters, and popular music. What a combination! I too am a feminist mom, and I recently hosted such a slumber party. I am not quite sure how I looked as I cooked the pancakes, but I was not in an unfestive mood. Girls singing and dancing somehow always perk me up. However, I do worry about the potentially distancing generation gap which might occur over the very terrain of popular music between my daughter and me. How do we navigate this difficult passage when my proclivities and interpretations differ from hers? How do we share a home without constant struggle? How does my daughter interpret the role of popular music in her life? These are all concerns which guide this essay.

Feminist research on popular culture reveals that while much of mainstream media is highly gendered, girls continue to create a space for negotiated, oppositional, and agency-creating meanings. However as Mazzarella (1996) notes, despite the growing amount of feminist scholarship on female fandom (e.g. Lewis, 1991), for instance, there is still very little research on usage and production of media and popular culture by the pre-adolescent/early adolescent (PEA) segment of the girl audience, especially in the United States. Thus while McRobbie (1991, 1994) and Nava (1992) have written extensively about theoretical issues of gender, class, race and ethnicity, culture, and adolescence in the British contemporary situation, there is little written about U.S. girls. In fact, Margaret Finders's *Just Girls* (1997) stands out as a lone beacon in the area of empirically based and critical-cultural-theory-inspired PEA girls and popular culture research.

As a subset, albeit a large one, of popular culture and feminist studies, popular music studies has traditionally focused on masculinity in theory and boys in practice. After all, isn't rock and roll a largely masculine endeavor and form of expression where boys and men reign supreme? However, as some scholars have begun to suggest, and as others have been assiduously documenting, there are both segments of the pop and rock and roll industry wherein girls and or women have been active, if not dominant, and other more contemporary components of the industry, such as hip hop and rap, where girls and women seek to make their mark either by joining the boys or staking out a more independent and sometimes feminist position (Rose, 1991, 1994; Gaunt, 1995). Other studies of MTV female stars in general (Lewis, 1990) and of Madonna in particular (Schwichtenberg, 1993) suggest both that certain female stars use predominantly masculine signifiers or generally devalued feminine signifiers to carve out a feminist space and that young girl fans respond to these moves by emulating these stars and experiencing empowerment as a result of [these stars'] role modeling (Douglas, 1997).

Little is written about the domestic struggle and negotiation over popular music between members of the family. While nearly all of us can remember conflict with our parents over our choice of music, the literature is nearly mum on this subject. The fact remains that while it's widely acknowledged that for the PEA girls peer groups ascend in importance and influence as other social institutions such as family, education, and church descend, most of these girls still live at home. Thus they listen to their music and watch their MTV either in their own or friends' homes. They may be listening to popular music, but as girls most of them continue do so in the confinement of freedom of domestic spaces. As McRobbie (1991) reminds us, precisely because girls have less access to freedom than their brothers, their cultural activities are incorporated into the "safe" spaces of the home and school. In part, we aim to address the gap in the literature that explores the intersection of popular music, generation, schooling, and domestic space.

As such this essay explores the tensions and pleasures in trying to navigate the terrain of mothering, for me, and daughtering and/or growing up, for Rhiannon, currently 13 going on 14 and experiencing the transition between junior and high school. Before continuing, we must both admit two things. First, the dominant voice will be mine, the mother. This is a decision made for strategic rather than for egalitarian reasons. Namely I want to and have to get this done whereas for Rhiannon this is yet one more demand on her busy schedule, social life, and dream world. As a friend, Dale Spender, so astutely put it, "Oh Rhiannon, I see your mother is reporting on your life!" Spender is both right and slightly incorrect. First, how else am I supposed to find out about PEA girls and popular music in general and about Rhiannon in particular? Second, we are constantly engaged in a multireflexive process in that we both read and react to popular press accounts of and academic scholarship about popular music. Rhiannon reacts to what I tell her the research says and quite often reads it herself to make sure I did not paraphrase too liberally. As a result she feels very strongly critical of the generalizations made about her age group and tastes in the literature. I try to be open about the groups she listens to, the stars she follows, but find myself stepping into the position wherein I remember my parents resided: "This Marilyn Manson stuff sounds and looks too weird, Rhiannon!" Thus Rhiannon has wanted to respond both to my comments about her and to research on adolescent girls for quite some time. In particular at this stage in her life, popular music occupies a very salient place.

The whole multireflexive process becomes even more complicated when you throw in the feminist mom and the cool but feminist daughter variables. This is yet another dynamic which is not simple. The bumps are there for both of us. For just as it is difficult to mother in this culture, it is no easier growing up with a feminist mother. My objections extend beyond mere issues of image to critiques of themes and worldview and possible alternatives in the construction of personhood for a female daughter. Rhiannon's defenses incorporate notions of female agency and self-expression, a PEA version of Butlerist performative theories both for herself and the artists she listens to. Furthermore, the same pressures which send me into spaces of parental despair send Rhiannon into defensive postures so she can fit into her peer group[s] despite the fact that somehow they all, or at least the close ones, know that Rhiannon has a "feminist" mother.

This will be a theoretically grounded conversation between a feminist mother and a PEA daughter about the place and role of popular music in our everyday lived experience (with Rhiannon's comments in italics). As such, we will weave through the domestic space of our home and into the school and after school worlds which Rhiannon inhabits. In all of these locations music occupies a place of both saliency and struggle, as we all seek to define and assert our identities partly through our musical choices and activities.

Theoretical Musings

That PEA girls are exposed to a huge amount of popular culture is undeniable. Research suggests that much of this exposure occurs during "leisure" hours, and the literature on this age group (see Hendry, Shucksmith, Love & Glendinning, 1993, for example) asserts that this is the one luxury "bestowed on adolescents" (p. 2). It is estimated that adolescents spend about eight hours per day with some sort of popular culture in primary, secondary, or tertiary form (Williams & Frith, 1994). In sum, at this age, media and peers replace family and parents as a source of influence and time. In particular, scholars suggest that popular music occupies a place of importance in many teenagers' lives, a place that may last for a lifetime.

Certainly the predominant place of popular music in adolescents' lives is a fact acknowledged by nearly all media industries. It is not just the rock and roll industry which targets the adolescent age group; the whole MTV phenomenon was built on the premise that the adolescent consumption of music was profitable enough to make it a viable competitor in today's media environment. Furthermore, as MTV execs soon found out, it wasn't the older but the younger target audience which would generate higher ratings and economic returns. Additionally, the Hollywood film industry, in a process widely known as synergy (Miller, 1997), links movie tracks to musical groups and hit songs so as to maximize exposure and sales of artists who are usually, though not always, owned by the same economic concerns. Judging from Rhiannon and her buddies' constant and frequent attendance to newly released movies, they are getting more than a healthy exposure to this synergy of film and music. This is not all, as any contemporary parent and more than the occasional colleague will tell you—there is everything from clothing to ads to any number of intertextual reminders of popular music and its synergistic connections.

The connections are ubiquitous. Though girls spend considerable amounts of time with popular culture, we ought not forget that their school time is laced, if not soaked, with interactions and representations which are masculine gendered. Research shows that girls are nearly erased as subjects within the schooling experience, whether it be in terms of how teachers and administrators pay attention to them or in terms of their representation within instructional materials such as textbooks and other classroom aids (Gilbert & Taylor, 1991; Mann, 1994; Pipher, 1994; Roman & Christian-Smith, 1988). Although "school is by no means the only site where people define themselves and their social worth . . . it is a formative one" (Luttrell, 1997, p. 5). Considering that nearly all adolescent girls attend school for about 7 hours a day, excluding extracurricular activities, this is an area of study which we must not forget for it is a public space in which girls are mandated to function.

Furthermore this essay represents an effort to work through the battleground that adolescence and popular music pose to mothers and their daughters—what has become an often talked about generation gap. However, very little of the literature talks to real parents and their children, let alone mothers and their daughters, adolescent angst being so often coded as a masculine enterprise. In this essay we seek to go beyond angst and into survival and creation as we explore the process of identity-formation of a PEA girl and the role of popular music in that process. We also assert a space of negotiation and struggle but not rejection, as much of the literature on PEA girls and their mothers suggests. Much of the support for such a utopian vision comes from the seemingly contradictory findings in the study of girls and popular culture. For example, while much of research suggests that adolescents generally reduce family interaction in favor of media and peer group involvement, recent feminist scholarship cautions us to consider the class biases of that finding (Finders, 1997).

In an ethnographic study of middle- and working-class girls as they crossed the passage from upper elementary to junior high, Finders (1997) challenges us to revisit our notions of adolescence and the popular media's role in it. In an impassioned plea for an awareness of the heterogeneity of the essentialist category of "adolescence," Finders argues that neither peer and media involvement nor resistance and rebellion are necessarily predominant components of adolescence. Additionally, her work suggests that the inevitable split between mothers and daughters in the adolescent period is not universal. The working-class girls in her study, in fact, remained close to their mothers or got even closer as a result of their entrance into the increasingly alienating experience of junior high school. This finding is supported in McLean, Gilligan, and Sullivan's study (1995), in which they find this to be true both of working-class and African American girls and their mothers. Finally, Finders rejects the divide between school hours and leisure hours, for she demonstrates that they are inextricably entwined. We agree with this as Rhiannon has MTV on as she does her math homework and girls in her peer group sometimes sketch or doodle instead of taking notes during, say, biology. Any study, and our conversation, needs to at least acknowledge both the heterogeneity of the adolescent girl population and the ubiquity of popular culture and music in their lives.

Topics of Conversation

The area of popular music is a huge one. Therefore we had to come up with some limits to our conversation, at least the published portion of it.[1] Drawing on the literature we've reviewed, we'll first discuss music at home and in Rhiannon's bedroom which is *different from music at home*. Second, we will discuss what Rhiannon's friends listen to. Third, we will discuss music video consumption as another expression of musical tastes.

Music at Home

As we began this discussion, we realized that "at home" is an already broad and heterogeneous category. While we do not live in a huge house, there are still times and spaces with different musical meanings. Furthermore, given that there are four of us living together, each of us with distinct if overlapping musical tastes and proclivities, our home is a series of spaces with very porous boundaries. Jazz, reggae, calypso, salsa, merengue, pop, "classic" rock, alternative rock (*we have very little truly alternative stuff*), opera, assorted soundtracks, old Sesame Street, and Christmas collections have to co-exist. As well, music systems follow the general economic power of their owners, with the "official" component system with the truly powerful speakers being set up in the living room, while each of the children have their own in their bedrooms. It is not surprising then that Rhiannon explicitly understands some of the possibilities of these spaces within the home.

There are three kinds of music at home. One is the music at home. The second is the music I listen to in my bedroom. The third is the music I listen to when I am the only one at home.

The music I listen to at home is stuff that my brother doesn't mind listening to or that he wouldn't kill me for listening to. Because Tobin likes Spice Girls, En Vogue, the Monkees, and the worst is Hanson. The only kind of Hanson I would listen to is Beck Hanson. When I am listening to music at home, I usually have to turn it down because Tobin gets upset if I don't listen to it quietly enough. But usually I end up turning it up because he makes a big point of turning the TV really loud so I can't hear my music. I generally don't listen to anything that he really hates and I only listen to a few songs because he doesn't like my music. He has a very preppy mainstream style of music; and our tastes conflict entirely.

In my bedroom I can listen to whatever I want. So I usually listen to Fiona Apple, Jewel, and maybe a little bit of Toni Braxton. Most of the music I listen to in my room is girl bands. Although never the Spice Girls. I usually don't listen to the music very loud because my stereo doesn't sound well at high volumes. It blares. If I had a better stereo, I'd play it louder. Although in my bedroom I usually only listen to slow songs.

Now when nobody else is at home, I take all my CD's downstairs to the living room and I play them at high volume, really high volume. So I can feel the bass when I am laying on the couch. I usually listen to Aerosmith, Guns 'n' Roses, Smashing Pumpkins, Live, Marilyn Manson, and anything else that can be played obnoxiously loud. I also play my opera CD's really loud because that's the way that opera is supposed to be. And so nobody can hear me sing.

What becomes apparent in this section is that the struggle at home is one of sibling rivalry. I haven't figured out which came first, the chicken or the egg—whether Rhiannon hates her brother's music because he likes it or because she hates it per se. She claims, *He likes it because I hate it. I was here first and I drew him into the music scene.* The fact remains that music is one of their major areas of struggle as they fight rather than negotiate their space and volume. Having little systems in their bedrooms has not necessarily settled the situation, as they sound battle each other in their rooms as well.

Maybe we have yet to reach the time when the main battle is a generational one between parents and children, but at this point the parental music collection remains a site of both poaching and exoticism. As popular music scholars have documented, new music technologies, such as vinyl records, cassette tapes, 8-tracks, and CD's, usher in new artists and new forms of marketing old artists. This is definitely the case in our home. Thus Rhiannon listens to Aerosmith, the new and the old stuff. She borrows our Aretha Franklin, B-52s, and Gloria Estefan. Tobin borrows and listens to the Beatles and the Bee Gees on vinyl. He had to purchase the Monkees because they are beyond even our eclectic collection. However, both Rhiannon and Tobin prefer to have their music on CD as that allows them to listen to it in their bedrooms or their CD-Walkmans. Vinyl choices mean the living room as that is where the sole record player resides. We all realize that the coveted sound system is in the living room—that is where the music sounds fine![2] That's where we all would rather listen to our music. One way of settling this desire is to wait, as Rhiannon does, till the rest of us are not around and crank that volume knob till we feel some form of physical reverberation.

There are some bands I feel a little uneasy about, such as Marilyn Manson. *I just don't know why you are worried about Marilyn Manson!* I saw their photograph in *Rolling Stone* magazine and thought, even as I knew I was thinking like my parents used to sound, "Now they've gone too far!" I exercise parental authority in that I refused to drive Rhiannon to the concert, thereby closing any opportunity for her to attend. Rhiannon acknowledges my misgivings and cooperates without giving up. I never hear their music in the living room stereo when I am home, but I know she watches MTV expectantly, hoping their videos will appear. There are many other groups she mentions which I don't recognize at all, but I just can't worry about these things.

The issue of exoticization occurs between us because we are not separated just by generation but by national and therefore cultural origin. Thus much of our parental music collection stems from Latin America and the Caribbean. Rhiannon does not find this music salient enough to mention in our conversation despite a couple of questions from me. She tolerates it as part of the territory. Tobin reacts to it more violently, so we engage in similar strategies to Rhiannon's—we try to listen to our stuff when Tobin is out of hearing reach.

Another issue that Rhiannon's account brings up is the role of female stars and girl bands in a PEA girl's music diet. Rhiannon has been attracted to female music stars from the beginning. The stars themselves may change. For example, last year Sheryl Crow and Alanis Morrisette reigned supreme (Valdivia & Bettivia, in press). However the fact that female stars continue to be popular does not change. Nonetheless not any girl band will do, as the following section will demonstrate in regards to the Spice Girls. *Actually I just don't like the Spice Girls because I find them obnoxious and silly. They are like Barbies.* Douglas (1997) ponders the very same thing as a feminist mother but the feminist discourse has seeped to the next generation as well. Furthermore, Rhiannon reserves her own private space, her bedroom, for listening to the "girls." We do not hear them outside except when she chooses to share a favorite song or guitar riff with us, which still leaves her as mistress of her own girl stuff.

Thus the home remains a site of active and dynamic musical activity, negotiation, and struggle. Implicit truces, in terms of space and time, have to be constantly reworked as musical tastes change and individuals have to assert their presence. However, we have worked out a system within which we all feel we sometimes get to listen to what we want to, how we want to.

Friends and Their Music

Scholarship on teens suggests that music is one of the major ways of being cool within the peer group (Danesi, 1994). Group as well as individual identity centers largely around musical choices. Donna Gaines's *Teenage Wasteland* (1991) documents one such group of boys as they use hard rock, often criticized for its suicidal tendencies, to build a sense of community in a hostile world. However her book does little to illuminate the position of the girls in that subculture. Indeed they are represented as passive followers and sideline actors in this largely male community. Thus we know little about PEA girls and their peer group popular music activities. Consequently, this part of the essay may read contradictorily in that it appears that Rhiannon says one thing but really practices another. This is not necessarily the case, as she refers to different levels of analysis, within her peer group and between peer groups.

I don't much care what kind of music my friends listen to because I know I have an odd style of music and we are just going to end up criticizing each other's taste in music anyway. I guess my all-around cool music friend is Andrea 'cuz she listens to anything and everything that's cool. So while she listens to the Spice Girls, *she also adores* Fiona Apple, Prodigy, *and* Marilyn Manson. *Plus she also enjoys and also agrees with my obsession for* Hole *and* Nirvana. *We both love Courtney and Kurt.*[3]

I guess my boyfriend and his friends as well as the majority of my guy friends listen to, of course, Marilyn Manson *and all the hard-core stuff like that. My incredibly odd boyfriend will buy and listen to any CD once, and then they'll just sit there in his CD case and rot till the end of time. Unless, of course, I show some interest in the CD and he'll give it to me.*

But as far as the rest of my guy friends, I don't know what they listen to other than Korn. *Melanie used to have a wild obsession with* Smashing Pumpkins, *then with* Aerosmith, *and now with* Marilyn Manson. *She knows like everything about him [Marilyn Manson], like even his birthweight, and has a pair of real expensive black boots just like him. I have no idea what Stefanie or Amber listen to.*

But there are groups at school who listen to different music. The preppie girls, airheads, listen to anything mainstream that comes along because they really don't take the time to listen to something they would really like. They listen to what everybody else is listening to because they want to be cool. The G's listen to stuff like the late Notorious B.I.G., Lil' Kim, Puff Daddy, Missy Elliott, Mariah Carey, *and other stuff like that—basically the kind of stuff you would find in* BET *[Black Entertainment Television]. The grungies listen to really hard-core and hard music like* Korn, Prodigy, Marilyn Manson, *and* Nine Inch Nails. *I don't know if there are other groups and what they would listen to.*

Within the peer group Rhiannon claims not to know tastes nor to listen to stuff when they are together. However the entire peer group explicitly identifies itself in relation to their overall general musical tastes and in rejection or reaction to other groups' tastes.

Within the peer group there are gendered but not mutually exclusive musical choices. Some girls listen to girl music, either when alone or together. Slumber parties consist, in part, of loud music. Thus they affirm their bonds by combining their collections and playing them selectively. Conversely, they confirm their bonds also by rejecting that which they don't like. Though Douglas (1997) convincingly argues for a defense of Spice Girls and their consumption by PEA girls, including her daughter and friends, Rhiannon and her friend Melanie absolutely loathe them. They are apparently not alone, as they can log on to a chat group on the net which allows them to join other anti-Spice Girls people. However other girls within the group absolutely love them.

The boys in the group tend to like hard rock. They don't demonstrate as much knowledge about girl music as the girls do about hard rock. When in mixed company the music is usually hard rock and so is the conversation. *Actually the girls like girl music and the boys don't care. Most of the guys have girlfriends and if their girls listen to girl music, then they will too.* Yet even within hard rock there is the occasional soft ballad which allows for romantic moments even within this very masculine of settings. *Like "Fade to Black!"*

The group, like their choice of particular artists, is both amorphous and dynamic. There appears to be much more tolerance within the group once you are in. *I am cool even though I hate Spice Girls.* As well, there is a tendency to avoid struggle within the group. There have been estranged friendships partly as a result of close friends parting because a third party was too different in terms of music among other things. As a result Rhiannon's group tries not to dwell explicitly on musical choice even as their membership in the peer group and their individual proximity to each other are determined partly by musical choice.

In terms of the group's relationship to other groups it ranges from tolerance to ridicule to unawareness. They tolerate the G's [short for "G-funks," or kids who listen to funk music] in a friendly manner even if asserting they are not one of them. This might be partly because they, as rock fans, listen to some R & B which overlaps with G tastes like Monica and Toni [Braxton]. Another reason is that they may see each other as yet another subculture or less powerful group than the preppies, which they and the G's really despise.[4] In fact while they describe themselves and the G's as agents in their musical choices, they ridicule preppies as followers of image not of substance. There are other groups of students who are neither G's nor grungies nor preppies. In fact Rhiannon and some of her friends describe themselves as independents but friends of the grungies. However, Rhiannon and her friends are unaware of groups beyond those three. Their universe revolves around each other, the three groups, and their home.

Music Videos

Music videos are as firmly entrenched a part of the television diet as talk shows, and Rhiannon would watch tons of both if I didn't check her. Furthermore, both MTV and VH1 have clearly segmented shows and times so that a regular viewer, such as Rhiannon or Tobin, knows with more or less certainty when to watch if they want to see particular artists. Rhiannon favors "Adult Videos" and the "Video Countdown" as a way of staying on top of what and how her favorite artists are doing.

As far as music videos go, I watch pretty much any of them. I mean, if I hear a song on the radio, I can tell you what song it is, who it's by, and what the CD is called. I watch Prodigy, Meredith Brooks, Fiona Apple, *of course,* Jewel, Verve Pipe, *and, of course,* Live—*basically anything that doesn't incredibly offend me like* Spice Girls *and* Third Eye Blind, OMC, En Vogue, *and basically anything else my brother likes. I find that all his music offends me, not just because he likes it, but because he has that kind of taste in music.*

I like the music videos because they have a nice way of showing things that the artists themselves like. For example Toni Braxton's *"You're Making Me High" video features Toni's six favorite things, some of them being martinis, olives, cigars, etcetera.*

I like to watch music videos because they give me a chance to listen to songs that I like that I don't have the CD to. I also like to see the artists, especially Fiona Apple, *because she is really pretty, and* Beck, *because he looks really good. And when you watch the videos, sometimes they have little interviews with the artists, so you get to hear them say silly things. Like one time, they were interviewing* Fiona Apple, *and they were asking her what the design on her little bowl from* Sarah McLachlan *was, and she said the important thing was that it was hers and nothing else mattered. I thought that was really cool.*

I guess "Pop Up Videos" are OK but they usually do older videos, which don't much interest me. Sometimes they play new videos like "Don't Speak" by No Doubt *but that song was so popular everybody knows everything about the video anyway. Other times you can get some pretty funny comments or some really odd statistics, which come in handy when you are trying to make a point to annoy your teacher.*

I usually watch videos with Tobin, as far as that goes. Because they play a mix—the kind of music I like, and the type of music he likes. It's like, if we're watching "The Top Ten Countdown" or just random videos, they'll play something like "2 Become 1" by Spice Girls which he really likes and something like "Turn my Head" by Live which I really like. Sometimes if I haven't heard a song that I like for a long time, then I'll just sit there and wait for them to play it. That usually happens to videos they don't like to play like "Sweet Dreams" by Marilyn Manson. I have to watch three weeks worth of "Adult Videos" (from midnight to 1 a.m. every morning) to find it once.

Surprisingly enough, the television through MTV softens the sibling rivalry as the shows themselves mix their music. As viewers with little control over when and what is played, Rhiannon and Tobin are left in a much more passive position and can let go of their animosity as they each wait for **their** video to be shown. While they may fight over music, they hang out together over MTV. They pretty much have to since the television is in the family room, and we resist any attempts to install sets in their bedrooms.

The generational struggle occurs over sheer viewing quantity rather than over content. For Rhiannon would leave MTV on all day and night if we don't object. It would be fairly easy for us to not butt in, after all we have TV's in our bedroom and office, but theoretically I believe too much of MTV is not good. While I am especially wary of the late night/early morning shows, the limits are largely exercised through the honor system and bedtime schedules. There have been times when, awake for a glass of water at 4 a.m., we'll find Rhiannon watching MTV. "I just couldn't sleep, Mommy!"

Rhiannon really enjoys "Pop Up Videos" though she won't confess to her pleasure. When a new one is announced, she'll remain riveted to the screen till it shows up. Usually she'll call us to come over and check it out. Later she'll call a friend and talk about it. I must admit that a few of them have been truly funny. I also learn little trivia which I can deploy on friends and students. "Did you know the Police hated each other?" Sometimes we even all sit together for this show, the only one on either MTV of VH1 which brings us together this way.

Rhiannon talks about videos much more than about music. We learn of fashion styles, themes, hair, and so on. She learns of new music or old music she'd like to own from videos. Radio does not really play a part in this particular universe. However, TV combines with telephone and friends for long conversations about what's on right now.

Conclusion

Most of the literature on popular music and adolescents centers on boys. Even within girl culture scholarship, there is little on PEA girls. Moreover, we have little about the terrain of the home as a site of negotiation and struggle over popular music. This essay explores the research gap through a conversation between a feminist mother and a feminist daughter. It is partial, in that the sample is small, but it is rich in that we can delve into some of the details of our particular lives. We propose that more work needs to be done in the space of the home and with the input of PEA girls. Following Finders (1997), we urge for studies to take into account the vast heterogeneity within a setting and a given age group of girls.

In terms of setting, this study demonstrates that the home can be divided up according to space and time so that a diverse set of musical tastes can co-exist more or less amiably under one roof. Granted, there will be struggle and occasional conflict, but, as we also suggest, musical tastes are not mutually exclusive. Children build on and poach from their parents' collections, and parents need not fear and reject every new musical trend nor development. As an example, "Pop Up Videos" are funny to all of us and in their eclectic recycling allow parents to access recent stuff and expose children to some of the old stuff in a very contemporary form. While none of us consider the home as "our own" musical space, we also all know that it's a place where at times we can enjoy our music with minimal or no interruption.

In terms of PEA girls, we also encourage increased focus on this group and their musical practices. The continuing presence and popularity of girl music, for example, show that the feminist documented effort to connect with the female audience remains successful. However, as we also discuss, not all PEA girls react to or integrate popular music in the same way. As with other forms of popular culture, these girls have to be "bilingual"—that is, they have to know their girl music and the boy music they'll have to discuss in the public spaces of school and parties. Furthermore there are a variety of tastes even within the same group at this age. Between peer groups, the lines of demarcation are largely defined by musical tastes, though not all groups are antagonistic to each other.

What we end up with is not the much touted generation gap but rather twisted roads with some firm and some shaky bridges. The new music as we all know is not so new, and the old music is new to those hearing it for the first time. Yet a girl today has plenty of stuff to listen to, and some funky stuff to watch. She also reserves a degree of autonomy within the predetermined diet—that is, Spice Girls might be targeted right at her but she can choose to disdain them or adore them. Granted, there is not a lot of evidence of independent cultural production but if we consider that everyone in Rhiannon's little group plays at least one instrument, these might well be some of the girl bands of the future. Given the variety of music with which they are familiar, I would not mind listening to their stuff in the living room, with the volume so high that my body would shake.

References

Danesi, M. (1994). *Cool: The signs and meanings of adolescence.* Toronto: University of Toronto Press.

Douglas, S. J. (1997, August 25/September 1). Girls 'n' Spice: All things nice? *Nation, 265*(6), 21–24.

Finders, M. J. (1997). *Just girls: Hidden literacies and life in junior high.* New York: Teacher's College Press.

Gaines, D. (1991). *Teenage wasteland: Suburbia's dead-end kids.* New York: Pantheon.

Gaunt, K. D. (1995). African American women between hopscotch and hip-hop: "Must be the music (that's turnin' me on)." In A. N. Valdivia (Ed.), *Feminism, multiculturalism and the media: Global diversities* (pp. 277–308) Thousand Oaks, CA.

Gilbert, P. & S. Taylor (1991). *Fashioning the feminine.* Sydney: Allen & Unwin.

Hendry, L. B., Shucksmith, J., Love, G. & Grlendinning, A. (Eds.). (1993). *Young people's leisure and lifestyles.* New York: Routledge.

Lewis, L. A. (1990). *Gender, politics, and MTV: Voicing the difference.* Philadelphia: Temple University Press.

Lewis, L. A. (Ed.). (1991). *Adoring audience: Fan culture and popular media.* New York: Routledge.

Luttrell, W. (1997). *Schoolsmart and motherwise: Working-class women's identity and schooling.* New York: Routledge.

Mann, J. (1994). *The difference: Growing up female in America.* New York: Warner Books.

Mazzarella, S. (1995). "The voice of a generation?" Media coverage of the suicide of Kurt Cobain. In *Popular Music and Society 19*(2), 49–68.

Mazzarella, S. (1996). Celebrity, romance, and fantasy: A critical reading of teen idol magazines. Paper presented at the meeting of the International Communication Association, Chicago, IL.

McLean, J., Gilligan, C. & Sullivan, A. M. (1995). *Between voice and silence: Women and girls, race and relationship.* Cambridge: Harvard University Press.

McRobbie, A. (1991). *Feminism and youth culture.* Boston: Unwin Hyman.

McRobbie, A. (1994). *Postmodernism and popular culture.* New York: Routledge.

Miller, M. C. (1997, August 25/September 1). The national entertainment state III: Who controls the music. *Nation, 265*(6), 11–16.

Nava, M. (1992). *Changing cultures: Feminism, youth and consumerism.* Newbury Park: Sage.

Pipher, M. (1994). *Reviving ophelia: Saving the selves of adolescent girls.* New York: Putnam.

Roman, L. G., Christian-Smith, L. K., with Ellsworth, E. (1988). *Becoming feminine: The politics of popular culture.* New York: Falmer Press.

Rose, T. (1991). Never trust a big butt and a smile. *Camera Obscura, 23,* 109–131.

Rose, T. (1994). *Black noise: Rap music and black culture in contemporary America.* Hanover, NH: Wesleyan University Press-University Press of New England.

Schwichtenberg, C. (Ed.). (1993). *The Madonna connection: Representational politics, subcultural identities, and cultural theory.* Boulder, CO: Westview Press.

Valdivia, A. with Bettivia, R. S. (1988). A guided tour through one adolescent girl's culture. In S. Mazzarella & N. Pecora (Eds.), *Growing up girls: Popular culture in the creation of identities.* New York: Peter Lang.

Williams, J. & K. T. Frith (1994). Introduction: Adolescents and the media. In R.M. Lerner (Ed.), *Early adolescence: Perspectives on research, policy, and intervention.* Hillsdale, NJ: Lawrence Erlbaum.

Notes

1. These are semirandom in that after taping conversations, we drew out these four categories as the most salient.

2. We hear of similar struggles in other generationally contested spaces. For example, we hear from students who change the radio dial whenever working at their faculty advisor's office. The faculty member changes it when working without the student. The radio stays on the faculty choice when both are in the office at the same time.

3. Here Rhiannon is referring to Courtney Love, lead singer of Hole and widow of Kurt Cobain, who was the lead singer of Nirvana until his suicide in 1994. For an elegant treatment of the coverage of Cobain's death and the characterization of his fans, see Mazzarella (1995).

4. There are far more than just musical choice differences between all of these peer groups. These choices include dress style, school activities, and proximity to the school administration approval in terms of their activities.

The "Sound" Identity:
Music-Making & Schooling

Glenn M. Hudak

So powerful is the desire to make music with others that one is tempted to conceive of music-making as an emergent, radical engagement with consciousness; an engagement which can "rattle" the hegemony of everyday life and open up the possibility of a common ground where differences might meet, mingle, and engage one another. Indeed, it is possible for one to speculate as to the formation of distinct musical identities located within the nexus of activities involved in the making of music and community—in the making of a musical "We."

To be sure, cultural studies already informs us that popular music plays a number of important social functions in the lives of children, adolescents, and adults. Simon Frith (1987), for instance, argues that the social functions of popular music include the formation of identity, the development of a sense of place and social context, and the management of feelings. Those listening to popular music often identify with a particular genre, and as "fans" or performers adopt certain modes of dress and ways of being-in-the-world based on the culture surrounding a particular genre of music. For students, musical identification is often linked with a particular group, clique, or gang. Popular music is related to styles of clothes and the expression of sexuality and racial identification. However, while cultural studies has opened the terrain of its investigations to include the varying dimensions of musical "consumption" and "use" in the lives of students (e.g., Hudak, 1993, 1994), the relations between music "making" and the formation of collective identities remains, the musical "We," opaque. To this project I now turn our attention.

The primary focus of my study is the relationship between music-making (with others) and the formation of what I define as the "sound" identity, a musical "We." As a way of comparison, the study has a secondary focus on the formation of the music fan, a musical "Us." To this end, I begin with a social phenomenology of music-making and identity formation. Here I focus, in detail, on the multiple ways in which music-making organizes lived-time within and between the musicians and listeners. In the concluding section I draw our attention, as educators, to the ways in which both music-making and schooling construct identities through the ways in which they organize lived-time of students. Here, I show how the sound identity, as a musical "We," is elaborated across the spectrum of schooling as a practice of love and freedom in the fight against racial discrimination.

The study is organized into five sections on music-making and the sound identity and a concluding section on schooling. The sections are:

1: The Social Space of Music (Making): Elaboration and Negotiation;
2: Music Making and the Alignment of Lived-Time;
3: Musical Interstices: The Sound Identity and The Fan;
4: The Zone of Occult Instability;
5: The Sound Identity and the Metonymy of Body and Soul;
6: Concluding Thoughts: The Sound Identity and Schooling (Racial Discrimination and Privilege).

The Social Space of Music (Making): Elaboration and Negotiation

It is possible for one to speculate as to the formation of distinct musical identities located within the matrix of activities involved in the making of music and community. In the making of musical "We's" (and "Us's"), all forms of music making have the potential to create collective identities. As Kobena Mercer (1992) observes, all identities, including musical "We's," are not fixed and to be discovered; rather, they are socially constructed within a specific historical context. Mercer writes, "Identities are not found but made; they are not just there, waiting to be discovered in the vocabulary of Nature, but they have to be culturally and politically constructed through political antagonism and cultural struggle" (p. 427). For Mercer and others identities are always constructed within a set of historically defined discourses. One's sense of self, expressed in terms of an identity, will always be situated and negotiated within parameters, a space of meanings that is already socially established through existing relations of power (Butler, 1990).

Edward Said's (1991) notion of "musical elaboration" demonstrates music's propensity to operate within existing relations of power without being "captured" or fixed. Here, music is able "to attach itself to, and become part of, social formations, to vary its articulations and rhetoric depending on the occasion and audience. . . ." (p. 70). Music is transgressive in its "nomadic" ability to be fluid, to travel. But, in its travels it nonetheless leaves traces, evidence, of its stay and hence alters the environment as it leaves. It "attaches itself" as it departs with no predetermined destination in mind. music is never stable; there is no final elaboration; it is always open to suggestion. In Beethoven's music, as Said points out, the compositional form elaborates a novel space where the patronage system is called into question. While Beethoven's music within one historical context elaborates a "revolutionary" sound, within a different period of history and/or different context his music becomes one of the "canons" of music.

The concept of elaboration situates music (and music-making) within a social space that is ever shifting, emergent, and contradictory. Said points out that elaboration is the way music "quite literally fills a social space, and does so by elaborating the ideas of authority and social hierarchy directly connected. . . ." (p. 64). Musical elaboration is never complete because it is contradictory, multiple, and unevenly developed as it fills a particular social space. (Social formations do not occur evenly, or at the same time.) Musical elaboration fills the social space by and through the ideas of authority and hierarchy, which are continually contested, shaped, and reshaped. This suggests that the concrete links between the presiding structures of authority and social hierarchy are never far from the composition and performance.

Musical elaboration allows, then, for transgressive elements to appear. Transgression is not the thief in the night stealing virtue, so to speak, nor is it the breaking of rules, nor a simple infraction of morality; rather the transgressor crosses over the limits of a historic situation, challenging, mixing, intermingling, testing—ultimately to shake free from the totalizing effort of seeing the world, its people, its cultures, its practices as monolithic. For example, no matter how conservative one may wish to theorize classical music as a social formation, it remains nonetheless an incomplete picture. "All retrospective historical analyses," writes Said (1991), whether of music or of any human activity, that judge, theorize, and totalize simultaneously, that say in effect that one thing (like music) = all things, or all music = one big summarizing result = it couldn't have happened any other way, seem to me to be intellectually and historically flawed (pp. 49–50).

Here Said is suggesting that music's transgressive elements are woven into discursive practices where its "final meanings" are endlessly deferred. That is, as a discursive practice music exists

within, not beyond, history; its site shaped by phenomenal shifting conditions, not a model, or a code; it makes meanings but the meanings are contingent rather than determinate, dispersed rather than unified, absent rather than present, and in the end uncontrollably prolific (Knoblauch & Brannon, 1993, p. 167).

Musical elaboration is a "leaky" system, so to speak, whose *presence* gives the appearance of the text (the music) as being solid, stable, and having foundation, but upon analysis it is sort of a "joker, forever composing and subverting the world" (p. 167). Here Said's notion of elaboration emphasizes the "presence" of music as a nomadic discourse whose meanings are continually (re)negotiated within a social space.

There exists a tension between music-making and the elaboration of music. While both are related, they are not reducible to each other. Elaboration articulates the nomadic travels of music within and through social formations. The performance, while elaborated within a social context, is further inscribed within the "temporalities of negotiation." Here Edward Said's notion of musical elaboration is complemented by Homi Bhabha's (1994) notion of "negotiation."

From Homi Bhabha's (1994) perspective, the notion of negotiation within a musical performance means that with each performance it is possible for new musical statements to be constituted/contested/domesticated, or to intervene with other existing (past or present) musical discourses.

When I talk of negotiation rather than negation, it is to convey a temporality that makes it possible to conceive of the articulation of antagonistic or contradictory elements: a dialectic without the emergence of a teleological or transcendent History (p. 25).

Prior to the performance, then, there are no absolute guarantees as to how the statements will be negotiated; there is no teleology. Within this framework the musical performance is viewed as a site of enunciation. During a performance, writes Bhabha (1994),

> the enunciative process introduces a split in the performative present . . . between the subject of a proposition and the subject of enunciation, which is not represented in the statement but which acknowledges [its] reference to a present time and a specific place (pp. 35–6).

The performance occurs in the present. During the performance, however, there is a split between the articulation of the music (its elaboration) and the production of musical statements (proposition) during the performance. The performative present, its "presence," splits to become a site where (e)merging temporalities from past musical discourses (re)negotiate their meanings within present contexts. The performance is constituted, in part, by its elaboration and is at the same time producing the live sound of music-making which enunciates the "present time and specific place." The music is same within different; it is old within new; it is global within local. The performative present announces, within the moment of enunciation, simultaneously different times and places as it announces a present and specific location.

Through its elaboration, music attaches itself, for instance, to past traditions, present realities, and future imaginative possibilities as a representation. Through its enunciation it announces its present sound. The relationship between elaboration and enunciation is one of multiple negotiations with/in past, present and future times. Here, the meanings of musical statements produced in performance are very much open to debate—more precisely, open to negotiation within the field of existing power relations. This negotiation is political in that the very framing of this musical expression is simultaneously a contested terrain and an ideological intervention (a sound investment!). For as Bhabha argues, "political positions are not simply identifiable as progressive or reactionary, bourgeois or radical, prior to the act of *critique engages,* or outside the terms and conditions of its discursive and textual address" (1994, p. 22). This means that the transgressive moment is that in-between moment (in between performance and representation) where music's "commitment to theorizing" about the world is negotiated within parameters of what is historically defined, and doubly inscribed, as constituting a "good" or "bad," "progressive" or "reactionary" engagement. Bhabha refers to the agonism constituted within the performative split as the "temporality of negotiation."

Music Making and the Alignment of Lived-Time

Indeed, in music making with others, the performance offers no guarantees as to its outcomes. The performance exceeds its elaboration at the very moment it articulates its elaboration. In the earlier, seminal article, "Making Music Together—A Study in Social Relationships," Alfred Schutz (1951) argues that musical knowledge and practices are always historically situated within a context, thus constituting the social setting within which a player performs his or her music. *However, and this is crucial, Schutz was quick to add that the social context does not exhaust the totality of the musical experience.* He wanted to expand the terrain of investigation to focus on music-making at the level of interpersonal relations through the alignment of lived-time within/between musicians and listeners of music. Here he claims that music-making is an "occurrence in inner time, which is the very form of existence of music" (p. 88). For Schutz it is precisely because music is temporal (as well as historical) in form that we can account for the way in which its brings together people, thus creating the possibility of a common experience between them: the creation of a common community—a "We."

A wonderful illustration of the way in which music-making brings people together was observed in a study of suburban high school students who use music (and drama) in their lives and at school (Hudak, 1993). One student musician, "Sam," told of a drumming concert he attended. The concert was organized by Grateful Dead drummer Mickey Hart. Drummers were from Africa, Brazil, and India.

> Hart had to get all these people from very different backgrounds, very conflicting religious backgrounds too, get them all on stage. They were all masters, so no one missed a beat, of course, but it was all these guys, and they got their shit together. They really, you know, they connected . . . all these very different styles combined into this one thing and its kinda cheesy in a sense to be saying this, but it was like a metaphor for world unity, I would think. . . . In my opinion, that's the only way people are able to unite, is when you put your ideologies aside. . . . The whole time I was thinking, I was seeing that there is hope for this world in a sense that people can put differences aside, and even if it's just for one night on stage (Hudak, 1993, p. 183).

Sam's example highlights the alignment of inner times between what Schutz refers to as the "beholder" (the listener) of music and the performer. This alignment of inner times between beholder and musician unites them within the "vivid present." The beholder, thus, is united with the composer by a time dimension common to both, which is nothing other than a derived form of a vivid present shared by the partners in a genuine face-to-face relationship—this sharing of the other's flux of experiences in inner time, this living through a vivid present in common, constituting the mutual tuning-in relationship, the experience of the "We," which is at the foundation of all possible communication (Schutz, 1951, pp. 90, 92).

What makes musical communication distinct from communication in general is the "polythetic characteristic of the communicated content" (Schutz, 1951, p. 92). The polythetic character means that music is understood, learned, in a step-by-step manner which cannot be summarized the way, for example, we can summarize a story. While I can call to your attention to the first four notes of Beethoven's *Fifth Symphony,* it is not possible to grasp the sounds themselves without hearing them through the temporal ordering of the score and/or performance. This temporal ordering of the notes coordinates the inner times between musicians and beholders.

For Schutz the alignment of inner time is characterized as a "tuning-in" relationship between the listener and performer/composer. The tuning-in relation holds good for all types of music (1951, p. 92). The process of tuning-in entails the reconstruction of musical content by the listener's stream of consciousness as he/she is either listening or imagining the music. This reconstruction creates in consciousness a "vivid present" where a "quasi-simultaneity" of events between listener/beholder and composer/performer is achieved. Central to this process of temporal alignment is the polythetic structure of the music itself.

Consider the following example. The composer writes a song; the song, in turn, represents notes, sounds, and so on, in time. The song-as-song occupies a specific amount of time when played. When the song is played, the sounds are heard by the beholder/listener in exactly the same time as intended by the composer/performer. This communication is in the "vivid present," now. As the beholder tunes in the sound waves, his/her inner time aligns with the composer. The more in tune the beholder becomes with the song, the closer alignment in temporal structure between listener-song-composer. In essence they become one on the "same wavelength," as the popular saying goes.

Schutz discussed intimacy in terms of the alignment of both inner and outer time. Intimacy between musicians and beholders occurs through the "pluridimensionality of time," as we make music together. Consider again Sam's example from the drumming concert. For Schutz, musical communication occurs in inner time. However, when performing together, making music with others, the drummers must live simultaneously both in inner and outer time for the performance to have a musical sense of coherence, that is, the drummers must be able to tune in to each other. Because, as Schutz argues,

> making music together occurs in a true face-to-face relationship—insomuch as the participants are sharing not only a section of time but also a section of space. The other's facial expressions, his gestures in handling his instrument, in short all the activities of performing, gear into the outer world and can be grasped by a partner in intimacy . . . This social relationship is founded upon the partaking in common of different dimensions of time simultaneously lived through by the participants. on the one hand, there is the inner time in which the flux of musical events unfolds . . . on the other hand, making music together is an event in outer time. . . . that is, a community of space, and it is this dimension which unifies the fluxes of inner time and warrants their synchronization into a vivid present (Schutz, 1951, pp. 95, 96).

Indeed, for the drummers, intimacy is constituted out of a merging of inner time and outer time—its "pluridimensionality"—within the space of the performance. This moment creates a unique situation where for performer and beholder (Sam in this case) the space creates an event, whereby a common experience is constituted, a "We." The We, in turn, means that communication of a sort has occurred across the bar of differences found in the auditorium. Within this space, a yearning is constituted where all in the auditorium can feel the sense of alignment. This created alignment between people sharing a common public space is intimacy, even as Sam suggests, "if only for a moment on stage."

The intimacy created in the formation of a musical "We" is, in part, experienced as a sensuous longing, a yearning to be with others. This yearning is erotic. For Audre Lorde (1978), the erotic has been misnamed and misused by men against women. The erotic is neither a "plasticized sensation" nor is it the pornographic—"sensation without feeling." Rather, the erotic "is an internal sense of satisfaction to which, once we have experienced it, we know we can aspire" (p. 2). This sense of satisfaction and the power of the erotic come from its ability to transcend the dichotomy between the spiritual and the political. For Lorde this dichotomy is false and results from an incomplete attention to our erotic knowledge. For the bridge which connects them is formed by the erotic—the sensual—those physical, emotional, and psychic expressions of what is deepest and strongest and richest within each of us, being shared: the passions of love, in its deepest meanings (p. 4).

This suggests that the formation of musical identities entails breaking down the dichotomy between the political and the spiritual. Indeed, at Sam's drumming concert the creation of a shared community is political as well as spiritual—the tender recognition of the fragileness of human endeavor. The very intimacy of the concert, for Sam, creates a connectedness that while momentary, nonetheless creates a yearning for similar experiences—a desire for more.

Indeed, to paraphrase Lorde, once we have experienced the erotic, we "Yearn" for more! This sense of yearning is "born of Chaos, and personifying creative power and harmony," found in any pursuit with another human being. The erotic is the sharing of joy, "whether physical, emotional, psychic, or intellectual, [forming] a bridge between sharers which can be the basis for understanding much of what is not shared between, and lessens the threat of difference" (1978, p. 5). We begin to see relations between the erotic, musical intimacy, and the formation of sound identities. Sound identities are constituted within a field of social intimacy with others. And as Sam's drumming example, cited earlier, vividly describes, this sharing is joyful while at the very same time the threat of difference is diminished. Literally, one yearns for such intimacy in the way the "body stretches to music and opens into response, hearkening to its deepest rhythms, so every level upon which I sense also opens to the erotically satisfying experience" (p. 5).

The very constitution of a "We" creates within the community a "yearning"; a specific longing to come together and make music, to make a community. I find that this yearning expresses similarities to bell hooks's definition of the term. bell hooks (1990) writes of community where "the shared space and feeling of 'yearning' opens up the possibility of a common ground where differences might meet and engage one another" (p. 13). Here members of the community feel connectedness, an intimacy, where differences might meet and engage one another. This sense of yearning-as-erotic is constructed (not discovered) in the social formation of a shared community which is linked together temporally through the music. This sense of yearning, grounded in the erotic moment, and the subsequent formation of a sound identity cannot be determined beforehand, nor can there be any guarantees as to the outcome. It is precisely the constitution of this shared sense of erotic intimacy created by and through music that begins to define the boundaries of a "sound" identity. Here sound identities are formed in what I refer to as the "temporality of alignment" in the making of music; it is the time of both synchronicity and uncertainty.

Musical Interstices: The Sound Identity and the Fan

Drawing upon Jerome Miller's (1992) investigations of wonder, yearning (the longing for another) is doubly inscribed within the structures of eros and desire. In yearning-as-erotic, Miller's work suggests that the erotic defines a specific relationship between self and other: one that lacks any sense of possessiveness towards the other. Miller's example is drawn from the experience of falling in love. When we fall in love, it is the erotic that moves us toward the other by, paradoxically, letting go of our desire to possess the person we love as an object of our affections. The act of "letting-go," however, is not a passive response toward the person we love. Rather, "the lover is filled with a spendthrift enthusiasm for the beloved which he does not want to suppress or inhibit" (p. 114). Eros then, is distinguishable from an appetite, a desire to consume the other. Indeed,

> eros, like desire, does not want to hold itself back; but whereas desire cannot restrain the urge for pleasure which effaces the other, eros cannot restrain its enthusiasm for the other in its otherness. Desire wants to possess the other; eros longs to spend itself wholeheartedly and unreservedly on the other's behalf. Desire makes us aware of a void to be filled, whereas enthusiasm springs from an overflowing heart that is eager to empty itself. Desire is a regressive impulse which leads to an effacement of the other, and the pleasure in which it culminates is as safe a haven as we can find. Enthusiasm, on the other hand, is a celebration of the other and urges us to throw caution to the wind—to risk everything on the other in a single act of self-abandonment (Miller, 1992, pp. 114–115).

As Miller suggests, the erotic embraces an enthusiasm-for-the other in the sense that we risk everything as we yearn to be with the other in a Subject-Subject relationship. This erotic relationship embraces both love and spirituality in our wholehearted attempt to let go of our egoistic desire to possess and control the other.

With these observations in mind, the formation of the sound identity is located within the field of yearning-as-erotic; it is a letting go of the self to be with another. The sound identity is constituted within a field of intimacy (the erotic) and through the alignment of heterogenous temporalities in music-making with others. In the formation of a sound identity we "give" ourselves over to the other as we let go of ego control and allow the music to align us temporally with others. This alignment with others creates an atmosphere of intimacy and genuine love. As noted, within the constitution of a sound identity there exists a sense of altruism, of giving towards the other articulated within the process of letting go. For this reason the sound identity is a spiritual as well as a political identity as Lorde noted. For the "We" lives, as Miller notes, "in human time precisely to the degree to which we give ourselves over to the spendthrift enthusiasm of this eros" (1992, pp. 115–116). It is precisely the formation of the sound identity *in time* that comes to constitute it as an identity, albeit a spiritual-political one at that. Eros paradoxically breaks down the barriers between Us/Them in the very act of letting go, of falling in love within time. For eros the alignment is constituted through a mutual sharing as a Subject-Subject relationship, an alignment of temporality with the other.

The second inscription of yearning is yearning-as-desire, where we extend ourselves to the other in the form of possessing the other as object. This relationship of control and possession defines a Subject-object relationship between ourselves and the other. Desire does not give itself over to the other; rather in its extreme forms our desire to possess the other can become an addiction, a fetish, as we attempt to efface the other through our desire to consume. For desire there is a moment of sharing. Here the act of sharing with others is constituted within the formation of "alliances." The alliance is formed by creating, marking off boundaries between "Us" and "Them." Here desire's intent to control is shared with select others as they decide who may, or may not, enter "their" space. This control of access, within the field of desire, marks off a boundary, a collective identity, an "Us."

Within the second inscription of yearning, yearning-as-desire, lies the formation of another collective musical identity: the "fan." Lawrence Grossberg (1987) defines the fan as constituted, in part, through these "affective alliances" where music works as an "affective" apparatus to encapsulate the nominal group in a pleasurable space:

> Marking itself as different and placing the fan within its spaces, the fan takes up a position of being different from those who don't "understand" the music and who cannot make the appropriate distinctions. . . . This practice of critical encapsulation divides the world into Us and Them, but that difference does not necessarily constitute an identity. While being a rock and roll fan sometimes does entail having a visible and self-conscious identity (such as punks, or hippies, or mods), it more often does not appear visibly on the surface of the fan's life, or even as a primary way in which most would define themselves. But it still functions as a way in which we mark our difference from others, especially from what is considered the straight adult, or boring world (pp. 185–186).

Here the impetus for the fan to draw up boundaries is linked to the marking of one's musical turf. In the marking of boundaries by fans, the musical world is divided into properties to be owned, so to speak. There is the marking of "our musical turf." And as such the marking off of "Them" who are not part of the group. The marking of boundaries by the fan affectively "encapsulates" the nominal group into a space of their own. While this affective alliance with others does not necessarily have to constitute an individual identity, however, it does constitute a identifiable group, collective musical identity: for example, punks, hippies, or mods. It is through their engagement with popular culture, and particularly music, that "affective alliances" are created to give the sense of group cohesion and a feeling of group solidarity within and between musicians and their "fans."

Indeed, Grossberg (1986) suggests that popular music can work within the affective domain to create the sense of a cohesive reality in the lives of children and adults, in part, through the (re)structuring of our feelings, our desires, through the "affective" apparatus of the popular. Grossberg claims that important differences have occurred in structure of popular culture from past periods to the present. He notes that one of the functions of popular culture "remains the same" (p. 186), its function as an affective structure which helps produce in us the feeling that the world is a coherent totality and that life has meaning. However, in prior historical periods the affective structure of popular culture was more stable and unified. Today, popular culture can no longer be counted on to project a stable and unified affective horizon. Instead the popular works by producing temporary "affective alliances . . . making whatever is incorporated into its space pleasurable" (Grossberg, 1986, pp. 186–187).

The affective structuring of our feelings-in-the-world points to the links between the popular culture and the affective in formation of an

affective alliance. Popular music works as an affective apparatus that miti-
gates the longing to consume the other, through the formation of temporary alliances linking together our desires within a pleasurable space.

Of importance however, is for us to take note of his definition of
"affect" itself, for

> it is necessary to recognize that the world is affectively as well as semantically
> structured. I am using the term affect to refer to the intensity or desire with
> which we invest the world and our relations to it. Desire, however, cannot be
> limited to sexual energy. This affective production is organized within and
> circulates around the body, understood as more than simply a semantic space
> and less than a unity defining our identity (Grossberg, 1986, p. 185).

Note that for Grossberg the "affective," while more than sexual energy, is nonetheless linked to our *desires* as it is woven into the fabric
of our energy investments-in-the-world. The affective is more than a
space of phenomenological meaning-making in our lives, the semantic, and less than a unified field of energy that we can point to as
defining our identity. The affective does not define us and yet it is:
immediate, circulating around the body, while structuring our feelings-
with-the-world. *The affective is located within the field of desire.*

A brief phenomenology of the fan's desire reveals a highly frustrat-
ing, unstable situation caused by the fan's desire to consume the other
and at the same time to let go and be with the other. The fan attempts
to solve this situation through the act of "taking-in" the other in the
formation of an alliance in an effort to stop time itself. The fan reasons that outside of time there can be no past or future, and without
time there can exist no pain of longing, no yearning. Despite the fan's
best efforts to form alliances, time continues and the fan's pain
continues.

The formation of a temporary affective alliance is often confused
by the fan as an act of falling in love. Because of the energy rush
generated, the fan momentarily loses him/herself within the desire to
"take-in-the-performance." This is a moment of hyper-self-absorption
on the part of the fan in the hope of ending the pain of longing. The
sheer energy of this sublime moment for the fan is both empowering
as well as addictive. On this account the fan attempts to accumulate
more "affective capital" in its investments with others through music
in the hope of "buying off" the pain of longing. This strategy fails for
the fan, in that the pain of longing continues to persist. Here the fan
yearns to consume more with each passing performance, as with each
performance the amount of energy consumed by the fan increases

until the fan "can't get no satisfaction" tho' they try and try and try.
. . .

Grossberg's discussion of the fan helps map out the different ways in which music making informs collective musical identities. The formation of the fan involves the creation of an "Us." The formation of a sound identity involves the creation of a "We." The descriptive overlaps between the musical "Us" and the musical "We" lies in the ways in which music making aligns lived-time with/in the performance.

The fan and the sound identity share similar descriptions, for Grossberg (1986) observes that "affective alliances work by making whatever is incorporated into its space pleasurable. Thus the fragments linked together need not be pleasurable outside of that space. . . . [T]hey are always local, fragile, and hesitant, and temporary" (pp. 186–187). Indeed, for Grossberg and myself both collective musical formations are generally described as: temporary, unstable, and fragile, and both define a site specific place that is pleasurable. The differences, the moments of displacement between these two formations, however, revolve around the specific configurations of "yearning" constituting each.

The overlaps and displacements in the descriptions between the sound identity and the fan point to what Bhabha (1994) refers to as the emergence of "interstices" in the formation of collective identities. Interstices are the "overlaps and displacements of domains of difference, that [occur in] intersubjective and collective experiences" (p. 2). The relationship between the sound identity and the fan is not one of mutual exclusion; rather these different musical formations overlap each other, and at times displace each other. The notion of interstices is helpful in that it defines a type of relationship that is not a causal link: instead the relationship is defined in terms of spaces, gaps in-between these two different musical formations. The notion of musical interstices helps clarify the possibility of simultaneous creation of an "Us" and a "We" at a musical performance.

The Zone of Occult Instability

At the center of music-making is the zone of occult instability marked within the performative split. This moment is a moment of uncertainty which has the potential to rattle the hegemony of everyday life. Here the performative split is analogous to the explosion of the Big-Bang in the creation of the universe. From an imaginary point in the center of a sphere, sound and energy waves emanate in every direction and at different temporal velocities through space. The moment of uncertainty constituted within the performative split is not monolithic. More precisely, at the moment of performance there is at least a double inscription of uncertainty where the process of enunciation produces something new, and possibly, even unrecognizable/unnamed. This moment of uncertainty for Bhabha (1994) is the moment of liberatio: "it is the time of liberation . . . a time of cultural uncertainty . . . of representational undecidability" (p. 35). It is at that moment of undecidability (at a conscious and unconscious level) that Bhabha (quoting Frantz Fanon) describes as *"the zone of occult instability* where people dwell (and where] cultural difference problematizes the binary division of past and present, tradition and modernity"(p. 35; emphasis in original).

Within each performance there is a doubling of the moment of "occult instability." One moment inscribes, opens the door for the formation of a hybrid, a third space. This moment articulates the elaboration as a new different musical formation, and occurs in the **temporality of negotiation**. The "Other" inscription closes the door on the moment and holds on to the moment in the formation of a sound identity. This moment occurs in the **temporality of alignment**. The former opens her/his arms to the logic of difference; in the latter s/he embraces the logic of sameness. The in-between is the zone of occult instability; a moment of profound interruption where one's everyday reality "stops."

The zone of occult instability suggests similarities to Carlos Castaneda's (1972) notion of "stopping-the-world." From the perspective of an individual's consciousness, stopping-the-world occurs when the flow of linguistic descriptions framing the parameters of everyday reality is "stopped," interrupted, by another alien set of circumstances. Hence, one's reality "stops." For the individual it is a time of liberation, a time of cultural uncertainty, of representational undecidability as reality is radically rendered problematic.

Castaneda (1972) uses the example of a child learning about reality as another way of explicating the concept of stopping-the-world. The child, he argues, learns a particular description of reality, out of many possible descriptions, as he/she grows up within a particular cultural context. According to Castaneda, "Everyone who comes into contact with a child is a teacher who incessantly describes the world to him, until the moment when the child is capable of perceiving the world as it is described" (p. 9). From that moment on, when the child lives out these descriptions, he/she becomes a member of the culture, where "membership becomes full-fledged, I suppose, when he is capable of making all the proper perceptual interpretations which, by conforming to that description, validate [it]" (p. 9). The notion of stopping-the-world defines a rupture in the fabric of everyday life, as common sense descriptions, which ordinarily run uninterrupted, have

> been stopped by a set of circumstances alien to that flow. . . . The precondition of stopping-the-world [is that one] learns a new set of descriptions for the purpose of pitting one against the other . . . [and] in that way break[s] the dogmatic certainty, which we all share, that validity of our perceptions, or our reality of the world, is not to be questioned (Castaneda, 1972, p. 17).

Within this framework, music-making analogously ruptures everyday reality in the constitution of heterogenous temporalities. In between the temporalities of negotiation and alignment is the zone of occult instability, which entails a stopping-the-world as everyday reality, our world of daily certainty, is interrupted by the formation of temporal anomalies within the field of social consciousness. Here the zone of occult instability is "the time of liberation" where musical statements produced, in performance, have yet to form a nomadic attachment to anything resembling commitment. Committed to what? It is an undecided, ambivalent moment which, like the "big bang" of the universe, created sounds, exploding on the scene.

In a study of high school musicians (Hudak, n.d.), "Jon" describes the performance as getting "lost" in the music:

> Well, when I'm performing, I'm really not anywhere. . . . if I'm conscious of where I am I get nervous, very nervous. . . . And I try to tone it down and get lost in the music, and when I do that, I'm not here, [or] there. I'm really within myself . . . trying to come through in the music (Hudak, n.d., unpublished).

Jon's observations clearly delineate the ambivalent, in-between zone where meaning/commitment has yet to be negotiated; that is, "I'm not here, [or] there." The force of this zone is like a temporal tidal wave, "displacing" and "stopping" prior moments. The "wow" of the performance has the potential for the formation of a "hybrid," third space. Bhabha (1990) explains hybridity:

> For me the importance of hybridity is not to be able to trace two original moments from which the third emerges, rather hybridity to me is the "third space" which enables other positions to emerge. The third space displaces

the histories that constitute it, and sets up new structures of authority, new political initiatives, which are inadequately understood through received wisdom (p. 211).

The formation of a "third space" displaces the histories that constitute it. Key is the process of displacement which occurs at one moment of occult instability, where new hybrid formations, the third space, reflect new meanings, constituted not through the dialect, but rather across the bar of difference.

As the zone "stabilizes," the temporality of negotiation becomes a site of intervention filling/framing the social space with a musical statement that is never complete, but nonetheless exudes a *presence*. This means that music's commitment is always partially oppositional, in the sense that the meaning of musical statements is always open to negotiation. It's all negotiated, hence there is a displacement that occurs which unsettles meanings, subverts the stability of meaning, and allows for multiple, non-essentialist readings of statements. Music's oppositionality is always partial also, because there is a doubling that occurs: subversion (via negotiation) is accompanied by replacement, the second inscription. To be fully oppositional the music must both subvert and replace the dominant ideology. However, replacement is itself always open to negotiation. There are no guarantees—no transcendental moments that allow one to see pregiven directionality toward "truth" and "progress." Within the zone of occult instability, all meanings and histories are displaced, nomadic, unstable, and hence "open to persuasion."

The second inscription of uncertainty within the zone of occult instability is that moment when the sound identity is constituted. Unlike music's commitment to negotiation, the formation of the sound identity *is* oppositional. As the erotic intimacy is constituted between musician/beholder there is a synchronization of time. That is, the temporality of alignment *subverts* nonsynchronicity and *replaces* it with alignment in the formation of a musical "We." It is of crucial importance to note that alignment is not standardization. The former "brings together" heterogenous temporalities in the way Sam observed, "if only for a moment on stage." The latter, standardization, is linear, serial time, whose hegemony is its teleology/ideology of control. The temporality of alignment is not about control; rather it is about being in the "right" place, at the "right" time, with the "right" people, and with the "right sound." Paradoxically, then, the temporality of alignment is very serendipitous, indeed!

There are at least two distinct temporalities constituted within the formation of a sound identity. One is during the performance; the other is after the performance. During the performance the sound identity is constituted within a public space, yet it is an intimate, communal experience. At once it is communal and private; it is inner time and outer time in sync; it is the temporality of alignment. However, as Jon observed, performing is public. It is filled with anxiety, until one "gets lost in the music." For Jon the publicness of the event suggests similarities to what Dick Hebdige (1988) refers to as "hiding in the light." For me, hiding in the light suggests intimacy in the spotlight, so to speak, where in Jon's terms he is trying to express himself "through the music." In Bhabha's terms, by making music with others at a public performance, the zone of occult instability occurs within a context that is "overdetermined from without"—a scene, an event. And in such a situation, there is always more occurring than what is seen. Here "something" is occurring that exceeds the frame of the image before us, eludes the eye/I. The sound identity is constituted at that moment of intimacy, where temporal alignment (re)collects our desires, ourselves, in the formation of a collective "We." And the "We" lasts til the music ends.

What remains, after the end? A yearning. A yearning that is at least doubly inscribed: it longs for the past, while looking forward to the future. This is similar to Shakespeare's "sweet sorrow" of parting, 'til it be "morrow." The second inscription is a yearning that is "a resistant trace, a stain of the subject, a sign of resistance" (Bhabha, 1994, p. 49). Yearning is a kind of a poetic evidence that there was a sound identity. For the formation of a sound identity is fleeting, nomadic, its stay is short, and when gone all that is left of this "pencilled in" identity is the erasure makings that leave a trace, a stain, a resistant desire, a yearning on the spirit. The sound identity is something of a "spell," the fragile alignment of time in a predominantly nonsynchronous world. In this sense it is alignment (which is distinct from standardization), that is marginalized, the rarity, in this "quantum" world of negotiations. Like "falling in and out" of love (which is a mode of the temporality of alignment!), one wonders if it really happened at all when it's over. Sometimes, our only evidence that it wasn't all a dream is the residual, the stain in time left behind, and articulated, doubly, as a "yearning."

The Sound Identity and the Metonymy of Body and Soul

I have defined the sound identity as being constituted within a field of intimacy (the erotic) and through the alignment of heterogenous temporalities in music-making with others. Here the sound identity leaves a trace, a stain on the spirit, the erasure markings of a "pencilled-in" identity, as it yearns to be together in time. The sound identity is temporary, unstable, fragile, and defines a site-specific place that is pleasurable. Unlike the fan, the sound identity marks no boundary with the other; it is neither controlling nor consuming. For the sound identity, making music with others acts as a "temporal apparatus" aligning inner and outer time in the formation of a "We." This particular alignment of "inner and outer" times through music-making shares similarities with Jamake Highwater's (1981) notion of "primal music."

For Highwater, primal music is a global phenomenon which includes Western music. Primal music is transcendental in that it articulates the spirit, the "soul" of music itself. The term *primal,* for Highwater, must not be confused with any outdated anthropological notion of the *primitive.* Indeed, the primal represents a dimension of spirit articulated in every culture, although differently within each. "The fundamentality of primal music," writes Highwater (1981),

> lies not in its originality or daring, in its complexity of harmonic development, but rather the intricate variations on the main themes and in the brilliant rhythmic complexities introduced by the lead drummer, who is "the Conductor" of the orchestra. . . . This primal music is a superstructure of redundant 4/4 beats surrounding a creative core of exquisite syncopations and added beats. . . . In primal music—of Africa, Oceania, Asia, and America—there is an outer composition, but there is also an inner pulsation, an inner core to the music's percussive and chordal life. What is often lacking . . . in Minimalist composers of the West is the essential core. . . . [T]he lesson to learn from primal music—from which they borrow so much and so little—[is that] there is an inner and outer music (p. 166).

For Highwater, the alignment of inner and outer music brings forth the "life-of-sound" (1981, p. 166) to the musician (and beholder) in performance. In the life-of-sound the musician discovers the immediacy of the sensual world as a unity of both body and spirit. Within the life-of-sound is constituted the "sound" identity. It is an identity of sound (inner and outer) that is not seen but rather felt and heard; it is an identity not of sight, but rather of sound itself. The sound identity is like a "missing person," we know of its existence, but are unable to locate his/her presence in space.

The reason the sound identity remains illusive, "pencilled in," is its location within the domains of a tribal culture: the life-of-sound. In fact, from Highwater's perspective the relationship between the life-of-sound and the sound identity is their mutual "centeredness" of self and others. For the Plains Indian, as an example, tribal centeredness is expressed as: "We are all related" (though not reducible to each other!) (1981, p. 189). In this statement the "We" means everything: rocks, plants, fish, trees, the Earth. We-are-all-related as brothers and sisters as framed within the formation of a tribal relationship. It is a relationship that moves beyond the current elaborations of race, class, gender, sexuality, age, and any other boundary marking off identification. As Highwater writes beautifully, "The tribal relationship of Indians is therefore never based upon the tolerance of others, but the experience of the self as part of others. *We are all related*" (1981, p. 189).

From Highwater's perspective the sense that "We are all related" occurs not out of tolerance (the Western notion of liberal democracy) but because of the centeredness of experiences between self and others. In this experience self is perceived as a part of others. This process, where self and other become interchangeable, is defined as a metonymic substitution (see Hudak, 1995). Homi Bhabha (1994) writes that metonymy is a

> figure that substitutes a part for a whole (an eye for an I), [which] must not be read as a form of simple substitution equivalence. Its circulation of part and whole, identity and difference, must be understood as a double movement that follows what Derrida calls the logic of the 'supplement': . . . [T]he supplement is an adjunct, subaltern instance which takes—the—place. As substitute it produces no relief, its place is assigned in the structure by the mark of an emptiness. Somewhere something can be filled up of itself . . . only by allowing itself to be filled through sign and proxy (pp. 54–55).

For Bhabha, the metonymic process of substitution is not a simple substitution of equivalents where A = B or where A determines B. Instead, the metonymic "resists the traditional causal links that explain" events brought together. For Bhabha, metonymy suggests the possibility of new understanding of events "based on shared symbolic and spatial structures, articulated within different temporal, cultural, and power relations" (1994, p. 55). Metonymic substitutions are always ambivalent precisely because the relationship between whole and part is more of a supplement, "an adjunct" to an already established, elaborated shared space.

In the metonymic substitution that occurs in the formation of a sound identity, the "We" offers "no relief" in part because this formation implicitly challenges the mythology of the "I" (the Western notion of a stable, "real" ego) in the moment it is supplemented by a "We." This tension, as Bhabha points out, is located in the "uncanny [formation of] sameness-indifference" (1994, p. 54). This common formation in contemporary Western society is often pushed into the margins of daily life. Within Western societies, as Miller observes, this moment is when "We" fall in love. However, as Lorde pointed out (1978), the erotic intimacy of the "We" is often subverted as the spiritual and the body are separated in the pornographic. In the formation of a sound identity, the "I" (as an individual body in space) resists letting go of itself so that it may (e)merge with others in the life-of-sound as a "We." This resistance on the part of the ego to let go is grounded within a culture that valorizes the ego and hence refuses to extinguish itself in fear of death. The irony of this situation is that when the ego lets go, a new terrain with others opens up. This tension is similarly found within the musical interstices between fan and sound identity. When there is an overlap between the fan (desire) and sound identity (eros) the body and soul (e)merge in the metonymy where the part (body) is supplemented by the whole (the soul)! When the body predominates in music-making, there is a displacement between the two formations where the soul is diminished as the boundary between egos, between "Us" and "Them," as constituted in performance.

Concluding Thoughts: The Sound Identity and Schooling. (Racial Discrimination and Privilege)

With regard to the sound identity in schooling, my concern is not with music education, or how we may enhance music-making within existing curriculums. Rather, I want to ask: How is the sound identity elaborated across the broad spectrum of schooling? To address this concern we have to realize that there exists a point of similarity between music-making and schooling: both act as "temporal apparatuses" organizing lived-time in the formation of identity.

Within the context of this paper, music-making acts as a temporal apparatus which structures our sense of yearning, longing to be together with others, through the alignment of lived-time. Indeed, music-making enters into the construction of self and consciousness via time, and as such it becomes a constitutive element in the formation of an identity. For Dwayne Huebner (1975), human beings "exist as temporal beings. This means that human life is never fixed but is always emergent as the past and future become horizons of a present" (p. 244). Music-making, as a specific structuring of temporality, then is connected with the constitution of what it means to be human. Without music making, then, the parameters of what it means to be a human being would be reduced, diminished in scope, for the shared intimacy created by music would be absent in social relations. The formation of a sound identity embraces this modality of intimacy.

The bureaucratic organization of schooling acts in many ways as a temporal apparatus, organizing the student's intersubjective experience of time and hence organizing the very way in which they think and act. For example, James Lofty (1992) found that the temporal organization of schooling structures the way students situate themselves as "writers." In related study on schooling and popular media (Hudak, 1994), I found that the temporal organization of the classroom (and popular media) plays an important role in the constituting of a "flexible-but-conforming subject," that is, a student who knows how to "play the game of schooling." The list could go on, for example, to include the temporal organization of gender and sexuality in schooling (e.g., Butler, 1990).

For my purposes, I want to focus, briefly, on how schooling organizes lived-time in the formation of a racial identity and how it pertains to race discrimination and privilege. Here racial identity is assumed to be neither a reductionist concept nor an essentialist notion, but rather racial formation is socially constructed (and continually contested) within the parameters of existing relations of power within the school (and societal) context. To this end, I want to focus on my study, "The Technologies of Marginality" (Hudak, 1993). For this study I interviewed two suburban high school students. One student was "Sam." Sam is white and from a upper-middle-class family; he is a musician. The other student is "Jorge." Jorge is Latino and is also from an upper-middle-class family; he is an actor. In this study I wanted to explore how these students use the arts to navigate the relations of power in schooling and to map out the different terrains of marginality occupied by two college-bound, upper-middle-class boys (keeping the variables of gender and class constant).

The interviews with Sam and Jorge suggested that they had different intersubjective experiences of schooling. The difference in their experiences was due, in part, to the formation of their racial identities as it pertained to race discrimination and privilege. That is, Sam experienced the privilege of choosing the margins, while Jorge's experience was one of his being placed within the margins of school life. With respect to the formation of their racial identities, I found that each boy not only had a different story to tell, but also that the temporal organization of their narratives was different. Sam told of his wanting to be a jazz musician and how he *looked forward* to exploring new cultures through music at a conservatory. Jorge, on the other hand, told of how he *looked backward* in time as an attempt to learn how to deal with present racist incidents in school. Here he used acting strategies to diffuse the racism he had experienced since entering the school district over a decade earlier. In their narratives I found a different set of mitigating circumstances defining their intersubjective experiences of self, society, and time.

Within the context of the study, I found that the formation of their racial identities paralleled the development of the different ways in which they situated themselves in the world temporally. For Jorge, past memories of discrimination framed present strategies in negotiating the realities of schooling. Here, Jorge situated himself in what I refer to as past-present time matrix in dealing with everyday events. Sam's story suggested a present-future matrix. This meant that Sam preferred to interpret present situations by looking to the future.

Of import, I asked what these different, socially constituted time matrices mean in terms of racial identity formation? I found that while Jorge and Sam occupied the same space, the margins, their worlds were bound together by different senses of time. Christoph Wulf (1989) writes that time and self-consciousness are intertwined in that "time is the medium that binds man's view of the world with his view of himself" (p. 49). That is, the "glue" (time) that binds their self-images and their worldview together are different; a difference that is grounded, in part, in the concrete material conditions of racial discrimination on the one hand and privilege on the other. My study suggests the ways in which schooling reproduces larger, societal patterns of discrimination and privilege through the temporal organization of the student's intersubjective experience.

Where does the sound identity fit into this picture? Sam and Jorge didn't know each other. My sense is that if they did, as artists, the sound identity would play an important role in aligning the heterogenous temporalities of discrimination and privilege. This alignment of time does not remove institutional structures that give rise discrimination and privilege. Rather, the sound identity, for, say, Sam, becomes an important communal experience which can be brought into other social contexts, "if only for a moment on stage." Here Sam's experience could link up with other similar formations that elaborate themselves as an ethic of love in the practice of freedom: "We are all related."

Consider Jorge's experience of the "actor's high." The actor's high is that state of being during a stage performance where there is no distinction between the actor, the character he/she plays, and the audience:

> You would be in this alternate state. You would be getting that actor's high, where you forget that you're you. You're just the character and nothing else could possibly come to your mind but the next word that the character is going to say. It just clicks in. Nothing else would work except that exact word and that exact thing. And that's happened to me twice in my life maybe . . . [I]t's incredible (Hudak, 1993, p.176).

The actor's high represents that stage experience where the subject and object merge in performance.

The actor's high is not an exact equivalent to the sound identity. However, my point is that they are similar with respect to letting go of the ego, and the (e)merging with others in performance. These similarities begin to form a backdrop in the overlapping experiences of student artists. Such overlaps in shared experiences create community. This community has the potential to elaborate a certain quality of love and freedom. In a recent article by bell hooks (1994), "Love as the Practice of Freedom," she points out that today there is no powerful discourse on love emerging from radical thought on the Left. She writes:

> My heart is uplifted when I read [Martin Luther] King's essay[s] . . . [They] lead us beyond resistance to transformation. King tells us that "the end is reconciliation, the end is redemption, the end is the creation of the beloved community.' The moment we choose to love we begin to move against domination, against oppression. The moment we choose to love we begin to move towards freedom, to act in ways that liberate ourselves and others. That action is the testimony of love as the practice of freedom (p. 250).

To hooks' statement we add Maxine Greene's (1988) observations on freedom, which shows itself, comes into being, when individuals come together in a particular way, when they are authentically present to one another (without masks, pretense, badges of office), when they have a project they can mutually pursue. . . . This means that one's reality, rather than being fixed and predefined, is a perpetual emergent, becoming increasingly multiplex, as more perspectives are taken, more texts are opened, more friendships are made (pp. 16, 23).

Taken together, the experience of the sound identity (e)merges with the actor's high, as they come together without masks, without pretense to control, based upon each student's different experience of letting go in performance.

I am fully aware that this picture "sounds" very idealistic. Perhaps. I am aware that Sam and Jorge's sense of racial identity has been informed, in part, through the complex processes found in schooling. However, identity formation is not a monolithic activity. And for now I want us to keep in mind the commitment, the worldview framed within the ethic of love, freedom, and the sound identity: We are all related. This commitment is found within the way Jorge and Sam frame their worlds. It is located in the contradictory lived-projects of high school students such as Jorge and Sam, who are searching for alternatives to the oppressive structures they experience in school. They are aware that there is more going on than the official school story. Life has mystery; it has soul. For the Sam and Jorge, performance affords them the potential space to explore "altered states" of being. As Sam states:

Nothing really moves me as far as music does. It's my only spiritual out. Some people have religion. Every now and then, when I play, there's an altered state in playing. . . . So I guess [I] tied music and spirituality, music is a healing thing.

I see it more as a means of expression, not as something that's going to lead me to something. . . . You know, physically and emotionally, it's a way of expressing how I feel, what I'm thinking and who I am.

When I talk about music expressing the way I feel, my emotions, and stuff, . . . it's the unspoken emotions and feelings, things that can't really be put into words, . . . I don't think you can say everything. . . . It's not all there is to the world. There's other forms. . . . there's more going on in your brain than you can speak about or understand (Hudak, n.d., unpublished).

Making music with others is by no means the solution to all the problems of privilege and oppression facing us in schools and society today. Music-making with others is not a monolithic activity; it is a contradictory, unstable, and a somewhat paradoxical human activity. There are no guarantees that creates harmony with ourselves or others.

However, the potential for the formation of a sound identity is always present. My goal has been to suggest how the sound identity, as a musical "we," elaborates itself across the spectrum of schooling as a practice of love and freedom in the fight against oppression. "We are all related." And where, to possibly state the obvious, "we" realize that there is more to life, and learning, than the desire to consume and control. "We" realize there's so much mystery, so much that's not definite or clear in our relations with ourselves and with others. So much that is not said; so much that remains unsaid; and so much that needs to be said in a way only music-making can . . .

So powerful is the desire to make music with others, that one is tempted to conceive of music-making as an emergent, radical engagement with consciousness—an engagement which can "rattle" the hegemony of everyday life and open up the possibility of a common ground.

References

Bhabha, H. (1990). The third space: An interview with Homi Bhabha. In J. Rutherford (Ed.), *Identity: community, culture, difference.* (pp. 207–221). London: Lawrence & Wishart.

Bhabha, H. (1994). *The location of culture.* New York: Routledge Press.

Butler, J. (1990). *Gender trouble: Feminism and the subversion of identity.* New York: Routledge.

Castaneda, C. (1972). *Journey to Ixtlan.* New York: Simon and Schuster.

Frith, S. (1987). Towards an aesthetic of popular music. In R. Leppert & S. McCleary (Eds.), *Music and society: The politics of composition, performance and reception.* Cambridge: Cambridge University Press.

Greene, M. (1988). *The dialectic of freedom.* New York: Teachers College Press.

Grossberg, L. (1987). Rock and roll in search of an audience. In J. Lull (Ed.), *Popular music and communication.* Newbury Park, CA: Sage Publications.

Grossberg, L. (1986). Teaching the popular. In C. Nelson (Ed.), *Theory in the classroom.* Urbana: University of Illinois Press.

Hebdige, D. (1988). *Hiding in the light.* New York: Routledge Press.

Highwater, J. (1981). *The primal mind.* New York: Meridian Books.

hooks, b. (1994). Love as the practice of freedom. In *Outlaw culture* (pp. 247–260). New York: Routledge.

hooks, b. (1990). *Yearning: Race, gender, and cultural politics.* Boston: South End Press.

Hudak, G. (1995, Fall). An Eye for an I: Metonymic substitutions between jazz, democracy and educational commitment. *Taboo: The Journal of culture and education.* Vol. 1(2).

Hudak, G. (1994). Critical pedagogy and the media-schooling couplet: Towards a grounded theory of popular media, language, and socialization. *Curriculum praxis: Occasional paper series* (No. 47). Edmonton, Canada: Department of Secondary Education, University of Alberta.

Hudak, G. (1993). Technologies of marginality: Strategies of stardom and displacement in adolescent life. In C. McCarthy & W. Crichlow (Eds.), *Race, identity, and representation in education* (pp. 172–187). New York: Routledge.

Hudak, G. (n.d.). Popular music and suburban youth: A qualitative study in identity formation. Unpublished.

Huebner, D. (1975). Curriculum as concern for man's temporality. In W. Pinar (Ed.), *Curriculum theorizing: The reconceptualist.* Berkeley, CA: McCutchan Publishing.

Knoblauch, C. & Brannon, L. (1993). *Critical teaching and the idea of literacy.* Portsmouth: Boynton/Cook Publishers.

Lofty, J. (1992). *A time to write.* Albany: State University of New York Press.

Lorde, A. (1978) *Uses of the erotic: The erotic as power.* Freedom, CA: Crossing Press.

Lusted, D. (1986). Why pedagogy. *Screen, 27,* 2–14.

Mercer, K. (1992). "1968": Periodizing postmodern politics and identity. In L. Grossberg, C. Nelson & P. Treichler (Eds.), *Cultural studies.* New York: Routledge Press.

Miller, J. A. (1992). *In the throe of wonder.* Albany: State University of New York Press.

Said, E. (1991). *Musical elaborations.* New York: Columbia University Press.

Said, E. (1994). *Re-presentations of the intellectual.* London: Vintage Press.

Schutz, A. (1951, March). Making music together—A study in social relationships. *Social research, 18*(1), 76–97.

Wulf, C. (1989). The temporality of world-views and self-images. In D. Kamper & C. Wulf (Eds.), *Looking back at the end of the world,* pp. 47–58. New York: Semiotext(e).

Subject Index

Name Index